Crusades
Volume 4, 2005

Crusades

Edited by
Benjamin Z. Kedar and Jonathan S.C. Riley-Smith
with Michael Evans and Jonathan Phillips

Editorial Board
Benjamin Z. Kedar (*Editor; Hebrew University, Jerusalem, Israel*)
Jonathan Riley-Smith (*Editor; University of Cambridge, U.K.*)
Jonathan Phillips (*Associate Editor; Royal Holloway, University of London, U.K.*)
Michael Evans (*Associate Editor; University of Reading, U.K.*)
Christoph T. Maier (*Reviews Editor; University of Zurich, Switzerland*)
Denys Pringle (*Archaeology Editor; University of Cardiff, U.K.*)
Karl Borchardt (*Bulletin Editor; University of Würzburg, Germany*)
Michel Balard (*University of Paris I, France*)
James A. Brundage (*University of Kansas, U.S.A.*)
Robert Cook (*University of Virginia, U.S.A.*)
Jaroslav Folda (*University of North Carolina, U.S.A.*)
Robert B.C. Huygens (*University of Leiden, The Netherlands*)
David Jacoby (*Hebrew University, Jerusalem, Israel*)
Catherine Otten (*University of Strasbourg, France*)
Jean Richard (*Institut de France*)

Crusades is published annually for the Society for the Study of the Crusades and the Latin East by Ashgate. A statement of the aims of the Society and details of membership can be found following the Bulletin at the end of the volume.

Manuscripts should be sent to either of the Editors in accordance with the guidelines for submission of papers on p. 253.

Subscriptions: Crusades (ISSN 1476–5276) is published annually in July.

Subscriptions are available on an annual basis and are fixed, until after volume 3 (2004), at £65, and £20 for members of the Society. Prices include postage by surface mail. Enquiries concerning members' subscriptions should be addressed to the Treasurer, Professor James D. Ryan (see p. 198). All orders and enquiries should be addressed to: Subscription Department, Ashgate Publishing Ltd, Gower House, Croft Road, Aldershot, Hants GU11 3HR, U.K.; tel.: +44 (0)1252 331551; fax: +44 (0) 1252 344405; email: journals@ashgatepublishing.com

Requests for Permissions and Copying: requests should be addressed to the Publishers: Permissions Department, Ashgate Publishing Ltd, Gower House, Croft Road, Aldershot, Hants GU11 3HR, U.K.; tel.: +44 (0)1252 331551; fax: +44 (0)1252 344405; email: journals@ashgatepublishing.com. The journal is also registered in the U.S.A. with the Copyright Clearance Center, 222 Rosewood Drive, Danvers MA 01923, U.S.A.; tel.: +1 (978) 750 8400; fax: +1 (978) 750 4470; email: rreader@copyright.com and in the U.K. with the Copyright Licensing Agency, 90 Tottenham Court Road, London, W1P 9HE; tel.: +44 (0)207 436 5931; fax: +44 (0)207 631 5500.

Crusades

Volume 4, 2005

Published by ASHGATE *for the
Society for the Study of the Crusades
and the Latin East*

© 2005 by the Society for the Study of the Crusades and the Latin East

All rights reserved. No part of this publication may be reproduced, stored in a retrieval system, or transmitted in any form or by any means, electronic, mechanical, photocopying, recording or otherwise without the prior permission of the publisher.

Published by
Ashgate Publishing Limited
Gower House
Croft Road
Aldershot
Hampshire GU11 3HR
Great Britain

Ashgate Publishing Company
Suite 420
101 Cherry Street
Burlington, VT 05401–4405
USA

Ashgate website: http://www.ashgate.com

ISBN 0 7546 5302 1

ISSN 1476–5276

Typeset by N^2productions

The paper used in this publication meets the minimum requirements of the American National Standard for Information Sciences – Permanence of Paper for Printed Library Materials, ANSI Z39.48-1984

Printed in Great Britain by MPG Books Ltd, Bodmin.

CONTENTS

Abbreviations ix

ARTICLES AND STUDIES

Some Reflections on the Failure of the Second Crusade 1
Graham A. Loud

Ermengol de Aspa, *Provisor* of the Hospital: 1188 15
Anthony Luttrell

Administrative Regulations for the Hospital of St John in Jerusalem
dating from the 1180s 21
Susan B. Edgington

The Templars and the Hospitallers, Christ and the Saints 39
Tom Licence

The Books of the Maccabees and the Teutonic Order 59
Mary Fischer

Aspects of Everyday Life in Frankish Acre 73
David Jacoby

The Naming Patterns of the Inhabitants of Frankish Acre 107
Iris Shagrir

Vassal and Faṣal: The Evidence of the Farkhah Inscription from 608/1210 117
Moshe Sharon

Inventio Patriarcharum 131
R.B.C. Huygens

REPORTS ON RECENT EXCAVATIONS

The Church of St John in Acre 157
Eliezer Stern

Latrun 159
Adrian Boas

REVIEWS

Thomas S. Asbridge, *The Creation of the Principality of Antioch, 1098–1130* (Martin Hoch)   161

The Canso d'Antioca*: An Occitan Epic Chronicle of the First Crusade*, ed. and trans. Carol Sweetenham and Linda M. Paterson; *The Old French Crusade Cycle Volume IV: La Chanson d'Antioche*, ed. Jan A. Nelson (Susan B. Edgington)   162

The Assizes of the Lusignan Kingdom of Cyprus, trans. Nicholas Coureas (Peter Edbury)   164

La Commanderie: Institution des ordres militaires dans l'Occident médiéval, ed. Anthony Luttrell and Léon Pressouyre (Klaus van Eickels)   166

The Crusades from the Perspective of Byzantium and the Muslim World, ed. Angeliki E. Laiou and Roy Parviz Mottahedeh (Ralph-Johannes Lilie)   168

Yvonne Friedman, *Encounter between Enemies: Captivity and Ransom in the Latin Kingdom of Jerusalem* (Alan V. Murray)   172

Thomas A. Fudge, *The Crusade against Heretics in Bohemia, 1418–1437: Sources and Documents for the Hussite Crusades* (Christoph T. Maier)   173

Norman Housley, *Religious Warfare in Europe, 1400–1536* (Claudius Sieber-Lehmann)   175

Nikolas Jaspert, *Die Kreuzzüge* (Christoph T. Maier)   177

Amnon Linder, *Raising Arms: Liturgy in the Struggle to Liberate Jerusalem in the Late Middle Ages* (Penny J. Cole)   179

David Marcombe, *Leper Knights: The Order of St Lazarus of Jerusalem in England, 1150–1544* (Andrew Jotischky)   181

David Nicolle, *Warriors and their Weapons around the Time of the Crusades* (John France)   183

Johannes Pahlitzsch, *Graeci und Suriani im Palästina der Kreuzfahrerzeit. Beiträge und Quellen zur Geschichte des griechisch-orthodoxen Patriarchats von Jerusalem* (Ralph-Johannes Lilie)   185

Jonathan Phillips, *The Crusades, 1095–1197* (Deborah Gerish)   187

Jonathan Riley-Smith, *What Were the Crusades?* (James A. Brundage)   189

Jürgen Sarnowsky, *Macht und Herrschaft im Johanniterorden des 15. Jahrhunderts. Verfassung und Verwaltung der Johanniter auf Rhodos (1421–1522)* (Karl Borchardt)   191

William Urban, *The Teutonic Knights: A Military History* (Sven Ekdahl)   193

The Templars: Selected Sources, trans. and annotated by Malcolm Barber and Keith Bate (Paul Crawford)   195

CONTENTS

Bulletin No. 25 of the SSCLE   197

Guidelines for the Submission of Papers   253

Membership Information   254

The Editors would like to express their gratitude to Dr Helen Nicholson for her sterling contribution as Associate Editor. They regret the fact that pressure of work has forced her to resign, but are pleased to announce the appointment of Dr Jonathan Phillips as Associate Editor in her place. They would also like to thank Dr Michael Evans for taking over the associate editorship of this volume while Dr Nicholson was on research leave. In addition, they are delighted to welcome Professor Denys Pringle as Archaeology Editor. And on behalf of the Society they are happy to announce the appointment of Professor James Ryan as Treasurer.

Abbreviations

AOL	Archives de l'Orient latin
Autour	Autour de la Première Croisade. Actes du colloque de la Society for the Study of the Crusades and the Latin East: Clermont-Ferrand, 22–25 juin 1995, ed. Michel Balard. Paris, 1996
Cart Hosp	Cartulaire général de l'ordre des Hospitaliers de Saint-Jean de Jérusalem, 1100–1310, ed. Joseph Delaville Le Roulx. 4 vols. Paris, 1884–1906
Cart St Sép	Le Cartulaire du chapitre du Saint-Sépulcre de Jérusalem, ed. Geneviève Bresc-Bautier, Documents relatifs à l'histoire des croisades 15. Paris, 1984
Cart Tem	Cartulaire général de l'ordre du Temple 1119?–1150. Recueil des chartes et des bulles relatives à l'ordre du Temple, ed. Guigue A. M. J. A., (marquis) d'Albon. Paris, 1913
CCCM	Corpus Christianorum. Continuatio Mediaevalis
Chartes Josaphat	Chartes de la Terre Sainte provenant de l'abbaye de Notre-Dame de Josaphat, ed. Henri F. Delaborde, Bibliothèque des Écoles françaises d'Athènes et de Rome 19. Paris, 1880
Clermont	From Clermont to Jerusalem: The Crusades and Crusader Societies 1095–1500. Selected Proceedings of the International Medieval Congress, University of Leeds, 10–13 July 1995, ed. Alan V. Murray. International Medieval Research 3. Turnhout, 1998
Crusade Sources	The Crusades and their Sources: Essays Presented to Bernard Hamilton, ed. John France and William G. Zajac. Aldershot, 1998
Setton, Crusades	A History of the Crusades, general editor Kenneth M. Setton, 2nd edn, 6 vols. Madison, 1969–89
CS	Crusade and Settlement: Papers read at the First Conference of the Society for the Study of the Crusades and the Latin East and Presented to R.C. Smail, ed. Peter W. Edbury. Cardiff, 1985
CSEL	Corpus Scriptorum Ecclesiasticorum Latinorum
Horns	The Horns of Hattin, ed. Benjamin Z. Kedar. Jerusalem and London, 1992
Kreuzfahrerstaaten	Die Kreuzfahrerstaaten als multikulturelle Gesellschaft. Einwanderer und Minderheiten im 12. und 13. Jahrhundert, ed. Hans Eberhard Mayer with Elisabeth Müller-Luckner. Schriften des Historischen Kollegs, Kolloquien 37. Munich, 1997

Mansi. *Concilia*	Giovanni D. Mansi, *Sacrorum conciliorum nova et amplissima collectio*
MGH	Monumenta Germaniae Historica
MO, 1	*The Military Orders: Fighting for the Faith and Caring for the Sick*, ed. Malcolm Barber. Aldershot, 1994
MO, 2	*The Military Orders*, vol. 2: *Welfare and Warfare*, ed. Helen Nicholson. Aldershot, 1998
Montjoie	*Montjoie: Studies in Crusade History in Honour of Hans Eberhard Mayer*, ed. Benjamin Z. Kedar, Jonathan Riley-Smith and Rudolf Hiestand. Aldershot, 1997
Outremer	*Outremer. Studies in the History of the Crusading Kingdom of Jerusalem Presented to Joshua Prawer*, ed. Benjamin Z. Kedar, Hans E. Mayer and Raymond C. Smail. Jerusalem, 1982
PG	Patrologia Graeca
PL	Patrologia Latina
PPTS	Palestine Pilgrims' Text Society Library
RHC	*Recueil des Historiens des Croisades*
Darm	*Documents arméniens*
Oc	*Historiens occidentaux*
Or	*Historiens orientaux*
RHGF	*Recueil des Historiens des Gaules et de la France*
RIS	Rerum Italicarum Scriptores
NS	New Series
ROL	*Revue de l'Orient latin*
RRH	Reinhold Röhricht, comp., *Regesta regni hierosolymitani*. Innsbruck, 1893
RRH Add	Reinhold Röhricht, comp., *Additamentum*. Innsbruck, 1904
RS	Rolls Series
SRG	Scriptores Rerum Germanicarum
WT	William of Tyre, *Chronicon*, ed. Robert B. C. Huygens, with Hans E. Mayer and Gerhard Rösch, CCCM 63–63A. Turnhout, 1986

Some Reflections on the Failure of the Second Crusade[*]

Graham A. Loud

University of Leeds

Greece did not send such a great army at the fall of Troy, nor was King Cyrus ever furnished with so large a force of men, but alas, the more and stronger they were, the less the consequences that resulted from their courage. Nothing that is worthy of record in a Royal Chronicle was done on this journey, so much was it filled with Roman blood and misfortune.[1]

Rhetorical they may be, but the words of the Cologne chronicler encapsulate the disappointment felt in the west after the failure of the Second Crusade in the Levant. The consequences of that failure were severe. William of Tyre, albeit with the advantage of a generation's hindsight, summed them up: "from this time on the conditions of the Latins in the East became visibly worse. Our enemies saw that the labours of our most powerful kings had been fruitless and all their efforts vain … their presumption and boldness rose to such heights that they no longer feared the Christian forces."[2]

The reasons for that failure are still much debated. Some at least appear obvious. There was the failure of the French and German contingents to co-operate in the march to the east: "the Germans were unbearable, even to us," as the French king's chaplain Odo of Deuil succinctly expressed it.[3] The armies were fractious and divided, "weakened by the jealousy of princes and the wrangling of priests."[4]

---

[*] A shorter version of this paper was given at the sixth conference of the Society for the Crusader States and the Latin East at Istanbul in August 2004. I am grateful to Dr. Alan Murray for discussion of the issues involved.

[1] *Chronica Regia Coloniensis*, ed. Georg Waitz (MGH SRG, Hanover, 1880), p. 83.

[2] WT 17.9, pp. 770–71. One should, however, note the cautionary observations about this passage by Martin Hoch, "The Price of Failure: the Second Crusade as a Turning Point in the History of the Latin East," in *The Second Crusade. Scope and Consequences*, ed. Jonathan Phillips and Martin Hoch (Manchester, 2001), pp. 184–85. For western reactions to the failure generally, Giles Constable, "The Second Crusade as Seen by Contemporaries," *Traditio* 9 (1953), 266–76, remains essential.

[3] *De Profectione Ludovici VII in Orientem*, ed. and trans. Virginia G. Berry (New York, 1948), pp. 42–43.

[4] *The Historia Pontificalis of John of Salisbury*, ed. and trans. Marjorie Chibnall (London, 1956), p. 54.

Discipline on the march was poor, indeed the French contingent had barely left their own country before they were scuffling with the burghers of Worms. Odo's throwaway comment that he would not record the ordinances that King Louis promulgated for his army, since nobody observed them properly, is immensely revealing.[5] Staff-work was rudimentary at best, as shown by the destruction of the German camp at Choirobacchoi; surely prudent commanders ought to have known the dangers of camping next to a river subject to flash floods?[6] Only when deep into enemy territory, and after sustaining heavy losses, were measures taken, under the direction of the Templars, properly and effectively to organize the conduct and tactics of the French army on the march.[7] When the Germans set out towards Iconium, "carrying as many supplies as they could," they ran short of food after a mere ten days, and according to one German chronicler were subsequently defeated by "hard labour, hunger and thirst," as well as Turkish harassment, without fighting a proper battle (*sine congressione*).[8] Yet it had taken the First Crusade some four months to march from Nicaea to Antioch, and if the crusaders were hazy about times and distances, surely the Byzantines who advised them were not? While it would clearly have been impossible to carry enough food for several months, Byzantine armies habitually carried a minimum of at least twenty days' provisions.[9] In 1190, during the Third Crusade, Frederick Barbarossa's army only ran short of food after almost a month of their march across Asia Minor, and even then still had bread (or the corn to make it), even if not much else.[10] Nor, of course, were the armies of 1147 helped by their hordes of imperfectly disciplined and ill-armed camp followers. Bernard of Clairvaux may well have urged "murderers, thieves, adulterers and perjurers" not to hesitate to secure their salvation, and boasted that so effective was his preaching that only one man was left for every seven women,[11] yet given the problems of supply and the breakdown of discipline in the armies, it might have been better for the success of the crusade had the recruiting been less all-embracing. As Odo commented, "the weak and helpless are always a burden to their commanders and a source of prey to their enemies."[12]

---

[5] *De Profectione Ludovici*, pp. 20–23.

[6] *De Profectione Ludovici*, pp. 48–49; *Gesta Friderici Imperatoris*, ed. Bernhard von Simson (MGH SRG, Leipzig, 1912), I.47, pp. 66–67; *Deeds of John and Manuel Comnenus, by John Kinnamos*, trans. Charles M. Brand (New York, 1976), p. 63; *O City of Byzantium, Annals of Niketas Choniates*, trans. Harry J. Magoulias (Detroit, 1984), pp. 37–38.

[7] *De Profectione Ludovici*, pp. 124–25.

[8] *Die Urkunden Konrads III*, ed. Friedrich Hausmann (MGH Diplomatum 9, Vienna, 1969), pp. 354–55 no. 195, at 354. *Annales Magdeburgenses*, MGH SS 16, p. 188.

[9] John Haldon, *Warfare, State and Society in the Byzantine World, 565–1204* (London, 1999), p. 167.

[10] Barbarossa's army set off from the mouth of the Dardennelles on 29 March 1190, by 22 April "all the supplies of the army except bread had been eaten," *Quellen zur Geschichte des Kreuzzuges Kaiser Friedrichs I.*, ed. Anton Chroust (MGH, SRG, n.s. 5, Berlin, 1928), pp. 72–74.

[11] *San Bernardo Opere*, 6/2 (Milan, 1987), pp. 142, 434, nos. 267, 363.

[12] *De Profectione Ludovici*, pp. 94–95.

Above all, the crusading armies of 1147 set out across Asia Minor at the beginning of winter. Not merely were they hampered by the cold, but pasturage for the horses and other baggage animals would have been poor and fodder hard to obtain, which in turn must have exacerbated their supply difficulties. This made the decision by Conrad to set off following the route of the First Crusade directly across Asia Minor all the more rash, since by following the coastal route (as the French eventually did) there would be the prospect of finding markets and obtaining supplies at those towns near the coast still in Byzantine hands. Byzantine armies, even in the days when Asia Minor was still all in imperial hands, had relied on the provision of supply dumps and careful arrangements in advance for obtaining fodder when mounting a major campaign.[13]

Yet for all this tale of woe, which could, if space permitted, be greatly extended, one could wonder whether, for example, the armies of the Second Crusade were any more disorderly, worse led, or more burdened with hangers-on than other medieval expeditions. Supply problems could hamstring military operations even in Christian territory, especially when undertaken in winter; as, for example, Henry IV of Germany discovered to his cost when he invaded Saxony during the winter of 1073–74, and similarly the Byzantine Emperor John Komnenos during his invasion of Hungary in 1129/30; and the First Crusade had suffered severely on its march to Iconium, even though this had been during the summer.[14] Furthermore, while the losses sustained in Asia Minor were undoubtedly heavy, we may concentrate on this phase of the crusade overmuch, simply because the only detailed eyewitness account of the crusade concluded with the arrival of the French army at Antioch. However, it needs to be remembered that both the kings involved, and at least some of their troops, did succeed in reaching the Holy Land. Nor should we assume that there was no prospect of successful military action once there, or that the fiasco that eventually ensued was inevitable.

This paper will focus on three aspects only of the failure of the Second Crusade in the east. One is an important issue raised in a recent study; the other two are factors which have been surprisingly neglected by modern historiography.

The first aspect is the involvement of Conrad III and the Germans. The long-established, indeed conventional, consensus of historical opinion has been that originally the plan for the crusade was of a primarily French expedition, led by Louis VII, and that the subsequent involvement of the Germans was the work of

---

[13] Haldon, *Warfare, State and Society*, pp. 166–74.

[14] *Lamperti Monachi Hersfeldensis Opera*, ed. Oswald Holder-Egger (MGH, SRG, Hanover, 1894), pp. 176–77. *Deeds of John and Manuel Comnenus*, p. 19. *Gesta Francorum et aliorum Hierosolimitanorum*, ed. Rosalind M. T. Hill (London, 1962), p. 23.

Abbot Bernard, acting on his own initiative, albeit in response to the preaching already undertaken by the renegade Cistercian Rodulf in the Rhineland. Only subsequently and reluctantly was this recruitment of a German army validated by Pope Eugenius III.[15] The implication at least is that, had the original plan been adhered to, while the troops involved may have been fewer, the difficulties of co-ordination and at least some of the supply problems that dogged the crusade's march would have been avoided. Nor would the French have been as likely to have received such a hostile reception from the Byzantine inhabitants on their route through the empire, had not the latter already suffered from the demands of the large and ill-disciplined German host.[16]

However, it has been recently suggested that, far from acting on his own initiative, Bernard's preaching in Germany and his enlistment of King Conrad was part of the papal plan for the crusade, or at any rate was positively encouraged by the pope, and that Conrad had good reasons to go on the expedition.[17] Furthermore, it is often forgotten that Conrad himself had already been to the Holy Land, in 1124/5; or at least had vowed to do so, which is what Ekkehard of Aura, our only source for this episode, actually said.[18] While there is no direct confirmation that he actually fulfilled this undertaking, it appears probable that that he did, both because of his apparent absence from the 1125 royal election in Germany (at which his brother was the defeated candidate), and since he only launched his own challenge for the kingship as late as December 1127. The presumption is that he had been absent up to that point.[19] In addition, had Conrad failed to fulfil his vow, it would surely have been remarked upon, either when he was excommunicated for his attempted usurpation of the German throne by Pope Honorius II or during the recruitment of the crusade in 1146/7.[20] Conrad therefore knew the Holy Land at

---

[15] See Hans E. Mayer, *The Crusades*, trans. John Gillingham (2nd ed., Oxford, 1988), pp. 93–99; Jean Richard, *The Crusades c.1071–c.1291*, trans. Jean Birrell (Cambridge, 1999), pp. 156–60.

[16] "Thus the Germans disturbed everything as they proceeded, and the Greeks therefore fled our peaceful king." *De Profectione Ludovici*, pp. 44–45.

[17] Jonathan Phillips, "Papacy, Empire and the Second Crusade," in *The Second Crusade. Scope and Consequences* [above, note 2], pp. 15–31.

[18] Ekkehard, *Chronicon Universale*, ad. an. 1124, MGH SS 6. 262: "An eclipse of the moon appeared on the Purification of St. Mary [2nd February]. Terrified by this, Conrad, the cousin of the emperor, undertook a change of his life (*conversionem morum suum professus*) and vowed that he would travel to Jerusalem to fight for Christ; through this he gained no little favour from everyone who had heard about this. Some people who had hitherto been given over to the study of wickedness promised to associate themselves with him in his following."

[19] Rudolf Hiestand, "Kingship and Crusade in Twelfth-Century Germany," in *England and Germany in the Middle Ages: Essays in Honour of Karl J. Leyser*, ed. Alfred Haverkamp and Hanna Vollrath (Oxford, 1996), pp. 244–45, 263–64; Wolfgang Giese, "Das Gegenkönigtum des Staufers Konrad 1127–1135," *Zeitschrift der Savigny-Stiftung für Rechtsgeschichte, Germanische Abteilung* 95 (1978), 202–20, at 203.

[20] For the excommunication: Robert Somerville, "Pope Honorius II, Conrad of Hohenstaufen and Lothar III," *Archivum Historiae Pontificiae* 10 (1972), 341–46.

first hand, and his half-brother, Bishop Otto of Freising, had also had discussions with an eastern envoy, the Bishop of Gibelet, at the papal court in 1145.[21] The summons to the crusade thus did not come "out of the blue," nor must we exaggerate the unfamiliarity of the crusade leaders with conditions in the east as a factor in the failure of the crusade (at least as regards the German contingent).

But to proceed from these contacts to assume that German involvement was part of the papal plan for the crusade from the first is a very long step indeed. It is of course easy, even tempting, to discount the tale in the *Vita Prima* of how Bernard, on his own initiative, persuaded the initially reluctant king and his great men to take the cross at Speyer in the last days of December 1146. His biographers were not, after all, disposed to underestimate the saint's role.[22] Yet it is worth noting how detailed and circumstantial the account of the *Vita Prima* is, and that it does not expressly connect Conrad's assumption of the cross with the miracles that Bernard was supposed to have wrought at Speyer – in his presence (and surely on the same occasion) – reported elsewhere in its narrative.[23] Furthermore, while few of the other contemporary German sources go into much, if any, detail, they too ascribe the responsibility for Conrad's assumption of the cross to Bernard.[24] Ultimately, the argument that Pope Eugenius was a party to, or actively sought, the recruitment of the king of Germany to the crusade rests upon the interpretation of one letter, sent by Conrad to the pope from the Diet of Frankfurt in March 1147. Dr Phillips has suggested that in the crucial passage of this letter Conrad was not apologizing for his hasty assumption of the cross without the pope's sanction, as has invariably been assumed, but was rather excusing his failure to delay the expedition as Eugenius had advised.[25] The problem here is that, while medieval Latin can often be ambiguous, it is really impossible to translate this passage in that sense. What it actually says is as follows:

> Indeed, the matter which was of concern to your good self, that we have assumed such a great task, namely the holy and life-giving cross and the intention of [making] so great and lengthy an expedition, without your knowledge (*absque vestra conscientia*), proceeds from a strong feeling of true love. But the Holy Spirit, which "bloweth where it listeth,"[26] and is accustomed to "coming suddenly"[27] allowed us to make no delay to take counsel

---

[21] *Ottonis Episcopi Frisingensis Chronica sive Historia de Duabus Civitatibus*, ed. Adolf Hofmeister (MGH SRG, Hanover, 1912), 7.33, pp. 363–65. Rudolf Hiestand, "The Papacy and the Second Crusade," in *The Second Crusade. Scope and Consequences*, pp. 35–36.

[22] *S. Bernardi Vita Prima*, 6.4, PL 185, cols. 381–83. Phillips, "Papacy, Empire and Second Crusade," 27.

[23] *Vita Prima*, 4.5, col. 338.

[24] For example, *Annales Palidenses*, MGH SS 16.82; *Chronica Regia Coloniensis*, p. 83; *Gesta Friderici*, 1.40, p. 59. Note especially the *Annales Magdaburgenses*, MGH SS 16.188: "Huius expeditione auctor et instigator exstitit Bernhart Clarevellensis abbas, qui tunc miraculis coruscare ferebatur."

[25] Phillips, "Papacy, Empire and Second Crusade," pp. 20–21.

[26] John, 3.8

[27] Mark, 13.36.

with you or anybody else; and immediately He touched our heart with His wondrous finger, He commanded our absolute obedience without their being any opportunity for delay interposing.[28]

One might also note that, if Eugenius was a party to Conrad's decision to take the cross, as Phillips claims, it seems odd that he did not follow the king's suggestion in this letter that the two should meet in Strassburg, during Easter Week. Even if his visit to Paris and St Denis at Easter (20th April) had been agreed in advance, he made no effort to encounter Conrad before the latter departed in May 1147. Since he had already met King Louis at Dijon at the end of March, before going on to Paris, his presence there was hardly essential.[29] Yet throughout the spring and early summer of 1147 the pope remained resolutely in France.

We may conclude therefore that the conventional view is justified. There is no clear evidence that Conrad's involvement in the crusade was planned, at least at the curia, and that by contrast this was indeed the work of St Bernard, first urging the king "with his customary gentleness," then convincing him with stern reminders of the Last Judgement, and finally personally giving him a holy banner "that he would with his own hand carry in the army of the Lord."[30]

The second issue to be considered here is the question of how far the losses sustained in Asia Minor prevented any subsequent military success, once the remnants (if such they were) of the two armies reached the crusader states. The casualties on the march in Asia Minor were undoubtedly very heavy, and contemporary chroniclers were not disposed to underestimate them. Conrad, we are told by the Pöhlde Annalist, "returned to Constantinople, bringing back with him few indeed of the great army that he had earlier had."[31] But can we necessarily accept, as Runciman for example did, William of Tyre's estimate that the German king lost nine-tenths of his army?[32] William was after all writing about thirty years later, and was certainly not an eyewitness – indeed in 1147/8 he was in Europe, not the Holy Land – hence he cannot even have spoken with the survivors who reached their destination. Conrad himself said that he returned to Constantinople through illness, and did not ascribe this to the losses incurred, and added that Manuel Komnenos and his German-born empress then "provided us and our princes with everything that we needed for our journey."[33] The phrase alluding to the princes is significant: for we know that when

---

[28] *Die Urkunden Konrads III*, pp. 332–33 no. 184.
[29] *Annales S. Benigni Divionensis*, MGH SS 5.44.
[30] *Vita Prima*, cols. 381–82.
[31] *Annales Palidenses*, MGH SS 16.83.
[32] WT 16.22, p. 747. Steven Runciman, *A History of the Crusades*, 2: *The Kingdom of Jerusalem* (Cambridge, 1952), p. 268.
[33] *Die Urkunden Konrads III*, p. 355 no. 195.

Conrad reached the Holy Land he was accompanied by, among others, his nephew Frederick of Swabia, his half-brothers Henry of Babenberg and Otto of Freising, Duke Welf, the Bishops of Basle, Metz and Toul, the Margraves of Montferrat and Verona, the Counts of Andechs and Biandrate, the son of the Count of Mons, and the exiled former Prince of Capua.[34] Such men did not travel alone, but with their *familiae* – their military households and bodyguards. In circumstances such as the chaotic retreat of the German forces after their confrontation with the Turks, the well-armed and armoured knights of these *familiae*, with their greater protection, cohesion and discipline, were far more likely to survive than the ill-armed, under-resourced and disorganized infantry and non-combatants. There is indeed some confirmation of this in the sources. Gerhoh of Reichersberg claimed that Conrad's expedition was joined by "a multitude of peasants and servants, abandoning their ploughs and their service," who lacked carts and horses to carry supplies and were already suffering badly from hunger during the journey through the Balkans.[35] The Pöhlde Annals noted that, once into enemy territory, "the footsoldiers were exhausted from hunger, unused to warfare and thus less attuned to dangers," while Conrad himself, writing home to Abbot Guibald of Stavelot, spoke of how "the Turks unceasingly harried and inflicted death upon the crowd of people on foot, who were unable to keep up." He then described how the French army "joined forces with us and our princes, although indeed some of our people were left behind, being unable to follow either because of illness or through lack of money. We then went without difficulty as far as St. John [*Ephesus*]."[36] Once again, those who lacked money were unlikely to be the great men and their immediate dependants, and Conrad's testimony is backed up by the Würzburg Annals, which said that, "the king came with all his princes and his whole knighthood (*omnique militia*) to Ephesus ... ready to set sail if a suitable opportunity should occur to take ship."[37] Even William of Tyre noted that, after abandoning his overland march, Conrad remained at Constantinople over the winter "with his princes (*cum suis principibus*)."[38] The prominence accorded in the sources to the death of Count Bernard of Plotzkau, while in part clearly due to his bravery, may also have been because casualties of his high social status among the German army were relatively rare.[39]

---

[34] WT 17.1, p. 760; *Gesta Friderici*, 1.62, p. 89. Robert of Capua was named by John of Salisbury, *Historia Pontificalis*, pp. 58–59. The death of Adolf IV of Mons (*Berge*) at the siege of Damascus was recorded by the *Chronica Regia Coloniensis*, p. 84.

[35] *De Investigatione Antichristi*, c. 59, ed. Ernst Sackur, MGH *Libelli de Lite* 3 (Hanover, 1897), 374–75.

[36] *Annales Palidenses*, MGH SS 16.83; *Die Urkunden Konrads III*, pp. 354–55 no. 195.

[37] *Annales Herbipolenses*, MGH SS 16.6.

[38] WT 16.23, p. 749; trans. Emily Babcock and August Krey, 2 (New York, 1943) 172, who render this 'nobles'.

[39] *De Profectione Ludovici*, pp. 92–95; *Annales Palidenses*, *Annales Magdeburgenses*, MGH SS 16, pp. 83, 188.

The French sources do indeed name a number of prominent nobles who perished, especially when traversing Mount Cadmus in January 1148, and casualties were heavy in the royal bodyguard, which was in the thick of the fighting.[40] But Odo of Deuil claimed that the French reached Anatalya "without suffering any loss to our forces except on the day when we made Geoffrey de Rancon our leader to death and destruction" (that is, on Mount Cadmus), and that it was the shortage of horses that then prevented the nobles continuing their journey overland.[41] William of Tyre, after an affecting account of the appalling losses the French had suffered, then contradicted himself by claiming that the food shortage at Anatalya was caused by "the great numbers of people who had come there." But, he noted, it was "above all the poor" who suffered from hunger.[42] (This was, of course, precisely what had occurred during the First Crusade, and was to happen once again in 1190.[43]) After Louis and his barons had set off by sea to Antioch, the poor who were left behind set out under the command of the count of Flanders to march there, and were very roughly handled by the Turks. But, again, we should note that the count of Flanders survived, and was one of those present at Acre in June 1148, "along with many other important nobles of high rank."[44]

Thus, while the forces which reached the Holy Land may have been much less numerous than those who set out – and we should not forget too that some of the Germans, disheartened and short of money, returned home from Constantinople after their travails in western Asia Minor[45] – at least some of the hard core of the crusader armies, the great nobles and their *familiae*, survived, and were available for military operations against the Turks in the summer of 1148. In addition, the funds provided by the Emperor Manuel enabled Conrad to hire troops in the Holy Land, largely from the pilgrims who had arrived there on the normal *passagium*, and to subsidize those of the German knights who were still with him, but were by now running short of money.[46] Louis VII had written from Antioch to his regent back home, Abbot Suger, that "we and the majority of our princes arrived safely by sea at the aforesaid city," and it was only shortage of cash that hindered him from

---

[40] *De Profectione Ludovici*, pp. 118–23; Louis VII to Abbot Suger (March/April 1148), RHGF 15.495–96. Cf. WT 16.25, pp. 750–52.

[41] *De Profectione Ludovici*, pp. 128–29, 134–35.

[42] WT 16.26, pp. 753–54.

[43] Cf. the account of the siege of Nicaea by the *Gesta Francorum*, p. 17: "many of the poor starved to death for the Name of Christ"; and in 1190 when "some of the infantry among our men had eaten up all their supplies," and "others among the infantry were so weakened that they lay down to await death," *Quellen zur Geschichte des Kreuzzuges Kaiser Friedrichs I.*, pp. 77, 79.

[44] *De Profectione Ludovici*, pp. 138–41; WT 17.1, pp. 760–61.

[45] *De Profectione Ludovici*, pp. 96–97; *Annales Herbipolenses*, p. 6.

[46] Rudolf Hiestand, "'Kaiser' Konrad III, der zweite Kreuzzug und ein verlorenes Diplom für den Berg Thabor," *Deutsches Archiv für Erforschung des Mittelalters* 35 (1979), 94–96. Otto of Freising noted that: "as the knights arrived, he [Conrad] induced all that he could by [gifts of] money to remain," *Gesta Friderici*, 1.62, p. 89.

"furthering Christ's business." He appears to have solved this problem, at least for a time, by borrowing from the Templars.[47]

We should also remember that however reduced the French and German armies of 1148 were, indeed even if they now comprised only "the few princes and other magnates for whom neither courage nor cash was lacking," by whom, according to Gerhoh of Reichersberg, King Conrad was accompanied,[48] they were still potentially a very significant reinforcement for the relatively small armies of the crusader states. For if the kingdom of Jerusalem could muster some 1,200 knights at the Battle of Hattin,[49] including those of the military orders, it is unlikely that the number available was anything approaching this forty years earlier. If the number of knights from the secular lordships was probably somewhat less than, but perhaps not far short of, the 670 recorded in the surviving late twelfth-century fief list, the contribution of the military orders, much less well-endowed in 1148 than later, was surely appreciably less, even though the two masters were already sufficiently significant to be present at the council that decided to attack Damascus.[50] Meanwhile, one plausible estimate suggests that Antioch and Tripoli could provide perhaps 500 knights between them.[51] Even a few hundred knights would therefore be a valuable addition to the troops available to the Franks of the East. And, whatever the losses in Asia Minor, what was left of the western armies probably provided at least those few hundred, and perhaps considerably more. Certainly Ibn al-Qalanisi claimed that, when the Franks besieged Damascus, they had at first a considerable advantage: "the infidels gained the upper hand over the Muslims owing to the superiority of their numbers and equipment."[52]

The ultimately ill-fated decision to attack Damascus is the third and final issue to be considered here. It is of course a much-discussed topic, yet there are still aspects of that decision that have not been sufficiently emphasized by modern scholars. Recent analysis has indeed stressed one important point – with the rapprochement between Damascus and Aleppo in the spring of 1147, and Frankish and Damascene forces clashing in the Hauran that summer, the attack in 1148 was in no sense an

---

[47] RHGF 15.496 [see above, note 37], ibid., 501–502.

[48] *De Investigatione Antichristi*, c. 59, MGH *Libelli de Lite* 3.376.

[49] *De Expugnatione Terrae Sanctae per Saladinum libellus*, in Ralph of Coggeshall, *Chronicon Anglicanum*, ed. Joseph Stevenson, RS 66 (London, 1875), p. 218.

[50] WT 17.1, p. 761. Peter W. Edbury, *John of Ibelin and the Kingdom of Jerusalem* (Woodbridge, 1997), pp. 133, 195–99.

[51] Claude Cahen, *La Syrie du Nord à l'époque des croisades et la principauté franque d'Antioche* (Paris, 1940), p. 328. At the Battle of the Field of Blood in 1119 the Antiochene army was estimated at 700 knights and 3,000 infantry, *Galterii Cancellarii Bella Antiochena*, ed. Heinrich Hagenmayer (Innsbruck, 1896), 2.5, p. 88. But after that disaster, and with the losses of territory in the 1120s and 1130s, it is most unlikely that the principality could have raised as many troops by 1148.

[52] *The Damascus Chronicle of the Crusades*, trans. Hamilton A. R. Gibb (London, 1932), p. 284.

unprovoked assault on a friendly city.[53] Yet, even if the former alliance between Damascus and the kingdom of Jerusalem was no longer in operation, that city and its ruler were not a significant threat to the crusader states, while Nur ad-Din, the ruler of Aleppo and son of the conqueror of Edessa undoubtedly was. Prince Raymond of Antioch clearly recognized this, and consequently urged the French king to take part in an expedition against Aleppo when Louis arrived in Antioch in February 1148. William of Tyre indeed suggests that he had had such a campaign in mind even before the king had set out, when the forthcoming expedition was only a rumour. But he goes on to add that what the prince wanted was to enlarge his own principality.[54] Was this, after all, what Louis had come to the east to do?

Edessa, the fall of which had been the ostensible cause for the Crusade, was not by 1148 a practical target, even though Conrad, in his letter from Constantinople in January still considered it the ultimate goal of the expedition. But it was too isolated, and the massacre or exile of most of the native Christian population after Count Joscelin's ill-fated attempt to recapture the city in November 1146 would have made it impossible to hold anyway.[55] Nor was this an enterprise that would probably have interested the prince of Antioch, who (according to William of Tyre) had "rejoiced in the count's misfortune" and done nothing to help him against Zengi in 1144.[56] However, there were other considerations that led to the French army leaving Antioch and marching south in April 1148.

The most sensational explanation for this move was the suspicion, genuine or imagined, that King Louis had begun to entertain concerning his wife's relations with her uncle, Raymond of Antioch. Yet, even though these rumours were reported by three separate and apparently unrelated sources, we would do well to remain sceptical. While such gossip was common in medieval courts (think of the slanders directed against the Empress Judith and Bernard of Septimania in the ninth century, the Empress Agnes of Germany during her widowhood in the 1060s,[57] Queen Melisende of Jerusalem and Hugh of Le Puiset only a few years before the Second Crusade, or Queen Margaret of Sicily and her minister Stephen of Perche in the

---

[53] Martin Hoch, "The Choice of Damascus as the Objective of the Second Crusade: a Re-evaluation," in *Autour*, pp. 359–69; Hiestand, "'Kaiser' Konrad III, der zweite Kreuzzug und ein verlorenes Diplom," pp. 91–92.

[54] WT 16.27, p. 754. Here he may have been thinking not so much of a direct attack upon Aleppo as of re-establishing the chain of fortresses that the principality had possessed around that city before the disastrous defeat of 1119; for which Thomas S. Asbridge, *The Creation of the Principality of Antioch 1098–1130* (Woodbridge, 2000), pp. 59–62, 65–67.

[55] WT 16.14–16, pp. 734–38. Runciman, *History*, 2.240; M. Hoch, *Jerusalem, Damaskus und der zweite Kreuzzug. Konstitutionelle Krise und äußere Sicherheit des Kreuzfahrerkönigreiches Jerusalem A.D. 1126–1154* (Frankfurt am Main, 1993), p. 106.

[56] WT 16.4, p. 720. Hiestand, "'Kaiser' Konrad III, der zweite Kreuzzug und ein verlorenes Diplom," pp. 88–89.

[57] *Lamperti Monachi Hersfeldensis Opera*, p. 79.

late 1160s),⁵⁸ the public nature of such courts rendered the reality unlikely, and in this particular case the relationship would also have been grossly incestuous. Furthermore, all three accounts, by Gerhoh of Reichersberg, John of Salisbury and William of Tyre, were written some years after the event – Gerhoh's *De Investigatione Antichristi*, from c.1161, was the earliest of the three. The authors therefore wrote in the knowledge that King Louis had later repudiated his wife, who had promptly married his main political rival – something which Gerhoh expressly mentioned – and would therefore be disposed to believe the worst about their marriage.⁵⁹

It has also been argued that Raymond's earlier acknowledgement of Byzantine suzerainty over Antioch would have made King Louis unwilling to co-operate with him in military operations, given the bad feelings towards Byzantium engendered in the French ranks by the passage through the empire and across Asia Minor. Louis would therefore have been reluctant to do anything that would contribute, even indirectly, to an increase in Byzantine territory or authority.⁶⁰

Much more significant, however, was the attraction exerted by Jerusalem. It has indeed been suggested that the pilgrimage to Jerusalem was the overwhelming reason why King Louis had set out on the expedition in the first place, that his wish to go on pilgrimage antedated the news of the fall of Edessa, and that he was far more concerned with the spiritual implications of his journey than with fighting for the faith.⁶¹ This argument might seem to be supported by the fact that Louis undertook two separate ceremonies before departing on the expedition, taking the cross at Vézelay at Easter 1146, but only receiving the pilgrim's wallet from the pope at St Denis in June 1147.⁶² However, at this early date in the evolution of Crusader ideology we should be cautious about drawing an artificial distinction between 'pilgrimage' and 'crusade', especially since the latter term was still only in embryo – Odo admittedly did use the phrase *militia crucis Christi*.⁶³ Rather, the ideal of pilgrimage was central to and permeated the whole expedition. Even the

---

⁵⁸ For this last, *La Historia o Liber de Regno Sicilie di Ugo Falcando*, ed. Giovanni Battista Siragusa (Fonti per la storia d'Italia, Rome, 1897), p. 118. In three of the four cases, a queen/empress was accused of having a sexual relationship with a political ally to whom she was distantly related; Agnes with a bishop who was a trusted adviser.

⁵⁹ *De Investigatione Antichristi*, p. 376; *Historia Pontificalis*, pp. 52–53; WT 16.27, p. 755; trans. Babcock and Krey, 2.180, who were convinced that adultery had taken place. But William was probably writing this in the 1170s. While there are indications that the marriage was not particularly happy, it was Eleanor's failure to produce a male heir that ultimately forced Louis to repudiate her, see Georges Duby, *The Knight, the Lady and the Priest. The Making of Modern Marriage in Medieval France*, trans. Barbara Bray (Harmondsworth, 1985), pp. 189–98.

⁶⁰ Jonathan Phillips, *Defenders of the Holy Land. Relations between the Latin East and the West, 1119–1187* (Oxford, 1996), pp. 92–96.

⁶¹ Aryeh Graboïs, "The Crusade of King Louis VII: a Reconsideration", in *CS*, pp. 94–104.

⁶² *De Profectione Ludovici*, pp. 8–9, 16–17.

⁶³ Ibid., pp. 12–13.

Anglo-Flemish attack on Lisbon was regarded as being part of a pilgrimage.[64] Louis himself wrote to Abbot Suger from Constantinople about "the wearisome journey of holy pilgrimage (*sacrosanctae perigrinationis iter laboriosum*)," and said to the envoys of the king of Hungary that "he must not do anything … which ill became a pilgrim." But when proposals were made to attack the Byzantines, it was other Frenchmen opposed to this who said that: "we are to visit the Holy Sepulchre."[65] Nor was this desire confined to the French, for the Germans, or at least those who described their expedition, saw this as the "way to Jerusalem" or "for the liberation of Jerusalem."[66] Conrad's first action on arriving in the Holy Land was to "venerate the Sepulchre of Christ with due honour," while Alfonso of Toulouse died "on his way to Jerusalem to give thanks for the successful accomplishment of his pilgrimage."[67] The Byzantine historian Niketas Choniates, albeit writing a long time after the event, was also clear that Jerusalem was the goal of the expedition.[68] Even Ibn al-Qalanisi noted that the Franks "repaired to Jerusalem and carried out the obligation of their pilgrimage."[69] One might suggest therefore that it was not simply Louis but his army who wished to press on to Jerusalem, visit the Holy Places and acquit themselves of their vow.

Once the French had marched the 250 miles (400 kilometres) south from Antioch to Jerusalem, it was highly unlikely that they would wish to retrace their steps for a campaign in the north.[70] Not only this, but Conrad and his "new army" were already in the kingdom of Jerusalem, and it was obviously in the interests of the Franks that they should work together. Given that Conrad was already in the south, it was thus inevitable that any military operation would take place in Palestine rather than in northern Syria.

In addition, it was also unfeasible that Baldwin III of Jerusalem, with his authority in his kingdom as yet weak and locked in dispute with his mother and her supporters, would be willing to take part in a campaign in the north, particularly when his predecessors' prolonged absences in Antioch – however necessary they may have been – had proved unpopular, and in the reign of his grandfather potentially destabilizing. Baldwin II had indeed put an end to such murmurings by

---

[64] *De Expugnatione Lyxbonensi*, ed. and trans. Charles W. David (New York, 1936), pp. 70–71, 108–109.

[65] RHGF 15.488 (soon after 4 October 1147); *De Profectione Ludovici*, pp. 36–39, 70–71.

[66] *De Investigatione Antichristi*, pp. 375–76; *Annales Herbipolenses*, MGH SS 16.3; *Annales Magdeburgenses*, ibid., 188.

[67] *Annales Palidenses*, MGH SS 16.83; WT 16.28, p. 756. Cf. *Deeds of John and Manuel Comnenus*, pp. 71–72: Conrad "performed appropriate rites at the life-giving tomb of Christ."

[68] *O City of Byzantium*, p. 36: "they declared and affirmed by oath that Jerusalem was [the] motive for their expedition. Later events proved their declaration was not false"; cf. also p. 43.

[69] *The Damascus Chronicle*, p. 282.

[70] William of Tyre considered the Principality of Antioch to be fifteen days' march from Jerusalem. This was surely an underestimate, unless he was referring to the southern border of the principality, WT 17.16, p. 782.

attempting the conquest of Damascus in the later 1120s.[71] In 1148, according to William of Tyre, "the chief men of the realm greatly feared that the king [of France] would be detained in the vicinity of Aleppo," and sent the patriarch to persuade him to come south to Jerusalem.[72] Their interest was to expand their own kingdom, not the northern states. Similarly, two years later a number of Baldwin III's nobles refused to accompany him on a campaign in Antioch, even though the principality was gravely threatened at the time.[73]

Otto of Freising indeed suggested that the decision to attack Damascus had already been taken, while Conrad was staying in Jerusalem after Easter, in a meeting with Baldwin III, the patriarch and the Templars.[74] In that case, therefore, the subsequent meeting at Acre was merely confirming a choice that had previously been made, before Louis had even arrived from the north. But, while some modern historians have noted that circumstance,[75] two other factors may also have been significant. First, assuming that Conrad had fulfilled his earlier pilgrimage, he would have been in the Holy Land either just before or at the time (early in 1126) when the first serious attack upon Damascus had been undertaken by Baldwin II, indeed it is not impossible that he may have taken part in it.[76] Thus Conrad might well have been predisposed to see Damascus as the obvious target for an attack by the crusaders. Secondly, Conrad was much the older and more experienced of the two western rulers and, while he had never gone to Rome to receive his imperial coronation, he still effectively enjoyed the prestige of that imperial status, shown not just by his own use of the title *augustus*, but by the way that Odo of Deuil described him as *imperator*.[77] Thus, if Conrad and the men of Jerusalem had decided to attack Damascus, it was unlikely that the king of France would oppose this – not that there is any indication that he did. Furthermore, there was nobody from the northern principalities present at Acre to put forward the case for military operations in the north, even had these been acceptable to the nobles of Jerusalem.[78]

Hence, far from being "incredibly stupid,"[79] the decision to attack Damascus in 1148 was all but inevitable. Having undergone all the trials and sacrifices of the journey, the westerners wanted to strike a blow for Christendom. Whether or not the

---

[71] Alan V. Murray, "Baldwin II and his Nobles: Baronial Factionalism and Dissent in the Kingdom of Jerusalem, 1118–1134," *Nottingham Medieval Studies* 38 (1994), 60–85.

[72] WT 16.29, p. 757.

[73] WT 17.15, p. 780.

[74] *Gesta Friderici Imperatoris*, 1.62, p. 89.

[75] Hans E. Mayer, "Studies in the History of Queen Melisende of Jerusalem," *Dumbarton Oaks Papers* 26 (1972), 127–28; Hoch, "The Choice of Damascus," p. 366.

[76] For this attack, WT 13.18, pp. 609–10.

[77] *De Profectione Ludovici*, pp. 34–35, 46–49, 102–103. Hiestand, "'Kaiser' Konrad III, der zweite Kreuzzug und ein verlorenes Diplom," pp. 113–19; Jonathan Phillips, "Odo of Deuil's *De Profectione Ludovici VII in Orientem* as a Source for the Second Crusade," in *The Experience of Crusading. 1 Western Approaches*, ed. Marcus Bull and Norman Housley (Cambridge, 2003), pp. 94–95.

[78] As perceptively noted by Hoch, *Jerusalem, Damaskus und der zweite Kreuzzug*, p. 120.

[79] Mayer, *The Crusades*, p. 103.

Franks of the East had sought the crusade to begin with,[80] they clearly did not wish to waste the opportunity that the arrival of western troops provided, and whatever the scale of the losses in Asia Minor, those westerners who did eventually arrive in the Holy Land still represented a substantial reinforcement for the relatively exiguous forces of the crusader states. While a campaign in the north against Aleppo might well have been in the best strategic interests of the crusader states, that was never a practical possibility, given both the lack of enthusiasm among the Jerusalemite nobility for a campaign in the north and the overwhelming significance of Jerusalem as a goal for the march of the westerners. Once the westerners had arrived at Jerusalem, Damascus was the obvious target, far more so than Ascalon, even though the latter town remained in Muslim hands.[81] Nor should we assume, whatever the later recriminations and accusations of treachery, that the siege of July 1148 was merely a token and half-hearted attempt on that city. Certainly the Damascus Chronicle of Ibn al-Qalanisi suggests that there was fierce fighting, with heavy casualties on both sides. He reported that when the Franks retreated the Muslims found numerous burial pits for both men and horses. He was also clear that it was the threat of being trapped by fresh Muslim forces coming to relieve the city that led to this withdrawal, and made no mention of the bribery or disaffection stigmatized by later western commentators.[82] Here the contemporary desire for scapegoats to explain an embarrassing failure has seriously muddied the waters.

What transpired in 1148 might indeed seem to fit the classic definition of tragedy: the disastrous consequences of a process that unfolded ineluctably, but into which the protagonists were drawn for entirely understandable and logical reasons. We should not, however, be misled; either by subsequent rationalizations by often ill-informed contemporaries, or by modern-day calculations of strategic interest that cannot be reconciled with twelfth-century realities, into assuming that it was simply the result of folly.

---

[80] The principal evidence to suggest that they had not is a letter from Pope Adrian IV to Louis VII, dated February 1159, in which he claimed that Louis and Conrad had undertaken the road to Jerusalem, *inconsulto populo terre*, PL 188, cols. 1615–17 no. 241, at 1616, discussed by Constable, "The Second Crusade as Seen by Contemporaries," p. 275. However, cf. Phillips, *Defenders of the Holy Land*, pp. 80–81.

[81] As Hoch ("The choice of Damascus," p. 366) notes, Ascalon had been largely neutralized by the chain of fortresses constructed by King Fulk *c.*1136–42. But in addition (a) Damascus was a larger city, and thus if hostile, potentially a much greater threat, (b) it was a wealthy city, and its conquest would give the Franks full control over the fertile area east of the Jordan and the Golan heights, (c) given its appearance in the Acts of the Apostles (especially chapter 9, the conversion of St Paul), if not in the Gospels, it had greater religious significance than Ascalon.

[82] *The Damascus Chronicle*, pp. 286–87. Cf. here Alan J. Forey, "The Failure of the Siege of Damascus in 1148," *Journal of Medieval History* 10 (1984), 13–23, for a more extended analysis.

Ermengol de Aspa, *Provisor* of the Hospital: 1188

Anthony Luttrell

Bath

Many things about Ermengol de Aspa, including his origins and the nature of his brief rule over the Hospital, remain uncertain and hypothetical,[1] but some new information is provided by the documentation from the Hospitallers' female monastery at Sigena, founded by Sancha of Castile, queen of Aragon, in 1187.[2] Ermengol seems likely to have been a Catalan from Aspa some 13 kilometres south of Lleida; a Saint Ermengol had been Bishop of Lleida and at least ten counts of Urgel bore the same name. The form Armengaud was, however, common in Southern France and there was a Valley of the Aspe in the Basses-Pyrénées south of Pau.[3] If he did come from Western Catalunya, that might have led to Ermengol's close association with Queen Sancha in the establishment of the house at nearby Sigena in which both the crown and the Order had deep interests.

Whether or not he owed his advancement to the queen, Ermengol was *magister* or castellan of Amposta, as the Hospital's prior in Aragon and Catalunya was entitled, in 1180 when, at Sancha's request, her husband Alfonso II addressed an important donation to him. Ermengol was also castellan in 1183 when he received another grant in Aragon.[4] In 1182, and again in 1184 when Sancha made an exchange with the Templars over properties which were intended to pass to Sigena, Ermengol was involved as prior of Saint-Gilles, while in 1184 he was described as *magister in Provincia et toto regno Aragonum*; a separate and presumably subordinate castellan of Amposta, Pedro Eximénez de Luna, was mentioned in the same text.[5] The prior of Saint-Gilles was the Hospital's overall provincial

---

[1] Jonathan Riley-Smith, *The Knights of St. John in Jerusalem and Cyprus: c. 1050–1310* (London, 1967), pp. 106–107.

[2] Agustín Ubieto Arteta, *Documentos de Sigena*, 1 (Valencia, 1972); these documents have been used by Luis García-Guijarro Ramos in a forthcoming study of Sigena's early years.

[3] Joseph Delaville le Roulx (*Les Hospitaliers en Terre Sainte et à Chypre: 1100–1310* (Paris, 1904), p. 101) proposes Asp in the Vivarais near Valence or Aspe in Biscay.

[4] *Cart Hosp*, nos. 586–88; María Luisa Ledesma Rubio, *La Encomienda de Zaragoza de la Orden de San Juan de Jerusalén en los siglos XII y XIII* (Zaragoza, 1967), pp. 230–31, 234–35.

[5] *Cart Hosp*, no. 677. Ermengol was prior of Saint-Gilles from 1182 to May 1188: *Cart Hosp*, nos. 619, 677, 781, 818, 820, 822, 829, 835; *Cartulaire du Prieuré de Saint-Gilles de l'Hôpital de Saint-Jean de Jérusalem: 1129–1210*, ed. Daniel Le Blevec and Alain Venturini (Paris, 1997), nos. 274, 290, 313–16, 318, 320, 369. The Aragonese Eximénez de Lavata was commander of Huesca in 1198, castellan of Amposta in 1201–05, prior of Saint-Gilles in 1205, grand commander in Spain in 1208–10 and grand commander in the West in 1208: *Cart Hosp*, nos. 1014, 1150, 1228, 1319, 1357; *Libro de Privilegios de la Orden de San Juan de Jerusalén en Castilla y León (Siglos XII–XV)*, ed. Carlos de Martínez Ayala et al. (Madrid, 1995), pp. 380–83, 385.

commander in much of France and Spain, and probably in England as well;[6] he could at the same time be castellan of Amposta. Four earlier priors of Saint-Gilles had acted in important matters in Aragon or Catalunya: at Lleida in 1149, at Tortosa in 1153, probably at Lleida in 1166 and at Barbastro in 1178.[7]

Ermengol de Aspa was apparently in southern France on 7 March 1187 when the count of Provence addressed a confirmation to him.[8] The document which regulated the foundation of Sigena was enacted with Queen Sancha eight months later in October 1187. Its text reflected two stages. At some time before that October Ermengol, using the titles of prior of Saint-Gilles and castellan of Amposta, was acting with Gaufridus, who was Treasurer of the Hospital and who had powers over all the Hospital in the West; he secured the consent to a decision concerning Sigena of a joint chapter attended by brethren from Cerisiers, that is from Burgundy-France, from Saint-Gilles or Languedoc-Provence and from Amposta or Aragon-Catalunya. The text of October 1187, evidently drawn up at a second stage somewhere in Aragon, concluded with various names including that of Ermengol, but in the second section of the document he was entitled only as prior of Saint-Gilles. Also named were Odo, as *magister* in Burgundy, and García de Lisa, as castellan of Amposta. The text also contained Sancha's promise to become a Hospitaller, either as a *consoror* or perhaps as a *donat*.[9] García de Lisa must have become castellan between the point, perhaps earlier than November 1186, of Ermengol's joint chapter and October 1187.[10] Ermengol de Aspa was actually in Syria in October 1187 and his name and *signum*, and possibly those of Odo *magister* in Burgundy, were presumably inserted in the Aragonese document in their absence.

Possibly because he was one of the senior officers in the West and was responding to the death on 1 May 1187 of the Master Roger des Moulins, or conceivably in order to secure recognition for the Rule of Sigena, Ermengol was by October 1187 at Tyre. He was still prior of Saint-Gilles; with him was Borrellus, the *preceptor* or grand commander of the Hospital, who had taken charge in the East following the death of Roger des Moulins.[11] The Latins were crushingly defeated at Hattin on 4 July 1187,

---

[6] Riley-Smith, *The Knights of St. John*, pp. 353–57.

[7] *Cart Hosp*, nos. 181, 220, 364, 541.

[8] *Cart Hosp*, no. 829. According to Jean Raybaud, *Histoire des Grands Prieurs et du Prieuré de Saint-Gilles*, 1 (Nîmes, 1904), p. 92, Ermengol was at Trinquetaille (Arles) in September 1187 but it seems that the date was 7 March 1187 at Saint-Gilles; *Cartulaire du Prieuré de Saint-Gilles*, pp. 260–61.

[9] *Cart Hosp*, no. 835. In 1178 Odin, prior of Saint-Gilles, held a chapter at Cerisiers, the prior of England being a witness: *Cart Hosp*, no. 528. There was a prior of France in 1181/2: *Cart Hosp*, no. 627.

[10] Ermengol de Aspa, prior of Saint-Gilles, and García de Lisa, *magister* of Amposta, were with Alfonso II at the siege of Roda in November 1186: Jesús Alturo i Perucho, *Diplomatari d'Alguaire i del seu monastir santjoanista, de 1076 a 1244* (Barcelona, 1999), no. 55.

[11] Four texts in Louis Méry and F. Guindon, *Histoire analytique et chronologique des Actes et des Délibérations du Corps et du Conseil de la municipalité de Marseilles*, 1 (Marseilles, 1842), pp. 100–102; Giuseppe Müller, *Documenti sulle relazioni delle città toscane coll'Oriente cristiano e coi Turchi fino all'anno MDXXXI* (Florence, 1879), pp. 26–31. A version of one of these four texts given

Jerusalem fell on 2 October and by November Tyre was under siege. No successor to Roger de Moulins was chosen, perhaps because it was not practical to arrange an election in the confusion of the desperate crisis during which the Hospitallers fought hard but suffered serious reverses in campaigns against Saladin's forces.[12] In May 1188 Ermengol de Aspa was still at Tyre and still prior of Saint-Gilles.[13] He may have been chosen to lead the Hospital soon after, and in October 1188, using the title of *provisor Hospitalis* and employing the *sigillum domus*, he and other Hospitaller officials formally confirmed the new Rule of Sigena in a covering act addressed to Sancha and Alfonso. In it Ermengol was entitled *Domini patientia Christi pauperum servus et fratrum sancti Hospitalis Jerusalem provisor humilis*; with him were the grand commander, the marshal and the priors of Italy, *Alamania* and Bohemia.[14] In about November 1188 Ermengol wrote, still as *provisor*, to the duke of Austria announcing the loss of Tortosa.[15] He possessed a magistral-type seal found at Tyre and inscribed ARMENGAVDVS CVSTOS.[16] The form *cvstos* was normally found on magistral seals in the twelfth century.[17] In 1184 the master had been entitled *pauperum Christi minister*; in 1184/5 the pope addressed him as *provisor*; in 1186 he was *magister ac custos humilis*; in 1192 *humilis minister*; and in 1193 *magister*.[18] Ermengol seems never to have used the title *magister* in relation to the whole order. He was back in the West by November 1190 when the king of Castile granted an exemption for the Hospital which was addressed to him as *magister* of Amposta; that text also mentioned a prior *in Hispaniis*, presumably the prior of Castile, who was clearly subordinate to Ermengol.[19] Ermengol was still castellan of Amposta in April 1191.[20]

---

in Ferdinando Ughelli, *Italia Sacra*, 3 (Venice, 1718), pp. 415–17, omitted the Hospitaller witnesses, including Ermengol.

[12] Delaville le Roulx, *Hospitaliers en Terre Sainte*, pp. 99–104.

[13] Müller, *Documenti*, pp. 34–35. Delaville le Roulx, *Hospitaliers en Terre Sainte*, p. 102, shows that other references to a master during 1188 are unreliable.

[14] *Cart Hosp*, no. 860 [giving October 1188 and Indiction VI instead of Indiction VII]. Delaville le Roulx, *Hospitaliers en Terre Sainte*, p. 102, argues that the copyist must have seen the name *Heremenga*.

[15] RRH, no. 678.

[16] [Comte] Chandon de Brialles, "Bulles de l'Orient Latin," *Syria* 27 (1950), 296; pl. xiv(17). This seal may have been the *sigillum domus* of 1188 and was perhaps the master's leaden seal, since the conventual seal is not known before 1221 or 1239: Riley-Smith, *The Knights of St. John*, pp. 278–79, 295.

[17] Edwin King, *The Seals of the Order of St. John of Jerusalem* (London, 1932), pp. 10–13.

[18] *Cart Hosp*, nos. 663, 693, 803, 919, 941.

[19] *Libro de Privilegios*, pp. 354–55; the Castilian king addressed another donation to Ermengol as castellan on 1 December 1190: *Cart Hosp*, no. 902.

[20] *Cart Hosp*, no. 908 [summary]. On 26 May 1188 and in June 1195 the castellan was García de Lisa; on 3 June 1188, in May 1189, on 7 March 1190 (but not on 3 May 1190), in April and October 1192, and in 1193 the castellan was Fortún Cabeça: *Cart Hosp*, nos. 918, 949 [with incorrect summary]; Alturo i Perucho, *Diplomatari d'Alguaire*, nos. 61–62, 66, 69, 73, 78; Carlos Laliena Corbera, "Documentos de Ordenes Militares en Barbastro," in *Annales número monográfico: 850 Aniversario acuerdo de esponsales entre Petronila de Aragón y Ramón Berenguer IV de Barcelona: 1137–1987* (2nd ed., Barbastro, 2002), nos. 8–9, 12.

There may have been some western pressure for the unusual choice of a Catalan as master; indeed the Catalan Arnau de Torroja, a competent military and political figure, had been the Templar *magister* in Provence and *Hispania* and then, also unusually for a Catalan, had become master of the Temple from 1180 to 1184.[21] Ermengol may have proved an unsatisfactory leader in critical times; possibly there was Franco-Provençal resistance to the choice of a Catalan, and indeed by June 1191 Garnier of Naples or Nablus had reached Syria from England and had become master of the Hospital.[22] Gilbert d'Assailly in 1170/2 and Alfonso of Portugal in 1206 both resigned the mastership, but they were indisputably masters. Ermengol may have been a temporary interim choice.[23] He had the title of *provisor* which had been used, though not as a title, for Gerardus the early ruler of the Hospital in a papal privilege of 1113 which used the word *prepositus*; the term *provisor* was also used of the master in a royal charter of 1149 and a papal text of 1184/5.[24] However, the phrase *Christi pauperum servus* used for Ermengol was similar to the more usual *Christi pauperum custos*; the word *custos* was also used on Ermengol's seal. At Huesca in Aragon in March 1188 a document of Queen Sancha and of the new castellan, García de Lisa, was enacted by the castellan "with the council and will of the Jerusalem master." In one place the text read "cum consilio et voluntate magistri Iherosolimitani et consilio et voluntate fratris Garssia de Lisa, magister [*sic*] Emposte ...;" in another it read "ego Garsia de Lisa, magister Emposte, iussu magistri nostro Iherosolimitano [*sic*]."[25] This "Jerusalem master" may have been Roger de Moulins who had died in May 1187, since some time before October 1187 Sancha had made "repeated requests" with regard to Sigena to the "Jerusalem master";[26] alternatively, the queen and those Hospitallers with her might have considered that Ermengol was then master, though he was in fact still prior of Saint-Gilles in May 1188. The next master, Garnier of Nablus, may have been elected in the second half of 1189. He was in Paris and still prior of England at some point in the first half of 1190 and he was at Messina, still not using the title of master, in October 1190; by June 1191 he had reached Syria.[27] Philip de Milly, a Frenchman

---

[21] Marie-Luise Bulst-Thiele, *Sacrae Domus Militiae Templi Hierosolymitani Magistri: Untersuchungen zur Geschichte des Templerordens, 1118/9–1314* (Göttingen, 1974), pp. 99–105. The Templars also had a province which covered Southern France and Northern Spain: Alan Forey, *The Templars in the 'Corona de Aragón'* (London, 1973), pp. 88–89.

[22] Delaville le Roulx, *Hospitaliers en Terre Sainte*, pp. 106–109.

[23] As Riley-Smith (*The Knights of St. John*, p. 107) suggests, noting that Jean de Joinville later used the title of *prevoz* for a Lieutenant Master: *Histoire de Saint Louis par Jean Sire de Joinvillle*, ed. Natalis de Wailly (Paris, 1868), p. 87.

[24] *Cart Hosp*, nos. 30, 180, 693.

[25] Ubieto, *Documentos*, no. 6.

[26] *Cart Hosp*, no. 835.

[27] Delaville le Roulx, *Hospitaliers en Terre Sainte*, pp. 106–109, 408–409, 426. In 1187 Garnier was also involved with Hospitaller sisters, being at Buckland in England where a female house was being founded: *A Cartulary of Buckland Priory in the County of Somerset*, ed. Frederick Weaver (London, 1909), p. 118.

from Picardy who was lord of Nablus and who was possibly a kinsman of Garnier, had been elected master of the Temple in 1169, perhaps because the Syrian establishment wanted an eastern Latin to hold the mastership.[28] For whatever reason, Ermengol was back in the West by late 1190.[29]

Ermengol de Aspa's situation remained obscure, so much so that the Hospital's brief Chronicle of the Deceased Masters, of which the earliest known manuscripts date to about 1300, listed him as master but wrongly placed him after Garnier of Nablus.[30]

---

[28] Bulste-Thiele, *Sacrae Domus*, pp. 73–86; Malcolm Barber, "The Career of Philip of Nablus in the Kingdom of Jerusalem," in *The Experience of Crusading*, 2: *Defining the Crusader Kingdom*, ed. Peter Edbury and Jonathan Phillips (Cambridge, 2003), pp. 73–75.

[29] *Cart Hosp*, no. 902. Ermengol possibly returned to the West and again became castellan perhaps somewhat earlier than late 1190, since a donation of 3 May 1190 addressed to Fortún Cabeza gave the latter no title, though he had been castellan on 7 March 1190: Alturo i Perucho, *Diplomatari d'Alguaire*, nos. 69–70.

[30] For example, Paris, Bibliothèque Nationale, Ms. franç. 6049, fol. 143; Ms. franç. 1978, fol. 168.

Administrative Regulations for the Hospital of St John in Jerusalem dating from the 1180s

Susan B. Edgington

Queen Mary, University of London

Codex Vat. Lat 4852 comprises important Hospitaller documents, most of which were reproduced by Delaville le Roulx in the four-volume cartulary of the Order (*Cart Hosp*). He overlooked, however, fos. 83r–104r, which contain a set of regulations for the Hospital in Jerusalem in an Old French translation which was almost certainly carried out for Guillaume de Saint-Etienne towards the end of the thirteenth century.[1] The original regulations may be dated on internal grounds to the 1180s: after 1181 (when Cola was acquired by the Order) and before the capture of Jerusalem in 1187. It is likely that they relate to the rule of Roger des Moulins, that is, before 1183.[2] No other version of these regulations is known to exist, in Latin or French, except a very fragmentary Latin manuscript in Marseilles.[3]

The interest of the regulations lies in their very detailed instructions as to the daily and yearly routines of the hospital; the descriptions of the roles of officials, including one – the *karavannier* – not found elsewhere; the procedure for admissions, and much else. These have been discussed in detail elsewhere.[4] It is possible only to speculate as to why the information is so chaotically recorded: the Latin original may have been notes of discussions, a draft, or have become disordered in the transmission. Although the title suggests the procedures are already in place (*qui a este uzei*), they may represent standing orders for the institution rather than formal statutes.

A full transcription and translation of the regulations follow. In the Old French, abbreviations have been silently expanded, and suggestions have been offered for lacunae (marked [ ]) where they are obvious. The orthography of the original has

---

[1] Vat. Lat. 4852, fo. 140v, has the colophon: "Ce livre fist escrire frere Guillaume de saint Estiene frere de lospital de saint Johan de Jerusalem." For much of the information about 4852 I am indebted to Dr Katja Klement (hereafter KK) and her unpublished doctoral thesis: *"Von Krankenspeisen und Ärzten ...": Eine unbekannte Verfügung des Johannitermeisters Roger des Moulins (1177–1187) im Codex Vaticanus Latinus 4852* (Salzburg, 1996). KK further believes that the translator was Jean d'Antioche, since the hand is identical with Chantilly, Musée Condé 590, which is known to be his work (p. 101).

[2] Cf. *Cart Hosp* no. 627, pp. 425–29.

[3] Marseilles, Archives départementales des Bouches-du-Rhône 56 H 4055 no. 2. See Anthony Luttrell, "The Hospitallers' Early Written Records," *Crusade Sources*, pp. 135–54, at 140. I am grateful to Dr Luttrell for bringing ms. 4852 to my attention, and for providing me with his transcript of the Marseilles ms.

[4] Susan B. Edgington, "Medical Care in the Hospital of St John in Jerusalem," *MO, 2*, pp. 27–33; eadem, "The Hospital of St John in Jerusalem," *Medicine in Jerusalem through the Ages*, ed. Zohar Amar, Efraim Lev and Joshua Schwartz (Tel Aviv, 1999), pp. ix–xxv.

been preserved, except that 'i' as initial consonant has consistently been changed to 'j'. Punctuation has been standardized, so that commas replace full points within sentences. It will be noted that at several points my transcription and/or translation differ from those of Klement.[5]

---

[5] I am grateful to Carol Sweetenham for checking my translation and for several suggested improvements.

Administrative Regulations / Vat. Lat. 4852 / fos 83r–104r / Text and Translation.

MS Vat. Lat. 4852

/89r/ *Des viandes as malades et des mieges et de lordenement qui a este uzei au palais des malades a Jerusalem*

Ordene fu dou maistre de lospital et dou general chapistre que chascun jor chascun malade ait demi pain mouflet[1] et dou pain de la maison assez, et tel vin com le covent. Les mieges d[o]ivent regarder ententivement les qualitez des malades et quelz maladies ils ont, et doivent regarder les orines et doner les syrops et les laituaires et les autres /89v/ choses qui sont necessaires as malades et desfendre les choses contraires et doner les profitables, et de tant com il les verront plus malades et plus febles, tant soient plus apareillielliez encor lor sante procurer. Les viandes d[e]s malades doivent estre teles. De Pasques jusques a la fiste[2] saint michiel aient char de poucins et autre volatile, et char de chevrel et daigneaus qui nont pas .i. an, et char de chastron dun an et plus sicom li fisicien deviseront lor /90r/ soit amenistre. De la feste saint michiel jusqua karesme char de poucins, et autresi com est devant dit. Et char de porc mahle dun an ensi come le miege devisera. De chars femeles de beste a .iiii. pies li malade ne manicent[3] en nul tems, ne les freres qui servent as malades ne lor doignent. En karehme peisson fres soit done as malades .iii. fois la semane,[4] se le malade loze mangier por sa maladie, et ce soit fait par conseil de miege. Joute et autres /90v/ [ ]nnaz[5] de leguns et farine dorge et autres viandes covenables a malade lor soit done par conseil de miege. Et bien apareilliez as jors establiz lor soient donez. Anguiles et fromage et lentilles et feves et chols et autres viandes qui sont contraires a malade nos defendons que ne lor soit done.

Des fruiz establi[6] por les malades

Des fruiz darbres sicome pomes grenates et autres[7] pomes, poires, prunes, fyes, et raisins sicome les mais- /91r/ tres qui furent devant nos establirent et ordenerent au chapistre de lospital de Jerusalem et a eus des povres et a lor profiz la tierte partie lor soit donee.

Des establissemenz des freres et des sergens par les rues

En chascune rue des malades ores et desoren avant ait .xii. sergens qui facent les liz des malades et qui les gardent de toute ordure et qui les mainent as chambres

---

[1] mouflet KK
[2] fest KK
[3] maiucent KK
[4] semaine KK
[5] cuisinaz KK
[6] establiz KK
[7] grenates et autres *om.* KK

Translation

Concerning foods for the sick and about doctors and about the arrangements which have been customary in the palace of the sick in Jerusalem.
It was ordained by the master of the hospital and by the general chapter that each patient[a] should have each day half a soft loaf and sufficient house-bread, and the same wine as the convent. The doctors should observe closely the condition of the sick and what illnesses they have, and should inspect their urine and give syrups and electuaries and other things which may be necessary for sick people and forbid contrary things and give them useful ones, and the more ill and more infirm are the patients they see, the more trouble yet they should take to restore their health. Foods for the sick should be thus: from Easter to Michaelmas they have the meat of chickens and other fowl, and meat of goats and lambs not yet one year old and meat of sheep one year old and more as often as the physician may instruct them to be provided. From Michaelmas to Lent meat of chickens and the same as was said before, and pork from the male animal one year old according as the doctor shall prescribe. Sick people should never eat female flesh from an animal with four feet, nor are the brothers who serve the sick ever to give them any. In Lent fresh fish is to be given to the sick 3 times a week, if the patient dare eat it for his sickness, and this is to be done on the advice of the doctor. Broth and other cooked dishes of vegetables and barley flour and other foods suitable for the sick are to be given to them on the advice of the doctor, and they are to be given to them well prepared on the days appointed. Eels and cheese and lentils and beans and cabbages and other foods which are contra-indicated for the sick, we prohibit them to be given to them.

Concerning fruits prescribed for the sick.
A third part of the tree-fruits, such as pomegranates and other apples, pears, plums, figs and grapes are to be given to them as the masters who were before us laid down and ordained in the chapter of the hospital of Jerusalem both for the use of the poor and for their profit.

Concerning the establishment of brothers and serjeants throughout the wards.
In each ward of sick people there are to be now and henceforth 12 serjeants who make the beds for the sick and keep them from any soiling and take them to the privies and guide them and support them closely. From procession to procession –

---

[a] The OF substantive 'malade' has generally been translated as 'patient'.

governant et soustenant estr[ ]ite[8] au passage de passage de Pasques et de la sainte croiz soient /91v/ mis plus de sergens selonc la disposicion dou frere hospitalier. Parmi les rues doivent estre les freres qui veillent de nuit, cest a savoir .ii. freres qui doivent veillier chascune nuit que nul contraire nen aviegne a noz seignors malades.

Des m. et v^c. bezants por les malades
Il est jugie et establi au chapistre general que m. et v^c. bezants soient donez au frere hospitalier qui a la cure des malades por louer mieges et por amandles as malades par an de la premiere aumone qui sera /92r/ aportee as .ii. passages en tel maniere, cest a savoir que la meitie de ceaus bezants aiant[9] nomez soient renduz a lospitalier au passage de Pasques, et lautre meitie au passage de la sainte croiz. Les quels bezants doivent premierement estre paiez sicom il est dit, et lautre aumone qui remaint doit etre[10] despendue au servise de la maison.

Les casaus des malades
Ces sont les casaus qui ai les avenemenz des fruiz et des boucs et des berbis et des chievres et des porcs et des gelines estre le co- /92v/ mun bienfait de la maison sont des malades, cest a savoir le casal de mont gabriel, Le casal sareth, le casal de cuisinat,[11] le casal sainte[12] marie, le casal Caphaer, Le casal cole, dont nul home ne soit ozei iceste constitucion troubler ou icestes possessions tolir ne amermer ne travaillier par aucune moleste, mais toutes les choses des malades soient gardees enteririement[13] au profit de lospital de Jerusalem.

Dou receivement et dou benefice /93r/ et de la garde des povres de Jesu Crist
Quant li malades vient a lospital saint Johan il doit entrer en liglise, et doit atendre tant que aucun des chapelains viegne selonc la coustume et lestabliment de la maison de la charite. Les chapelainz qui a cest office sont mis, vienent au malade et le confessent, le cumenient et le mainent au palais. Li sergent soient apareillie qui le receivent. Et sil est tems de dihner ou de souper il le man-/93v/nient as tables qui sont dejouste lautel dou palais des malades et la manicient[14] et boivent se il veulent.[15]

Apres sont menez en la chambre de la karavane et sont despoillie et les robes liees fermement et moustrees as malades que chascun sache conoistre le sac[16] quant

---

[8] estreice KK
[9] avant KK
[10] estre KK
[11] tuisinat KK
[12] saint KK
[13] enterinement KK
[14] maniuent KK
[15] voulent KK
[16] so(c?e?) [*sic*] KK

that is, from Easter to the feast of the Holy Cross – more serjeants are to be appointed as the brother hospitaller orders. Among the wards there are to be brothers who keep watch at night, that is to say 2 brothers who are to keep watch each night in order that nothing adverse should happen to our sick lords.

Concerning the 1500 bezants for the sick.
It was judged and decided in the chapter general that 1,500 bezants should be given to the brother hospitaller who has the care of the sick to hire doctors and for almonds for the sick every year from the first almsgiving, which is to be brought at the 2 processions in such a way: that is to say: half of these bezants aforementioned are to be paid to the hospitaller at the procession at Easter, and the other half at the procession of the Holy Cross. These bezants are in the first place to be paid as has been said, and the other alms which remain should be spent in the service of the house.

The casales *of the sick.*
These are the *casales* which produce fruit and bucks and ewes and goats and pigs and hens, not for the common advantage of the house but for the sick, that is to say: the *casale* of Mount Gabriel; the *casale* Sareth; the *casale* of Tuisinat; the *casale* St Mary; the *casale* Caphaer; the *casale* Cola.[b] Regarding these, let no man dare to disturb these arrangements or steal our possessions, nor diminish, nor damage them in any way, but all the things for the sick are to be kept entirely for the benefit of the hospital of Jerusalem.

Concerning the reception and the privileges and the care of the poor of Jesus Christ.
When the sick come to the hospital of St John they must enter the church and wait for one of the chaplains to come according to the custom and establishment of the house of charity. The chaplains who have been appointed to this task come to the patient and confess him and give him communion and lead him to the palace. The serjeants should be ready to receive him. And if it is time for dinner or supper they should take him to the tables which are next to the altar of the palace of the sick and there he will eat and drink if he wants to.

Afterwards they will be taken into the room of the *karavane*[c] and undressed and their clothes tied up tightly and shown to the sick so that each one can recognize his own bundle when he wants to leave. And the *karavannier* is to give each a pair of linen sheets and 1 cover and 1 pillow[d] and 1 goblet and 1 spoon and 1 barrel to put

---

[b] Cola was acquired by the Order in 1181 and thus its inclusion here gives a *terminus post quem* for the original document: see Denys Pringle, *Secular Buildings in the Crusader Kingdom of Jerusalem: An Archaeological Gazetteer* (Cambridge, 1997), no. 180, p. 87, *s.v.* Qula.

[c] This office and the official in charge – the 'karavannier' – are unique to this document.

[d] KK's suggestion for 'profinel'.

il vodront departir. Et le karavanier doint a chascun .i. paire[17] de linceaus et .i. covertour, et .i. profinel,[18] et .i. hanap, et une cuillier, et .i. baril a metre son vin, et li doint .i. sergent /94r/ qui le maine couchier, puis li demandent sil a monoie quil la doint a garder a lospitalier. Le testament soit fait devant lospitalier, ou par devant aucun de ses compaignons, et selonc le pooir de la maison le testament soit tenu .i. frere et le Notaire soufisant au testament, et se le malade veaut il puet apeler .i. chapelain ou une autre persone et face sa devise sicom dex li enseignera, et le notaire doit metre en parchemin quoique[19] il li dira. Le frere qui est present li doit moustrer /94v/ les bienfaiz de la maison, et li amoneste que premierement doint a la maison.

Touz les jors apres la messe matinal soient apareillie li sergent qui doignent dou vin as malades de celui dont le covent boit et ausi temprei et chascun en preigne demi litre en son baril. Et se le malade ne veaut dou vin ait dou sucre le pois de la quarte part. Apres mannicent[20] li sergent lor matinel [ ] .i. pain et .i. hanap de Berrie plain de vin de covent et u- /95r/ ne escuele de cuisinat. Endemetiers que cil mangeront lospitalier et ses compaignons et cil qui repaireront en sa chambre servent as[21] plus febles qui sont es chambres des meillors et des plus delices viandes qui sont en la maison.

Quant li sergent auront mangie len doit soner une campane qui pent sur lius[22] de la bouteillerie, et soit donee laigue as malades por laver les mains, par tout le palais et mete len napes devant eaus longues /95v/ et lees, et li frere et li sergent portent la viande devant eaus.

Touz les jors soit achete dou plus blanc pain qui porra estre trove en la place et chascun malade en ait [ ] et dou pain dou covent tant com mestier sera.

Trois jors en la semaine le dimenche et le mardi et le juesdi doivent avoir char de porc ou de moton. De la rote de porc soit fait .v. mes et de la rote de moton .iiii. tansoulement.

En ces .iii. jors soient apareilli- /96r/ ez poucins ou gelines en bon broet tresbien conduit et safrane. La geline soit departie en .iiii. parties et le pucin[23] en .ii. Et qui ne vodra de la char de porc ou de moton, si doit avoir de la geline ou dou pocin sil veaut, et sil ne veaut ne de lun ne de lautre, il prendra .ii. deniers et une escuele de cuisinat de lospitalier ou dautre deparlui.

Quant li malade ont mangie le remenant de la char soit done as sergens.[24] Les greignors /96v/ pieces et les plus beles a ceaus qui charitablement servent les malades.

---

[17] pair KK
[18] profiriel KK
[19] quonque KK
[20] maniucent KK
[21] al KK
[22] luis KK
[23] poucin KK
[24] sergent KK

wine in and he is to be handed over to a serjeant who takes him to lie down. Then they ask him if he has any money which is given to the hospitaller to look after. His testament may be made in the presence of the hospitaller or before one of his colleagues, and according to the means of the house the testament is to be upheld; one brother and the notary sufficing for the testament, and if the patient wants to he can call one chaplain or one other person and make his will as God will instruct him, and the notary should put onto parchment whatever he says. The brother who is present should point out the privileges of the house to him and tell him that he has a first duty to the house.

Every day after the morning Mass the serjeants should be ready to give wine to the sick from that which the convent drinks and diluted in the same way, and each will take half a litre of it in his barrel. And if the patient does not want wine he may have sugar, the weight of a quarter. Afterwards the serjeants shall eat their breakfast: 1 loaf and one Berrie[e] goblet full of the wine of the convent and one cooked dish. While they are eating, the hospitaller and his colleagues and those who surround him in his room serve to the weakest patients who are in their rooms the best and the finest foods which are in the house.

When the serjeants have eaten one of them should ring a bell which hangs above the door of the *bouteillerie*[f] and all over the palace water is given to the patients to wash their hands and long, wide cloths are put in front of them, and the brothers and the serjeants carry the food into their presence.

Every day there should be bought the whitest bread which can be found in the place and every patient shall have some of it and as much from the convent as shall be necessary.

Three days a week, Sunday and Tuesday and Thursday, they should have pork or mutton. From roast pork 5 portions are made, and from roast mutton only 4.

On these 3 days chickens or hens should be prepared in a good sauce, very well seasoned and done with saffron. The hen should be divided into 4 portions and the chicken into 2. And anyone who does not want pork or mutton, he should have hen or chicken if he wants, and if he wants neither the one nor the other, he shall take 2 deniers and a cooked dish from the hospitaller or from another in his place.

When the patients have eaten the rest of the meat is to be given to the serjeants; the larger pieces and the nicest to those who serve the sick charitably.

---

[e] KK has 'Beirut'.
[f] The 'buttery'. The official ('boutellier') appears later.

Chascun soir soit done semenel au palais a touz ceaus qui prendre en vodront, et as febles doint len amandelei bien soutil au gruel dorge ou lait damandeles ou aucun legier pulment et fruit et autres choses que mestier lor est. Et quant li malade manivent au souper si lor doint len le vin ausi temprei com au matin a .iii. demi litre.

Les mercrediz et les samedi[z] /97r/ aient les malades generaument au souper herbes crues, et .ii. fois le mois soient remiez[25] les linceaus et les napes.

Au lundi et au mecredi et au venredi et au samedi soient serviz de chichres et damandelei ou de deliez [ ], et chascun ait une escuele et qui ne veaut de lun ait de lautre. Apres aient de eus cuiz en aigue, et qui en veaut si en ait .iiii. et qui rien[26] veaut receive .i. denier de lospitalier ou autre chose en leu deus, et as febles apareille len ce que il de- /97v/ mandent.

Es jors des granz gehunes sicome sont li .iiii. tens et autres granz gehunes aient li malade double cuisinat. Amandelei ou trie ou ris aveuc les chichres et pitance general de fruit se len en treuve a plantei. Es simples jors de venredi quant li fruit sont fres sovent aient pitance general.

Alentree dyver baille len a chascun malade .i. paire[27] de soliers, et par tout yver covertors et carpites tant come mestier /98r/ est.

Chascune nuit doivent veillier au palais .xvi. sergens[28] por garder les malades. Le .viii. veillent de complies jusques amienuit, et les autres .viii. veillent de [ ][29] jusques au jor. Les .iiii. veillent en .i. chief dou palais et .iiii. en lautre et .iiii. en une chambre entour les febles et .iiii. en lautre chambre.

Touz les sergenz voisent toute nuit par les malades et cuevrent les descovers, et portent /98v/ laigue fresche et dient a basse voiz seignors malades vez ci laigue de pardeu.

Les sergens mainent as chambres les malades et les soustiegnent et mainent[30] et ramainent a lor liz, et se[31] mestier est si les portent et raportent, et lor baillent lor

---

[25] remuez KK
[26] nen KK
[27] pair KK
[28] sergent KK
[29] KK *supplies* [mienuit]
[30] as chambres les malades et les soustiegnent et mainent *om.* KK
[31] ce KK

Each evening fine bread[g] may be given at the palace to all those who want to take it, and for the frail there should be almonds very finely ground in a barley gruel or almond-milk or some light food and fruit and other things as they need. And when the patients eat at supper, they should be given wine diluted as in the morning, 3 half-litres.

On Wednesdays and Saturdays the patients may generally have for supper salad,[h] and twice a month the linen sheets and the tablecloths should be changed.

On Monday and on Wednesday and on Friday and on Saturday should be served chickpeas and almonds or fine [...][i] and everyone may have one bowl and anyone who does not want the one may have the other. Afterwards let them have eggs cooked in water, and whoever wants them may have 4 of them and whoever does not want them may receive 1 denier from the hospitaller or some other thing in place of eggs. And for the frail should be prepared whatever they ask for.

On the days of the great fasts such as Ember days[j] and other great fasts the patients have double rations of cooked food. Almonds or choice food[k] or rice with chickpeas and the normal portion of fruit if it is to be found on the plants. On simple Fridays when the fruits are fresh they may often have the general serving.

At the beginning of winter there shall be handed to each patient 1 pair of slippers,[l] and all winter covers and rugs, as many as are needed.

Every night 16 serjeants are to keep watch in the palace to take care of the patients. Eight watch from compline through to midnight, and the other 8 watch from [midnight][m] until day. Four watch at one end of the palace and 4 at the other and 4 in one room[n] over the frail patients and 4 in the other room.[o]

All the serjeants watch over the patients all night and replace covers on any who are uncovered and bring fresh water and say in a low voice: "Sick lords, see here this water which comes from God."[p]

The serjeants take the sick to the (privy) chamber and support them and take them and bring them back to their beds, and if it is necessary they carry them there and

---

[g] For 'semenel' KK has 'Grieß' (groats), but see Godefroy, *s.v.* 'seminal': 'pain ou gateau de fleur de farine cuit deux fois, que l'on mangeait surtout en careme'.

[h] Literally 'raw herbs'.

[i] lacuna

[j] 'Quatre tens': literally 'four times'.

[k] KK has 'Nudeln' (noodles) for 'trie'.

[l] 'soliers'

[m] lacuna

[n] Elsewhere 'chambre' means the privy chamber, and this may be the case here in view of the duties detailed for the night watch below.

[o] 'chambre'

[p] KK has, 'Ihr Herren Kranken, wollt ihr Wasser von Gott?' (Your sick lordships, will you have water from God?)

orinaus se mestier est, et portent vuidier as chambres et les recintent et les metent souz les liz des malades.

Les autres malades qui par feblece font lor nature dessouz eaus en lor liz, les sergenz /99r/ le netoient et tendent[32] doucement et metent dessouz eaus blans linceaus et molz et delyez, et ensi lor facent jor et nuit toutes les fois que mestier lor est, et non tansoulement li sergent mais li frere meisme le facent volentiers.

Et doivent avoir .i. fisicien por les febles qui se preigne garde ententivement[33] de chascun selonc ce que mestier est.

Quant li frere receivent celui fisicien por la cure des malades il doit jurer sur sains /99v/ ou fiancier que il a son pooir se prendra garde[34] des malades sanz riens demander dou lor.

Le jor de la chandelor done lospitalier a chascun des sergens une chandoile.

Le jor de karehme prenant ont les malades au matin porree et char de porc fresche, et au soir gelines en broet en .iiii. parties la geline.

Le mecredi de la cendre le priour et les clers et les freres et la gent dou siecle qui vienent la cel jor vont a la procession entour les /100r/ malades chantant les saumes et la letanie, et la procession sareste devant lautel et face len le sarmon as sains et as malades au salu de lor armes. Apres le prior aveuc les chapelains voist par les malades et lor doinst[35] la cendre.

En karehme ont les malades peisson fres .iii. fois la semaine se len en puet trover ausi com il ont char en charnage, et a la fyee salei quant len ne puet trover fres. Es autres .iiii. jors il ont double cuisinat /100v/ amandelei ou trie, ou ris aveuc chichres et raizins secs ou autre fruit.

Au dimenche quant le vin est livrei sont les malades covers de covertours lonc et larges et precious de porpre et de soie et telz ya dorez, et lors vient la procession et vait entour les malades et puis sareste devant lautel et lors dit len lepistre et levangile dou saint esperit et puis sen retorne la procession a liglise.

Chascune nuit de tout lan /101r/ vait la procession entour les malades, et le karevanier vait devant .i. cierge ardant en sa main et cuevre les descovers, et amoneste doucement les malades quil se tiegnent en pais et honestement tant que la procession soit passee. Apres vait .i. frere le bouteillier[36] des malades qui porte .i. encensier et vait entensant. Apres celui vait .i. frere et fait la priere por toute

---

[32] cerdent KK
[33] enterinement KK
[34] deaus *expuncted*
[35] doist KK
[36] boutellier KK

back, and give them their urinals if necessary and take them to the chamber and empty them and rinse them out[q] and put them under the patients' beds.

The other patients who from weakness relieve themselves[r] beneath them in their beds: the serjeants shall clean them and wipe them gently and put beneath them white linen sheets which are soft and fine,[s] and they do this day and night every time it is necessary, and not only the serjeants but the brothers themselves should do it willingly.

And they should have 1 physician for the frail who will take care of each one diligently[t] according to his need.

When the brothers accept this physician for the care of the sick he must vow by the saints or swear that he will do all in his power to take care of the sick without asking anything of them.

On Candlemas Day the hospitaller gives each of the serjeants a candle.

On the day Lent begins the patients will have in the morning leek and fresh pork, and in the evening hens in their cooking liquid, each hen in 4 portions.

On Ash Wednesday the prior and the clerks and the brothers and the lay people who come there on this day go in a procession around the patients singing the psalms and the litany, and the procession stops in front of the altar and a sermon is preached to the healthy and the sick for the salvation of their souls. Afterwards the prior with the chaplains goes among the patients and gives them the ash.

In Lent the patients have fresh fish 3 times a week if it can be found, as well as having meat on meat (days), and as a general rule[u] salted when one cannot find it fresh. On the other 4 days they have double rations of cooked food, almonds or choice food[v] or rice with chickpeas and raisins or other fruit.

On Sunday when the (communion) wine is administered the patients are covered with long and wide and precious covers, made of purple and of silk and decorated with gold, and the procession comes to them and goes around the patients and then stops in front of the altar and there they are told the epistle and the gospel of the Holy Spirit and then the procession returns to the church.

Every night all year long the procession goes around the patients, and the *karavannier* goes in front with a burning candle in his hand and covers the uncovered and gently exhorts the patients to behave peaceably and reverently until the procession has passed. Afterwards comes 1 brother, the patients' *boutellier*, carrying a censer and as he goes he censes. After him comes a brother who says a prayer for all Christendom and for all the benefactors of the house of the hospital,

---

[q] For 'recintent' KK has 'zurückbringen' (bring back).
[r] 'font leur nature'
[s] KK translates 'delyez' as 'saubere' (clean).
[t] KK has 'en enterinement' which she translates as 'völlig' (thoroughly), while I read 'ententivement'.
[u] For 'a la fyee' KK has 'ausnahmsweise' (exceptionally).
[v] 'trie' – see above.

crestiente[37] et por touz les bienfaitours de la maison de lospital, et plus especiaument /101v/ por les plus especiaus. Apres cestui vait lospitalier portant .i. grant cierge alumei. Apres lospitalier vait le prior et les chapelains et les clers. Apres vait le comandeor et les autres freres. Apres[38] vont les sergens de touz les offices.

Deus fois en lan ou plus est rompue la karavane selonc ce que mestier est la ou les robes des malades sont, en tele maniere. Toutes les robes des malades sont aportees en une place grant et large, et lors /102r/ se lievent li malade en ordre. Premierement cil qui gisent en une rue, et apres li autre[39] qui gisent en une autre rue, et conoist chascun sa robe et la dessoivre des autres. Et ci qui sen veaut eissir il porte sa[40] robe et sen puet eissir se il li plaist, et ci qui veaut remanoir, recomande rechief sa robe a garder et sont remises les robes en la karavane. Et sil ya aucun qui ne puisse sa robe trover lospitalier li rent sicom il puet meaus, et sil ne sont telz que lon /102v/ les doie croire par simple parole, len lor fait dire sur lor pelerinage combien la robe perdue valoit, et se il la perdue en[41] la maison. Et quant cest servise[42] est fait, les robes de ceaus qui sont mors sont portees en une chambre, et lendemain lospitalier vient aveuc ses sergens ou il meaus se fie et entre en cele chambre et deslient celes robes et serchent diligenment se il ya point dargent cosu. Les robes de laine sont mises par eles en une part /103r/ et celes de linge en une autre part. Et sont traiz les brayers hors des brayes et les pelices ensement, les soliers et les autres choses toutes. Quant il ont ce fait lospitalier prent des meillors robes de[43] lange et de linge tant come li plaist et les garde por doner a ceaus qui ne peuent trover lor robes en la karavane.

Des meenes robes done lospitalier a lentree dyver as sergens qui servent les malades a chascun une. Les povres /103v/ robes et les robes qui poi valent sont vendues.

Le jor dou grant venredi ont li malade pain et aigue et qui veaut vin si en prent en son hanap.

La veille de Pasques ont li malade peisson par tout le palais.

Et se la feste de saint marc levangeliste vient en charnage si ont cel jor li malade flaons de eus et de fromages, ou peisson se len le treuve ou eus.

Le lundi des Rovoisons vie- /104r/ nent les processions de toute la vile et vont entor le palais des malades, et sont estendu sur eaus les covertours de soie, en cel jor ont eus et ce quil suelent avoir.[44]

Lendemain ont peisson se len le puet trover, et se len ne le puet trover si ont flaons.

---

[37] crestience KK
[38] apree KK
[39] lautre KK
[40] la KK
[41] an KK
[42] sevise KK
[43] de *repeated* KK
[44] ce q(ue) si velent KK

and more especially for the most outstanding ones. After him comes the hospitaller carrying a large lighted candle. After the hospitaller comes the prior and the chaplains and the clerks. After comes the commander and the other brothers. After come the serjeants from all their posts.

Twice a year or more the *karavane* is broken open according to necessity – there where the patients' clothes are – in the following way. All the patients' clothes are brought into an area which is big and roomy, and then the patients get up in turn. First those who lie in one ward, and afterwards the others who lie in another ward, and each one recognizes his clothing and picks it out from the rest. And whoever wants to leave wears his clothing and he can leave if he wants to, and whoever wants to stay entrusts his clothes to be guarded again and the clothes are sent back to the *karavane*. And if there is anyone who cannot find his clothes, the hospitaller will compensate him as best he can. And if he is not the sort of person who can be believed simply on his word, then he is made to say on his pilgrimage how much the lost clothing was worth, and if he lost it in the house. And when this service has been done, the clothes of those who have died are carried into a room, and the following day the hospitaller comes with his serjeants or those whom he most trusts and they enter this room and undo these clothes and investigate carefully whether there is any money sewn into them. Woollen clothes are put on one side by them, and those of linen on another side. And the belts are drawn out of the breeches and likewise the robes, the shoes and all the other things. When they have done this the hospitaller takes the best clothes of wool and of linen, as many as he likes, and keeps them to give to those who cannot find their clothes in the *karavane*.

The middling clothes are given by the hospitaller at the beginning of winter to the serjeants who serve the patients, one to each. The poor clothes and the clothes which are worth little are sold.

The day of Good Friday the patients have bread and water, and whoever wants wine has it in his goblet.

On the vigil of Easter the patients have fish everywhere in the palace.

And if the feast of St Mark the Evangelist falls on a meat day, then on such a day the patients have tarts[w] made with eggs and cheeses, or fish if it is to be found, or eggs.

On Monday of Rogationtide processions come from all the town and go around the palace of the sick and they have covers of silk spread over them, and on this day they have eggs and what they would normally have.

The next day they have fish if it can be found, and if it cannot be found they have tarts.

---

[w] KK translates 'flaons' as 'Auflauf' (soufflé): see her note 380, p. 213.

Le jor de Noel le jor de Pasques[45] et le jor de la pentecouste ont li malade morterolz[46] de char et les autres choses que il y covient, et char fresche a la sausse. /104v/

Le jor de saint Johan baptiste sont serviz tout autressi. Se la feste vient en dimenche ou en mardi ou en juesdi. Et se ele vient en autre jor, si ont cuisinaz et aucun fruit.

Li malade doivent gehuner la vigile de saint lorens, et la vigile de notre dame de la myaoust, et le jor vait la procession sollempnel entour eaus et doivent gehuner la vigile de saint bertholomei, et la vigile de pentecouste, et la vigile de touz[47] sains, et les quatre tens /105r/[48] de may gehunent li malade.

Par tout lan ont li malade le mecredi et le samedi eus generaument se il ni afiert vigile, et le venredi ont chichres et amandelei, et de noveaus fruiz se len enpuet trover.

---

[45] le jor de Pasques *om.* KK
[46] morterols KK
[47] tuoz KK
[48] *ms has 104r*

On Christmas Day, Easter Day and the day of Pentecost the patients have bread and milk[x] and other things which are suitable for them and fresh meat done with sauce.

On the day of St John the Baptist everything is served in exactly the same way if the feast falls on a Sunday or on Tuesday or on Thursday, and if it comes on another day they have cooked dishes and some fruit.

The patients are to fast on the vigil of St Laurence, and the vigil of Our Lady in mid-August, and on the feast day the solemn procession goes around them, and they are to fast on the vigil of St Bartholomew, and the vigil of Pentecost, and the vigil of All Saints, and the patients fast on the Ember days in May. All year round on Wednesdays and Saturdays the patients have eggs generally if it is not deemed a vigil, and on Fridays they have chickpeas and almonds, and new fruits if they are to be found.

---

[x] 'morterols': see Frédéric Godefroy, *Lexique de l'ancien français*, ed. Jean Bonnard and Amédée Salmon (Paris, 1964), *s.v.* 'morteruel' and *The Oxford English Dictionary* (1971), *s.v.* 'mortress'; KK translates as 'Fleischröllchen' (little meat rolls).

The Templars and the Hospitallers, Christ and the Saints*

Tom Licence

Magdalene College, Cambridge

Shortly before the dissolution of his order, a young Templar lay dying in Cyprus. Clutching a crucifix in his hand, he cried out to the one whose death was depicted upon it: "You are the true God, son of God, O my saviour, my creator, and of the whole world! You alone, Christ, do I summon in my need, knowing that you can save me in this world and the next."[1] Seldom are we offered such a haunting insight into the devotion of an individual Templar, which had impressed itself so firmly upon the memory of the witness that he would recount it during the Process. The young Templar's plea to Christ was personal and intense, the plea of one far from home and facing death. Behind it lay the human need for a comforter who had shared in his sufferings and conquered death on the cross, but the plea also drew upon a tradition of devotion to Christ that had inspired the Templars since their beginnings. Generally this devotion reflected the preoccupations of an increasingly Christocentric era, but its expression in the Temple, far from being a microcosm of contemporary piety, was nurtured by the order's unique background. Despite Bernard of Clairvaux's imaginative commentary upon this devotion we must be careful not to strip what was an instinctive spiritual bond between the Knights of Christ and their Lord of its potency by attempting an intellectual model of Templar Christology. Instead we can turn to the various images of Christ which both the Templars themselves and other religious employed to motivate the brethren. Three were central: the lordly Christ, whom the Templars served in battle; the suffering Christ, whom they emulated with their deaths; and the vulnerable Christ, whom they defended by defending his people.

During the eleventh century the metaphor of soldiering for Christ began to be equated with physical warfare against Christ's flesh-and-blood enemies.[2] Warriors embarking upon the First Crusade understood their enterprise in these terms, devotedly seeking to avenge Christ, a fatherly lord "who had lost his inheritance, his

---

* From Tom Licence, "The Spiritual Appeal of the Military Orders," unpublished MPhil thesis (Cambridge, 2003). This article addresses those figures especially venerated by the Templars, namely Christ and Mary, with some parallels from the Hospital, and concludes with a discussion of Templar and Hospitaller sanctity. Military order devotion to St George, St John the Baptist, and other favoured saints awaits investigation. My especial thanks are owed to Jonathan Riley-Smith.

[1] Konrad Schottmüller, ed., *Der Untergang des Templer-Ordens*, 2 vols. (Berlin, 1887), 2:156–57.
[2] Alan Forey, "The Emergence of the Military Orders in the Twelfth Century," in *Military Orders and Crusades*, ed. Alan Forey (Aldershot, 1994), pp. 175–95.

haereditas or *patrimonium*, to the pagans."³ The new paradigm of the warring *miles Christi* enabled the knightly class to forge a meaningful bond with Christ. For those whose status in society was that of warriors not intercessors, turning their weapons to Christ's service could be more comprehensible than attempting it solely through enclosure. This militant form of devotion probably brought the Templars' knightly founders to Jerusalem in the first place, inspired or enabled their adoption of a military function, and provided the shared tradition from which their spirituality grew.⁴ Alain Demurger defined the resulting order as "a permanent incarnation of the model of Christ's militia."⁵ In effect, a vigorous and appealing new trend in knightly piety had been provided with an outlet for communal, regular expression. Although it had its roots in the rhetoric of crusade, it would now receive continual nourishment through the devotional lives of the Knights Templars.

The Latin rule of the Templars opened with a bold summons to those who, secretly despising their own wills, wished to make Christ their cause and serve him as knights. In this conversion, Christ was the postulant's first point of reference, his inspiration and his lord for evermore. The radical summons itself was no novelty. Six centuries earlier Saint Benedict's rule had also begun by challenging its audience to "renounce their wills" and "serve the Lord Christ in battle with the weapons of obedience."⁶ Whereas Benedict, on the one hand, had envisaged an enclosed community, resisting demonic temptations with Saint Paul's spiritual armoury, the Templars, on the other, took up steel and traded blows with Christ's enemies in the Holy Land. Of the two appeals, Christ's interests in the 1120s loomed larger in the Templar summons, associated as it was with the urgent, personal entreaty of a vulnerable lord for Christ's new temporal dominions were constantly under threat.

According to Bernard, these Templars were "the elect troops of God," gathered under his banner "from the ends of the earth." Employing a similar image, Innocent II wrote in 1139 that these troops had "consecrated their hands to the Lord's service in the blood of his enemies," while Peter the Venerable viewed them as "the militia of the eternal king, the army of the Lord of Hosts, set to wage war against the prince of this world and overthrow the enemies of Christ's cross."⁷ Where would the

---

³ Jonathan Riley-Smith, "Crusading as an Act of Love," *History* 65 (1980), 177–92, at p.180.

⁴ *Cart Tem* no. 141; Anthony Luttrell, "The Earliest Templars," in *Autour*, pp. 193–202, esp. p. 199.

⁵ Alain Demurger, *Vie et mort de l'ordre du Temple 1118–1314* (Paris, 1985), p. 31; "Qu'est-ce, en fin de compte, que l'ordre du Temple? Une institution originale qui incarne en permanence le modèle de la chevalerie du Christ."

⁶ Justin McCann, ed. and trans., *Rule of Saint Benedict* (London, 1952), prologue, p. 3.

⁷ Bernard of Clairvaux, "Liber ad milites Templi de laude novae militiae," in *Opera Omnia*, ed. Jean Leclercq, Henri M. Rochais and Charles H. Talbot, 8 vols. (Rome, 1957–77), 3:214–39, at p. 221; Rudolf Hiestand, ed., *Papsturkunden für Templer und Johanniter*, Vorarbeiten zum Oriens Pontificius 1 (Göttingen, 1972) (hereafter Hiestand) no. 3; Peter the Venerable of Cluny, *The Letters of Peter the Venerable*, ed. Giles Constable (Cambridge, Mass., 1967), no. 172, "Ad Ebrardum Templi Domini" (1148x53), pp. 407–409, at p. 407.

Christians be now, demanded the Templars' founder, if Christ's apostles had told him they wished "to clear off and contemplate"?[8] Simon, bishop of Noyon, took the point further. In 1130 or 1131 he described the Templars as Christendom's defenders, one of "the three orders of the Church," which he listed as the intercessors, the defenders and the labourers. The defenders, Simon wrote, had almost disappeared, but merciful Christ had re-established them by infusing the Holy Spirit into our hearts. Christ, in sum, was abundantly supplied with monks (of whom Bernard also observed that "the world was full") but needy of warriors. For Simon, the Templars' significance within the Church was such that he had placed the nascent order on a par with the whole of institutional monasticism, "the intercessors."[9] Cloistered warfare was thriving, as it had never done before, but for some Benedict's metaphor was losing its potency through the observation that battle was demonstrably raging elsewhere. Christ himself had summoned the Templars to fight alongside him in his patrimony: they obeyed in faith and love. It was a simple spiritual bond, but a powerfully evocative one among the leaders of Christendom.

More emotive, however, was the Templars' willingness to emulate Christ's tribulations. As Giles Constable, Colin Morris and others have observed, devotion to the suffering Christ was central to twelfth-century spirituality.[10] The Templars made a novel and impressive contribution by combining regular vows with daily willingness to shed their blood. Willingness to die was one thing, the desire for death was another, but enthusiastic commentators soon bridged the gap. Bernard's declaration that "he who desires to die does not fear death" might have sounded bold in the cloister but there is no evidence that Templars actively sought martyrdom.[11] Hugh of Payns, who knew his knights' devotional temperament better than Bernard, made no reference to seeking death in his letter and suggested only that the brethren should offer themselves "as sacrifices to God," a traditional metaphor of trust and obedience. Bernard's tactics of edification were more psychological: to intensify the Templars' dependence on Christ by emphasizing their constant proximity to death. The Templars, he wrote, "for whom to live was Christ and to die was gain," should

---

[8] Jean Leclerq, ed., "Un document sur les débuts des Templiers," *Revue d'histoire ecclésiastique* 52 (1957), 81–91, at p. 88; "Si Apostoli dixissent Christo; Uolumus uacare et contemplari ... a contradictionibus et contentionibus hominum longe esse ... ubi nunc esset Christiani ?" Little doubt can remain that Hugh of Payns is the letter's most likely author. See Simonetta Cerrini, "La fondateur de l'ordre du Temple à ses frères: Hugues de Payns et le sermo Christi militibus," in *Dei gesta per Francos: études sur les croisades dédiées à Jean Richard*, ed. Michel Balard, Benjamin Z. Kedar and Jonathan Riley-Smith (Aldershot, 2001), pp. 99–110; Dominic Selwood, "Quidam autem dubitauerunt: the Saint, the Sinner, the Temple and a Possible Chronology," in *Autour*, pp. 221–30 at pp. 223–24.

[9] *Cart Tem* no. 31. Simon was adapting the old Carolingian model by replacing *bellatores*, for whom he found no role in the Church, with *defensores*. For Bernard's comments on monks see "De laude," p. 214.

[10] Giles Constable, *Three Studies in Medieval Religious and Social Thought* (Cambridge, 1995), p. 279; Colin Morris, *The Papal Monarchy: The Western Church from 1050–1250* (1989; repr. Oxford, 2001), p. 376.

[11] "De laude," p. 214.

desire and embrace death, knowing that if they trusted in Jesus they would finally participate in the mystery of his empty Sepulchre.[12] Danger stimulated devotion, and Bernard, whose theology Morris has summarised as "almost completely Christ-centred," hoped that devotion to Christ would become so instinctive to the Templars in their perilous vocation that they would be emboldened in battle. Christ had died but in doing so he had conquered. Here as elsewhere "the Cistercians appear deliberately to have promoted devotion to [his] crucified humanity as an appropriate path for simple Christians to follow."[13]

Influential as it was, Bernard's *De laude* was only the signpost on what, I suggest, was a spiritual path already well trodden by the Templars. Prior to the Council of Troyes (1129) the brethren had spent up to nine years risking their lives for others and it is inconceivable that they would not, as a community, have already considered the religious significance of their peculiar sacrifice. Ideas would have formed in the East without Bernard's input and some of them might still be detectable.[14] One scriptural text which adhered to the order from an early stage and inspired both faith in and emulation of Christ's love was John 15.13: "Greater love has no man than this; that he lay down his life for his friends." The text, in which Christ was thought to prophesy his own death, forged a strong link between his redemptive sacrifice and Templar spirituality and might have played an unknown role in inspiring the order's foundation. By 1129 it had been lifted from the rhetoric of crusading and glossed for the Temple.[15] This is revealed by an allusion to the text in the Latin rule, which states that a Knight Templar should be ready to "lay down his life for his brothers as Christ had done for him." Behind this reference we can detect theological thought patterns that had observed Christ's fulfilment of his own words, equated a Templar's "friends" with his brother knights, and enrolled the text as an exemplum for the brethren. They added moreover that in his death a Templar "would imitate Christ's," likening death to receiving "the cup of salvation," and that a Templar's death (like Christ's) would be "a pleasing sacrifice" to God.[16] It is possible that John 15.13 received this gloss at Troyes, but the fact that such an apposite text was only alluded to suggests that it was already familiar to the Templars. Indeed it had circulated

---

[12] "De laude," p. 214, cf. Phil. 1.21; also pp. 215, 236.

[13] Morris, *Papal Monarchy*, pp. 376–77.

[14] Bernard does not seem to have known much about the Templars in 1125 when he wrote to their latest recruit, his temporal lord Count Hugh of Champagne, praising his decision to become "a simple soldier"; see *Opera*, vol. 7, letter 31.

[15] Bernard never referred to John 15.13 in "De laude." As for the rule, Dominic Selwood ("Quidam autem dubitauerunt," p. 221) has rightly asserted that Bernard's authorship – another historical myth – "cannot be substantiated."

[16] Gustav Schnürer, ed., *Die ursprüngliche Templerregel* (Freiburg, 1903) (hereafter Schnürer) no. 6. The Templar "sapientissimo prophetarum in hoc se equipollere ualeat: 'Calicem salutaris accipiam', id est mortem, id est morte mea mortem domini imitabor, quia sicut Christus pro me animam suam posuit, ita et ego pro fratribus animam meam ponere sum paratus. Ecce competentem oblationem, ecce hostium uiuentem Deoque placentem."

during the First Crusade and, as with other aspects of crusade spirituality, was inherited, embraced and developed by their order.

Senior churchmen assisted in this process. Joscelin, bishop of Soissons, wrote to Hugh of Payns, commending his brethren for exposing their lives to defend Christianity.[17] Innocent II proclaimed that the Templars had "abandoned all to follow Christ" and were "assiduously prepared to lay down their souls for their brothers."[18] Elsewhere he quoted John 15.13 in full and argued that the Templars, through their ready sacrifice, were not only "ablaze with the flame of true charity," but were even fulfilling gospel works.[19] Peter the Venerable laboured this point, explaining that his great love and admiration for the brethren welled up from his conviction that they were "truly participants in that pinnacle of charity" which he then defined by citing John 15.13.[20] Effectively, as with Benedict's metaphor of warring for Christ, an old image, reinvigorated by crusading, helped to mould the new order's spirituality. At the same time John 15.13's gloss identified Christ with the vulnerable pilgrims protected by the brethren. Christ, observed the archbishop of Braga in 1145, was the true recipient and beneficiary of such charitable behaviour and would reward the Templars according to his words: "whatever you did for the least of mine, you did for me."[21] The Templars' Latin rule required that the sick be treated like Christ for the same reason, so that at the Judgement Christ should be able to say "I was sick and you visited me."[22] This injunction suggests that, although the Templars were not a hospital order, where an opportunity to serve Christ among the sick brethren of their own infirmaries presented itself they were inspired to act upon it. The developing model of true knighthood was already laden with ideals of protecting the poor, the sick, widows and orphans, but the Templars peered through it to the image of Christ, whom they viewed not only as its instigator but also as dwelling in the vulnerable. This Christ was far from being a distant figure, presiding over his earthly patrimony in heaven, since the Templars shared in his sufferings and earned his gratitude by protecting his people.

Monasticism had always, at least in theory, revolved around Christ. Augustine's second rule, popularly adopted among regular canons in the central Middle Ages, ended with the instruction that it should be followed in Christ's name. Benedict's lengthy rule similarly concluded that its adherents "should prefer nothing

---

[17] *Cart Tem* no. 59 (1133x4); "animas uestras pro Xpistianitatis defensione exposuistis."

[18] *Cart Tem* Bulls III (1138x42); "relicti omnibus, secuti sunt Christi, et assidue pro fratribus animas ponere sunt parati."

[19] Hiestand, no. 3; "uere karitatis flamma succensi, dictum euangelium operibus adimpletis quod dicitur: 'maiorem hac dilectionem habet' ..." (John 15.13). See also no. 8 (January 1144), in which Celestine II employs and develops the same text.

[20] Peter the Venerable, *Letters*, p. 408, "Ad Ebrardum" (1148x53); "Estis uere participes illius summe et precipue caritatis de quo saluator 'maiorem hac dilectionem habet' ..." (John 15.13).

[21] *Cart Tem* no. 363; "quod uni ex minimis meis fecistis, michi fecistis" (Matt. 25.40).

[22] Schnürer, no. 50; "quasi Christo eis [the sick] seruiatur, ut euangelium: 'Infirmus fui et uisitastis me' memoriter teneatur" (Matt. 25.36).

whatsoever to Christ." While Christ's name appeared once in the former and fifteen times in the latter, in the Templars' Latin rule alone (modelled on Benedict's but shorter in substance) it made eighteen appearances. Before we view this as merely reflecting the preoccupations of a Christocentric era we should observe that in the roughly contemporary Latin Hospitaller rule Christ's name appeared only twice. Eight of its appearances in the Templar rule form part of the Templars' preferred title, referring to "a knight," "knights," "co-knights" (*commilites*) and "the militia" of Christ. This dedication is significant in itself but other references, some of which do not name Christ, reveal his specific roles in Templar spirituality. Christ was seen as "our great provider," to whom the brethren should humbly give thanks when saying grace. On Fridays his Passion was to be reverenced by the communal distribution of Lenten food and on Sundays his Resurrection was honoured with two meat meals for the brethren.[23] None of these Christological images or associations was present in any of the other rules mentioned earlier (we can only speculate as to their sources), but their emphasis on Christ's provision, Passion and Resurrection pointed towards his redemptive sacrifice. Some images of Christ, such as his presence in the sick, a Hospitaller obsession, had been borrowed; others had been slightly adapted. When discussing the role of abbot, Saint Benedict had emphasized his responsibility to model himself upon Christ, whereas the Templars reversed the emphasis, urging obedience to their master as to Christ: "since nothing was dearer to Christ than obedience."[24] All of these images, as well as Christ the vulnerable lord, Christ the sacrifice for his friends and Christ the poor pilgrim, were devised, borrowed or adapted to motivate the Templars. The fact that all were Christ-centred implies that Christ himself was their motivation.

When the Latin rule was translated into French, Christ's name made another six appearances. All except one referred to "Jesus Christ," although this two-part appellation had only appeared once in the Latin. "The Holy Resurrection" therefore became "the Holy Resurrection of Jesus Christ," while "the dominical Passion" became "the Passion of Jesus Christ."[25] Jesus Christ made a new appearance as "the strict judge," who would call sinners to account, and was named as the authority behind two scriptural quotations, one of which lacked an attribution in the Latin, where the other was cited as "that saying of the Lord."[26] To receive the cup of salvation, furthermore, was no longer to imitate Christ's death but to avenge it with one's own, while John 15.13, which had surfaced once in the Latin, appeared twice in the French as a testimony to its adoption by the order.[27] At least among the French

---

[23] Schnürer, nos. 14, 13 and 10.

[24] The ideas in their rule (Schnürer, no. 46) combined elements from chapters 2 and 5 of Benedict's rule, on the abbot and obedience respectively.

[25] Schnürer, no. 10; Henri de Curzon, ed., *La règle du Temple*, Société de l'histoire de France (Paris, 1886) (hereafter Curzon) no. 26; Schnürer, no. 13; Curzon, no. 28.

[26] Curzon, no. 49; Schnürer, no. 33; Curzon, nos. 39, 40 and 41. The first was described in the French as "said by Jesus Christ through David's mouth" and the second became "that saying of Jesus Christ."

[27] Schnürer, no. 6; Curzon, no. 63; Schnürer, no. 6; Curzon, no. 56 and 63.

Templars, who restructured and translated the Latin rule, enthusiasm for Christ had grown since Troyes and by 1147 the brethren had emblazoned themselves permanently with his cross.[28]

Why did the Templars look to Christ over any other saintly patron? The answer may lie in the spiritual climate of Mount Moriah. Sylvia Schein has argued that Temple Mount became one of the most important centres of sanctity in Latin Jerusalem.[29] Opposite the Templars' headquarters in the Al-Aqsa mosque ("the Temple of Solomon") was the Dome of the Rock, which Godfrey of Bouillon had converted into "the Temple of the Lord" in 1099 and invested with a community of Augustinian canons. From their arrival the canons thrived upon the promulgation of a Christocentric cult, covering the Dome's walls with biblical texts and paintings to remind the faithful of Christ's life, and selling lumps of its rock, from which Christ was supposed to have ascended into heaven, as relics. Apart from the significance of its location, this cult, like the fervent devotion to Christ exhibited by the first crusaders, was probably intensified by the constant proximity of Muslim enemies who denied Christ. By 1102 or 1103 the pilgrim Sæwulf associated the Dome with all the episodes of Christ's life that took place in the Temple and some that did not, while four great Christ-centred feast days became linked with the mount. On Palm Sunday (Christ's entry into Jerusalem), the Purification of the blessed Virgin (Christ's presentation at the Temple) and the Exaltation of the Holy Cross, large processions of Latin clergy set out on a roundabout route from the Holy Sepulchre towards it. When they arrived they entered through the Golden Gate, circled the Templars' headquarters and concluded their procession with prayers in the precinct of "the Temple of the Lord." A similar procession occurred at Easter. The Templars themselves actively disseminated apocryphal legends associated with the Mount, where it was believed that Christ would make his final triumphant return. Between 1161 and 1174, the Templar Henry d'Arci of Lincoln commissioned the production of a vernacular poem for the edification of his brethren based on an old prophecy concerning Antichrist.[30] This poem repackaged solemn and foreboding information.

---

[28] Anthony Luttrell ("The Earliest Templars," p. 197) suggests that the Templars first adopted this symbol in 1120, following the date given by the chronicler, Bernard the Treasurer. From the order's foundation, some of the brethren may indeed have been *crucesignati* as crusaders, but had their order consciously adopted the cross as an official symbol prior to 1129 it would surely have featured in their rule, which discussed their dress in detail. William of Tyre's date of 1147 is more likely.

[29] See Sylvia Schein, "Between Mount Moriah and the Holy Sepulchre: the Changing Traditions of the Temple Mount in the Central Middle Ages," *Traditio* 40 (1984), 175–95. Aryeh Grabois ("La fondation de l'abbaye du Templum Domini et la légende du Temple de Jérusalem au XIIe siècle," in *Autour*, pp. 231–37) has summarized some further evidence which supports Schein's findings.

[30] Robert Fawtier and E.C. Fawtier-Jones, "Notice du Manuscrit French 6 de la John Rylands Library, Manchester," *Romania* 49 (1923), 321–42, at pp. 331–40. See also Keith Sinclair, "The Translations of the Vitae Patrum, Thaïs, Antichrist and Vision of St Paul made for Anglo-Norman Templars: Some Neglected Literary Considerations," *Speculum* 72 (1997), 741–62. For the Latin original see "Epistola Adsonis ad Gerbergam reginam de ortu et tempore Antichristi," in *Sibyllinische Texte und Forschungen*, ed. Ernst Sackur (Halle, 1898), pp. 97–113.

Antichrist would come to Jerusalem and set up his throne in Christ's Temple (the Dome), after which he would proceed to dismantle Christ's works. Taking an interest in these affairs, the Templars probably viewed their defence of Mount Moriah as an eschatological duty and devoted themselves to Christ and his cult at the Dome rather than to Solomon, after whom their own residence was named. Indeed, as Schein has observed, the Templars preferred "the Temple of the Lord" as their emblem, and its image appeared on their seal with the legend "the seal of the Knights of Christ's Temple."[31]

We may compare the Templars' Christ with the Christ who appears in the Hospitallers' legends.[32] The legends, a hagiographic advertisement for the order and edifying narratives for its members, showed Christ's intervention in the Hospital's affairs prior to his incarnation and the Hospital's importance as a centre for his earthly ministry. Christ to the Hospitallers was no ethereal, symbolic figure – the Christ upon whom a Cistercian might meditate – but a corporeal, compelling exemplum, commanding his disciples always to serve their fellow human beings. With an audience interested in Christ's actions, the legends wasted no time contemplating his theological significance. Like the Hospitallers themselves, their Lord was a doer. He appeared on earth, gathered his disciples, came to the Jerusalem Hospital, preached salvation to the people and miraculously healed the sick.[33] Far from merely expressing devotion to him, the Hospitallers believed that their vocation followed directly from Christ's commands, "love the Lord your God with all your heart" and "sell all you have and give to the poor," which they claimed he had given in the Hospital itself.[34] Commitment to those commands moreover had to be complete and uncompromising, long before Saint Francis founded the Franciscans on similar principles. Ananias and Sapphira, the legends warned, were struck dead not for lying to the Holy Spirit (as Saint Peter had claimed) but because they had failed to render all their possessions to God and the poor.[35] Their doom, in the Hospitaller narratives, was inserted immediately after Christ's command to abandon everything for the poor; a juxtaposition which can only have alarmed the order's more hesitant donors. Lest those donors channel their charity elsewhere, one

---

[31] "Sigillum Militum de Templo Christi." Ulger, bishop of Angers, can be forgiven for believing that the Templars were in fact based there; "Isti enim sunt ... commilitones militantium Christo, in sacrosancto Templo Domini Ierusalem." *Cart Tem* no. 21.

[32] Antoine Calvet (*Les légendes de l'Hôpital de Saint-Jean de Jérusalem*, Centre d'enseignement et de recherche d'Oc 11 (Paris, 2000)) argues the legends were composed in Jerusalem between 1140 and 1160 at the latest, and published several versions. See also *RHC Oc*. 5:401–27 for Hospitaller legends, and Keith Sinclair, ed., *The Hospitallers Riwle*, Anglo-Norman Text Society (London, 1984), for a twelfth-century version.

[33] *RHC Oc*. 5:407; "per presentiam corporalem ibidem adueniendo, discipulos et apostolos suos fouendo, populis uiam salutis predicando, in infirmis miracula faciendo."

[34] Matt. 22.37 and 19.21; *RHC Oc*. 5:407, cf. Calvet, *Légendes*, pp. 120, 152.

[35] Acts 5.1; *RHC Oc*. 5:408, cf. Calvet, *Légendes*, pp. 112, 121, 133 for variants.

version observed that the unlucky couple's crime lay in neglecting God, the poor *and the Hospital*; "as a result of which they were struck by sudden death".[36]

Perhaps the chief reason the Hospitallers cherished the poor was that in them they saw the personification of Christ. In their legends Christ had bidden Zacharias go to Jerusalem and "feed me in the person of the poor". Blessed Gerard, the first master, was alternatively described as a "serf of Christ" and "a serf of the poor", indicating that the two were interchangeable, while postulant Hospitallers had to vow obedience as slaves to their lords the sick.[37] The legends also tampered with gospel narratives to exalt the poor by forging additional links between them and Christ. Whereas Christ in the gospel had told his disciples "whoever honours you honours me; whoever receives you receives me", according to the Hospitallers he had uttered those words with hands outstretched over not only the disciples but also the poor.[38] The Hospitallers' lordly Christ, however, did not appear vulnerable. Except for one known claim that the Last Supper had taken place and the Eucharist been instituted at the Hospital, and another that fasting was mandatory for Hospitallers on Fridays because Christ had suffered on that day, the Hospitallers, unlike the Templars, placed no emphasis upon his tribulations or his death.[39] Instead they selected scriptural texts and gospel episodes that illustrated his life, his commands and his daily plight in the poor and sick, against which his earthly patrimony appeared only of secondary importance. Indeed the order's founders had not been warriors, and the lordly Christ of knightly piety, as far as we can tell, had never established himself in its early spirituality.

At some point during their career the Templars developed the idea that their order had been established in honour of the Blessed Virgin Mary. The instructions on conventual life and admission in which this idea appears are difficult to date. Our Lady, they inform us, was the beginning and end of the order (a motherly equivalent of Christ's Alpha and Omega), which had been founded in her honour.[40] The later Templars invoked Mary's mercy at chapter and accompanied their paternosters with Hail Marys, while postulants joined "for love of God and Our Lady" and promised

---

[36] Calvet, *Légendes*, p. 133; italics mine.
[37] Calvet, *Légendes*, p. 110; ibid., pp. 134–35; "seruus Christi", "seruus pauperum"; Jonathan Riley-Smith, *The Knights of St John in Jerusalem and Cyprus 1050–1310* (London, 1967), p. 24.
[38] Cf. Luke 10.16; *RHC Oc.* 5:407.
[39] Karl Borchardt, "Two Forged Thirteenth-Century Alms Raising Letters used by the Hospitallers in Franconia," in *MO*, 1, pp. 52–57, at p. 54. The pilgrim's tour appended to the *Gesta Francorum* placed the Last Supper elsewhere, for which see *Gesta Francorum et aliorum Hierosolymitanorum*, ed. Rosalind Hill (London, 1962), p. 100. See also Sinclair, *Riwle*, p. viii. On admission, however, the Hospitallers were told to wear their crosses in honour of Christ's passion and death for them (like the Templars). Riley-Smith, *The Knights*, p. 24.
[40] Curzon, nos. 306 and 685.

obedience, chastity and poverty to "Our Lady."[41] During the Process, a Templar composed a prayer to Mary as his advocate.[42] Although we may be unable to chart the chronology of this escalating Marian devotion, a few observations can be made about its origins. First, the Templars were not founded in Mary's honour. Mary only appeared three times in the Latin rule, twice when the brethren received instructions for feast days, including the Marian feasts, and once in relation to conduct appropriate during the Matins of the Marian office.[43] None of these references, unlike the many to Christ, discussed her role or invested her with importance. All monastic establishments celebrated the Marian feasts in this period and the Little Offices of the Virgin were also popular. In the customs of La Grande Chartreuse, set out in 1127 by Prior Guy I, each Carthusian had to recite not only the Matins but also the Lauds of the Marian office in his cell. During the day each canonical hour was to be preceded by the Office of the Virgin.[44] Cluny had also introduced the Little Offices of the Virgin, which had been prescribed by Urban II in 1095 as an intercession for the First Crusade. The early Cistercians, on the other hand, who rejected accretions to the liturgy, would not recite the Marian offices in choir; the activity was still prohibited in the time of Abbot Raynald of Citeaux (c.1134–50).[45] When placed in this context it can be seen that Templar devotion to Mary in 1129 was pretty average.

During the later 1130s, however, dedications to Mary began to proliferate in Templar charters. Of the 600 published by the Marquis d'Albon, dating between c.1124 and 1150, the first 319 provide a sample of the twenty years of Templar documentation up to January 1144. Examining their dedication formulae, we find that grants were usually made "to God and the Knights of Solomon's Temple" or "to the Knights of Christ."[46] The first 118 of these charters pre-date, or in a few instances might pre-date, March 1136 and only two of them include Mary in their formulae. One grants land "to almighty God, blessed Mary ever virgin and the holy Jerusalem militia of Solomon's Temple," the other to "Lord God, blessed Mary and the militia of the Jerusalem Temple."[47] Of the 200 charters that fall between March 1136 and January 1144, however, 51 refer to Mary as a grantee.[48] Eleven of these

---

[41] Ibid., nos. 339, 401, 537, 542, 660, 668, 675 and 676.

[42] Jules Michelet, ed., *Procés des Templiers*, 2 vols. (Paris, 1841–51), 1:122–23.

[43] Schnürer, nos. 10, 13 and 7.

[44] Hubertus P. J.-M. Ahsmann, *Le culte de la Sainte Vierge et la littérature française profane du Moyen Âge* (Paris, 1935), p. 24.

[45] Bede Lackner, "The Liturgy of Early Citeaux," in *Studies in Medieval Cistercian History*, ed. Basil Pennington (Shannon, 1971), pp. 1–34, at p. 32.

[46] For example, *Cart Tem* no. 9; "Deo militibusque Templi Salomonis," and no. 17; "militibus Xpisti."

[47] *Cart Tem* no. 43 (Toulouse, 1132); "Deo omnipotenti et beate semper virginis Marie et sancte militie Iherosolimitane Templi Salomonis," and no. 95 (Toulouse, 1134); "Domino Deo et beate Marie et militie Iherosolimitani Templi."

[48] Charter dedications to Mary become noticeable in March 1136; January 1144 is an arbitrary date chosen for this sample.

date from the first two years of this eight-year period, twenty-six pre-date March 1139, and in them grants to the Virgin occur in Toulouse, Provence, Roussillon, Arles, England and Barcelona.[49] One donor even referred to "the militia of blessed Mary in Jerusalem," although this was exceptional.[50] Most simply made grants "to God, blessed Mary and the Temple," or "to Christ and his mother."[51] The dedication formula "to Jesus Christ and his mother" emerged in Provence by November 1138 at the latest.[52]

Who or what instigated this explosion of Marian devotion in the Temple? Bernard and the Cistercians are unlikely candidates, because Abelard, writing c.1131–33, complained that they neither commemorated Mary nor any other saint, even though they dedicated their churches to her.[53] Neither can the popular trend in Marian devotion, revealed by Abelard's complaint, account for the suddenness of the Templar shift towards her. Our answer, after a closer look at the origins of the earliest Marian grants, may lie in Southern France. Cristina Dondi has argued that individual Templar preceptories adopted the liturgies and calendars of their provinces rather than those of the mother-house in Jerusalem (which took the liturgy of its diocesan cathedral, the Holy Sepulchre).[54] Building upon her argument, let us venture the same hypothesis for Templar devotion. Had the Templars established a network of early bases in a region where devotion to Mary was already popular, recruiting among the pious aristocracy and acquiring existing churches with Marian dedications, it follows that Mary would have been incorporated into their spirituality naturally, at least on a regional level. We cannot say whether she attained a contemporary prominence in the East.

The least that can be said for this hypothesis is that it fits the facts. In 1136 an important Templar preceptory was founded at Richerenches after several members of the landowning family surrendered an entire lordship and joined the order. The fervour spread south to Roaix, where a second preceptory was established between 1138 and 1141.[55] Mary was a saintly patron in both locations. At Richerenches the Templars would gather in the church of St Mary to witness knightly benefactors confirm their gifts by oath upon the Virgin's altar, or at the church door. At Roaix, grants were made to the Templars from the tithes of another Marian church.[56]

---

[49] For example, *Cart Tem* nos. 129 (Toulouse), 120 (Provence – Richerenches), 170 (Provence – Roaix), 128 (Roussillon), 281 (Arles), 124 (England) and 180 (Barcelona).

[50] Ibid., no. 139 (Mas-Deu – Roussillon, May 1137).

[51] For example, ibid., nos. 119 and 125.

[52] See ibid., no. 170 (Roaix), but also nos. 125, 152 and 164 (Richerenches).

[53] Lackmer, "Liturgy," p. 17.

[54] Christina Dondi, "The liturgy of the Holy Sepulchre in Western Europe, c.1100–c.1500. With special reference to the practice of the order of St John of Jerusalem," unpublished PhD thesis (London, 2000), pp. 112–15. (The thesis has since been published: see Bulletin, page 205.)

[55] Jonathan Riley-Smith, "The Origins of the Commandery in the Temple and the Hospital," in *La commanderie: institution des ordres militaires dans l'Occident médiéval*, ed. Anthony Luttrell and Léon Pressouyre (Paris, 2002), pp. 9–18, at p. 12.

[56] *Cart Tem* nos. 520, 469 and 470. For the church at Roaix see nos. 527 and 586.

Turning back to our charter sample, we can see that Richerenches and Roaix, in the main part, account for the proliferation of Marian grants after March 1136. From its foundation until 1144, Richerenches supplied thirty-five extant charter grants for d'Albon's cartulary, twenty-seven of which included Mary as a grantee, while Mary appeared in half of the eight associated with Roaix. Seven Marian grants hailed from Toulouse, with its priories of St Mary Deaurate and St Mary Dealbate, and the earliest of these (1132) probably established the Marian formula that crept into the Douzens cartulary.[57] At the Mas-Deu preceptory in Roussillon (founded 1137) a church of blessed Mary sat in the middle of the Templars' new estates, as did the one at Richerenches.[58] As with Richerenches, Roaix and Douzens, the Marian formula also appeared in its grants.[59]

Were the new Templar recruits in Toulouse, Provence and Roussillon orchestrating a campaign to elevate Mary within the order? This seems unlikely. Rather, they were continuing to express devotion to a locally popular saint and probably promulgating the Marian formula by copying each other's charter protocol. When Queen Matilda employed this protocol to grant the Templars Cressing (1136 or 1137) she might have done so advisedly, replicating either a Marian dedication at Temple Holborn or the practices of Southern France. After that early grant, only two of the twenty-one English charters pre-dating 1144 included Mary.[60] The fact that Barcelona managed one Marian grant out of twenty, while Madrid, Lisbon and Flanders produced ten, eight and three grants respectively without mentioning her at all, suggests that Marian devotion in the Temple was initially only regional or sporadic. Neither was the French version of the Latin rule, completed about this time, particularly innovative in this respect. True the Templars like other religious were multiplying the Marian offices, probably through the adoption of provincial liturgies, for the French speaks of "all the hours of Our Lady" and not just "the Matins of holy Mary." It also describes the pagans as "enemies of the Virgin Mary's son," at least in this instance shifting its emphasis from Christ to his mother.[61] Mary, however, appears no more in Templar legislation, while the several new references to Jesus show that he was still at the heart of Templar devotion.

When placed on trial, the Templar knight Raymond of Gardia, preceptor of Mas-Deu, was adamant that the Templars were orthodox in their devotion to Christ. Each year on Good Friday, with neither sandals nor weapons nor head covering, the

---

[57] Ibid., no. 43 (Toulouse, 1132). Douzens was founded in 1133 and must have administered the Templars' early estates in this region. This particular charter was included in its cartulary, which produced six Marian grants out of twenty-five between 1136 and 1144. For the church of St Mary Deaurate, given to the Templars by Raymond of Toulouse, see no. 19 and, for the priory, no. 93.

[58] Ibid., nos. 98 and 339, cf. no. 152 (Richerenches).

[59] For example, ibid., nos. 128, 139 and 295.

[60] Some of these Marian grants could have been random. Mary occurs rarely and randomly in Hospitaller charters.

[61] Curzon, nos. 16 and 56.

brethren would adore the Holy Cross upon bended knees. On the two feasts of the Holy Cross in May and September, albeit wearing sandals, they would do the same, chanting the standard liturgy: "we worship you Christ and bless you, because through your Holy Cross you have redeemed the world."[62] Their three annual communions coincided with the feasts of Christ's resurrection (Easter), his sending of the Holy Spirit (Pentecost) and his nativity (Christmas), and Brother Raymond himself "placed his firm hope in the body of Christ, so that through him he might be saved." When denying later allegations about idols, he added that the Templars worshipped "the one true God, Lord Jesus Christ."[63] Other Templars and their witnesses protested the same orthodoxy. One had frequently heard his brethren sing "Jesus saviour of the world" and wondered how they could deny Christ, as was alleged, in their admission ceremonies.[64] A second had seen Templar chaplains cast out evil spirits by the power of the cross at Acre, while "the noble and powerful lord" Roupen of Montfort testified that he had seen the Templars honour and worship Christ's cross devotedly "for many years."[65] Raymond of Benthe, a knight from Nicosia deputed to guard the Templars in captivity on Cyprus, declared that he had never seen anyone revere the cross more and even spoke of having witnessed the host miraculously expand during a Templar Mass.[66] Were these the characteristics of men who spat upon Christ's image, trampled it underfoot and denied him as their saviour?

By the early fourteenth century the Templars were in a muddle over their identity. Perhaps they were confused because they lacked their own corpus of literature or because any written and oral legends had been disrupted by the fall of Jerusalem in 1187, or the fall of Acre in 1291. Apart from believing that their order had been founded in Mary's honour, the Templars also hailed Bernard as its founder, and the accretions to their rule contained contradictions such as the presence of three alternative formulae for admission.[67] Hugh of Payns had been forgotten, and was mentioned only once in the trial as the possible identity of a mysterious head statue or reliquary.[68] As for the charges, Geoffrey of Gonville, preceptor of Aquitaine, suggested that the Templars might deny Christ three times in honour of Saint Peter.[69]

---

[62] Michelet, 2:458; "Adoramus te, Christe, et benedicimus tibi, quod per sanctam crucem tuam redemisti mundum."

[63] Michelet, 2:460; "adiciens quod dicti fratres omnes et singuli eiusdem ordinis adorant solum Deum unicam Dominum Jhesum Christum." *Adiciens* in this text usually precedes personal commentary by its subject.

[64] Michelet, 2:229.

[65] Michelet, 1:647, cf. Schottmüller, 2:392–93; Schottmüller, 2:158.

[66] Schottmüller, 2:157–58.

[67] Bernard is described as the order's founder and instigator of customs in Michelet, 1:120, 122, 145 and 615. For the three formulae of admission see Curzon, nos. 1, 274–78 and 657–74.

[68] Heinrich Finke, *Papsttum und Untergang des Templerordens*, 2 vols. (Münster, 1907), 2:336–37. Hugh of Payns never appears in Michelet or Schottmüller.

[69] Michelet, 2:400. Surprisingly, this is the only instance in the extant trial proceedings when this inherently likely explanation occurs.

If this exercise had originally been designed to stimulate devotion it had quite spectacularly backfired. The detail of repentant Templar confessions nevertheless obliges us to conclude that it probably did go on. One knight confessed to denying Christ in Acre to a certain Brother Julian of the order of Saint Augustine's hermits, vicar to the Jerusalem patriarch. Initially incredulous, the friar eventually instructed the knight to fast every Saturday for the rest of his life on bread and water. The Templar protested that the master did not freely give the brethren licence to fast, so Julian instructed him instead to wear an iron *lorica* over his shirt throughout Lent, and both men wept. Twenty-four years later, the repentant knight still retained the letters from his confessor that confirmed his confession and absolution.[70] Although we may suspect the Templars under examination of having exaggerated their devotion to Christ (given the charges against them) and of having access to friendly witnesses who would do the same, it can be said in their favour that Christ had always been central to their spirituality. If some explanation had ever existed which reconciled that spirituality with the symbolic denial of its object, then it had already been forgotten by the time of the Process.

In 1139 the Christians suffered a defeat at Thecua. Many had been slain, but William of Tyre eventually recorded the name of only one, Eudes of Montfaucon, an illustrious Knight Templar whose death caused widespread grieving.[71] How had his memory been preserved? Did he find his way into oral legends, written history or an obit roll, or was some magnificent tomb constructed which attracted a posthumous cult? There is no way of knowing. Many tales of great heroes and their pious deeds circulated in Latin Jerusalem. Its kings sat upon the throne of David, traced their lineage to Charlemagne and chose to be interred below Calvary in the church of the Holy Sepulchre. Joscelin I of Edessa died, according to William, giving thanks to God like some Old Testament patriarch, and Melisende had an altar built outside her tomb in the Valley of Jehoshaphat where daily masses were celebrated for her soul and all the faithful departed.[72] To shape events in the Holy Land was to participate in sacred history; to die in its defence was to follow the martyrs and the Maccabees. As a result the boundaries between history and hagiography were more fluid than in the west. Were valiant martyrs like Eudes of Montfaucon ever invoked before battle as heavenly patrons by warriors who knew they might soon follow in their footsteps? An army of ghostly warriors was believed to have helped the Frankish armies on the First Crusade.[73] This was the climate in which the Templars shed their blood for Christ, but did any of them achieve sanctity?

---

[70] Schottmüller, 2:47.
[71] WT 15.6, p. 683.
[72] WT 14.3, 18.32, pp. 634–35.
[73] *Gesta Francorum*, p. 69.

There is no proof that any Templar attracted posthumous veneration. Crusaders like John of Montfort (d. 1246) and Eudes of Nevers (d. 1265), whose shrine at Acre miraculously healed the sick, were able to attract posthumous cults in the east, while Hospitallers managed the same in the west.[74] Why then, uniquely among the religious orders, did the Templars apparently fail to do either? The answer probably lies in the subsequent destruction of evidence. Small cults in the east, where there was a high turnover of Templar personnel, could easily have been destroyed without a trace, while western Templar saints may have fallen from favour at almost any point after the dissolution and disgrace of the order. Indeed the appearance of a head reliquary of Hugh of Payns during the Process is perhaps the only survival of such a cult devoted to the Templars' first master. Alternatively an answer may lie in the nature of the order itself. The Temple possessed neither the literary expertise nor the devotional coordination to promote its own to sanctity.[75] Warriors, administrators and farmers were not hagiographers, and where they did seek to promulgate local cults, such as that of the hermit Bevignate in Perugia (with the support of the Perugian commune and the Templars at Modena), they seem to have failed.[76] Moreover, the adoption of provincial liturgies, calendars and saints, usually the patrons of the churches which came into Templar possession, would not necessarily have led to the recognition of an individual within the order as a whole. For any religious order this normally required an orchestrated effort, but the Templars may also have lacked the inclination, because their rule, as Simonetta Cerrini has argued, placed obedience before individual valour.[77] If a pious Templar ever did develop a posthumous cult, we can probably conclude that it was local, short-lived and soon forgotten.

This conclusion is illustrated by the case of Blessed Gerland.[78] In 1327 "St Constantine" appeared before a Hospitaller in Syracuse to reveal that the remains of a saintly knight lay buried in a ruined Templar church outside the city. Digging in its nave, the Hospitaller unearthed a burial of such heavenly aroma that he was

---

[74] John of Montfort's cult was first attested in the fifteenth century, but the Count of Nevers's cult was observed at Acre in 1265. For the former (he was not a Templar as the *Acta Sanctorum* suggests) see *AASS* May 5:270–71 and Nicholas Coureas, *The Latin Church in Cyprus, 1195–1312* (Aldershot, 1997), p. 206. For the latter see Laura Minervini, ed., *Cronaca del templare di Tiro (1243–1314)* (Naples, 2000), p. 104; "et sachés que Nostre Seignor fist pour luy miracles, car tous malades quy atouchoi[en]t a son monyment estoient tant tost guaris de lor maladie."

[75] For literacy in the Temple see Alan Forey, "Literacy and Learning in the Military Orders in the Twelfth and Thirteenth Centuries," in *MO*, 2, pp. 185–206.

[76] Christina Dondi, "The liturgy of the Holy Sepulchre," pp. 102–3. Hagiographies are usually our only evidence of such cults and many must have disappeared from record for lack of them.

[77] Simonetta Cerrini, "I Templari: una vita da fratres, ma una regola anti-ascetica; una vita da cavalieri, ma una regola anti-eroica," in *I Templari, la guerra, e la santità*, ed. Simonetta Cerrini (Rimini, 2000), pp. 19–48, at p. 35; "L'obiettivo di un cavaliere di Cristo non è di diventare un eroe, ma di obbedire!"

[78] From Giacomo Bosio et al., "De B. Gerlando, equite Hierosolym. Templarione an Hospitalario? Calatagironi in Suracusana Siciliae diocesi," *AASS*, Jun. 3:651–55.

confident it contained the relics he sought. Three days later, on 21 June, those relics began to effect miraculous cures and by 20 July about a hundred miracles had been recorded. So went the story discovered by the Hospitaller historian Giacomo Bosio during his researches in 1616. Bosio, who completed a book on Hospitaller saints in 1622, offered further information, although his sources are unknown.[79] The mysterious knight was called Gerland of Germany, or John of Poland or maybe Gerland of Poland or John of Germany. His life had been exemplary: abstinent, disciplined and prayerful. Gerland himself had protected widows, defended orphans, helped the needy and worn a hair shirt under his splendid knightly attire. He had died c.1244 and an icon from the 1580s showing Gerland in Hospitaller garb deceived Bosio into believing that Gerland had been a Hospitaller. In fact, until 1310 the Templars had owned the church where Gerland's relics were allegedly found. Since Gerland was believed to have died before this date, he could well have been a Templar saint.[80] On the other hand he may never have existed. Churches are full of burials and visions elide with dreams. Bosio's account cannot be accepted as reliable and his description of the saintly knight's life is as predictable as it is brief. Would the Hospitallers, finally, have been able to resurrect a Templar saint so soon after the Templars' shameful demise? Perhaps they might. Gerland's rapid acceptance and the miraculous powers of his relics would have amounted to an extraordinary coup for the Hospitallers had he never existed. Behind the fog and myth there does seem to loom some figure, vaguely recalled in the locality, of a saintly calibre. Assuming a popular Templar cult had been suppressed after 1310, its revival and adoption by the Hospitallers some years later was a shrewd and successful move.

If the Templars had produced a saint, how would they have portrayed him? A likely extant model lies in the hagiography of Blessed Gobert.[81] Gobert, count of Apremont (c.1187–1263), died in the Cistercian abbey of Villiers in the diocese of Liège, where a fellow monk wrote his hagiography. Although Gobert ended his days a Cistercian, the count and his entourage had helped protect the Templars and Hospitallers of Acre from a hostile Frederick II in 1228. This episode is prominent in his hagiography where Gobert's arrival is presented as the answer to the Templars and Hospitallers' prayers, causing them to rejoice and thank God. The hagiographer, moreover, adds a number of details that suggest he was modelling his depiction of Gobert upon a paradigm of Templar spirituality. He confronts us, for example, with the Templar image of the twofold warfare. Gobert, we read, attended Matins before daybreak girt with his sword, thereby starting his day equipped against the twofold enemy of body and soul.[82] His devotion in prayer was such that the warrior "now

---

[79] Giacomo Bosio, *Le imagini dei beati e santi della sacra religione di S. Giovanni Gerosolimitano* (1622; repr. Rome, 1860).

[80] For German and Polish Templars and their donors in the 1230s and 40s see Winfried Irgang, ed., *Urkunden und Regesten zur Geschichte des Templerordens im Bereich des Bistums Cammin und der Kirchenprovinz Gnesen* (Cologne, 1987), especially nos. 6, 7 and 34.

[81] Anon., "B. Gobertus, Ordinis Cisterc.," *AASS* Aug. 4:370–95.

[82] Ibid., 382E; "Contra duplicem quippe hostem, uisibiliter scilicet et inuisibiliter, arma arripuit."

appeared more like a monk" and he preached to his companions on the world's empty vanity, the transience of the flesh, the devil's cunning temptations, God's gracious bountiful goodness and the glory of eternal life.[83] At Villiers the monks would have heard the monastic office of Twelve Lessons but Gobert, his hagiographer observed, attended the canonical office with the Templars, as well as reciting the hours of Blessed Mary (customary among both Templars and Cistercians by this date).[84] This makes the account convincing, while the image of Gobert fully armed, rising before dawn for prayers in the Holy Land, may provide an insight into the devotional lives of eastern Templars. When Gobert joined Villiers he became "a new knight of Christ," and a prayer to the saint preserved in a manuscript there, along with its antiphon, cried "Pray for us, unconquered knight."[85] Even without these final details, if the narrative of Gobert's eastern adventures is taken alone, one can be forgiven for thinking that it is the *vita* of a Templar.

I suggest a Templar and not a Hospitaller (although Gobert served with both orders) because sanctity in the Hospital was never defined by the paradigm of saintly knighthood as it was in the Temple, through the Templar rule and *De laude*. Of five known Hospitaller saints who died before 1350 – Hugh of Genoa, Ubaldesca, Toscana, Flora and Gerard – not one was said to have lifted a sword.[86] The first four achieved sanctity in western preceptories while Gerard, although present at the fall of Jerusalem, was never depicted as a combatant. Only Blessed Gerland was modelled as a knight, but his cult might have been Templar, and Bosio's hagiography falls well outside our period. Surprised by the Hospital's peaceful western calendar, Jonathan Riley-Smith has offered three possible explanations. The Church might have been reluctant to sanction the martyrdom of warriors, evidence of cults in the east might have been destroyed, or "the bustling environment of the compounds and castles in Palestine and Syria" might have

---

[83] Ibid., 380B.

[84] Ibid., 380B; Gobert is likely to have observed the canonical hours when accompanying the military orders, although "horasque canonicas" can refer to either the monastic or canonical offices.

[85] Ibid., 380C; 370B.

[86] See Jonathan Riley-Smith, "Hospitaller Spirituality in the Middle Ages," Sovereign Military Order of Saint John of Jerusalem of Rhodes and Malta, *Journal of Spirituality* 2 (Rome, 2002), pp. 2–3. Hugh of Genoa died in *c.*1230 and his fifteenth-century hagiography appears to be based on a contemporary life commissioned by Gregory IX and the archbishop of Genoa, for which see Anon., "De S. Hugone Confessore," *AASS* Oct. 4:362–64. Ubaldesca (died *c.*1207) was a servant in a nuns' hospital in Pisa which affiliated to the order during her lifetime. For her, see Anon., "S. Ubaldesca, Virgo," *AASS* May 6:854–59 and Gabriele Zaccagnini, *Ubaldesca, una santa laica nella Pisa dei secoli xii–xiii* (Pisa, 1995). Toscana, a Hospitaller *consoeur*, died "many years" before her translation in 1343, but her earliest extant *Life* dates from 1474, for which see Celsus Mapheus, "De S. Tuscana Vidua," *AASS* Jul. 3:860–66. For Flora, a Hospitaller sister who died in 1347, see *AASS* Jun. 6, "appendix ad diem XI Jun.," 97–117. The remains of blessed Gerard (whose skull now resides on Malta) were being venerated at Manosque in 1283, for which see Anthony Luttrell, "The Rhodian Background of the Order of St John of Jerusalem of Rhodes and Malta," in *The Sovereign Military Hospitaller Order of St John of Jerusalem of Rhodes and Malta: the Order's Early Legacy in Malta*, ed. John Azzopardi (Valletta, 1989), pp. 3–16, at p. 9.

prevented Hospitallers from developing the saint within.[87] A fourth possible explanation is that the Hospital saw warfare as only one expression of its charitable vocation. Its various legends, which originated and circulated in the east, never took the opportunity to present either Gerard or Raymond of Puy as saintly knights, an opportunity that surely would have tempted the Templars had one of their founders been present in 1099. The legends also downplayed the Hospital's military function. One Latin version mentioned it only among the Hospital's other charitable activities.[88] Likewise William of Saint Stephano, writing a more historical account of his order's origins at the turn of the fourteenth century, paid scant attention to its military role.[89] In the fifteenth century an anonymous priest offered a scathing account of the Hospital's militarization, describing how early Hospitaller priests, driven by madness and greed, had abandoned their duties, to become knights![90] With a strong spiritual identity of its own to preserve, distinct from that of the Templars, the Hospital therefore might have pursued paths of sanctity other than the paradigm of saintly knighthood, at least until the dissolution of the Temple, which was the original and definitive military order.

How then was sanctity achieved in the Hospital? Extant hagiographies suggest that Hospitaller spirituality engaged with action, contemplation and mysticism. The first is no surprise, for the Hospital's Christ was a doer and charity was its hallmark. Toscana attended the sick daily, washed their feet and gave alms. Ubaldesca never let the poor depart from her doorstep without offering them what little she had and her charity shone forth as she served the sisters with industrious efficiency. Gerard was a slave to the sick and risked punishment to feed the hungry crusaders, while the brother-chaplain Hugh was not only a good administrator but also a model of charity, humbly ministering to the needy, washing their feet and burying the dead. Commenting upon Hugh's miracle of changing water into wine, his hagiographer quoted Christ: "whoever believes in me will do my works."[91] Here was that same simple faith in the literal interpretation of scripture which we have observed in the order's legends, and which seems to have been characteristic of the early Hospital. After his death, Hugh's shrine was able to exorcize a demoniac, who vomited up a fat stinking toad, and win grateful converts to the Hospital from among the cured, including one lady who spent the rest of her life serving the sick with great love and

---

[87] Riley-Smith, "Hospitaller Spirituality," pp. 3–4.

[88] *RHC Oc.* 5:404; "Ille ordo multotiens postea pauperibus christianis uictum et uestitum pariter et hospitium exhibuit, mortuosque honorifice sepeliuit multaque alia charitatis opera exercuit. Fratres etiam Hospitalis hostes fidei christiane uictoriosissime debellauerunt, et multa grauamina eis intulerunt."

[89] William de St Stephano, "Comment la sainte maison de l'hospital de S. Johan de Jerusalem commença" (*c*.1303), in *RHC Oc.* 5:422–27.

[90] Anon., "De primordiis et inuentione sacrae religionis Jerosolymitanae," in *RHC Oc.* 5:428–29, at p. 429.

[91] *AASS* Oct. 4:363F; "Qui credit in me, opera, que ego facio, et ipse faciet." Ubaldesca also followed Christ's example by changing water into wine, for which see *AASS* May 6:858B.

charity.[92] Inwardly the saints were as devoted as their outward deeds suggested. Toscana found time for contemplation as well as work, prayer and battling demons. Flora also fought demons, as did Hugh, whose Hospitaller cross was only "an external symbol of the inner cross he had carved upon his heart."[93] Many medieval saints donned *cilicia*, and Hugh, Ubaldesca, Gerland and Gobert all punished their flesh with these unpleasant garments. Charity, fervour in prayer, devotion in the office or in performing the Mass and spiritual warfare were all orthodox saintly characteristics of the age, but they could only be combined in an order that was able and willing both to engage with the world and withdraw from it.

Saintly Hospitallers furthermore found comfort, inspiration and guidance in mysterious visions. At fifteen Ubaldesca went to Pisa on the instructions of an angel. At Pisa her future abbess and some forty nuns awaited her, having been forewarned of her arrival by the angel in a dream. After Ubaldesca correctly predicted her own death, the sisterly community saw a host of angels bear her soul aloft, singing: "Come bride of Christ, receive the crown God has prepared for you from the beginning of the world."[94] Seven days later with crowds pressing at her tomb a Hospitaller priest "of proven sanctity" saw a vision of Ubaldesca in heaven. Convinced of her blessedness, he subsequently had her body translated to a new tomb. A former Hospitaller prior, Brother Bartolus, distressed at having been removed from his post by the Hospital's commander, humbly beseeched Ubaldesca to help him regain it. In return he promised to celebrate her feast day every year. Ubaldesca appeared during the night with instructions to prepare for her feast and soon afterwards Brother Bartolus was reinstated. Flora was similarly blessed with heavenly visions, seeing divine mysteries in the Spirit and levitating in front of all the sisters while at prayer during Pentecost.[95] Indeed throughout the Hospital's history visions appeared in its religious literature. From the legendary tales of founders like Zacharias and Julian the Roman to whom Christ appeared, to the Hospitaller on Syracuse who dug up blessed Gerland's remains, the order had developed a tradition of acting upon them. Of course the use of visions to direct hagiographic narratives and sanctify their subjects was no Hospitaller novelty and the Templars' interest in the vision of Antichrist suggests they too might have embraced mystical spirituality. Nevertheless a recurrent formula is evident in Hospitaller hagiography where the direct intervention of Christ and heavenly beings is the input, simple obedience is the process and a life of uncompromising charity and devotion is the result. Through this formula the Hospitallers attempted to replicate the exciting narratives of the gospels, the Acts of the Apostles and perhaps their own spiritual experiences in the Holy Land.

---

[92] *AASS* Oct. 4:363F and 364A.
[93] *AASS* Oct. 4:363D; "gestans crucem foris in pectore, quam intus cordi insculpserat."
[94] *AASS* May 6:855D–E and 858D; "Veni sponsa Christi, accipe coronam, quam tibi parauit Deus ab origine mundi."
[95] *AASS* May 6:858C and E; *AASS* Jun. 6:109E and 111F.

The Books of the Maccabees and the Teutonic Order

Mary Fischer

Napier University, Edinburgh

After the fall of Acre in 1291, the Teutonic Order removed its headquarters first to Venice, and then to Prussia in 1324. Shortly thereafter, during the first third of the fourteenth century, two chronicles recounting the order's origins and its wars in Prussia were written. Peter of Dusburg's *Chronicon Terre Prussie*[1] describes the Teutonic Order's origins and its wars in Prussia up to 1330. It was commissioned by Werner von Orseln, the first grand master to be based solely in Prussia (1324–30). It is generally acknowledged that this chronicle was written in an attempt to influence opinion in the order, as part of a wider aim to reinvigorate the order's sense of identity and purpose. According to Hartmut Boockmann, in his discussion of the historiography of the order:

> dieser Text war auf einen praktischen Zweck hin geschrieben. Er wollte moralische Wirkungen erzielen, er sollte die Ordensritter seiner Zeit, des frühen 14. Jahrhunderts, durch das Beispiel ihrer Vorgänger zur Regeltreue mahnen, sie aufrufen, der ursprünglichen Bestimmung ihres Ordens gerecht zu werden, also die Heiden zu verfolgen und zu bekämpfen.[2]

This chronicle is not the only evidence that there was a concerted effort to restate the order's crusading ethos for the new situation in which it found itself at the beginning of the fourteenth century. Karol Gorski detects a *Frömmigkeitsbewegung* within the order, which he dates from 1291 to approximately 1340.[3] Evidence in the statutes and elsewhere suggests that Grand Masters Karl von Trier (1311–24) and Werner von Orseln both attempted to enforce higher standards of religious observance and observance of the Rule. New regulations forbade the knight brothers to buy their own horses or use ornate weapons or saddles.[4] There were also

---

[1] Peter von Dusburg, *Chronik des Preußenlandes*, trans. and annotated by Klaus Scholz and Dieter Wojtecki, Ausgewählte Quellen zur Geschichte des deutschen Mittelalters 25 (Darmstadt, 1984).

[2] Hartmut Boockmann, "Geschichtsschreibung des Deutschen Ordens im Mittelalter und Geschichtsschreibung im mittelalterlichen Preußen. Entstehungsbedingungen und Funktionen," in *Literatur und Laienbildung im Spätmittelalter und in der Reformationszeit*, ed. Ludger Grenzmann and Karl Stackmann (Stuttgart, 1984), pp. 79–93, p. 82.

[3] Karol Gorski, "Das Kulmer Domkapital in den Zeiten des Deutschen Ordens," in *Die Geistlichen Ritterorden Europas*, ed. Josef Fleckenstein and Manfred Hellmann, Forschungen und Beiträge 26 (Sigmaringen, 1980), pp. 330–37.

[4] *Die Statuten des Deutschen Ordens nach den ältesten Handschriften*, ed. Max Perlbach (Halle, 1890), pp. 147–48.

regulations which required religious observances to be kept "mit grôzerem vlîze ... dan bisher ist geschen."[5] The commissioning of Dusburg's chronicle appears to have been part of this movement.[6]

However, a Latin chronicle was evidently not sufficient for the role the Order's leadership intended it to play. Dusburg's chronicle was translated into the vernacular almost immediately at the express wish of the next grand master, Luder of Brunswick (1330–35) and his successor Dietrich of Altenburg (1335–41). This new version by Nicolaus von Jeroschin, a chaplain in the order, was completed in c.1340.[7] The reason for the translation, as cited in the text,[8] was to make the work available to a wider audience:

> ... und hîz dî sinne mine
> mich darûf arbeitin
> unde in dûtsch bereitin,
> ûf daz er sus bedûten
> mug allen dûtschin lûten
> dî wundir unde zeichin gots,
> dî nâch gûte sîns gebots
> in Prûzinlande sîn geschên.[9]

The need to make learning and participation in worship accessible to the growing numbers of knights and laymen who could read German, but not Latin, posed a particular challenge for a military order such as the Teutonic Order. New provisions in the order's rule at this time acknowledge this: "Ouch setzen wir ein igelich brûder, der nit gelêret ist, spreche sîn âve Maria unde den gelouben zu Tûtsche."[10] It has been suggested that the proliferation of vernacular texts in the order's libraries at this time, including Jeroschin's translation of Dusburg's chronicle, served not only as a resource for the mealtime readings, which were required by the order's statutes,[11] but may also have been used for individual study.[12]

---

[5] *Statuten*, p. 147: "... with greater diligence ... than has hitherto been the case."

[6] Karl Helm and Walther Ziesemer, *Die Literatur des Deutschen Ritterordens* (Giessen, 1951), p. 150.

[7] Nicolaus von Jeroschin, *Krônike von Prûzinlant*, ed. Ernst Strehlke, *Scriptores rerum Prussicarum* 1 (Leipzig, 1861), pp. 3–219.

[8] Ibid., lines 146–68.

[9] Ibid., lines 158–65: "... and called on me to work on the preparation of a German translation, so that it might explain to all Germans the significance of all God's wonders and signs which have come about in Prussia according to his goodness."

[10] *Statuten*, Rule 13, p. 41: "We also decree that every Brother who cannot speak Latin should say his Hail Mary and the Creed in German."

[11] *Statuten*, p. 147.

[12] Jelko Peters, "Zum Begriff: 'Deutschordensdichtung'. Geschichte und Kritik," *Berichte und Forschungen* 3 (1995), 7–38, 30; Arno Mentzel-Reuters, "Literatur im Deutschen Orden 1275–1550," in *Deutsche Literatur und Sprache im östlichen Europa*, ed. Carola Gottzmann (Leipzig, 1995), pp. 40–41.

It is written in Middle High German rhyming couplets and is 27,738 lines in length. The first approximately three and a half thousand lines (up to line 3392) are introductory in nature, while the bulk of the chronicle deals with the order's wars in Prussia up to the death of Grand Master Werner of Orseln and the election of Duke Luder of Brunswick as grand master of the order in 1330.

The chronicle's aim is to place the conquest of Prussia unequivocally within the context of the traditions of crusading warfare to glorify the order's role as part of a divinely ordained contest between the godly and the heathen. It restates themes and terminology familiar since the First Crusade and develops the order's own traditions. The Order's cult of the Virgin Mary as its patron and defender figures prominently, and the chroniclers also draw on the tradition of biblical justification of warfare in the name of the church, which had built up throughout the crusading period. The traditional range of Old Testament heroes, as well as the Gospels and the teachings of St Paul, underpin the theological justification of these particular wars. However, it is clear that, although all the usual references are present, the Books of the Maccabees are accorded far greater importance here than at any time since the preaching of the First Crusade. Indeed, Helmut Bauer, writing on the order's historical writing, suggests that the order was unique in its almost exclusive use of Judas Maccabaeus as a model.[13] To what extent did the Teutonic Order use the acknowledged links between the wars of the Maccabees and those of the medieval military orders to give its own wars in Prussia legitimacy and to reinvigorate the idea of the *militia Christi* for its members in the fourteenth century?

The Maccabee material is only preserved within the Apocrypha of the Bible. The texts were treated with suspicion by the early church fathers. St Jerome omitted the books from the canon. Augustine had reservations about their usefulness to the Church but he nonetheless recognized the mother and her children depicted in 2 Maccabees 7.11 as the first Christian martyrs, despite having lived under the laws of the prophets, by virtue of the coming death of Christ.[14] He only discusses this aspect of the stories and not the actual wars of the Maccabees themselves and this sets the pattern for future exegesis.

There is no interest in treatment of religious warfare in the texts of the stories until the ninth century, presumably as a result of increased persecution of the Church by Vikings and the new need for the Church to defend its institutions. The first illustrations of the warring Maccabees appear at this time, in the *Book of the Maccabees*[15] written in Saint Gallen in the ninth century. The exegesis written by Hrabanus Maurus (d. 856)[16] interprets the books in terms of the *psychomachia*, a

---

[13] Helmut Bauer, *Peter von Dusburg und die Geschichtsschreibung des Deutschen Ordens im 14. Jahrhundert in Preußen* (Berlin, 1935), p. 33.

[14] "martyres eos fecit moriturus Christus." St Augustine, Sermo 300, "In solemnitate martyrum Machabaeorum," PL 38.1377.

[15] Reproduced in *Geschichte der deutschen Kunst* 1, ed. Georg Dehio (Berlin, 1930), p. 61.

[16] "Commentaria in libros Machabaeorum," in PL 109.1125–1256, col. 1127.

spiritual battle between good and evil and as a prefiguration of the Christian conquest of the world. The elder Maccabee, Mathathias, is interpreted as a prefiguration of Christ, while his sons are prefigurations of the apostles and the saints. Judas Maccabaeus' name is interpreted as "evangelist" and his role prefigures that of the first preachers of the gospel. Conversely Antiochus represents the Antichrist and his generals are motivated by arrogance and insolence. They are defeated by the Maccabee army, which takes its motivation from its faith and its God. This interpretation is maintained in its essentials throughout the Middle Ages. The Maccabees constituted one of the main Old Testament prefigurations of the crusaders during the preaching of the First Crusade. According to Penny Cole, in her analysis of the role of the Maccabees as a model for the preaching of the First Crusade, "in all essential ways the struggles of the Maccabees against the persecutor Antiochus ... and by association, of the crusaders against the Muslim infidel, are substantially identical."[17]

In view of these parallels, and the validation of the just war in the wars of the Maccabees, it is unsurprising that the Books of the Maccabees featured prominently in the preaching of the First Crusade. All accounts of Urban II's sermon at Clermont include frequent references to the Maccabees. The poem "De Templo Domini," written in Jerusalem in the mid-twelfth century is largely a paraphrase of the first Book of the Maccabees.[18] Later preaching of the crusade refers to the Maccabees texts,[19] as do Eugenius III, Gregory VIII, Henry of Albano, Honorius III, James of Vitry and Humbert of Romans.[20] The example of Mathathias is frequently used as a model of the attitude and state of readiness required of a crusader. Henry of Albano, for example, emphasizes the need for Christians to transcend the deeds of the Maccabees because of the new Covenant in Christ.[21]

Judas Maccabaeus is used typologically throughout the crusades as a prefiguration of the warrior leader – the inscription on Baldwin I's tomb records him as "the new Maccabaeus."[22] The comparison of warlike princes with Maccabaeus is common throughout the twelfth century. The wording of Judas Maccabaeus' exhortation to his men on the eve of a battle became a rallying cry which is repeated throughout the crusading period:

---

[17] Penny J. Cole, *The Preaching of the Crusades to the Holy Land, 1095–1270* (Cambridge, Mass., 1991) pp. 31–32.

[18] Rudolf Hiestand, "Gaufridus abbas Templi Domini: an Underestimated Figure in the Early History of the Kingdom of Jerusalem," in *The Experience of Crusading* 2, ed. Peter Edbury and Jonathan Phillips (Cambridge, 2003), pp. 48–59.

[19] Cole, *The Preaching of the Crusades*, pp. 1–36.

[20] Ibid., pp. 63–65, 134 and 206.

[21] Henry of Albano, "De peregrinante civitate Dei: Digressio, qua lamentatur auctor Jerusalem ab infidelibus captam," PL 204.350, ch.12.

[22] Elias Bickerman, *Der Gott der Makkabäer* (Berlin, 1937), p. 37.

And Judas said, Gird yourselves and be valiant, men and be in readiness against the morning, that ye may fight with these Gentiles, that are assembled together against us to destroy us and our holy place: for it is better for us to die in battle, than to look upon the evils of our nation and the holy place. (I Maccabees 3.58–59)

However, in every case the emphasis is on spiritual rather than physical warfare. Even Bernard of Clairvaux, in spite of his advocacy of the idea of the *militia Christi* and of the military orders, stops short of explicitly recognizing the Books of the Maccabees as a justification for physical warfare in the service of the Church. In his response to an unknown correspondent, to the question as to why the Maccabees, alone of all the Old Testament heroes, are accorded an annual feast day and venerated as Christian martyrs, while he does implicitly acknowledge contemporary parallels, he does not allude directly to the crusading movement or to the concept of the *militia Christi*.[23] According to his reply, the Maccabees can be considered martyrs because they died for the right to profess their faith, not because they were proto-Christian warriors: "Just as our martyrs, they too were forced to pour out libations to strange gods, to forsake the laws of their country or rather of their God, and they died because they refused to do so."[24] In fact, it has been suggested that the Maccabee material remained essentially alien to the Middle Ages. According to Carl Erdmann,[25] the Old Testament models seem to have been of greatest importance for establishing the principle of crusade at the beginning of the crusading movement. Thereafter they appear to have become established as part of the general clerical discourse about the crusades, but lose their immediacy and vividness.

The extent to which the Maccabees are used as models in Jeroschin's *Krônike von Prûzinlant* is worthy of investigation both on account of the frequency of allusion as well as the manner and context in which they are used. They feature most prominently in the theoretical introduction, which attempts to set out the theological basis of the wars and to provide a justification for the use of armed force in the service of the church. This introduction, which is unique to this chronicle and Dusburg's original, can be roughly divided into two parts. The first 2,000 lines deal with the foundation of the order, give a general justification for armed warfare in the name of the Church and give specific papal endorsement of the order's role in this warfare in the text of an exhortation attributed to Gregory IX. The second section, which comprises approximately 1,500 lines, lays out the conditions for just war, in part through an extended development of St Paul's metaphor of spiritual weapons.

---

[23] Bernard of Clairvaux, "Epistola XCVIII, De Machabeis," in *S. Bernardi Opera* 7, ed. Jean Leclercq and Henri Rochais (Rome, 1974), pp. 248–53.

[24] Ibid., pp. 249–50; translation by Bruno Scott James, *The Letters of Saint Bernard of Clairvaux* (Stroud, 1998), p. 145.

[25] Carl Erdmann, *Die Entstehung des Kreuzzugsgedankens* (Stuttgart, 1935), p. 253.

In overall terms the Maccabees are clearly the most important models for the clerical writers of the chronicle. An examination of the Old Testament models in these sections reveals that the Maccabees are mentioned fifteen times, as against eight for David, the next most mentioned Old Testament hero, five for the Israelites, three for Solomon, two for Daniel and one each for Gideon, Joshua, Abraham and Saul.

Not only do references to the Maccabees dominate in purely numerical terms; their importance is also highlighted by their use at crucial key points in the text which attempt to define and sanction the order's wars. These are: the list of biblical prefigurations of the crusades, the chronicle's text of the papal bull sanctioning their wars, the section defining the physical weapons whose use is sanctioned in a holy war and, finally, a list defining circumstances in which the use of these weapons is justified.

In the section which lists biblical prefigurations of the crusades in general, and of the order's wars in particular,[26] the chronicle identifies Abraham's campaign to free his brother Lot from the rulers of Sodom and Gomorrah and his subsequent blessing by Melchizedech, "king of Salem and priest of God most high,"[27] as the origin of just warfare against the heathen in the name of the church. Jeroschin then lists the Apocalypse of St John and the "church militant," the Israelites under Moses and Joshua, and King David and his servants, and the section ends and culminates in a long passage on the wars of the Maccabees. The Teutonic Order is expressly presented as the successor to the wars against the heathen and defilers of the holy places:[28]

> Disen strîtin ebin hât
> Gevolgit nâch mit vrechir tât
> Der heilige ordin rittirlîch
> Des dûtschin hûsis.[29]

Secondly, the chronicler justifies the wars by citing the text of Gregory IX's sermon.[30] This passage does not correspond to any known historical document and may well have been written by the order to fill a need felt for a document initiating and sanctioning their wars in Prussia, in the form of a traditional crusading bull. It begins with a description of the threat to Christianity, using the text from I Maccabees 3.58–59 in which Judas Maccabaeus exhorts his men to choose death rather than accept the desecration of the holy places:

---

[26] Nicolaus von Jeroschin, *Krônike von Prûzinlant*, lines 607–834.
[27] Gen. 14.10–20; Nicolaus von Jeroschin, *Krônike von Prûzinlant*, lines 615–64.
[28] Nicolaus von Jeroschin, *Krônike von Prûzinlant*, lines 781–834.
[29] Ibid., lines 825–28: "these battles were continued by the bold exploits of the holy chivalric Order of the German House."
[30] Ibid., lines 2004–129.

Sune, gurtit ûwir swert
Und sît an creftin wert;
...
wan uns bezzer ist dî nôt
daz wir in strîte ligin tôt
wenne daz wir sûllen sêhn
und in jâmikeite spêhn
unsir volc bemeilgin
und ouch unsir heilgin.[31]

The account attributed to Gregory IX goes on to exhort the brothers to emulate the example of the Israelites and especially of Judas Maccabaeus. With the exception of two quotes from Deuteronomy, the entire text is made up of quotations from the Books of the Maccabees. The final passage comes from Mathathias' final speech, which in traditional exegesis prefigures Christ sending out the apostles to evangelize the world.[32] Here the knights who are to conquer Prussia for Christendom take the role of the apostles. The passage is repeated at the end of the chronicle, where it has become an appeal to contemporary knights to remember the sacrifices of their predecessors and to continue their work in Prussia:

Bedenkit ûwerre vetre werc
Dî sî tâten sundir geberc
In ires lebins zîten
An tugenthaften strîten;
Und um der vetre erbe
Stêt in strîte bederbe;
Sô nemit ir grôz achberkeit
Und eines namen êwichkeit! [33]

The third key section is that listing and interpreting the meaning of the weapons which may be carried by the *militia Christi*.[34] It has references to the Maccabees among other Old Testament models and culminates in a reference to the Maccabees' defence of the Temple in Jerusalem.

Finally, and most significantly, in the list of circumstances in which the bearing of arms is sanctioned, the Maccabees are the sole Old Testament reference in the section on open warfare.[35] The section explicitly refers to the Maccabees' success in battle:

---

[31] Ibid., lines 2040–41, 2046–51: "Sons, gird on your swords and be strong; ... for it is better for us to suffer death in battle than to look on wretchedly as our people and our saints are dishonoured."

[32] I Macc. 2.50–51 and 64.

[33] Jeroschin, *Krônike*, lines 27115–22: "Think of the deeds of your predecessors, the virtuous battles they fought in their day, unstinting in their efforts; and for the sake of your fathers' inheritance be bold in battle; in this way you will achieve great respect and lasting renown!"

[34] Ibid., lines 2274–3057.

[35] Ibid., lines 3058–392.

> Des irhûbin sî ouch sich
> An dî vîende vîentlich
> Und irslûgin in der stunt
> Vûzgenger wol eilftûsent
> Und darzu gesundirt
> Tûsint und sechshundirt
> slûgin sî der rîten.[36]

The section ends again with a direct comparison between the Maccabee wars and the Teutonic Order's wars.[37]

In the body of the chronicle, which relates the events in Prussia from 1225 to 1340, references to the Maccabees also occur at significant points in the narrative. The knights are twice directly compared to the Maccabees, once in the introduction to the description of the first Prussian rebellion.[38] Here the specific link may have been intended as a means of pre-empting any criticism which might have been levelled at the order because of its apparent failure. Later in the chronicle, a commander is implicitly compared with Judas Maccabaeus when he uses Judas's words from I Maccabees 3.18 to encourage his men.[39]

Therefore, although both Peter von Dusburg and Nicolas von Jeroschin were both clerics, the references to the Maccabees are almost exclusively in relation to warfare. The only exception is the use of Mathathias' lament (1 Maccabees 2, 7) on the destruction of churches. In this chronicle, therefore, in a distinct break with church tradition, the Maccabees are emphatically seen as an explicit justification for warfare in the name of the Church and are exploited to this end more unambiguously than at any time since the beginning of the crusading movement.

The order's use of the material is not confined to these chronicles. The earliest reference to the Maccabees comes in the revised statutes of the order, probably undertaken by William of Modena, the papal legate to Prussia at the time of the Council of Lyons, and written at some time between 1244 and 1251.[40] In the prologue of the Statutes a list of Old Testament precedents is brought forward to demonstrate the existence of a body of knights active in the service of the Church since Abraham culminating in the Maccabees. The Maccabees are used here explicitly as a precedent for religious warfare and far more directly than in earlier literature of the crusades:

---

[36] Ibid., lines 3188–94: "And so they rose against the enemy and within a short time they slew eleven thousand infantry and, in addition, sixteen hundred knights."

[37] Ibid., lines 3202–12.

[38] Ibid., lines 5871–77.

[39] Ibid., lines 20011–31.

[40] *Statuten* (see above, note 4), pp. 23–25.

[41] Ibid., p. 25: "We remember too, the praiseworthy battles, honourable in the sight of God, of the knights called the Maccabees, and how bravely they fought the heathen for the sake of their honour and their beliefs."

Wir gedenken ouch des lobelichen strîtes, der wert vor gote was, der rittere, die da heizent Mâchabei, wie stercliche die durch ir ê unde umme den gelouben striten mit den heiden ...[41]

In wording similar to that which Jeroschin uses in his chronicle, the Teutonic Order is presented as their heirs and successors: "Disen strîten hat nâchgevolget herteclîche dirre heilige ritterliche orden des spitâles sente Marien von dem Thûschen hûse."[42] There is also a Middle High German translation of the Books of the Maccabees,[43] dating from the first half of the fourteenth century and written at approximately the same time as Jeroschin's chronicle, which was widely disseminated in the order's libraries. The one extant copy of this manuscript bears the arms of the duke of Brunswick, and it was thought at one time that the grand master who commissioned Jeroschin's chronicle, Luder of Brunswick, may himself have been the author of the translation. While this now seems unlikely, it is probable that the order or one of its members commissioned the translation, given the importance of the model for the order's self-image.[44]

The overriding importance the order gives to the Maccabees and the explicit use of their example to justify warfare is not reflected in other preaching or writing about the northern crusades. We know that the preaching of these crusades was entrusted to the Dominicans. Crusading sermons were seldom recorded; however, the general themes can be found in collections of sermons written as source material and guidance for preachers by eminent preachers of the day. Versions of crusade sermons survive in collections of so-called *ad status* sermons. A recent study by Christoph Maier[45] allows an informed guess about the likely content of these sermons. Maier has made a detailed study of the *ad status* model sermons of a number of preachers, including Humbert of Romans, who was the general master of the Dominicans from 1254 until he retired to write his collections of sermons in 1263. Maier describes the mendicant orders as being the closest the Middle Ages came to mass media. If the identification of the Maccabees with northern crusades reflected popular belief, or if the Church felt it was particularly apposite, then presumably it would be reflected in their sermons. Maier's findings, however, shows that the sermons emphasize the moral and devotional aspect of the crusade for the individual, while "[in] contrast, military, material or political aspects of crusading are less prominent features of these texts."[46] The two main Old Testament contexts serving as a foil for the crusades are the stories of the conquest of the

---

[42] Ibid., p. 25: "The bold successor to these battles is the holy chivalric Order of the Hospital of St Maria of the German House."

[43] *Das Buch der Makkabäer*, ed. K. Helm (Tübingen, 1904).

[44] Helm and Ziesemer, *Die Literatur des Deutschen Ritterordens*, pp. 95–100; Jelko Peters, "Zum Begriff 'Deutschordensdichtung'," pp. 28–29.

[45] Christoph T. Maier, *Crusade Propaganda and Ideology. Model Sermons for the Preaching of the Cross* (Cambridge, 2000).

[46] Ibid., p. 54.

Promised Land by the Israelites after the Exodus from Egypt and the fights of the Maccabees. However, the references to the Maccabees are relatively few in number in comparison to the overall use of Old and New Testament models and vocabulary. The most frequent quotation is from I Maccabees 2, lamenting the destruction of the holy places. The one sermon Maier discusses which is based entirely on the Maccabee texts is by Eudes of Châteauroux. It takes as its text II Maccabees 15.15–16:

> And Jeremiah stretching forth his right hand delivered to Judas a sword of gold and in giving it addressed him thus: Take the Holy sword, a gift from God, wherewith thou shalt smite down the adversaries.

However, the emphasis here is again, as it is in the official exegesis, on the spiritual rather than the physical side of warfare. In the words of the sermon: "He armed each of them not with shield and lance for defence but with excellent words and exhortation."[47] This is a very selective use of the text, which in fact describes Maccabaeus and his army in prayer before setting out against the enemy and concludes:

> And contending with their hands and praying unto God with their hearts, they slew no less than thirty and five thousand men, being made exceeding glad by the manifestation of God. (II Maccabees 15.27)

As one would expect from a theologian, the endorsement of their wars is implicit, rather than explicit as it is in Dusburg's and Jeroschin's chronicle.

Humbert of Romans, as master general of the Dominicans from 1254 to 1263, might have been expected to have had influence on the preaching of the crusade to Prussia. However, his collection of sermons contains only one slight reference to the Maccabees, and only to the martyrdom of the mother and children (II Maccabees 7.11) and not the wars. Therefore although the Maccabee material still has a place in the general preaching of crusades, it is by no means as central as it was during the First Crusade but, along with the rest of the biblical ideological substructure, has become part of the clerical shorthand of writing and preaching about the crusades. The content of these model sermons in themselves gives no indication of why the texts are so central to the order's chronicles.

These sermons were aimed at a specific group of people: those who were able to consider undertaking a crusade, and not at members of a military order. It is likely that the Teutonic Order's interest in the material stems partly from the fact that it provided a clear and unambiguous endorsement – for those who chose to interpret the texts literally – for the existence of crusading orders.

Although there is no evidence that the Maccabees came to be associated solely or primarily with the military orders, there is evidence that their analogous role as

---

[47] Eudes of Chateauroux, "Sermon 2,1," in Maier, *Crusade Propaganda and Ideology*, p. 277.

priest-warriors was recognized by contemporaries. Honorius III called the Teutonic Knights the "new Maccabees under the new Covenant"[48] while earlier Adrian IV wrote of "God's brave and honourable warriors, the Knights of the Temple, the new Maccabees in the time of grace."[49]

However, of all the military orders, it does seem that it was only the Teutonic Order for whom the Maccabees became central to their self-image and who fully exploited their potential as a prefiguration of the orders' role in the crusades. The Templars apparently did not feel the need for a foundation myth of the kind the Teutonic Order establishes in its Statutes and in the chronicles. The support of Bernard of Clairvaux and *De laude novae militiae*[50] presumably made any such effort on their part redundant. The Knights of St John, however, did write an account of their foundation known as the Miracles or Legends,[51] apparently to supplement the account of their origins by William of Tyre. The Miracles date from the twelfth century, were translated into several languages and validated by Innocent IV. By the mid-fourteenth century this text is found at the beginning of all collections of the statutes of the order as the only authentic account of the origins of the order. The Maccabees are mentioned among Old Testament prefigurations of the order in all the versions of the Miracles. In the earliest version Judas Maccabaeus makes a donation to the Hospital for the souls of the dead. At this stage he is not associated with the warrior element in the order. The latest version of the Miracles, which dates from the period after the loss of Acre in 1291, is the only one which deals specifically with the order's military function. This version claims that the Hospital was founded by Judas Maccabaeus during the wars for the liberation of Jerusalem, as a refuge for the wounded and a place of prayer for the souls of the dead. The connection between Judas Maccabaeus and the knights of the Hospital is implicit in the text but, crucially, unlike the comparable writings of the Teutonic Order, the link is not exploited explicitly at any point in the text. The emphasis instead is on the Hospital's charitable function.

It appears, therefore, that the Teutonic Order was alone in its almost exclusive identification with the Maccabees and its explicit use of the texts to justify warfare. In this they may have identified and been building on a specifically German tradition. There is evidence that the Maccabee material had particular resonance in Germany. Other studies have noted the preponderance of references to the Maccabees in Helmold of Bosau's *Chronica Slavorum*,[52] written in the mid-twelfth century and describing the first missions and wars of conquests against the Slavs.

---

[48] *Tabulae Ordinis Theutonici*, ed. Ernst Strehlke (Berlin, 1869; repr. Toronto, 1975), no. 321, p. 290.

[49] "Quantum Strenui (13.11.1157)," *Veterum Scriptorum at Monumentorum amplissima collectio*, ed. Edmond Martène and Ursin Durand (Paris, 1724–33), 2.647.

[50] Bernard of Clairvaux, "Liber ad milites Templi De laude novae militiae," in *S. Bernardi Opera*, 3.213–39.

[51] "Exordium Hospitalorium," *RHC Oc.* 5.399–435.

[52] Helmold von Bosau, *Slawenchronik*, ed. Heinz Stoob, Ausgewählte Quellen zur Geschichte des deutschen Mittelalters 19 (Darmstadt, 1963).

Similarly, Henry of Livonia's Chronicle of Livonia,[53] begun in around 1224 by a mission-priest to record the conquest of Livonia by the Sword Brothers, who were later absorbed into the Teutonic Order, also runs counter to the trend noted in other chronicles written at this time, in which the influence of Old Testament prefigurations of the crusade is declining. The editor of the German edition of the chronicle highlights the importance of the Maccabee borrowings for the text.[54] A separate study establishes a striking predominance of references to the Books of the Maccabees, although the borrowings are stylistic rather than thematic.[55] Nonetheless this suggests that the author was deeply imbued with the spirit of the material and regarded it as being particularly relevant to his chronicle. These parallels suggest that the Saxon church schools may have seen the Maccabees as a key text, and one which was particularly relevant for that area, even before the arrival of the Teutonic Order.

The *Krônike von Prûzinlant* and its source, Dusburg's chronicle, were both written by clerics, in the clerical tradition. They can usefully be contrasted with the *Livonian Rhymed Chronicle*,[56] written in the vernacular at the end of the thirteenth century by an anonymous knight, possibly a member of the order. The stated aim of this chronicle was to describe how Christianity came to Livonia. Although relatively close in chronological terms to Dusburg's Latin chronicle, the *Livonian Rhymed Chronicle* owes more to the vernacular epic than it does to the learned tradition of the clerical authors of the earlier Latin chronicles. Biblical references are rare. Instead the chronicle focuses on the technical details of warfare. Stylistically the chronicle has more in common with the tradition of the lay epic, the *Spielmannsepos* and the work of Wolfram of Eschenbach. This suggests that, even for those associated with the order, the original aims of the *militia christi* were being superseded by a lay, purely worldly ethic. Seen within this context, and in that of the grand masters' attempts to reinvigorate the order's mission, Jeroschin's vernacular reworking of Dusburg's Latin text represents a pivotal point in the development of the vernacular historiography of the northern crusades, reflecting the reality of fourteenth century crusading for the order.

The Teutonic Order was uniquely successful in the fourteenth century in attracting large numbers of lay crusaders to support its wars in Prussia and against the Lithuanians. Crusaders came not only from Germany, but, for a hundred years at the height of the order's influence, from England, Scotland, France, Italy, Spain and beyond to take part in the wars against the "heathen" in north-east Europe. It

---

[53] Heinrich von Lettland, *Livländische Chronik*, ed. Albert Bauer, Ausgewählte Quellen zur deutschen Geschichte des Mittelalters 24 (Darmstadt, 1975).

[54] Ibid., p. xxix.

[55] Willi Bilkins, *Die Spuren von Vulgata, Brevier und Missale in der Sprache von Heinrichs Chronicon Livoniae* (Riga, 1928); cited in Leonid Arbusow, "Das entlehnte Sprachgut in Heinrichs Chronicon Livoniae," *Deutsches Archiv für Erforschung des Mittelalters* 8 (1950), 100–53, here pp. 108–11.

[56] *Livländische Reimchronik*, ed. Leo Meyer (Paderborn, 1976).

became, as Werner Paravicini has said, "ein Phänomen europäischen Ausmaßes."[57] Participation on such campaigns became perceived as part of what it meant to be a rounded knight in the fourteenth century, in much the same way as later members of the aristocracy took part in the "Grand Tour." Chaucer's Prologue to the Canterbury Tales alludes to his Knight's campaigns in Prussia and Russia[58] and the term *Reise* entered both French and English as a loan word, meaning a campaign on behalf of the Order.[59]

This phenomenon is all the more impressive because of the context in which it was achieved. The Teutonic Order survived the loss of Acre in 1291 to prosper in the changed circumstances of the fourteenth century and is generally judged to have reached the zenith of its influence under the leadership of Winrich von Kniprode, Grand Master from 1351 to 1382. The precise motivation of the participants in the campaigns of the fourteenth century, so long after the original call to arms of the First Crusade, has long been a subject of debate.[60] Axel Ehlers, in his study of the Lithuanian Crusade, surmises that, like earlier crusaders, it is "likely that they were driven by a mixture of devotional and worldly aims that merged in the idea of Christian chivalry. The Teutonic Knights did their best to make this idea a reality."[61] He concludes: "Prussia developed into a popular battleground because the Teutonic Knights offered all options, both religious and secular."[62]

Jeroschin combined the popular appeal of vernacular lay epics like the *Rhymed Chronicle*, and their accessibility to the lay crusader, with the scholarly tradition of the Latin chroniclers, and the uncharacteristically literal use of the Books of the Maccabees appears to be the bridge which allows him to combine the two. This combination of piety, spirituality and acknowledgement of the realities of chivalric warfare, disseminated by the order via this chronicle and reconciling the idea of warrior and priest in a way unique to the order, may well have contributed in no small part to the popularity of the northern crusade in the fourteenth century.

---

[57] Werner Paravicini, *Die Preußenreise des Europäischen Adels*, 2 vols to date (Sigmaringen, 1989–), 1.11.
[58] *The Riverside Chaucer*, ed. Larry D. Benson (Oxford, 1988) p. 24, lines 53–55.
[59] Paravicini, *Preußenreise*, 2.13.
[60] Axel Ehlers, "The Crusade against Lithuania Reconsidered," in *Crusade and Conversion on the Baltic Frontier 1150–1500*, ed. Alan V. Murray (Aldershot, 2001), p. 22.
[61] Ibid., p. 22.
[62] Ibid., p. 42.

Aspects of Everyday Life in Frankish Acre*

David Jacoby

Hebrew University of Jerusalem

The crusader occupation of Acre in 1104 generated political, social, economic and cultural developments that altered the urban texture of the city and the composition of its population, as well as the nature and dynamics of its everyday life. Shortly after its conquest Acre became the main port of the Frankish Levant, as well as the main destination of merchants and immigrants and the exclusive one of crusaders and pilgrims in the region until its fall to the Muslims in 1291, except for four years of Muslim occupation. In 1191 the city returned to Frankish rule and replaced Jerusalem as the political and ecclesiastical centre of the Latin Kingdom. It absorbed displaced institutions and individuals, as well as new immigrants, and reached the peak of its urban, demographic and economic growth within the following century. This is the period upon which the present paper focuses.

The urban environment was one of the important factors shaping Acre's everyday life. Acre was a walled city divided into two sections, one inherited from the pre-crusader period, which for the sake of convenience may be called the Old City, and the suburb of Montmusard, which expanded to the north of it after 1191.[1] Two maps of Acre drawn around 1320, one by Pietro Vesconte and the other by Paolino Veneto (Figs. 1 and 2, respectively),[2] as well as architectural surveys and

---

* An earlier version of this paper was read to a symposium entitled *Historic Acre as a Living City*, held in July 2003 in Acre under the auspices of the Old Acre Development Company.

[1] On the urban development and the quarters of crusader Acre, see David Jacoby, "Crusader Acre in the Thirteenth Century: Urban Layout and Topography," *Studi medievali* 3a serie, 20 (1979), 1–45; David Jacoby, "Montmusard, Suburb of Crusader Acre: the First Stage of its Development," in *Outremer*, pp. 205–17; David Jacoby, "Les communes italiennes et les Ordres militaires à Acre: aspects juridiques, territoriaux et militaires (1104–1187, 1191–1291)," in Michel Balard, ed., *Etat et colonisation au Moyen Age* (Lyon, 1989), pp. 193–214; David Jacoby, "L'évolution urbaine et la fonction méditerranéenne d'Acre à l'époque des croisades," in Ennio Poleggi, ed., *Città portuali del Mediterraneo, storia e archeologia. Atti del Convegno Internazionale di Genova 1985* (Genoa, 1989), pp. 95–109. The first two papers are reprinted in David Jacoby, *Studies on the Crusader States and on Venetian Expansion* (Northampton, 1989), nos. V and VI, respectively; the last two appear in idem, *Trade, Commodities and Shipping in the Medieval Mediterranean* (Aldershot, 1997), nos. VI and V, respectively. Some of the views expressed in these studies have been revised in the present one in the light of new evidence. Benjamin Z. Kedar, "The Outer Walls of Frankish Acre," *'Atiqot* 31 (1997) [= *'Akko (Acre): Excavations Reports and Historical Studies*], 157–80, argues that Frankish Acre extended well beyond the territory ascribed to it by previous studies. His approach has been partly vindicated by some recent archaeological finds, yet various problems await further clarification.

[2] On the two maps and their sources from the last decade of Frankish rule, see Jacoby, "Crusader Acre," 2–7. The Venetian Marino Sanudo commissioned the Vesconte map. For further evidence on his presence in Acre in 1286, see David Jacoby, "Three Notes on Crusader Acre," *Zeitschrift des Deutschen Palästina-Vereins* 109 (1993), 95 and n. 76.

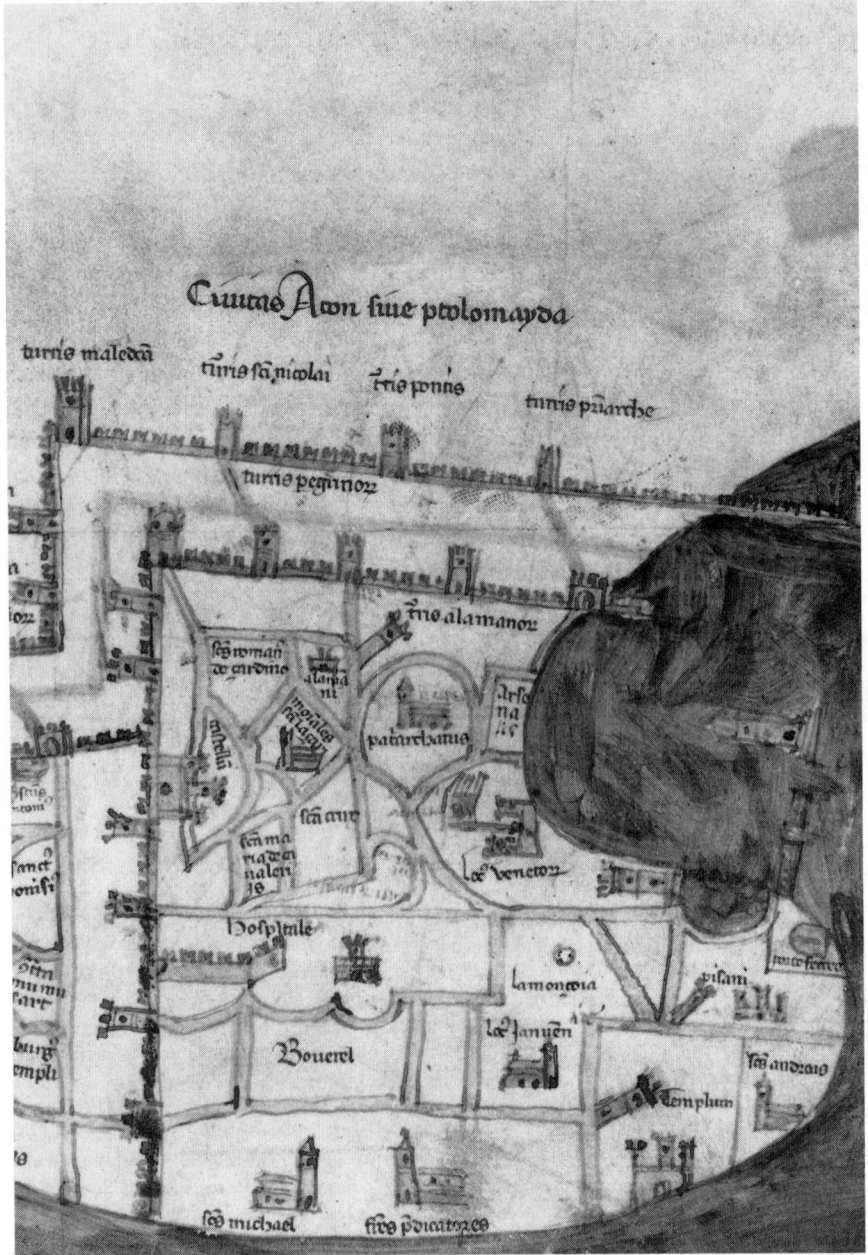

Fig. 1 Map of Acre by Pietro Vesconte (*c*.1320). London, British Library, MS Add. 27376, fol. 190r (Reproduced by kind permission of the Trustees of the British Library)

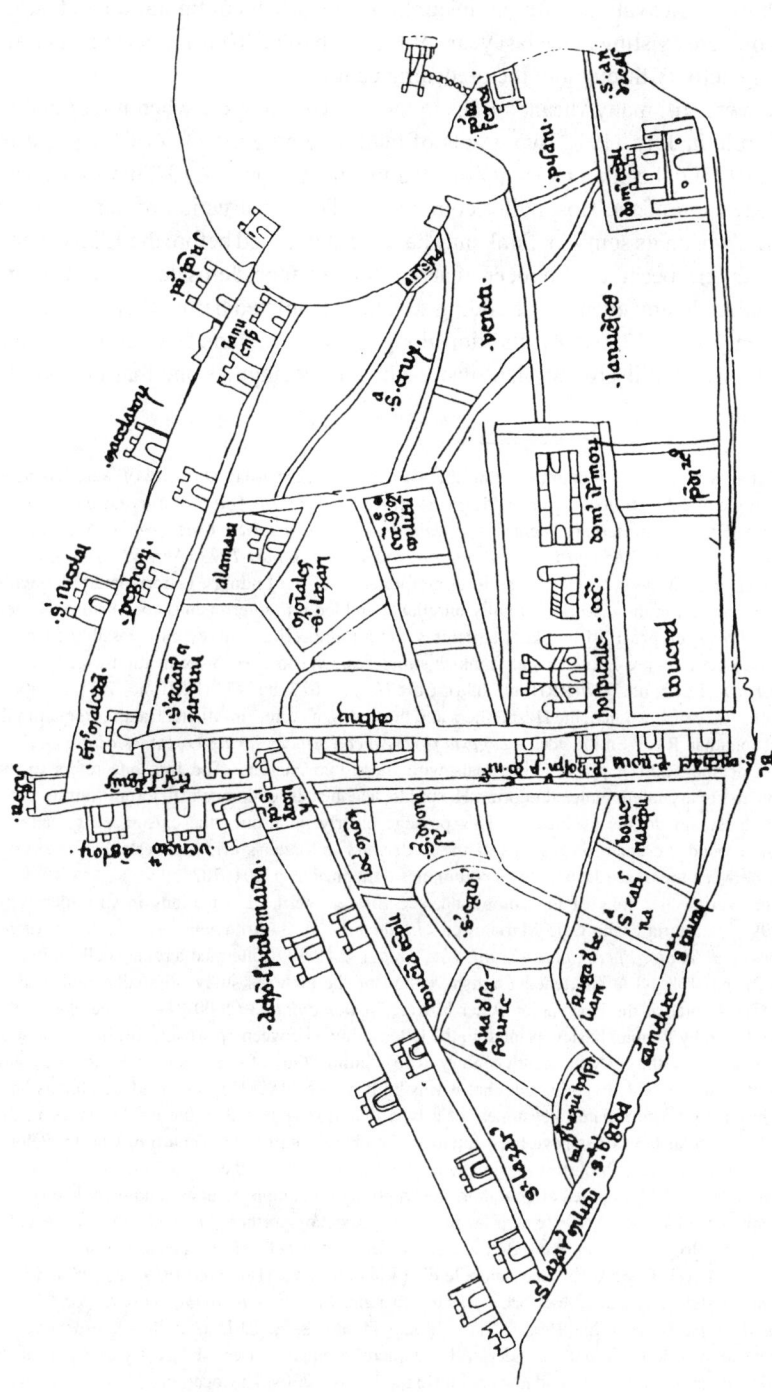

Fig. 2   Map of Acre in the chronicle of Paolino Veneto (1323?). Vatican City, Biblioteca Apostolica Vaticana, MS Lat. 1960, fol. 268v

archaeological excavations offer an insight into the urban configuration and street network of Acre existing in the last years of Frankish rule.³ They reflect the outcome of building activity throughout the preceding century.

There were still many vacant spaces in the Old City of Acre when it returned to Frankish rule in July 1191. Two grants of land, one by King Guy of Lusignan in January 1192 and the other by Henry of Champagne in January 1194, paved the way for the extension of the Hospitaller compound.⁴ The construction of the so-called *crypt of St John* on its southern flank may have been initiated before the 1220s, when the Hospitallers became convinced that a return to their Jerusalem headquarters was excluded. In any event, the building was not completed before that decade and possibly only in the 1230s.⁵ An addition along the western flank belongs to the same period.⁶ Its rhomboid ground plan, instead of the rectangular one that one would

---

³ An extensive survey of buildings within the walls of the present-day Old City of Acre has been carried out under the direction of architect Alex Kesten: see his *Acre, The Old City. Survey and Planning* (Jerusalem, 1962); repr. in Bernard Dichter, *The Maps of Acre. An Historical Cartography* (Acre, 1973), pp. 70–98. Alex Kesten, *The Old City of Acre. Re-examination Report 1993* (Acre [?], 1993), offers further evidence from the survey and a revised interpretation of the findings. Unfortunately, Kesten's use of historical data in these works is totally unreliable and led him to erroneous conclusions. Kesten distinguished between pre-1291 and later structures, yet a more refined survey may possibly enable a differentiation between pre-Frankish and Frankish structures. On some recent excavations, see below.

⁴ *Cart Hosp*, 1:582, no. 917 (RRH, no. 698); *Cart Hosp*, 1:617, no. 972 (RRH, no. 717). Jonathan Riley-Smith, "Guy of Lusignan, the Hospitallers and the Gates of Acre," in Michel Balard, Benjamin Z. Kedar and Jonathan Riley-Smith, eds., *Dei gesta per Francos. Études sur les croisades dédiées à Jean Richard* (Aldershot, 2001), pp. 111–15, deals with these two charters. The first one refers to the "districtionem et parvitatem platee domorum Hospitalis acconensis, et domos officiorum fratrum extra curiam et clausuram domus hospitalis." This passage clearly underlines the existence of scattered possessions around the enclosed nucleus of the Order and the latter's efforts to establish territorial continuity between them: see Jacoby, "Les communes italiennes," pp. 201–202.

⁵ On the various sections of the compound, see Eliezer Stern, "Excavations in Crusader Acre (1990–1999)," in Maria Stella Calò Mariani, ed., *Il cammino di Gerusalemme, Atti del II Convegno Internazionale di Studio (Bari-Brindisi-Trani, 18–22 maggio 1999)*, Rotte mediterranee della cultura 2 (Bari, 2002), pp. 163–68, a shortened English version of the author's study originally published in Hebrew: "The Center of the Hospitaller Order in Acre," *Qadmoniot* 33 (2000), 4–13. The plan of the compound drawn by Raanan Kislev, printed in the latter volume between pp. 16 and 17, fig. 1, ascribes the *crypt of St John* to the early thirteenth century. Riley-Smith, "Guy of Lusignan, the Hospitallers and the Gates of Acre," p. 111, hypothesizes that it was built before 1187. Decisive evidence for its later dating is provided by its foliated keystones, of a type that first appeared in the Ile-de France in the 1220s–1230s. Similar keystones have been found in the church built in the suburb of Chastel-Pèlerin in the 1230s or later and at Montfort, the castle of the Teutonic Order, the construction of which was initiated in 1226 or 1227, pursued after a short interruption and completed at an unknown date before 1240. On this type of keystone, see Zehava Jacoby, "The Impact of Northern French Gothic on Crusader Sculpture in the Holy Land," in Hans Belting, ed., *Il Medio Oriente e l'Occidente nell'arte del XIII secolo*, Atti del XXIV Congresso internazionale di storia dell'arte 2 (Bologna, 1975), p. 125 and figs. 110–12. On Chastel-Pèlerin and Montfort, see Denys Pringle, *The Churches of the Crusader Kingdom of Jerusalem. A Corpus* (Cambridge, 1993–), 1:75–79, esp. 75 and 78, fig. XLI, and 2:40–43, respectively.

⁶ The western addition is buried under still-occupied Ottoman houses, yet the style of two of its engaged Gothic capitals above ground level points to the 1220s–1230s. The location of this addition west of a line going southwards from the Gate of the Hospital appears to coincide, at least partly, with the

expect, clearly points to the constraints imposed by space limitations. After that large-scale building campaign, which may have come to an end around 1235, the Order had exhausted the vacant land at its disposal. Its further territorial expansion by construction in the Old City was prevented by the neighbouring built-up areas and, therefore, it resorted to the purchase of houses in the vicinity of its possessions.[7] Any additional major building project of the Order could only be carried out in Montmusard.[8]

Further construction after 1191 is indirectly attested in the western-northwestern section of the Old City, called Boverel on the Vesconte and Paolino maps, an area under royal authority.[9] The terms *boverel* and *boveria* were generally applied to a farm, a cattle market, and a stable lodging cattle or horses.[10] The first two meanings may be excluded, considering the urban context of Acre and the association of Boverel with the Templars, to which we shall soon return. Indeed, it is unlikely that the Templars had a farm or a cattle market in the Old City before 1187 or later in Montmusard. Rather, the name Boverel seems to point to an area in which one or several stables sheltered warhorses behind the city wall. These horses presumably belonged to the Temple Order, the compound of which was located further south along the western flank of the Old City.[11] At one point the stables were removed from Boverel to an area of Montmusard just north of the Old City wall, labelled *boveria Templi* on Paolino's map (Fig. 2). Boverel became afterwards a residential neighbourhood, although retaining its original name. It is noteworthy that the houses in that long and narrow area are aligned along an almost straight street, which their respective entrances face. Both L-shaped entrances apparently had

---

territory granted to the Hospitallers in 1192. I shall return elsewhere to this issue. The enlargement or reconstruction of the Order's church in Gothic style seems to be contemporary with the constructions just mentioned: see next note. On an excavated section of the church beneath the Serai, see Eliezer Stern, "'Akko, the Old City," *Excavations and Surveys in Israel* 109 (1999), 11–12, and map in the Hebrew section, 15, fig. 17; another section of the church has recently been uncovered: see Eliezer Stern, "The Church of St John in Acre," *Crusades 3* (2004), 183.

[7] See Jacoby, "Les communes italiennes," pp. 202–204.

[8] Marie-Luise Favreau, *Studien zur Frühgeschichte des Deutschen Ordens*, Kieler historische Studien, Band 21 (Stuttgart, 1974), pp. 44–46, states that the German knights erected new buildings on vacant land soon after the Frankish recovery of Acre. Given conditions in the city at that time, it seems very unlikely that the Germans could have succeeded in doing so within less than the seven months extending between the city's reconquest in July 1191 and February 1192, when Guy of Lusignan mentioned these buildings, including one serving as a hospital. Since the charter he delivered to the Germans mentions the grant of the land on which the buildings stood, these must have already existed prior to 1187. See Jacoby, "Les communes italiennes," pp. 206–207 and 213, n. 62.

[9] Its location appears to be more accurate on Paolino's map, where it is depicted as close to the seashore, than on Vesconte's, as evidenced by the Frankish buildings identified by the Kesten survey: see his map of Crusader remains in *Acre, The Old City*; repr. in Dichter, *The Maps of Acre*, p. 72.

[10] See Meron Benvenisti, *The Crusaders in the Holy Land* (Jerusalem, 1970), pp. 259–61; idem, "Bovaria-babriyya: A Frankish Residue on the Map of Palestine," in *Outremer*, pp. 132–34.

[11] This suggestion is strengthened by the later connection of two areas in Montmusard called *boveria* or *bovaria* with the Templars, on which see below. On the location of the Templar compound, see Jacoby, "Les communes italiennes," pp. 204–206.

guard-houses. To the west the houses abut a wall three metres thick, of which eighty metres can still be traced.[12] These features clearly imply planned construction requiring a substantial investment yet, unfortunately, we do not know whether this was a royal or a private enterprise. The whole disposition of the neighbourhood clearly contrasts with the tortuous medieval streets uncovered by the Kesten survey and the lack of planning in the excavated thirteenth-century quarter (see below). There is good reason to believe that population pressure soon after 1191 generated the change in the function of Boverel, and that this urban section was the first one to be built up at that time.[13]

Vacant land in the Old City is also attested by references to *gastine* in 1230.[14] In the urban context of Acre the term referred to land void of structures or with ruined buildings. The late twelfth and the thirteenth century witnessed the addition of a residential neighbourhood, devoid of urban planning, on vacant land in the north-eastern corner of the present-day Old City.[15] By 1257 there was no more land available for large-scale construction in the Frankish Old City, except for the garden of the royal castle close to the northern city wall and the one belonging to the monastery of St Romanus, located in the north-eastern corner of that urban section. This is clearly illustrated by the charter granted to the Anconitans by John of Ibelin, lord of Arsur, constable and bailli of the kingdom of Jerusalem. It suggested that they erect a church, a communal building and a hostel for the accommodation of their merchants either on the grounds of a Genoese garden or orchard in Montmusard, or else buy large houses in the suburb and receive vacant land between them.[16] At some unknown date before 1273 it was the turn of the garden of the royal castle to be invaded by houses, after one of the rulers of the kingdom allowed their construction on its soil, presumably for financial reasons.[17]

---

[12] See Kesten, *Acre, The Old City*, pp. 18–19; repr. in Dichter, *The Maps of Acre*, pp. 78–80, and Kesten, *The Old City of Acre*, pp. 57–58 and map 14. However, this was not the *burgus novus*, as stated by that author. The appellation was applied to the suburb: see Jacoby, "Montmusard," p. 208.

[13] On that pressure, see Jacoby, "Crusader Acre," 44, and idem, "Montmusard," p. 210.

[14] Ernst Strehlke, ed., *Tabulae Ordinis Theutonici* (Berlin, 1869), pp. 57–58, no. 73 (RRH, no. 1020).

[15] See Danny Syon and Ayyelet Tatcher, "'Akko, Ha-Abirim Parking Lot," *Excavations and Surveys in Israel* 20 (2000), 11–17 (English section); for plan and illustrations, see the Hebrew section, 17–24.

[16] New edition of the charter by D. Abulafia, "The Anconitan Privileges in the Kingdom of Jerusalem and the Levant Trade of Ancona," in Gabriella Airaldi and Benjamin Z. Kedar, eds., *I comuni italiani nel regno crociato di Gerusalemme*, Collana storica di fonti e studi, diretta da Geo Pistarino 48 (Genoa, 1986), pp. 560–63, esp. 562–63. The precise location of the area is not mentioned, yet its siting in Montmusard is obvious, considering the following factors: the Genoese garden is described as being close to the city wall and the seashore, which the Genoese quarter did not reach; there is no evidence of such a Genoese garden in the Old City; finally and more decisively, the Anconitans were promised that they would be allowed to transit with their goods free of charge through the nearest gate under royal authority, obviously from and to the harbour, which clearly implies that the site was not in the Old City.

[17] Charter of 1273 ed. by Marie-Luise Favreau-Lilie, "The Teutonic Knights in Acre after the Fall of Montfort (1271): Some Reflections," in *Outremer*, pp. 283–84: "dedenz le jardin qui fu dou chastiau."

The garden of the monastery of St Romanus was possibly the only large vacant space left in the Old City in the last years of Frankish rule. By itself the name, St Romanus "of the gardens", *a zardini* or *de zardinis* on maps of Acre (Figs. 1 and 2), does not prove that such was the case, considering the construction of houses in the royal garden attested in 1273.[18] However, there is convincing evidence that the monastery's garden was preserved until the fall of Acre to the Mamluks. Indeed, during the final defence of the city in 1291 it provided ample space for the positioning of the large Pisan stone-throwing machines and their copious ammunition.[19]

Eventually, then, the Old City became densely built-up, yet the distribution of population within its walls was uneven. The quarter of the Chain close to the harbour must have witnessed a heavy concentration of inhabitants.[20] By contrast, density must have been relatively low in the Hospitaller and Templar compounds, despite their multi-storied buildings, since they contained vast halls, numerous storerooms, and spacious apartments for their leaders.[21] Low population density may also be assumed for the royal castle and for some monasteries.

Another important feature of the Old City was the physical partitioning of its space in the course of the thirteenth century, as a result of political and military confrontations between the major maritime powers. Pisa and Venice built walls surrounding their respective quarters, and Genoa fortified the entrances to its own. In addition, the compounds of the Hospitallers and the Templars became self-contained urban entities clearly separated from their surroundings.[22]

Montmusard expanded gradually after 1191.[23] The first phase in that process must have taken place within the same decade, once the erection of a protective system on the land front of the suburb had begun, its future course on the ground had been determined, and its completion could be expected in the near future. Its construction, accomplished some time before 1212, undoubtedly furthered and hastened residential building in the suburb.[24] Displaced ecclesiastical institutions and individuals resettling in Acre after 1191 were presumably among the first to establish themselves in Montmusard. The *Ruga Bethleemina* and *Ruga de Saforie* marked on the Vesconte and Paolino maps locate respectively the new residence of the bishop and clergy of Bethlehem and that of former inhabitants of Sephoria in Galilee. It is noteworthy that these areas were not contiguous, the first being in the

---

[18] On which, see previous note.

[19] Laura Minervini, ed., *Cronaca del Templare di Tiro (1243–1314). La caduta degli Stati Crociati nel racconto di un testimone oculare* (Naples, 2000), p. 214, no. 261, and p. 218, no. 263.

[20] On this quarter, see Jacoby, "Crusader Acre," 15–19.

[21] The Hospitaller compound also had a large courtyard, visible today, which apparently was not the case of the Templars.

[22] See Jacoby, "Crusader Acre," 19–36; idem, "Les communes italiennes," pp. 194–98.

[23] On the suburb before 1187, see Jacoby, "Montmusard," pp. 205–208.

[24] For the dating of the construction, see the Appendix to this study, pp. 99–102.

western and the second in the eastern part of Montmusard.[25] The hospital and church of St Thomas Becket, established in the Old City, were relocated in 1227–28 in the northern section of the suburb, later known as the English neighbourhood.[26] Some time after the 1230s, yet before 1270, the Hospitallers built a large compound which became the new residence of the conventual brothers.[27] Known as the *auberge*, it appears as *hospicium Hospitalis* on Vesconte's map and as *albergum Hospitalis* on the Venetian copy of Vesconte's map, between St Lazarus to the north and the *Ruga Bethleemina* to the south.[28]

The function of the area along the shore just north of the Old City wall also underwent some changes. A charter issued in 1198 mentions the *porta boverie Templi* in an area close to the *porta nova*,[29] which suggests that the stables established in the suburb just north of that gate and of Boverel were still located there. This was apparently also the case in 1237, when Pope Gregory IX listed property held by the monastery of the Holy Trinity along the shore of Montmusard *juxta bovariam Templi*.[30] The proximity of the monastery to that area is also borne out by the maps of Vesconte and Paolino. However, three years later a charter mentioned the *boveria Templi* as being close to the house of the Order of St Lazarus "of the knights" situated in the English neighbourhood. This location concurs with the one along the suburb's double wall provided by Vesconte's map (Fig. 1).[31] It follows that the Templars' stables had again been transferred, this time apparently

---

[25] Vesconte's map is undoubtedly more accurate than Paolino's in this respect, as proven by documentary evidence. Vesconte's map in Oxford, Bodleian Library MS. 10,016 (Tanner 190), fol. 207r, has the erroneous inscription *Ruga Sancti Forie*: see Jacoby, "Montmusard," p. 209.

[26] See Alan Forey, "The Military Order of St Thomas of Acre," *English Historical Review* 92 (1977), 481–95; repr. in idem, *Military Orders and Crusades* (Aldershot, 1994), no. XII. On the *vicus Anglorum* and its location, see David Jacoby, "Some Unpublished Seals from the Latin East," *Israel Numismatic Journal* 5 (1981), 87–88; David Jacoby, "Pilgrimage in Crusader Acre: The *Pardouns dAcre*," in Yitzhak Hen, ed., *De Sion exibit lex et verbum domini de Hierusalem. Essays on Medieval Law, Liturgy and Literature in Honour of Amnon Linder*, Cultural Encounters in Late Antiquity and the Middle Ages 1 (Turnhout, 2001), pp. 110–11.

[27] For the dating, see below, Appendix.

[28] Venice, Marciana, MS Z. lat 399 (colloc. 1610), fol. 84v. The inscription has been distorted in the two other copies. Paris, Bibliothèque Nationale, MS Lat. 4939, fol. 113v, has *albergum hospicium*, and Vatican City, Biblioteca Apostolica Vaticana, MS Palat. lat. 1362, fol. 9r (here Fig. 2), [?]*bazium Hospi*[*talis*]. The maps of the first two copies are reproduced in Joshua Prawer, "Historical Maps of Akko," *Eretz Israel* 2 (1953), 175–84 (Hebrew), Pl. XXI, fig. 2 and Pl. XXII, fig. 1, respectively.

[29] Sebastiano Paoli, *Codice diplomatico del sacro militare ordine gerosolimitano oggi di Malta* (Lucca, 1733–37), 1: 287, no. 8 (RRH, no. 746). The gate's name is attested only once. On the *porta nova*, see Jacoby, "Crusader Acre," 21, n. 103.

[30] Lucien Auvray, ed., *Les registres de Grégoire IX*, Bibliothèque des Écoles françaises d'Athènes et de Rome, 2e série (Paris 1896–1955), 2:col. 843–44, no. 4014.

[31] Comte de Marsy, "Fragment d'un cartulaire de l'ordre de Saint Lazare en Terre Sainte," *AOL* 2 (1884), part B, 155–57, no. 39. For the location of St Lazarus "of the knights," see Jacoby, "Pilgrimage in Crusader Acre," pp. 110–11. Paolino's map (Fig. 2) is less reliable. It locates the *boveria Templi* further south along the double wall and to the south-east of the *Rua* or *Ruga de Saforie*.

between 1237 and 1240 within Montmusard itself.[32] The vacated area along the northern wall of the Old City became a residential neighbourhood, called *burgus Templi* on Vesconte's map.[33]

Aerial photographs taken in 1918 and 1923 have revealed the outline below ground of a more or less rectangular and elongated building complex of particular interest, which must have been located north of the *burgus Templi*, between the seashore and the *Ruga Bethleemina* (Figs. 1 and 2). It is divided in its midst by a street, faced by units that seem to have served as shops and were possibly topped by a second, residential floor. The southern entrance appears to have been protected by a fortified gatehouse. The disposition of this complex recalls to some extent that of the residential neighbourhood of Boverel.[34] It was clearly built in a single, well-planned construction campaign that unfortunately cannot be dated, and implies that the area had previously been completely vacant.

On the whole, however, construction in Montmusard was inordinate and proceeded spontaneously, as evidenced by the establishment of ecclesiastical institutions in various parts of the suburb until the late Frankish period. Patches of built-up areas alternated with open spaces, upon which single-standing structures existed. Some areas of the suburb retained for a long time a semi-rural character.[35] The ample territory of the suburb was so large that it could easily absorb the growing population of Acre after 1191 and was never entirely covered by structures. The absence of the main maritime nations from Montmusard accounts for an additional contrast between the suburb and the Old City. The former lacked the physical partitioning gradually imposed upon the latter by the rivalry between these nations in the course of the thirteenth century.

The quality of life in Frankish Acre was obviously affected by the nature of the urban environment and by ecological conditions.[36] As noted earlier, there were several autonomous quarters and compounds in the Old City, each of which

---

[32] However, one should not rule out an earlier transfer and the persistence of the old name for some time, like that of Boverel, on which see above.

[33] A charter issued by Guy of Lusignan in 1189 mentions a *domus Templi* in an area corresponding to the *burgus Templi*, close to the Gate of the Bath of the Old City: Giuseppe Müller, ed., *Documenti sulle relazioni delle città toscane coll'Oriente cristiano e coi Turchi fino all'anno MDXXXI* (Florence, 1879), p. 38, no. 32. However, since that charter may be a forgery or its topographical data may have been changed between 1192 and 1200, it is unclear whether the house indeed existed in 1189, or whether it was built after 1191: see Jacoby, "Montmusard," pp. 208–10. A house in the *burgus Templi* is mentioned in the will of the Syrian Saliba, drafted in 1264: *Cart Hosp* 3:91, no. 3105.

[34] See Adrian J. Boas, "A Rediscovered Market Street in Frankish Acre?" *'Atiqot* 31 (1997), 181–86. Its location is presently occupied by a police station built in the period of the British mandate over Palestine and by a health clinic, some 50 metres from the sea and some 210 metres north of the present-day Old City. See the reproduction of the photographs in Kedar, "The Outer Walls of Frankish Acre," 163, figs. 3 and 4.

[35] The property held by the monastery of the Holy Trinity in 1237 included "vineam quoque, ortum et terram cultam et incultam, turrim et domos in eis edificatas": see above, n. 30.

[36] For the following two paragraphs, see Jacoby, "Three Notes," 88–91.

apparently disposed of its own garbage and waste. It is unclear how this was carried out in the urban territory under royal authority, which lacked territorial continuity. In the winter rainwater may have carried down to the harbour some of the refuse dropped by the inhabitants in the streets, as the city was built on a gradient. On the other hand, there appears to have been an overall sewage system serving the entire Old City, which implies co-operation in both planning and maintenance between the various political institutions operating within its walls. The sewage channel underneath the Hospitaller compound and its latrines, the so-called tunnel proceeding westwards from the Templar compound under the Pisan quarter, as well as individual houses in the excavated thirteenth-century neighbourhood mentioned earlier were apparently all linked to that urban sewage system, which carried waste into the harbour.[37] Leavings from the royal slaughterhouse and fishmarket, both of which were close to the harbour, were most likely dumped in the latter's waters. The harbour area must have been particularly polluted. In 1261 Venice decided to seal off the main windows in the apse of the church of St Demetrius, situated close to that area, in order to prevent the wind from projecting filth upon the altar. The water circulation in the harbour was not sufficient to clear it from the accumulated waste. Significantly, the harbour was called in French "Lordemer" ("the filthy sea"), a term also implying a foul smell.

Conditions deteriorated especially in May–June and September–October, when the easterly wind blows and temperatures rise substantially. This was precisely the period in which thousands of merchants and pilgrims arrived with the seasonal maritime convoys or were in the city to embark on their way home.[38] Conditions were conducive to the spread of disease and to a seasonal rise in mortality, especially among visitors unaccustomed to the local climate and food. Not surprisingly, their judgment was harsh. The Greek pilgrim John Phokas, who presumably arrived in Acre in 1177, reports that "the air is being corrupted by the enormous influx of strangers, various diseases arise and lead to frequent deaths among them, the consequence of which is evil smells and corruption of the air."[39] Deeply biased against Christians, the Muslim traveller Ibn Jubayr, who visited the city in September and early October 1184, provides a similar picture: "The roads and

---

[37] Personal communication from Eliezer Stern, Archeological Supervisor for Western Galilee, Israel Antiquities Authority. See Miriam Avissar and Eliezer Stern, "'Akko, the Old City," *Excavations and Surveys in Israel* 14 (1995), 24–25, on the drainage system beneath the Hospitaller compound, and 18 (1998), 14, on the "Templar" tunnel; for the recently excavated neighbourhood, see above, n. 15.

[38] See David Jacoby, "Pèlerinage médiéval et sanctuaires de Terre Sainte: la perspective vénitienne," *Ateneo veneto* 173 (n.s. 24) (1986), 27–30, repr. in Jacoby, *Studies on the Crusader States*, no. IV; idem, "Pilgrimage in Crusader Acre," pp. 105–107; David Jacoby, "Il ruolo di Acri nel pellegrinaggio a Gerusalemme," in Calò Mariani, *Il cammino di Gerusalemme*, pp. 31–50.

[39] "Ioanna Foki Skazanie vkratce o gorodach i stranach ot Antiochii do Ierusalima," ed. I. Trojckij, *Pravoslavnyi Palestinskij Sbornik* 8/2 (fasc. 23) (1889), 6, chap. 9. English trans. by Aubrey Stewart, *The Pilgrimage of Joannes Phokas in the Holy Land*, PPTS, 5/3 (London, 1896), p. 11, used here; slightly different trans. in John Wilkinson with Joyce Hill and W.F. Ryan, eds., *Jerusalem Pilgrimage, 1099–1185*, Hakluyt Society, Second Series 167 (London, 1988), p. 319.

streets [of Acre] are choked by the press of men ... Unbelief and unpiousness there burn fiercely, and pigs [by which he meant Christians] and crosses abound. It stinks and is filthy, being full of refuse and excrement."[40] The complaints of both foreigners are amply confirmed by the name "Lordemer," coined by the local Frankish population.

Industrial activity added fumes and bad smells. A sugar plant was operating in the Old City in 1187. After the occupation by Saladin's forces, the latter's nephew, Taqi al-Din, dismantled the plant, seizing its implements and transferring the ovens out of the city.[41] Several glass and metal workshops were apparently also active in Acre, although we do not know in which sections of the city.[42] A soap plant existed in the Genoese quarter around the mid-thirteenth century.[43] A street bordered by tanneries was located in Montmusard on land belonging to the bishopric of Hebron, close to the St. Catherine neighbourhood situated north of the *burgus Templi* (Figs. 1 and 2).[44] The environmental conditions in Acre must have worsened in the thirteenth century with the extension of construction and the increase in population, especially in the Old City.

Respite from the dreary urban conditions could possibly be gained in some sections of Montmusard retaining a semi-rural character, and in any event in the "green belt" to the east of Acre. The plain located in the immediate vicinity of the city and the nearby mountainous area of Lower Galilee were covered with fields, gardens, orchards, vineyards and farms, supplying the city with wheat, fruit and vegetables, and providing grazing grounds for cattle and horses.[45] The large sandy

---

[40] *The Travels of Ibn Jubayr*, trans. Ronald J.C. Broadhurst (London, 1951), p. 318.

[41] Imad ad-Din in Abu Shama, "Livre des Deux Jardins," *RHC Or*, 4:296. Although sugar was usually processed in the vicinity of the fields growing sugar cane, there were also some refineries in cities. A large one is attested in Cairo in 1240: see Shelomo D. Goitein, *A Mediterranean Society. The Jewish Communities of the Arab World as Portrayed in the Documents of the Cairo Geniza*, 6 vols. (Berkeley and Los Angeles, 1967–93), 1:81, 367, no. 26.

[42] I shall deal with them elsewhere.

[43] See David Jacoby, "Mercanti genovesi e veneziani e le loro merci nel Levante crociato," in *Genova, Venezia, il Levante nei secoli XII–XIV*. Atti del Convegno internazionale di studi, Genova–Venezia, 10–14 marzo 2000, ed. by Gherardo Ortalli and Dino Puncuh = *Atti della Società Ligure di Storia Patria*, n.s. XLI (CXV)/1 (Venice, 2001), p. 249. High-grade soap produced in Acre was exported to Alexandria and Montpellier, according to a trade manual compiled in Acre around 1270; on which see David Jacoby, "A Venetian Manual of Commercial Practice from Crusader Acre," in Airaldi and Kedar, *I comuni italiani*, pp. 403–28, repr. in Jacoby, *Studies on the Crusader States*, no. VII.

[44] The tanneries are attested in 1253 and 1273: Strehlke, *Tabulae Ordinis Theutonici*, p. 83, no. 104 (instead of *tavaria*, read *tanaria*), and *Cart Hosp* 3:296–97, no. 3514 (respectively RRH, nos. 1207 and 1389). The property mentioned in the first document was located in the vicinity of the monastery of the Holy Trinity, which itself was situated close to the church of St Catherine, according to a letter of Pope Gregory IX: see above, n. 30.

[45] There is abundant evidence in that respect. See *The Travels of Ibn Jubayr*, pp. 317, 325, for 1184. Three stones bearing the inscription IANVA, which located the boundaries of a rural estate belonging to the Commune of Genoa in 1255, have been found north-east of Acre. The property was adjacent to a vineyard of the Templars and a field of the Hospitallers, all within a range of around 8 kilometres from

plain extending along the bay south-east of Acre was also favoured by the city's residents. It served as a course for horses and training ground for knights.[46]

The heterogeneous population of Acre's was an important feature of the city's life.[47] After 1104 Latin settlers hailing from numerous regions in the West rapidly became the largest and dominant element in Acre. Diversity among them became even more pronounced after the city's recovery in 1191, when Jerusalem remained under Muslim rule and Acre became the focus of western immigration in the Levant. The Frankish population included speakers of both French and Provençal,[48] in addition to a mercantile component overwhelmingly of Italian origin, mainly concentrated in the privileged quarters of Genoa, Venice and Pisa.[49] Further population clusters based on common origin and language came into being after 1191. It will suffice to mention two of them: the Teutonic Order, settled in the Old City, which presumably attracted German-speakers; and the English neighbourhood in the northern section of Montmusard.[50] Ethnic and linguistic diversity was also conspicuous among the merchants, pilgrims and men-at-arms temporarily residing in Acre or passing through the city. Yet French appears to have been the common language of many pilgrims. The prayers recited by the Hospitaller priests in the conventual hospital for its benefactors and for the sick, probably composed at Acre in 1197, are written in French,[51] and so is the itinerary of the city's pilgrimage, recorded in the *Pardouns dAcre*.[52]

The Oriental Christians, called Syrians by the Franks, remained in Acre after its conquest. They were divided among several religious communities, each of which retained its own churches and monasteries. The number of these institutions was small compared with the Latin ones, yet it is highly significant that several of them were situated in Montmusard.[53] Their location implies an influx of Oriental Christians after 1191, when construction in the suburb expanded. Some Oriental Christians must have been attracted by the economic opportunities offered by Acre.

Acre: see Rafael Frankel, "Three Crusader Boundary Stones from Kibbutz Shomrat," *Israel Exploration Journal* 30 (1980), 199–201, with map.

[46] *The Travels of Ibn Jubayr*, p. 325.

[47] For this paragraph, see Jacoby, "Il ruolo di Acri nel pellegrinaggio," pp. 38–39; David Jacoby, "Society, Culture and the Arts in Crusader Acre," in Daniel H. Weiss, ed., *France and the Holy Land: Frankish Culture at the End of the Crusades* (Baltimore, 2004, pp. 98–100).

[48] See Cyril Aslanov, "Languages in Contact in the Latin East: Acre and Cyprus," *Crusades* 1 (2002), 156–75, 180–81.

[49] See Laura Minervini, "La lingua franca mediterranea. Plurilinguismo, mistilinguismo, pidginizzazione sulle coste del Mediterraneo tra tardo medioevo e prima età moderna," *Medioevo Romanzo* 20 (1996), 237–39, 244–45. On the quarters, see Jacoby, "Crusader Acre," 19–36.

[50] On the possessions of the Teutonic Order, see Jacoby, "Les communes italiennes," pp. 207–208. On the English neighbourhood, see above, n. 26.

[51] See Léon Le Grand, "La prière des malades dans les hôpitaux de l'Ordre de Saint-Jean de Jérusalem," *Bibliothèque de l'École des Chartes* 57 (1896), 325–38, esp. 329–32, for dating and location.

[52] On which see below, n. 116.

[53] See Jacoby, "Three Notes," 83–88. Those in Montmusard are attested in the second half of the thirteenth century, yet for lack of evidence it is impossible to determine when they were established there.

Others were presumably refugees, mostly from Frankish territories conquered by the Muslims in 1187 or in the thirteenth century, or else from Syrian cities threatened or attacked by the Mongols around 1260.[54] There was also much diversity among the Oriental Christian peasants, pilgrims and merchants visiting the city. Byzantine pilgrimage to the Holy Land continued unabated throughout the two centuries of Frankish presence in the Levant, though on a much smaller scale than western pilgrimage.[55] Byzantine merchants traded in the city or passed through it on their way to and from Egypt in the twelfth, and presumably also in the thirteenth century.[56] An Arabic–Old French phrase-book of the thirteenth century written in Coptic characters suggests that Coptic pilgrims and merchants from Egypt visited Acre.[57] There is good reason to believe that many, if not most visiting merchants and especially resident commercial agents from cities under Muslim rule who operated in Acre were Oriental Christians, like the Nestorians from Mosul, rather than Muslims.[58]

Some Jews also remained in Acre after the conquest of 1104, and a Jewish community existed in the city throughout the Frankish period. According to the Jewish traveller Benjamin of Tudela, it numbered some two hundred members when he visited Acre in 1163 or somewhat later.[59] The Jewish population was reinforced in the thirteenth century by immigration, both from Muslim territories and from the Latin West.[60]

---

[54] For the latter, see Robert Irwin, "The Supply of Money and the Direction of Trade in Thirteenth-Century Syria," in Peter W. Edbury and David Michael Metcalf, eds., *Coinage in the Latin East. The Fourth Symposium on Coinage and Monetary History*, British Archaeological Reports, International Series 77 (Oxford, 1980), pp. 74–75; also, Jacoby, "Society, Culture and the Arts," pp. 102–104.

[55] Alice-Mary Talbot, "Byzantine Pilgrimage to the Holy Land from the Eighth to the Fifteenth Century," in Joseph Patrich, ed., *The Sabaite Heritage in the Orthodox Church from the Fifth Century to the Present*, Orientalia Lovaniensia Analecta 98 (Leuven, 2001), pp. 97–110, esp. 101–107, deals with individual cases; for a broader perspective, see Jacoby, "Society, Culture and the Arts," pp. 104–105.

[56] See David Jacoby, "Byzantine Trade with Egypt from the Mid-Tenth Century to the Fourth Crusade," *Thesaurismata* 30 (2000), 62–64.

[57] See Aslanov, "Languages in Contact," 156–67, esp. 157–58.

[58] On their trade, see below, n. 89. Also Jean Richard, "La confrérie des Mosserins d'Acre et les marchands de Mossoul au XIIIe siècle," *L'Orient syrien* 11 (1966), 451–60; repr. in idem, *Orient et Occident au Moyen Age: contacts et relations (XIIe–XVe s.)* (London, 1976), no. XI. On the settlement of Nestorians in Acre after 1261, see David Jacoby, "The Kingdom of Jerusalem and the Collapse of Hohenstaufen Power in the Levant," *Dumbarton Oaks Papers* 40 (1986), 99, n. 112; repr. in Jacoby, *Studies on the Crusader States*, no. III.

[59] Marcus N. Adler, ed. and trans., *The Itinerary of Benjamin of Tudela* (London, 1907), Hebrew, p. 21, trans., p. 19. Benjamin was in Antioch and Gibelet (Jubail) in 1163: see David Jacoby, "Benjamin of Tudela in Byzantium," in Peter Schreiner and Olga Strakhov, eds., *Chryse Porta/ Zlatyia Vrata: Essays presented to Ihor Ševčenko on his Eightieth Birthday by his Colleagues and Students*, Palaeoslavica 10/1 (Cambridge, Mass., 2002), p. 181. He afterwards proceeded southwards, yet we do not know how much time elapsed until he reached Acre.

[60] Joshua Prawer, *The History of the Jews in the Latin Kingdom of Jerusalem* (Oxford, 1988), refers to the Jews of Acre, yet his location of their residences (pp. 103, 262–64), must be rejected. I shall return to that issue elsewhere. In the meantime, see below, n. 64.

On the other hand, there was no permanent Muslim community in Frankish Acre.[61] Exceptionally, though, a few Muslims resided in the city for some years. A tale included in *The Thousand and One Nights*, which apparently reflects an authentic story, records the activity of an Egyptian Muslim who in 1184 rented a shop in Acre and sold flax in the following three years, until the city's conquest by Saladin.[62] The small space set aside for Muslim worship in a section of the cathedral of the Holy Cross, formerly a mosque, was clearly intended for visiting Muslims, as explicitly stated by Ibn Jubayr.[63] These included peasants bringing their products for sale, merchants coming from Syria, Egypt and other countries under Muslim rule, and pilgrims like Ibn Jubayr returning from Mecca to Muslim countries in the western Mediterranean.

In the Frankish Levant religious affiliation was the basic criterion of social stratification, group identity and individual status. Despite the social and legal cleavage separating Latins from non-Latins, there was a constant economic and social intercourse between the members of all communities in Acre. Daily contacts were also furthered by the absence of enforced residential segregation, of which there is no trace.[64] However, group identity was clearly expressed in visual terms. Oriental Christian, Jewish and Muslim men were bearded, whereas Frankish laymen were clean-shaven like their brethren in the West, as attested by sculpted heads, manuscripts and ceramics produced in the Frankish Levant.[65] In contrast to local Franks, crusaders were not acquainted with local mores. Shortly after their arrival in Acre in 1290 some of them attacked and killed several local Orthodox Christians whom they mistook for Muslims because they were bearded and, obviously, dressed in Oriental clothes.[66]

---

[61] See Jacoby, "Society, Culture and the Arts," p. 102.

[62] See Robert Irwin, "The Image of the Byzantine and the Frank in Arab Popular Literature of the Late Middle Ages," *Mediterranean Historical Review* 4 (1989), 232–33.

[63] *The Travels of Ibn Jubayr*, p. 318.

[64] See David Jacoby, "The *fonde* of Crusader Acre and its Tariff. Some New Considerations," in Balard, Kedar, Jonathan Riley-Smith, eds., *Dei gesta per Francos*, pp. 287–89; for evidence on the scattered residence of non-Franks in Acre, see Jacoby, "Three Notes," 83–88, esp. 87–88.

[65] Giles Constable, Introduction to the *Apologia de barbis* in Robert B.C. Huygens, ed., *Apologiae duae. Gozechini epistola ad Walcherum. Burchardi, ut videtur, abbatis Bellevalis Apologia de barbis*, CCCM 62 (Turnhout, 1985), pp. 94–102. References to shaving and beards appear in a treatise composed within the two decades preceding 1187: Benjamin Z. Kedar, ed., "The *Tractatus de locis et statu sancte terre ierosolimitane*," in *Crusade Sources*, p. 124, and for its dating, see ibid., p. 119. See depictions of Frankish men in Silvia Rozenberg, ed., *Knights of the Holy Land. The Crusader Kingdom of Jerusalem* (Jerusalem, 1999), pp. 125–26, 128, figs. 1–2, 4–6, a sculpted head from the castle of Montfort belonging to the Teutonic Order, a scene in the Boulogne manuscript of William of Tyre's *Histoire d'Outremer*, executed in Acre, and knights on three ceramic bowls belonging to the group of Port St Symeon ware, manufactured in the area of Frankish Antioch. On two of the bowls and this group, see Edna J. Stern, "Excavation of the Courthouse Site at *'Akko*: The Pottery of the Crusader and Ottoman Periods," *'Atiqot* 31(1997), 56–58. For a depiction of a bearded Jew, see below, n. 77.

[66] *Cronaca del Templare di Tiro*, p. 200, § 244: "tuerent pluissors Suriens qui porteent barbes et estoient de la ley de Gresse, que pour lor barbes les tuerent en change de Sarazins."

Clothing was indeed another distinctive feature of ethnic-cultural identity. The Muslim historian Ibn al-Athir offers a convincing illustration in that respect in his report on the unusual behaviour of Henry of Champagne. In order to improve his relations with Saladin, the Frankish ruler requested from him in 1192 the gift of a robe of honour and said: "You know that to wear the *qaba* (a kind of robe) and the *sharbush* (a hat with a high-domed crown) is a disgrace among us, but I shall put them on if they come from you, because of the regard I have for you." Saladin sent these precious pieces, and Henry of Champagne wore them in Acre.[67]

Cotton, wool, silk and linen fibres are all recorded in the Acre tariff, a list of taxes imposed on imported or exported goods passing through the royal *fonde* or *funda*, the customs monitoring the city's land trade.[68] Textiles made of these materials were undoubtedly widely used in Acre, regardless of community affiliation or social standing. The city imported silken cloth, wimples and garments from Antioch, which produced both Byzantine and Islamic silks.[69] In 1184 the Arab traveller Ibn Jubayr saw in Tyre a Frankish bride "most elegantly garbed in a beautiful dress from which trailed, according to their custom, a long tail of golden silk," in fact gold-interwoven silk.[70] There was also a demand for silks manufactured in Muslim countries, both among local Franks and visitors. The Nestorians active in Acre came from Mosul, a renowned manufacturer of silk and gold-interwoven fabrics, as attested by Marco Polo.[71] The so-called "Tartar cloths," both plain and figured silk and gold textiles from Central Asia and the Middle East, were available in the city from the 1260s onwards.[72] As usual, the quality and cut of the clothes worn in Acre reflected to some degree the social hierarchy. Such was also the case of footwear. Shoes were manufactured in the city, sandals presumably too.[73] More modest

---

[67] Ibn al-Athir, "Kamel Altevarykh," *RHC Or*, 2/1:59. In the Muslim world rulers granted since the ninth century a robe of honour or several clothing items to those they wished to distinguish, whether subjects or foreigners. The Franks were well acquainted with this practice, common in Egypt in the Fatimid and later periods: see Paula Sanders, "Robes of Honor in Fatimid Egypt," in Stewart Gordon, ed., *Robes of Honor. The Medieval World of Investiture* (New York, 2001), pp. 225–39. On the *sharbush*, see Leo A. Mayer, *Mamluk Costume, a Survey* (Geneva, 1952), pp. 27–28.

[68] Edition of the tariff by Arthur A. Beugnot, "Livre des Assises de la Cour des Bourgeois," in *RHC, Lois*, 2:173–81, chaps. 242–43. On its nature, content and the dating of its sections, see Jacoby, "The *fonde* of Crusader Acre," pp. 283–93.

[69] Imports from Antioch to Acre are attested by the tariff (see previous note): *RHC, Lois*, 2:179, chap. 243, pars. 8–9. This section of the Acre tariff belongs to the post-1191 period. On the nature of Antioch's silks, see David Jacoby, "Silk crosses the Mediterranean," in Gabriella Airaldi, ed., *Le vie del Mediterraneo. Idee, uomini, oggetti (secoli XI–XVI)*, Università degli studi di Genova. Collana dell'Istituto di storia del medioevo e dell'espansione europea 1 (Genoa, 1997), pp. 63–64; repr. in David Jacoby, *Byzantium, Latin Romania and the Mediterranean* (Aldershot, 2001), no. X.

[70] *The Travels of Ibn Jubayr*, pp. 320–21.

[71] Marco Polo, *Il Milione. Prima edizione integrale*, ed. F. Benedetto (Florence, 1928), pp. 17–18.

[72] See David Jacoby, "Silk Economics and Cross-Cultural Artistic Interaction: Byzantium, the Muslim World and the Christian West," *Dumbarton Oaks Papers* 58 (2004), 234–35.

[73] Incidentally, individuals living under Muslim rule bought shoes in Acre: see Jacoby, "The *fonde* of Crusader Acre," pp. 280, 291–93.

customers were content with clogs, although fashion was respected. In 1284 a merchant in Acre ordered from Venice 1,000 pairs of thick wooden soles for clogs, half of them for men and half for women.[74] Yet beyond social standing, Frankish clothes also displayed distinctive characteristics consonant with Western fashion.[75] Their function as social and cultural markers was particularly important in the multi-ethnic and multi-cultural context of Frankish Acre.

A depiction of Oriental garbs worn in Acre appears in the Arsenal Old Testament, a manuscript apparently produced in the city between the spring of 1250 and the spring of 1254, the period in which King Louis IX of France stayed in the Kingdom of Jerusalem.[76] Its pictorial cycle partly derives from the Oxford Moralized Bible, in which the three figures seated with Job wear the traditional garb of European Jews, long-sleeved tunics with hooded mantles and pointed caps. By contrast, in the Arsenal Old Testament these figures wear long robes and turbans. The one in the foreground holds in his left hand the tsitsith, fringes made of knotted blue and white threads as prescribed in the Bible. Although not affixed to the corners of the outer garment or to the prayer shawl, as was the custom, the tsitsith clearly identifies the figure as a Jew.[77]

Acre witnessed a movement of people, goods and pack animals the whole year round. Commercial life was concentrated in the Old City. There were several focuses of activity furthering the encounter between various sections of the local population, as well as between residents and visitors. One of them was the royal *fonde*, already mentioned above. It was situated at the gate of St Nicholas, inserted within what became the inner wall of the Old City in the thirteenth century. This was the gate through which "one enters and goes out of the city," as stated in a charter issued by King Amaury of Lusignan in 1198.[78] The harbour area and the maritime toll station called *catena* or *chaene*, on account of the chain protecting the harbour, were also a major focus of activity. The location of these customs corresponds to that of the existing Khan al-Umdan, built on medieval foundations.[79] The main urban arteries joined the harbour to the royal *fonde*, and these installations to the Italian quarters.[80] Paolino's map (Fig. 2) seems to offer a more accurate representation of

---

[74] See David Jacoby, "New Venetian Evidence on Crusader Acre," in *The Experience of Crusading*, 2: *Defining the Crusader Kingdom*, ed. Peter Edbury and Jonathan Phillips, eds., (Cambridge, 2003), 2:254–55.

[75] Urban T. Holmes, "Life among the Europeans in Palestine and Syria in the Twelfth and Thirteenth Centuries," in Setton, *Crusades*, 4:22–23, is far from exhausting the topic of Frankish dress.

[76] See Daniel H. Weiss, *Art and Crusade in the Age of Saint Louis* (Cambridge, 1998), pp. 202–204.

[77] Weiss, *Art and Crusade*, pp. 120–21, 188; see p. 125, fig. 63 and colour plate VII, left column, bottom. On the relation between the pictorial cycles of Job in the two manuscripts, see ibid., pp. 115–17, esp. 116.

[78] See Jacoby, "The *fonde* of Crusader Acre," pp. 281–83. The Gate of St Nicholas was renamed Gate of the Pilgrims in the thirteenth century, and the appellation St Nicholas was transferred to the gate directly in front of it in the outer wall, close to the cemetery bearing the same name: see Jacoby, "Pilgrimage in Crusader Acre," pp. 108–109.

[79] See Jacoby, "Crusader Acre," 16–17.

[80] See Jacoby, "L'évolution urbaine," pp. 105–106.

these thoroughfares than Vesconte's map, though still a very schematic one. Another important artery passing east of the Hospitaller compound and the Genoese quarter linked the harbour to Montmusard.[81]

Trade at the *fonde* was primarily related to the provisioning of Acre in basic victuals, such as grain, cheese, poultry, fruit and vegetables from Acre's rural hinterland, marketed daily by Oriental Christian and Muslim peasants or by middlemen.[82] They also brought raw materials and half-finished goods like flax, wool, silk, hides, straw for baskets and feathers for cushions and mattresses, in addition to wood used as fuel. Other products came from more distant regions, for example, wine from the area of Nazareth in Lower Galilee dates from around Tiberias and the Jordan Valley, and sugar from sugar cane plantations in widely scattered regions.[83] The peasants also collected plants growing in coastal or arid and saline areas, from which soda ashes with high alkali content were produced. Soda ashes were one of two basic ingredients required for glassmaking and also entered in the production of soap and colourants for textiles.[84] The peasants bought in Acre salt, ceramic containers and leather straps, among other goods.[85] Warhorses were raised in the Frankish Levant and brought to Acre by land to replace those lost during maritime journeys, by disease, or in combat.[86] The royal *fonde* also handled

---

[81] Its course can be more or less reconstructed by a comparison of its depiction on the maps of Vesconte and Paolino with Frankish buildings appearing on Kesten's map of crusader remains: see Kesten, *Acre, The Old City*, reproduced in Dichter, *The Maps of Acre*, map no. 4 facing p. 73. It is not impossible that this thoroughfare corresponded more or less to the Byzantine *mese* or main trading street, recorded in a seventh-century source, the course of which was somewhat altered by encroachments over the centuries and by Hospitaller construction in the first half of the thirteenth century: see Jacoby, "L'évolution urbaine," p. 96.

[82] In 1290 crusaders massacred the Syrian and Muslim peasants who had come to sell their products: *Cronaca del Templare di Tiro*, p. 200, § 244. On the existence of both Muslim and Oriental Christian villages around Frankish Acre, although the former were more numerous, see Ronnie Ellenblum, *Frankish Rural Settlement in the Latin Kingdom of Jerusalem* (Cambridge, 1998), pp. 232–33, 274–75, 282–83.

[83] See above, n. 7. Sugar arrived in Acre through the royal *fonde*, yet was also imported by sea for re-export; see Jacoby, "The *fonde* of Crusader Acre," pp. 284–85. A list of sugar mills in the Kingdom of Jerusalem has been compiled by Brigitte Porëe, "Les moulins et fabriques de sucre de Palestine et de Chypre: histoire, géographie et technologie d'une production croisée et médiévale," in Nicholas Coureas and Jonathan Riley-Smith, eds., *Cyprus and the Crusades. Papers given at the International Conference "Cyprus and the Crusades", Nicosia, 6–9 September, 1994* (Nicosia, 1995), pp. 397–430; however, the author's references to written and archaeological evidence are not always accurate or complete and must be updated. See also Edna J. Stern, "The Excavations at Lower Horbat Manot: A Medieval Sugar-Production Site," *'Atiqot* 42 (2001), 277–308, and the map of sites at ibid., 277.

[84] See Eliyahu Ashtor and Guidobaldo Cevidalli, "Levantine Alkali Ashes and European Industries," *Journal of European Economic History* 12 (1983), pp. 475–522, repr. in *Technology, Industry and Trade: The Levant versus Europe, 1250–1500*, ed. Benjamin Z. Kedar (Aldershot, 1992), no. VII; David Jacoby, "Raw Materials for the Glass Industries of Venice and the Terraferma, about 1370 – about 1460," *Journal of Glass Studies* 35 (1993), 67–68, repr. in idem, *Trade*, no. IX; idem, "Mercanti genovesi e veneziani," pp. 232, 255. The plants collected in the Frankish Levant have not been securely identified so far.

[85] See above, n. 68.

[86] See David Jacoby, "The Trade of Crusader Acre in the Levantine Context: an Overview," *Archivio Storico del Sannio* n.s., 3 (1998), 111, repr. in David Jacoby, *Commercial Exchange Across the*

merchants and goods arriving from Damascus. Ibn Jubayr, who travelled in 1184 with one of the caravans coming from that city, provides a colourful description of the *fonde*. He was surprised to find there Oriental Christian officials, who dealt with Arabic-speakers.[87] The use of donkeys and camels for transportation was so common that for many items trade taxes at the royal *fonde* were calculated according to donkey- or camel-load. Both pack animals are depicted above the map of Acre ascribed to Matthew Paris that appears in Cambridge, Corpus Christi College, MS. 26, fol. 3v–4r (Fig. 3).[88]

Until 1187 merchants from the Muslim hinterland dominated trade between that region and Acre. After the Christian recovery of the city in 1191, growing numbers of Latin merchants passed through the royal *fonde* on their way to Damascus and returned with cotton thread, high-quality silk textiles and precious stones, among other commodities. Royal officials in Acre imposed dues on Venetian merchants engaged in overland trade with Frankish and Muslim territories, although Venice considered that they were entitled to full fiscal exemption. Bribery in exchange for full or partial evasion of taxes, openly stated in a Venetian report of 1243, must have been a daily occurrence, despite royal regulations threatening officials involved in such deals with the penalty of death by hanging.[89] In the late years of Frankish rule Venetian settlers in Acre purchased cotton directly from local growers around Tiberias, which was then under Muslim rule.[90]

Intensive activity also took place in and around the harbour during the whole year. Fish supplied part of Acre's diet. Native Pisans were particularly active in fishing, yet there were also some Genoese working under contracts for a limited period of up to one year.[91] Since local demand for fish could apparently not be met, imports of salted fish from Egypt were necessary.[92] Jewish fishermen from

---

Mediterranean: Byzantium, the Crusader Levant, Egypt and Italy (Aldershot, 2005), no. IV; idem, "The Venetian Privileges in the Latin Kingdom of Jerusalem: Twelfth and Thirteenth-Century Interpretations and Implementation," in *Montjoie*, pp. 168–69; Malcolm Barber, *The New Knighthood. A History of the Order of the Temple* (Cambridge, 1994), pp. 235–38.

[87] See Jacoby, "The *fonde* of Crusader Acre," pp. 278–80.

[88] However, the inscription above the donkey reads *mulus*, mule.

[89] See Jacoby, "Mercanti genovesi e veneziani," pp. 233–36; idem, "The Venetian Privileges," p. 168, repr. in David Jacoby, *Commercial Exchange Across the Mediterranean: Byzantium, the Crusader Levant, Egypt and Italy* (Aldershot, 2005), no. IV.

[90] *Zibaldone da Canal. Manoscritto mercantile del sec. XIV*, ed. Alfredo Stussi, Fonti per la storia di Venezia, sez. V – Fondi vari (Venice, 1967), p. 63: "all te[m]po ch'Acre iera in pie," (at the time Acre was standing), thus before its destruction by the Muslims in 1291.

[91] Native Pisans are mentioned in *Cronaca del Templare di Tiro*, p. 182, § 218: "barques de pesqours, poulains pizans." For the Genoese, see Laura Balletto, *Genova nel Duecento. Uomini nel porto e uomini sul mare*, Collana storica di fonti e studi, diretta da Geo Pistarino, 36 (Genoa, 1983), pp. 195–206. It is likely that these Genoese also engaged in trade while in Acre. Interestingly, in 1267 a merchant leaving Genoa for the Levant received an investment in ropes or lines used in fishing, *in cordis piscandi*: Laura Balletto, "Fonti notarili genovesi del secondo Duecento per la storia del Regno latino di Gerusalemme," in Airaldi and Kedar, *I comuni italiani*, p. 207.

[92] See above, n. 68.

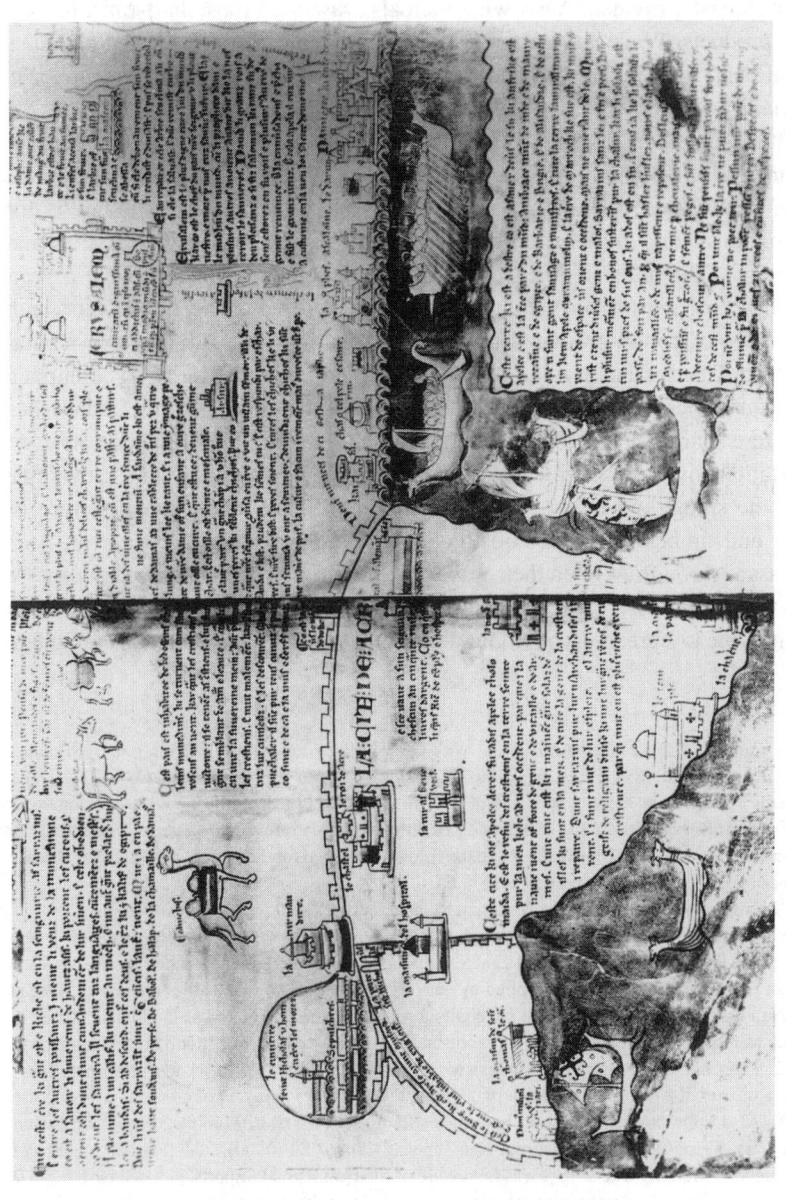

Fig. 3 Map of Acre by Matthew Paris (1252 or shortly later). Cambridge, Corpus Christi College, Ms. 26, fols. 3r–4v (Reproduced by kind permission of the Master and Fellows of Corpus Christi College, Cambridge)

Alexandria occasionally drank beer in the taverns of Acre. They operated along the Levantine coast under Frankish rule to collect murex shells, from which the precious purple colourant was extracted.[93] Local ships practising cabotage along the Levantine coast provided Acre with victuals, raw materials, half-finished and finished products. Wine came from Antioch and Laodicea, silk stuff and ceramics from Antioch,[94] spices, salt fish and flax from Egypt,[95] planks, scrap iron and iron ingots, nails and horseshoes from Ayas in Cilician Armenia.[96]

Cabotage and short-distance navigation along the Levantine coast were firmly linked to the operation of the east–west and north–south Mediterranean trade systems, as well as to trans-Asian routes. Acre was a major warehouse for goods in transit and fulfilled an important function in their concentration and distribution.[97] The trans-shipment of cargo was particularly intense twice a year, during the short periods in which western ships visited Acre. In the thirteenth century bales of cotton produced in regions extending from the city's own rural hinterland to Tiberias and Syrian Aleppo were brought to Acre in order to be shipped in large quantities to Italy. The grouping of silk bales, sugar and soda ashes from different areas in Acre followed a similar pattern. This rationalization of transportation lowered freight costs.[98] Acre also served as the major Levantine port for the smuggling of war materials to Egypt. Iron for the manufacture of weapons and timber for naval construction originating in the West and in Asia Minor passed through Acre on their way to Alexandria.[99] In 1246 Pope Innocent IV blamed the Venetians, the Genoese and the Pisans for shipping slaves from Constantinople to Acre, most of whom would be transferred to Egypt and strengthen

---

[93] New edition of the Judaeo-Arabic text with Hebrew trans. by M. Gil, *Erets Israel ba-tequfa ha-muslemit ha-rishona* (634–1099) [= *Palestine during the First Muslim Period (634–1099)*] (Tel Aviv, 1983), 3:511–14, no. 599, who dates the document to *c.*1115, instead of *c.*1180 as Goitein, *A Mediterranean Society* 1:126–27 and 430, n. 87. The letter explicitly refers to the taverns. The activity of these fishermen may have been partly related to the colourant needed for the tsitsith, on which see above.

[94] See above, n. 68, and for ceramics, also n. 65.

[95] See above, n. 68, and Jacoby, "A Venetian Manual," pp. 419–20.

[96] David Jacoby, "The Supply of War Materials to Egypt in the Crusader Period," *Jerusalem Studies in Arabic and Islam* 25 (2001), 109–10, 122–25. Although there is no direct evidence for deliveries to Acre in that respect, these are clearly implied by various commercial contracts, the function of Acre as transit port to Egypt, and the use of Acre's weights for iron shipments from Ayas in Cilician Armenia. Horseshoes were also imported from Genoa, for instance in 1267: see Balletto, "Fonti notarili genovesi," pp. 231–32. Three horseshoes from the Frankish period have been discovered in an area corresponding to the Genoese quarter of Acre: see Eliezer Stern, "'Akko, the Old City," *Excavations and Surveys in Israel* 109 (1999), 12–13. On thirteenth-century horseshoes found south-west of Montfort, see Jochai Rosen, "Crusader Period Horseshoes from Horbat Bet Zeneta," *'Atiqot* 39 (2000), 204 (English summary), 107–108 (Hebrew section). The author was not aware of the commercial imports adduced here.

[97] See Jacoby, "The Trade of Crusader Acre," 111–16; idem, "Mercanti genovesi e veneziani," pp. 238–40, 255–56.

[98] See Jacoby, "A Venetian Manual," pp. 415–16, 420–21, 425; idem, "The Trade of Crusader Acre," 118–19. For sugar and ashes, see above, n. 83 and n. 84, respectively.

[99] See Jacoby, "The Supply of War Materials," 106, 114–18, 122–25, 127.

its army.¹⁰⁰ A large number of local porters, merchants, middlemen and sailors must have been involved in the storage of goods in Acre and in cabotage, as well as in the loading and unloading of ships in the harbour and in the bay, where large vessels were moored. Barks also transferred to Venetian ships anchoring in the bay the fine-grained sand found at the mouth of the Belus river (now called Na'aman) southeast of Acre, for use as a vitrifying agent in Venice's glass workshops.¹⁰¹

The building and repair of barks and small boats, and also the careenage of larger ones, was partly carried out on strips of sandy beach. An arsenal or shipyard is mentioned in three charters issued in favour of the Pisans, respectively in 1187, 1189 and 1200.¹⁰² An active shipyard is attested in Acre in the Byzantine and early Arab period. The localization of this installation east of the Venetian quarter on both the Vesconte and Paolino maps (Figs. 1 and 2) seems to reflect topographical continuity in this section of the city since the late sixth century, if not earlier.¹⁰³ A structure divided into six berths beneath the Burj Kapu courtyard, at a location corresponding to the one indicated on the medieval maps, was excavated a few years ago. In the thirteenth century the dry-dock was unsuitable for large vessels. It may have been used for the construction and repair of small and medium-sized ships.¹⁰⁴ Significantly, in 1182–83 Saladin's navy caught a large western vessel on its way to Acre with planks, carpenters and shipwrights on board.¹⁰⁵ This suggests that Acre lacked then a supply of timber adequate for naval construction and skilled workers required for continuous shipbuilding. Conditions in that respect must have worsened after 1187, with the loss of some of the remaining forests in Lebanon to Saladin.¹⁰⁶

The movement of people and goods in Acre reached its peak twice a year with the arrival of the seasonal maritime convoys from the West, one before Easter and the

---

[100] E. Berger, ed., *Les registres d'Innocent IV* (Les registres des papes du XIIIe siècle. Bibliothèque des Ecoles françaises d'Athènes et de Rome, 2e série) (Paris, 1884–1921), 1:316, doc. 212. See also Jacoby, "The Venetian Privileges," pp. 168–69; and, on Acre as an important slave market, Benjamin Z. Kedar, "The Subjected Muslims of the Frankish Levant," in James M. Powell, ed., *Muslims under Latin Rule, 1100–1300* (Princeton, 1990), p. 153.

[101] This sand was used in the production of glass since Antiquity, as reported by Pliny the Elder. I shall deal elsewhere with its export in a study on the contribution of the Levant to the Venetian glass industry in the thirteenth century.

[102] Müller, ed., *Documenti*, p. 30, no. 25; p. 38, no. 32; p. 82, no. 52, *ad portam tarsane*, which implies that there was access to the shipyard and that *tarsana* was not just a toponym inherited from the Arab period preceding the crusades.

[103] See Jacoby, "L'évolution urbaine," pp. 97–98.

[104] On the excavated site, see Eliezer Stern, "'Akko, the Old City," *Excavations and Surveys in Israel* 109 (1999), 10–11, and for the location and the plan of the building, see Hebrew section, 15, figs. 17 and 18. The berths are about 10 m wide and between 12 and 20 m long and, therefore, offer space insufficient for large vessels.

[105] See Jacoby, "The Supply of War Materials," 126.

[106] Marie-Luise Favreau-Lilie, *Die Italiener im Heiligen Land vom ersten Kreuzzug bis zum Tode Heinrichs von Champagne (1098–1197)* (Amsterdam, 1989), pp. 21–23, ascribes undue importance to shipbuilding in the royal arsenal, and her assumption that the Hospitallers had a shipyard is unwarranted. These issues require a renewed investigation.

other in late summer. Dozens of ships carrying thousands of passengers, mostly pilgrims, anchored in the harbour or in the bay within a few days. Western pilgrimage had become a mass movement soon after the First Crusade, expanded after 1191, and, despite Muslim rule over Jerusalem during most of that period, remained substantial in the following century until the collapse of the Frankish states in 1291. Travelling merchants stayed in Acre for a month at most, pilgrims a few days only, unless they were prevented from access to the holy sites. However, some merchants and pilgrims extended their stay from one sailing season to the other, especially over the winter.[107]

Life in Acre acquired a frantic pace during the two peak periods of the year. As in tourist centres nowadays, residents eagerly offered services to visitors. Money changers and bankers awaited their exit from the maritime customs to supply local currency and loans, and middlemen to arrange accommodation in public buildings or private homes. Ecclesiastical institutions assisted poor and sick people and provided religious services. The Old City in particular was flooded by pilgrims, merchants, soldiers and sailors, roaming and choking the streets, haggling and shouting. Resident merchants, interpreters and notaries were particularly busy. Guides escorted tours in town or took pilgrims to Jerusalem and additional holy sites. Other residents hired horses and donkeys for transportation or served as armed escorts. Acre's role was crucial for pilgrimage, as it provided most of the logistics required for the visit of the holy sites.[108]

The heterogeneous composition of Acre's population was also reflected by the hybrid material culture of the city. There was a ready market for both Western and Oriental commodities. The Frankish demand for western woollens was aimed both at local consumption and at re-export in order to finance the purchase of Oriental goods.[109] Prunted glass beakers were apparently first imported from Italy and later imitated by local workshops.[110] A specific type of enamelled glass-beakers with Latin inscriptions, apparently produced in Venice from the second half of the thirteenth century, circulated widely in the West and also reached Acre.[111]

---

[107] For this paragraph and the following, see above, n. 38.

[108] Laura Minervini, "Les contacts entre indigènes et croisés dans l'Orient latin: le rôle des drogmans," in Jens Jüdtke, ed., *Romania arabica. Festschrift für Reinhold Kontzi zum 70. Geburtstag* (Tübingen, 1996), pp. 57–62, deals only with one aspect of interlingual communication. On Syrians in the Frankish administration, see above, n. 87.

[109] For instance, large quantities of woollens were shipped to Acre on Marseillais ships in 1248: see A. Schaube, *Handelsgeschichte der romanischen Völker des Mittelmeergebiets bis zum Ende der Kreuzzüge* (Munich, 1906), pp. 204–205.

[110] See Yael Gorin-Rosen, "Excavation of the Courthouse Site at 'Akko: Medieval Glass Vessels (Area TA)," *'Atiqot* 31(1997), 82–84, and p. 79, figs. 20–26; see also a fairly well preserved piece in Rozenberg, *Knights of the Holy Land*, p. 266, fig. 1.

[111] Moshe Dothan, "'Akko: Interim Excavation Report. First Season, 1973/4," *Bulletin of the American Schools of Oriental Research* 224 (December, 1976), 37, mentions two fragments of a beaker found in a building of the Frankish period excavated to the east of the present Old City: see 39, fig. 41. They belong to the so-called 'Aldrevandin' group, judging by the likeness in enamel painting, motifs,

On the other hand, the Franks accommodated to some extent to their Levantine surroundings within their own private space. They acquired devotional objects and various artefacts such as ceramics, including Chinese celadon and porcelain which were clearly luxury items,[112] in addition to brass vessels,[113] glassware,[114] jewellery and textiles,[115] some of which reflected Oriental culture and artistic traditions in the Levant and further east. The numerous visitors passing through Acre were also sensitive to the aesthetic and exotic appeal of these objects. They generated a sharp rise in demand which furthered substantial local production all the year round, in expectation of new customers.

Until 1187 pilgrims acquired at the major holy sites or in their vicinity most of the relics, reliquaries, icons, crosses, and pilgrims' flasks or ampullae with which they returned home. However, some of these objects must have been produced and sold in Acre, a transit station to these sites. Acre's function in that respect expanded after the loss of Jerusalem to the Muslims in 1187, and became decisive after the renewed loss of the Holy City and other holy sites in 1244 and the establishment of an institutionalized pilgrimage in Acre itself some time after 1258. This pilgrimage, promoted by the accumulation of relics brought from other locations, linked some forty Latin churches, monasteries and hospitals in the city, among the seventy or so existing there at that time. Its itinerary is recorded in the *Pardouns d'Acre*.[116]

The growing output of devotional objects in Acre in the second half of the thirteenth century is confirmed by the discovery of moulds and materials in a workshop of the Frankish neighbourhood excavated in the north-eastern corner of the present-day Old City.[117] This workshop produced on a large scale lead-alloy ampullae bearing a standardized decoration, consisting of geometric, floral, scale or cross motifs. Such motifs were particularly appropriate for Acre, which lacked shrines and pilgrimage stations related to sacred history or to saints. Earlier pilgrims' flasks display shrines with distinctive, widely-known monumental

---

colour, execution and the band of Latin inscription. On this group, see Ingeborg Krueger, "A Second Aldrevandin Beaker and an Update on a Group of Enameled Glasses," *Journal of Glass Studies* 44 (2002), 111–32.

[112] Summary of findings by Edna J. Stern, "Ceramic Ware from the Crusader Period in the Holy Land," in Rozenberg, *Knights of the Holy Land*, pp. 258–65; see also Edna J. Stern, "Excavation of the Courthouse Site," 35–70. On thirteenth-century finds of celadon, see Syon and Tatcher, "'Akko, Ha-Abirim Parking Lot," 13, 15. The Chinese porcelain has been excavated in the Hospitaller compound and in the north-eastern corner of the present-day Old City: personal communication from Edna Stern, Israel Antiquities Authority.

[113] On "Islamic" contemporary production, see Eva Baer, *Ayyubid Metalwork with Christian Images*, Studies in Islamic Art and Architecture. Supplements to *Muqarnas* 4 (Leiden, 1989); Esin Atil, *Renaissance of Islam. Art of the Mamluks* (Washington, D.C., 1981), pp. 50–79.

[114] See Gorin-Rozen, "Excavation of the Courthouse Site," 75–85.

[115] On which see above, n. 69.

[116] See Jacoby, "Pilgrimage in Crusader Acre," pp. 105–17.

[117] On which see above, n. 15.

features, such as those existing in Jerusalem, or religious representations associated with holy sites.[118]

The ampullae of Acre illustrate the nature of devotional objects such as icons and other artefacts as marketable goods and the need to examine their artistic production in Acre in the city's economic context.[119] The attempts of art historians to ascribe icons and artefacts to a definite ethnic-cultural and geographic setting, namely "Latin," "Byzantine-Orthodox" or "Islamic," has created rigid mental moulds and artificial barriers, which obscure the dynamics of artistic creation and their connection with production and consumption patterns.

These patterns must have been duly reflected by a growing activity of local workshops producing painted panels and portable icons in Acre. The earliest known depiction of a shop selling icons appears in the manuscript of the *Cantigas de Santa Maria* of King Alfonso X of Castile, illuminated soon after 1265.[120] It illustrates an episode in the story of the Virgin's icon bought in Jerusalem for the Orthodox convent of Our Lady at Saydnaya, to the north-east of Damascus.[121] The depiction offers a faithful rendering of an icon shop in the Holy City, also valid for thirteenth-century Acre, and surely reflects the experience gathered by pilgrims purchasing icons from existing stock.

Three distinct patterns in the marketing of painted panels and icons may be envisaged. The first one involved patrons who commissioned works bearing particular features in accordance with their wishes. Other individuals presumably bought icons displayed in a shop and had some distinctive personal marks, such as names, portraits or heraldry added to them. However, the vast majority of customers must have been content with the finished product. Once we take these alternatives into account, it is quite conceivable that several thirteenth-century icons considered as made in Acre for members of the Orthodox community because they lack distinctive Latin marks, were in fact produced for Latins or in any event were used by them. It is obvious that in the Frankish Levant the religious devotion of Christian worshippers and benefactors, whether local or foreign, cut across religious denominations.

The production and marketing of manuscripts in Acre must have followed patterns similar to those of devotional objects. Richly illuminated manuscripts were clearly commissioned by wealthy individuals or by ecclesiastical institutions.

---

[118] Danny Syon, "Souvenirs from the Holy Land: A Crusader Workshop of Lead Ampullae from Acre," in Rozenberg, *Knights of the Holy Land*, pp. 112–15. On earlier ampullae, see Jaroslav Folda, *The Art of the Crusaders in the Holy Land: 1098–1187* (Cambridge, 1995), pp. 294–97.

[119] For this paragraph and the next three ones, see a more detailed treatment in Jacoby, "Society, Culture and the Arts," 101–102, 108–11.

[120] José Guerrero Lovillo, *Las Cántigas. Estudio arqueológico de sus miniaturas* (Madrid, 1949), Pl. 12, left col., middle. The inscriptions accompanying the six miniatures illustrating Cant. IX appear ibid., p. 379.

[121] On the story and its context, see Benjamin Z. Kedar, "Convergences of Oriental, Christian, Muslim, and Frankish Worshippers: the Case of Saydnaya," in Hen, *De Sion exibit lex*, pp. 59–69.

Yet the continuity of manuscript and illuminator workshops could not have been ensured only by occasional commissions for luxury manuscripts.[122] It clearly depended on a fairly constant stream of demand, furthered by the production of manuscripts differing in quality and adapted to the purchasing power of prospective buyers. Some knights and commoners such as lawyers with fairly modest means were surely content to own manuscripts only sparsely decorated. This is illustrated by two copies of legal texts from the last decades of Frankish rule, one of which is adorned with a single miniature and the other with illuminated initials.[123] Numerous fictional and historical works in French, such as the *Histoire d'Outremer*, which reflected class attitudes and values, enjoyed a wide circulation within the ranks of the nobility and in other circles in Acre and, more generally, in the Frankish Levant, as well as among Western visitors.[124] There is good reason to believe that copies of these works with minimal or even no decoration were produced for rather modest customers, more numerous than those acquiring luxury books.

In sum, the presence of a clientele in the Frankish Levant and the constant stream of visitors who were potential customers called for commercial book production in Frankish Acre.[125] One may envisage, therefore, that various works enjoying a fairly wide circulation were copied and stored, like devotional objects and artefacts, in anticipation of customers. Some of these were foreigners who stayed in Acre for a short time only, namely crusaders, diplomatic envoys, official representatives of foreign powers, merchants and especially pilgrims. They would have been unable to acquire the manuscripts they were interested in or had been asked to purchase, unless these were readily available.

The arts and crafts of the Frankish Levant exhibit at times a genuinely original blending and fusion of heterogeneous elements, some indigenous and others imported. There can be no doubt that the so-called "Islamic" techniques, visual vocabulary, iconographic formulae and styles were not restricted to Muslims and were shared by their indigenous Christian counterparts, whether in Muslim or

---

[122] On one or several *scriptoria* in Acre, see Laura Minervini, "Produzione e circolazione di manoscritti negli stati crociati: biblioteche e *scriptoria* latini," in *Medioevo romanzo e orientale. Il viaggio dei testi*, III Colloquio internazionale Medioevo Romanzo e Orientale, Colloqui 4 (Soveria Mannelli, 1999), pp. 88–96.

[123] See Peter Edbury and Jaroslav Folda, "Two Thirteenth-century Manuscripts of Crusader Legal Texts from Saint-Jean d'Acre," *Journal of the Warburg and Courtauld Institutes* 57 (1994), 243–54.

[124] See David Jacoby, "La littérature française dans les états latins de la Méditerranée orientale à l'époque des croisades: diffusion et création," in *Essor et fortune de la chanson de geste dans l'Europe et l'Orient latin. Actes du IXe Congrès international de la Société Rencesvals pour l'étude des épopées romanes (Padoue-Venise, 1982)* (Modena, 1984), pp. 617–46; David Jacoby, "Knightly Values and Class Consciousness in the Crusader States of the Eastern Mediterranean," *Mediterranean Historical Review* 1 (1986), 158–86. Both papers have been reproduced in Jacoby, *Studies on the Crusader States*, nos. II and I, respectively.

[125] Unfortunately, there is no documentation on commercial book production in Acre, similar to that bearing on Paris in the years 1175–1291; on which see Richard H. Rouse and Mary A. Rouse, *Illiterati et uxorati. Manuscripts and their Makers: Commercial Book Producers in Medieval Paris, 1200–1500*, 2 vols. (Turnhout, 2000), 1:17–91.

in Frankish territories. The "Freer canteen," apparently produced in Syria in the mid-thirteenth century, displays Christian scenes, including the Nativity of Christ and the Entry into Jerusalem, as well as Christian figures under arches, but the technique is "Islamic."[126] Two "Islamic" glass beakers preserved at the Walters Art Museum in Baltimore display haloed figures and what appear to be Christian iconographic motifs, accompanied by Arabic inscriptions.[127]

It is likely that indigenous artists and artisans producing "Islamic" objects were attracted to Acre by favorable economic prospects. Others, displaced by political and military events, among them the Mongol invasion of Syria, settled from 1259 onwards in Frankish coastal cities such as Acre.[128] It is not excluded, therefore, that various "Islamic" brass and glass vessels, including some bearing Christian motifs and iconography such as those just mentioned, were also manufactured by indigenous workers in Frankish territories for Christian and Muslim customers living under Muslim rule.[129] Their mobility entailed a diffusion of technology, designs, iconographic formulae and styles. Together with the movement of goods, they generated at times new fashions, new market demands, and the manufacture of new products. Frankish Acre was a fertile ground for such developments. Its local merchants and craftsmen must have been keenly aware of the heterogeneous composition of the clientele for Oriental artefacts. The potential customers included Frankish and other Christian residents, local ecclesiastical bodies, charitable institutions, confraternities and crusaders, as well as foreign merchants and pilgrims from Byzantium and Muslim countries.

We may conclude this brief survey, which is far from exhaustive, with a few observations. Everyday life in Frankish Acre was shaped and continuously reshaped by the dynamic interaction between the various communities residing in the city, their respective attitudes, cultures and artistic traditions, and by their collective encounter with a large and transient population of visitors. Its evolution generally followed a seasonal pattern, the rhythm and intensity of which were connected more with the sea and the movement of ships, than with the city's own hinterland. Relatively few of those partaking in urban everyday life are known to us. The others, many in lowly occupations, remain anonymous. Written sources seldom reflect the decisive contribution of that silent majority, active at sea and in the city's institutions, houses, offices, workshops, streets and markets.

---

[126] See Baer, *Ayyubid Metalwork*, pp. 19–23, figs. 73–74.

[127] See Atil, *Renaissance of Islam*, pp. 118–27, figs. 44 and 45, and the peripheral view of fig. 45 on p. 144; also John Carswell, "The Baltimore Beakers," in Rachel Ward, ed., *Gilded and Enamelled Glass from the Middle East* (London, 1998), pp. 61–63.

[128] See above, n. 54.

[129] Among the potential customers one should also take into account Copts coming from Egypt: see above, n. 57.

Appendix: Dating construction in Montmusard

The double wall of the suburb

The restoration of Frankish rule over Acre in 1191 was followed by the erection of a double wall protecting the suburb of Montmusard. The double wall extended from the seashore on the northwest to St Antony's Gate, opposite the royal castle in the Old City, to the south-east. From there a second wall was added, parallel to the existing one on the northern flank of the Old City to the east of the castle and along its entire eastern flank. These major construction operations, the outcome of which is illustrated by the maps of Vesconte and Paolino (Figs. 1 and 2), required a large labour force and a considerable financial investment, yet no written record of them has survived. This is all the more surprising, since similar large-scale building on two other Frankish sites is duly documented, namely on the castle of Chastel-Pèlerin ('Athlit) within the year 1218 and at Safed in the early 1240s.[130] As a result, neither the precise nature, extent nor dating of the work carried out in Acre is known, nor can the exact course and length of the double wall of Montmusard be determined for the time being.[131]

In 1987 Rafael Frankel discovered the foundations of a cylindrical tower located on the foreshore some 800 metres north of the present Old City wall. He suggested that it was the tower marking the north-western tip of the outer wall of Montmusard depicted on the Venice and Vatican copies of the Paolino map (Fig. 2), while insisting at the same time that there was no archaeological proof that the tower's foundations were from the Frankish period.[132] In a later personal communication to me he envisaged the possibility that these foundations may be Hellenistic and that the Franks took advantage of them. This leaves the dating of the tower's foundations an open question. A recent salvage excavation has revealed the section of a Frankish wall built in the vicinity of the tower, which vindicates Frankel's initial suggestion.[132a]

It is rather puzzling that the Franks walled a substantial space to the north of the Old City, well beyond the one required after 1191 for the resettling of displaced institutions and individuals and the addition of new immigrants, even in the foreseeable future. As noted above, the territory of Montmusard was never entirely

---

[130] Oliver of Paderborn, *Historia Damiatina*, in *Die Schriften des Kölner Domscholasters, späteren Bischofs von Paderborn und Kardinalbischofs von S. Sabina Oliverus*, ed. H. Hoogeweg, Bibliothek des literarischen Vereins in Stuttgart 202 (Tübingen, 1894), pp. 169–72, chap. 5, and that author's letter no. 3, ibid., pp. 288–89; R.B.C. Huygens, *De constructione castri Saphet. Construction et fonctions d'un château fort franc en Terre Sainte* (Amsterdam, 1981).

[131] However, Kedar, "The Outer Walls of Frankish Acre," 160–62, and 159, plan 4, has suggested a possible course, based on various archaeological remains.

[132] Rafael Frankel, "The North-West Corner of Crusader Acre," *Israel Exploration Journal* 37 (1987), 256–61 and pls. 31–32. On the copies of Vesconte's map, see above, n. 28.

[132a] See A. Tatcher, "Acre: Northern Sea Promenade," *Crusades 3* (2004), 183–84.

filled with structures. However, if the tower discovered by Frankel on the foreshore is indeed Hellenistic, it may provide a solution to the problem. It suggests that, in addition, the Franks possibly made use of a section of the Hellenistic wall protecting Acre when constructing the outer one enclosing the new suburb, and that the latter's course was partially determined by the remnants of that Hellenistic wall. However, the Frankish outer wall of Montmusard did not follow the earlier one along its entire length, since the Frankish digging of a moat in front of a tower inserted within the outer wall on the so-called Courthouse Site, northeast of the Old City, led to the destruction of Hellenistic buildings.[133] The use of the tower and the possible reliance upon a section of the Hellenistic wall in the construction of the outer one enclosing the suburb imply that the latter's construction began on its northern tip on the seashore, and not at the Old City wall existing in 1191. This would not have been the only instance in which the Franks took advantage of earlier structures. The course of the Frankish wall protecting Caesarea was apparently determined by a pre-existing Abbasid or Fatimid wall, and in 1218 the builders of Chastel-Pèlerin reached after six days of digging the foundations of a long and thick ancient wall, on top of which they presumably erected a section of their own.[134]

We may safely assume that the first priority of the Franks after the recovery of Acre was the repair of the battered wall of the Old City. Indeed, extensive work was carried out from August 1191 onwards on the orders of King Richard I of England.[135] It is only afterwards that work on the protection of Montmusard and on the second wall of the Old City could have begun. In 1982 I suggested that this work was carried out after 1198 and completed by 1212, when Wilbrand of Oldenburg saw a double wall protecting the entire land front of Acre.[136] Most recently Jonathan Riley-Smith has proposed an earlier dating. Montmusard, he writes, must have already been walled by January 1194, when Henry of Champagne granted the Hospitallers a section of the northern wall of the Old City, "because otherwise no ruler would have given a stretch of the wall away so insouciantly."[137] Several objections may be raised against that argument. First, the grant of 1194 did not entail a complete surrender of royal rights, since Henry of Champagne retained control over the *porta S. Johannis* and the royal rights pertaining to it. Moreover, he could count on the Hospitallers to repair, fortify, maintain and defend the section of the

---

[133] See Moshe Hartal, "'Akko," *Excavations and Surveys in Israel* 13 (1993), 22–23.

[134] See Denys Pringle, "Town Defences in the Crusader Kingdom of Jerusalem," in Ivy A. Corfis and Michael Wolfe, eds., *Medieval City Under Siege* (Woodbridge, 1995), pp. 89–90, 95–96; and for Chastel-Pèlerin, Oliverius Scholasticus, as above, n. 130,

[135] Ralph of Diceto, *Ymagines historiarum*, ed. W. Stubbs, RS 68 (London, 1876), 2:95; Ambroise, *Estoire de la guerre sainte. Histoire en vers de la Troisième Croisade*, ed. Gaston Paris, Collection de Documents inédits sur l'histoire de France (Paris, 1897), p. 144, lines 5384–92.

[136] See Jacoby, "Montmusard," pp. 211–14. This hypothesis requires some qualifications, presented below.

[137] Riley-Smith, "Guy of Lusignan," pp. 111–12. The grant appears in *Cart Hosp* 1:617, no. 972 (RRH, no. 717).

wall which he granted them, since it abutted their compound. The construction of a tower above the gate, envisaged by the grant, had been most likely requested by the Order itself. The safety of the Old City along that section of wall was thus ensured. Secondly, Henry had already granted earlier, in 1193, a section of the eastern wall of the Old City to the Hospitallers and another, adjacent one, to the German knights, including the outer defences of their respective sections, on condition that they repair and improve them.[138] Denys Pringle has pointed out that the defence system of the Old City in the 1190s consisted of a wall with towers and gates, preceded by a ditch, a "barbican" and a forewall.[139] It is clear that by 1193 there was no additional defence beyond the one just described, and such was still the case in 1198, as the Gate of St Nicholas retained then its function as main passage in and out of the city, both for people and for goods. Incidentally, the section granted to the German knights did not include that gate, in the vicinity of which the royal *fonde* was situated.[140] In sum, the grant of a section of the wall along the northern flank of the Old City to the Hospitallers in 1194 cannot be adduced as an argument for the existence of a wall protecting Montmusard.

The early dating of Montmusard's fortification, suggested by Jonathan Riley-Smith, encounters additional objections. There is good reason to believe that architectural and military considerations led to the simultaneous erection of both walls, rather than to the construction of a single one and the later addition of the other, a far more complex enterprise. Since the southern tip of the outer wall of Montmusard reached the northern flank of the Old City, it must have been more than 1,100 metres long, if we rely on Kedar's suggestion about its course.[141] It seems highly unlikely that the construction of two parallel walls of that length, with their towers, fortified gates and a barbican in the sixty metres or so between them, should have been completed within less than fifteen months.[142] Indeed, the work could not have begun before the completion of the repairs on the Old City wall initiated in August 1191 (see above), the only large-scale building activity after Acre's recovery mentioned by contemporary sources. On the other hand, the construction of the double wall should have been completed before January 1194, if we accept the dating proposed by Riley-Smith. It is noteworthy that the renewed fortification of Caesarea by King Louis IX of France was carried out from March 1251 to May 1252, and similar work in Jaffa, though on a larger scale, was conducted from May

---

[138] This condition is explicitly stated in the grant to the Teutonic Order: Strehlke, *Tabulae Ordinis Theutonici*, pp. 24–25, no. 28 (RRH, no. 717). Only a summary of the grant to the Hospitallers has been published, yet we may safely assume that it contained the same condition: *Cart Hosp* 1:594, no. 938 (RRH Ad, no. 716a).

[139] Pringle, "Town Defences," pp. 82–83.

[140] See above, n. 78.

[141] See Kedar, "The Outer Walls of Frankish Acre," 159, plan 4.

[142] An excavated section of the northern inner wall of the Old City is located some 60 m southwest of the Courthouse site, on which a tower inserted within the outer wall has been found: see Eliezer Stern, "'Akko (Acre), the Eastern Moat," *Excavations and Surveys in Israel* 110 (1999), 11–13.

1252 to June 1253.[143] These construction operations required far less labour and financial investments than the double wall of Montmusard.

Denys Pringle has raised the possibility that the double wall seen by Wilbrand of Oldenburg in 1212 along the Old City may have represented no more than a rebuilding and strengthening of the defence system existing before 1187.[144] This is excluded, since Wilbrand clearly describes an arrangement along the entire land front of Acre, by which towers were inserted both within the inner and outer wall, those of the former being lower than the latter's. No such towers existed in front of the wall surrounding the Old City before 1187, and their building as isolated structures after 1191 would have been an aberration from a military point of view.

In sum, there is good reason to believe that the construction of the walls of Montmusard did not begin shortly after July 1191. It may be safely assumed that the main reason prompting Henry of Champagne to grant sections of the Old City wall to the Hospitallers and to the German knights in 1193 and 1194, in return for their repair, reinforcement and maintenance, was the inability of the royal treasury to fund such work. It is unclear whether resources were lacking or whether they were being invested at that time in the larger construction project of Montmusard. It would seem, however, that this project was not initiated until shortly before 1198, or even after that year. Indeed, once the construction of the outer wall along the suburb had begun, it was imperative for military reasons to complete it rapidly along the Old City.[145] This was not yet the case in 1198, yet definitely so by 1212, as attested by Wilbrand of Oldenburg. It follows that the reference to the city's two walls in a charter of King John of Brienne issued in 1217 implies the existence of an outer wall fortified by towers along the Old City's eastern flank, in front of the Gate of Geoffroy le Tor opening in the inner wall.[146]

The auberge *of the Hospitallers in the suburb*

The coronation in Tyre on 15 August 1286 of King Henry II of Lusignan as king of Jerusalem was followed by lavish festivities. In Acre these took place in the *herberge* of the Hospitallers situated in Montmusard. The building was "a very large *palais*," "very long and very beautiful," which was supposedly 150 *canes* long and had a very large inner courtyard.[147] It is likely that the various pageants enacted

---

[143] Pringle, "Town Defences," pp. 89–91, 93–94.

[144] Ibid., p. 83, with Wilbrand's description.

[145] See Jacoby, "Montmusard," p. 213.

[146] Strehlke, *Tabulae Ordinis Theutonici*, p. 41, no. 50 (RRH, no. 899). On this gate, see Jacoby, "Montmusard," pp. 211–12.

[147] *Cronaca del Templare di Tiro*, p. 170, § 203, and p. 222, § 266. The figure refers to the length of the building, and not to that of a hall, as in Jonathan Riley-Smith, *The Knights of St. John in Jerusalem and Cyprus, c. 1050–1310* (London, 1967), p. 248. The *cane* can only be the one used in the Kingdom of Jerusalem or that of Cyprus, where the chronicler lived after 1291. It measured 2.20 m: see Huygens, *De constructione castri Saphet*, pp. 26–28. The building would thus have been 330 m long, which is

during the festivities, which included jousting, were staged in that courtyard.[148] There is no direct evidence regarding the period at which the building was erected. Since the terms *herberge* and *alberga/albergum* were also used for the Hospitaller compound in the Old City (as we shall see below), they do not offer any clue in that respect, nor does the office of *auberger*, attested in 1239.[149]

Jonathan Riley-Smith considers that the conventual brothers had been moved by 1230 from the compound in the Old City to the new *auberge* in Montmusard.[150] The charters on which he relies in that respect locate the *alberga hospitalis sancti Iohannis* at a short distance from the *curia* or residence of the archbishop of Nazareth, which must have been close to the latter's church of St Mary of the Knights. This church appears on both the Vesconte and Paolino maps, to the east of the Hospitallers' compound in the Old City. The pilgrimage itinerary known as *Pardouns dAcre* places it on the way between the abbey of St Lazarus of Bethany, which also appears on both maps, and the church of the Holy Sepulchre.[151] In 1267 a bull of Pope Clement IV mentions the houses of the archbishop of Nazareth *juxta Sepulchrum*, near the church of the Holy Sepulchre. Even if the *curia* of the archbishop was included among those houses, it would still have been in the Old City. Its location in Montmusard in 1230, far from the Nazareth church, is therefore excluded. It follows that the documents of that year mentioned earlier refer to the Hospitaller *auberge* in the Old City. This conclusion is enhanced by the fact that they deal with a transfer of land and houses between the Teutonic Order and the monastery of St Mary of Josaphat, both of which were situated in the Old City and pursued a systematic acquisition policy aimed at creating clusters of property around their respective main buildings.

---

excluded. Since no width is mentioned, one may wonder whether *longesse* does not stand here for 'perimeter' which, for instance, would imply measurements of a rectangular building 100 m long and 65 m wide.

[148] After referring to the building, the chronicle adds that it *avoit mout grant propris de court, e la fu fait la feste*. The language is somewhat ambiguous, as it is not clear whether the festivities took place in the building or, rather, in the courtyard. In any event, the existence of the latter definitively rules out the identification of the *auberge* with the rectangular neighbourhood in the suburb, mentioned above, a possibility raised by Boas, "A Rediscovered Market Street," 185, yet ruled out by him for the wrong reasons, namely the supposed length of the hall in the building, as interpreted by Riley-Smith (see previous note).

[149] See Riley-Smith, *The Knights of St. John*, pp. 309–10.

[150] Riley-Smith, ibid., p. 248, referring to Strehlke, *Tabulae Ordinis Theutonici*, pp. 57–60, nos. 73–74 (RRH, nos. 1020–21). His assumption rests on the reference to *gastine* in that document. As noted earlier, open spaces still existed in the Old City in the 1230s, and the term *gastina* could very well have been applied to them. There is no reason to believe that it was only used for Montmusard.

[151] H. Michelant and G. Raynaud, eds., *Itinéraires à Jérusalem et descriptions de la Terre Sainte rédigés en français aux XIe, XIIe et XIIIe siècles* (Geneva, 1882), p. 235. On the nature of the itinerary, see "Pilgrimage in Crusader Acre," pp. 107–110, 112. The *palatium* of the archbishop in Acre, which must have been identical with the *curia*, is mentioned yet not located in a charter of 1255 : E.G. Rey, ed., *Recherches géographiques et historiques sur la domination des Latins en Orient* (Paris, 1877), pp. 36–38.

There are additional arguments strengthening the assumption that the *auberge* of the Hospitallers was still in the Old City by 1230. The construction of the new *auberge* before that year, as well as around that time, may be discounted. The enlargement of the Order's main compound, completed in the 1220s or 1230s (a dating suggested above), was expected to fulfil its expanded needs.[152] It is hardly plausible, therefore, that the Hospitallers should have engaged in additional large-scale building in Montmusard at the same time or shortly afterwards. The financial outlay in each of these enterprises was considerable, and it is unlikely that the Order should have mustered the resources to cover both of them within a relatively short period, considering its other commitments. Incidentally, the enlargement of the compound, whether still underway or already completed, must have been one of the decisive factors that prompted the Hospitallers to retain their headquarters at Acre, rather than moving back to Jerusalem after the Frankish recovery of the Holy City in 1229. Soon after that event the Order immediately took possession of its conventual buildings in Jerusalem,[153] which implies that some of the brothers and servants must have been stationed there. It is likely, therefore, that there was no need for additional buildings in Acre until after the fall of Jerusalem to the Khorezmians in 1244.

One may wonder whether the map of Acre ascribed to Matthew Paris and drawn in or shortly after 1252 offers some evidence regarding the *auberge* in Montmusard (Fig. 3).[154] This map is far more schematic than those of Vesconte and Paolino with respect to the configuration and topography of Acre, it omits the urban street network and depicts only a few architectural landmarks, the siting of which is not always accurate. It nevertheless provides evidence not found on the two other maps about the approximate location of three buildings, the *chaene* or maritime customs, the house of the Patriarch, and the house of the royal constable, which could be seen from ships approaching the harbour.[155] The map depicts *la maisun del Hospital* as straddling the northern wall of the Old City. This position may create some confusion regarding the siting of the Order's headquarters either in that urban section or in the suburb. However, since the structure representing it is located north of the Genoese fortified building in Cambridge, Corpus Christi College, MS. 26 (Fig. 3),[156] the reference is clearly to the Order's compound in the Old City, and not to the *auberge* in Montmusard. The only two structures depicted in the suburb are

---

[152] E. Jordan, ed., *Les registres de Clément IV (1265–1268)* (Paris, 1904), p. 163, no. 511. I wish to thank Denys Pringle for discussing with me the topographical issues regarding the location of the Nazareth church and houses.

[153] See Riley-Smith, *The Knights of St. John*, p. 247.

[154] For that dating and those of the five extant copies, see Richard Vaughan, *Matthew Paris* (Cambridge, 1958), pp. 238–39 and 244–45. Suzanne Lewis, *The Art of Matthew Paris in the* Chronica Majora (Berkeley and Los Angeles, 1987), p. 357, suggests a date somewhat after 1253–54.

[155] See Jacoby, "Crusader Acre," 10–11.

[156] British Library, MS Royal 14 C vii, fol. 4v–5r, wrongly identifies that structure as Pisan.

those of St Lazarus and of St Thomas Becket.[157] If the new *auberge* had existed by 1252, one would expect it to be reflected on Matthew Paris's map, as on the Vesconte and Paolino maps,[158] given its size and the fact that the Hospitallers were the only military order having an additional large building in the suburb. It may be argued, however, that Matthew Paris depicted only a few landmarks representing buildings or institutions and saw no need to underline the Hospitallers' presence both in the Old City and in the suburb. In short, his map does not offer any clue with respect to the new *auberge*.

A statute adopted by the Order in 1265 deals with the lodging of the Order's bailiffs coming from overseas in the dormitory of the *herberge*, which seems to imply that there was yet another dormitory elsewhere. If this interpretation is correct, this statute may well provide the earliest testimony regarding the new *auberge*.[159] Yet incontrovertible evidence regarding the latter appears only in 1270. One of the Order's statutes adopted in that year refers to the building housing the conventual refectory, in which the brothers ate their meals, as *premier couvent*, which implies the existence of a second one.[160] We may safely assume, therefore, that the construction of the new *auberge* took place after the 1230s and most likely after 1244, and was possibly completed by 1265 and in any event by 1270. Jonathan Riley-Smith has recently suggested that the housing of large numbers of mercenaries and servants in the Order's compound in the Old City resulted in construction in two different ways. On the one hand, it prompted the Hospitallers to build numerous latrines in the northern section of their compound and, on the other, to erect a new sumptuous building in Montmusard for the lodging of the conventual brothers.[161] These projects must have been undertaken around the mid-thirteenth century or shortly afterwards.

---

[157] On which see above, nn. 26 and 31.
[158] See above, n. 28.
[159] *Cart Hosp* 3:119, no. 3180, § 4: "que les bailliz qui venront d'outremer ... se herbergent au dortor à la herberge." However, the Marshal could lodge the bailiffs in his room, which obviously was in the same structure.
[160] *Cart Hosp* 3:228, § 13.
[161] On the latrines, see above, n. 37. The stationing of turcopoles of the Order in Acre is attested in 1258: *Cronaca del Templare di Tiro*, p. 70, § 47. However, it does not enable a narrower dating, as we do not know their numbers. On the employment of mercenaries by the Order, see Riley-Smith, *The Knights of St. John*, pp. 324–26.

The Naming Patterns of the Inhabitants of Frankish Acre*

Iris Shagrir

Ben Gurion University

The anthroponymic method and analyses that have been developed and used in medieval studies in recent decades perceive the personal name as one of the means by which a social group may express itself. These methods enable researchers to trace socio-cultural evolutions within groups and to explore the differences between them. Using evidence from name-giving patterns from the Latin kingdom of Jerusalem and from crusader Acre in the twelfth and thirteenth centuries, I will attempt to examine whether there were any special characteristics of the naming patterns of the inhabitants of Acre, both in comparison with the rest of the Latin kingdom, and in comparison with Italian maritime towns in the thirteenth century. I will also attempt to verify whether a so-called "urban anthroponymy," a phenomenon described in European contemporary studies, can be identified in thirteenth century Acre. I will first present briefly the basic terminology and the main findings on the naming patterns of the Latin kingdom of Jerusalem. I will then examine the findings from a sample of people specifically identified as inhabitants of Acre, and compare these findings with Franks from the rest of the Latin kingdom. A third section attempts to compare Acre and the Italian maritime cities in the thirteenth century, mainly Venice and Genoa, and intends to identify an "urban phenomenon" in the naming patterns in Acre.

The Naming Patterns of the Latin Kingdom in the Twelfth and Thirteenth Centuries

The sources for the study of the naming patterns in the Latin kingdom are formal documents, acts and transactions, related to the kingdom, from which around 6,200 personal names were extracted. A structured data file was designed based on these names, and was used for a qualitative and quantitative analysis of the name-giving practices and preferences of the people who lived in the Latin kingdom between 1100 and 1291.[1]

A basic assumption of the anthroponymic approach is that the choice of a personal name reflects social and cultural orientations; that giving a name is an

---

* An earlier version of this paper was read to a symposium entitled *Historic Acre as a Living City*, held in July 2003 in Acre under the auspices of the Old Acre Development Company.
[1] Iris Shagrir, *Naming Patterns in the Latin Kingdom of Jerusalem* (Oxford, 2003).

individual decision embedded in a social, cultural and religious context. The naming patterns of a defined group (in other words a group with a social meaning, like diocese, town, region), thus serve as indirect indicators for tracing meaningful trends and fashions in that group. The patterns are likely to reflect changes evolving from socio-cultural interaction between groups, and can serve as a basis for comparisons between different groups. Name studies offer a novel way of examining the question of identity, in the specific context of an immigrating society in the process of creating a new group identity. In sociological research, three models are used to analyse the behaviour of immigrant or colonizing groups: (a) adaptation – the immigrants adjust to the host society; (b) segregation and isolation – in other words minimal or no interaction between groups; and (c) acculturation – which means that, through the encounter with the indigenous society, the immigrant group will gradually develop a special pattern, which is not identical either to the original old culture or to the local one.[2]

The anthroponymic analysis of the naming patterns in the Latin kingdom has revealed the following major evolutions:

1. The Frankish naming pattern shared the major evolutions observed in the naming patterns in contemporary Catholic Europe.
2. The convergence of various European traditions in the Latin East is evident in the Latin kingdom's more heterogeneous and dynamic pattern, compared to specific localities in western Europe.
3. The name preferences of the indigenous oriental Christians made an impact on the preferences of the Franks. This impact was limited to oriental Christian names that were then familiar, but not frequent, in western Europe. The findings support the hypothesis that Frankish culture integrated some European and oriental elements.
4. The preference of names of Christian connotation, mainly saints' names, over names of Germanic and Latin origin without a distinct Christian connotation, is an evolution common to western Europe and the kingdom. However, there are differences in its pace: among the Franks of Outremer central saints' names gained prevalence relatively early.
5. Contrary to the process of shrinkage of the name stock, characteristic of western Europe, it appears that the Frankish name stock did not shrink significantly over the period of the kingdom's existence.

---

[2] John W. Berry, "Acculturation and Adaptation in a New Society," *International Migration* 30 (1992), 69–85.

The Naming Patterns in Acre Compared to the Rest of the Latin Kingdom

The comparison of the naming patterns of the inhabitants of Acre with the patterns of the whole kingdom shows that the prevalent trends in the kingdom were present in Acre, and even seem to be more pronounced. The analysis of the naming patterns of the inhabitants of Acre is based on a sample of people identified specifically as *habitatores* or *burgenses* of Acre in the twelfth and thirteenth centuries. The names of these people were drawn from the documents in Reinhold Röhricht's *Regesta regni hierosolymitani* and from the *Documenti del commercio veneziano*.[3] The sample does not include members of the military orders.[4] It consists of 287 people, who are unevenly divided over the two centuries of study, with 41 people in the twelfth century and 246 in the thirteenth. The findings therefore reflect more strongly the thirteenth century, due to its relative weight in the total sample.

The major characteristics of the naming behaviour in the kingdom as a whole, are also observed in the data relating to Acre alone. The common development is perceived in the trend of the increasing popularity of Latin names in Acre as well as in the rest of the kingdom. In both groups the rates of Latin names increased constantly: in Acre from 41 per cent to 63 per cent over the twelfth and the thirteenth centuries, compared with the slightly more moderate increase in the rest of the kingdom of 32 per cent to 53 per cent. It is notable that the percentage of Latin names is higher in Acre than in the rest of the kingdom. This evolution coincides with a decrease in the prevalence of Germanic names, in Acre from 59 per cent to 35 per cent between the twelfth and the thirteenth centuries; the rates were decreasing also in the whole kingdom from 65 per cent to 44 per cent. Here, too, it should be noted that the rates of Germanic names are lower in Acre than they are in the rest of the Latin kingdom.

An evident corresponding evolution occurred in the application of saints' names. In Acre the rates of saints' names rose from 34 per cent to 56 per cent over the whole period (Fig. 1), while in the rest of the kingdom they rose from 28 per cent to 46 per cent. In the case of saints' names it can be seen as well that in Acre both the minimum and the maximum rates are higher than in the rest of the kingdom. When the patterns relating to Acre are compared to the Latin kingdom they show similar phenomena, yet in Acre they seem stronger and more pronounced. The proportion of saints' names in Acre is elevated compared both to the rest of the kingdom and to contemporary western European localities, such as Genoa 1261 (48 per cent) and English towns of the beginning of the thirteenth century (Winchester, Canterbury and Leicester range between 25 per cent and 30 per cent). The pattern in Acre also

---

[3] *Documenti del commercio veneziano nei secoli XI–XIII*, ed. Raimondo Morozzo della Rocca and Antonino Lombardo, 2 vols. (Turin, 1940); *Nuovi documenti del commercio veneto dei secoli XI–XIII*, ed. Antonino Lombardo and Raimondo Morozzo della Rocca (Venice, 1953).

[4] Rates given for the Latin kingdom also exclude the military orders. This is based on the assumption that most of the brothers were recruited in western Europe.

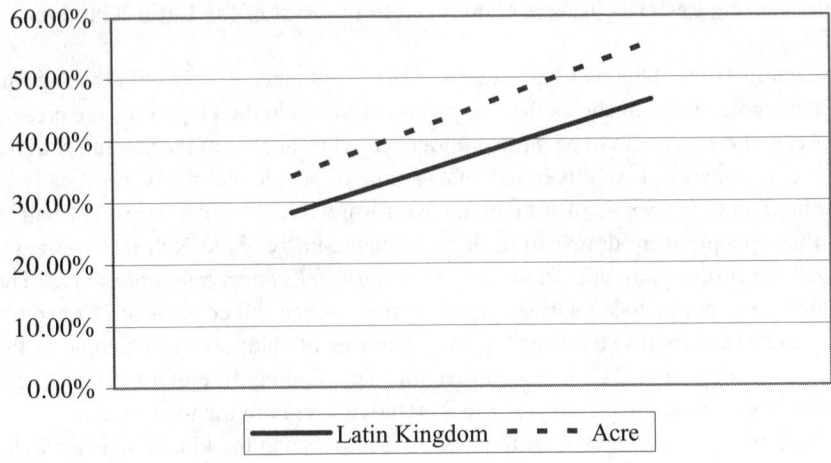

Fig. 1 Increase in preponderance of saints' names: twelfth to thirteenth centuries

shows a lower rate of Germanic names than in contemporary western Europe. It seems to bend even more than the Latin kingdom itself towards the "Mediterranean" naming pattern, which, more than its western European counterpart, favoured Latin names and saints' names as opposed to the Germanic names that were dominant in early medieval Europe.

This can also be observed in the list of the most popular name choices. Figure 2 presents the top choices in Acre and in the rest of the Latin kingdom (excluding Acre), showing the names with more than a 2 per cent rate of popularity. The four top names are identical: John, James, William, Peter. Yet in Acre the higher rates of other well-known saints' names are noticeable: Nicholas, one of the most popular saints in the east, patron of seafarers, merchants, cities, and an especially popular saint in Italy; Thomas, Stephen, and Andrew, saints specifically related to the Holy Land, being two apostles and the first martyr; and Anthony, a desert father, founder of Christian monasticism as well as a popular Italian saint, Anthony of Padua.

It should be pointed out that the total sample of the Latin kingdom probably contains more people from Acre (but not identified as such) than the smaller pool of individuals clearly identified as living in Acre. Therefore, in order to refine the comparison between inhabitants and non-inhabitants of Acre, the group hitherto defined as the "rest of the kingdom" was broken down into those individuals who clearly lived in places other than Acre (such as Gerald Rufus of Mahomeria; RRH no. 302), and those whose place of residence remains unknown. In this manner, the individuals who may be from Acre but are not identified by their place of residence are isolated into a residual sample of "unidentified persons."

This more focused comparison between residents of Acre and those who are clearly not from Acre yields interesting results. The new group, consisting only of

Latin Kingdom		Acre		Venice		Genoa	
Name	%	Name	%	Name	%	Name	%
John	12.31	John	13.8	John	16.5	William	8.8
William	5.6	William	4.9	Mark	13.2	James	7.9
Peter	4.8	Peter	4.1	Marinus	11.2	Simon	6.3
James	3.7	James ⎫	3.7	Peter	9.4	Nicholas ⎫	5.9
Hugh	2.9	Nicholas ⎭		Nicholas	5.6	John ⎭	
Nicholas	2.3	Thomas	3.3	James	5.1	Lanfranc	5.4
Guy ⎫		Stephen	2.8	Philip	3.3	Henry ⎫	4.2
Philip ⎬	2.1	Hugh	2.4	Andrew	3.1	Obertus ⎭	
Henry ⎬		Andrew ⎫		Leonard ⎫	2.8	Peter	3.0
Thomas ⎭		Anthony ⎬	2.0	Thomas ⎭		Paschal	2.5
		Godfrey ⎬					
		Robert ⎭					

Fig. 2   Top name choices in the thirteenth century

people with a defined place of residence other than Acre, includes 1,488 individuals: 1,055 in the twelfth century and 433 in the thirteenth. Comparing it again with the findings of Acre, the results point towards a less robust difference between the groups, though a difference still exists. In the case of Latin names in the thirteenth century, where Acre shows a rate of 63 per cent, the group of people not from Acre shows 53 per cent (compared to 53 per cent in the rest of the kingdom comprising those who lived in places other than Acre and those of unidentified location). The rate of saints' names in Acre is 56 per cent in the thirteenth century, as reported above, and is 51 per cent among the people not from Acre (compared to 46 per cent in the unfiltered group). It appears that the better identified group has a rate of saints' names higher than those people whose first names are not accompanied by a toponymic descriptor. This may be explained by a probable link between the preponderance of by-names and greater homonymity, since a growing use of popular saints' names may, given the limited choices, promote homonymity.

The results also show clearly that in Acre there were more people carrying Latin names which are not saints' names (for example, Bonaventura, Homodeus), a pattern generally typical of Italian name repertories of the period.[5] This Italian impact on the naming pattern in Acre can be ascertained by deducting the individuals who lived in Acre and are clearly designated as Italians by origin (such

---

[5] For example, Olivier Guyotjeanin, "L'onomastique émilienne," *Mélanges de l'École Française de Rome* 106 (1994), 381–446, table 13, 411.

as Johannes Pisanus): without the Italians the discrepancy between holders of Latin names (57 per cent) and holders of saints' names (53 per cent) diminishes significantly compared to the sample including them (in other words there are fewer individuals carrying Latin names which are not saints' names). An additional finding is that the percentage of saints' names among the people who have a defined location other than Acre is closer to that of inhabitants of Acre. This presents a question regarding the composition of the group. Clearly it is the better-identified sub-group of those who lived in places other than Acre, which may mean that they are better recognized, as a result of being more prominent members of society.[6] The assumption that this group contains a significant proportion of members of the Frankish nobility may be supported by its top name preferences. Notably, the rise of the name John was specifically strong and significant among the Franks in the Levant, a predilection reflected both in its high frequency compared to contemporary European name stocks and in its lead rate over the second most popular name. Furthermore, the preference for John was especially striking among the Frankish nobility, peaking to about 19 per cent at the middle of the thirteenth century.[7] In the sample of people living in places other than Acre the frequency of John, the top name, is 16 per cent, compared to 14 per cent in Acre and to 11 per cent among those individuals of undefined place of residence.

In sum, the comparison between the inhabitants of Acre and those who do not live in Acre shows that the evolutions taking place throughout the kingdom also occurred in Acre, and appear to be more prominent in Acre, especially in the thirteenth century. However, the attempt at a more focused comparison between those who lived in Acre and those who definitely did not produced mixed results. They may be a consequence of the significant Italian presence in thirteenth-century Acre and from the particular composition of the filtered group, which may contain a greater proportion of nobles.[8]

The Naming Patterns in Acre Compared to Italian Maritime Cities

The patterns of the personal names of the inhabitants of Acre were compared with the findings on the naming practices available from contemporary Venice and Genoa. For the comparison with Venetian names I used the personal names of

---

[6] This phenomenon is documented in medieval western Europe. See Heinrich Rüthing, "Der Wechsel Personennamen in einer spätmittelalterlichen Stadt. Zum Problem der Identifizierung von Personen und zum sozialen Status von Stadtbewohnern mit wechselnden oder unvollständigen Namen," in Neithard Bulst and Jean-Philippe Genet, eds., *Medieval Lives and the Historian. Studies in Medieval Prosopography* (Kalamazoo, 1982), pp. 215–26.

[7] Shagrir, *Naming Patterns*, chap. 3.

[8] In other words, the more focused comparison inserted an additional, probably significant, variable into the procedure; namely how well individuals are identified in the documents and who are the better-defined ones.

the 127 *boni homines* who attested the granting of assets in Constantinople to the monastery of S. Giorgio Maggiore in 1090,[9] and a list of 393 people elected for the General Council (*Maggior Consiglio*) of 1261–62.[10] The comparison with Genoa is based on the data made available by Alain Birolini's study of Genoese anthroponymy and by Kedar's study of saints' names in Genoa.[11]

Birolini asserts that in Genoa, from around 1100 to around 1220, Germanic names predominated in the Genoese name stock, with Obertus and William as the most dominant names. This is also demonstrated in the lists provided by Kedar for 1157 and 1188 (the first of which is "more aristocratic," the second less so). The Germanic names, specifically those without a Christian content, were being replaced towards the middle of the thirteenth century by Latin names, with a remarkable rise of John and especially of James. On the other hand, in Venice the levels of Latin names at the end of the eleventh century (1090) and in the middle of the thirteenth – 96 per cent and 97 per cent, respectively – were extremely high and unparalleled elsewhere. This exceptional proportion of Latin names in Venice correlates with an outstanding rate of saints' names as well, to which the closest figure is the 56 per cent rate of saints' names in Acre. The most frequent names in thirteenth-century Acre are John, William, Peter, James and Nicholas (in equal fourth place), and Thomas (see Fig. 2). The list has much in common with the most popular names of both Venice and Genoa (Fig. 2). John and Nicholas are very popular across the samples, as well as James and Peter to a lesser degree.[12] Each list also has its unique characteristics: William is absent in Venice but ranks first in Genoa, whereas Mark and Marinus rank high in Venice but not elsewhere. The

---

[9] The document is reproduced in Vittorio Lazzarini, *Scritti di paleografia e diplomatica* (Venice, 1938), pp. 171–77. The name list and count appear in Gianfranco Folena, "Gli antichi nomi di persona e la storia civile di Venezia," *Atti dell'Istituto Veneto di Scienze* (1971), pp. 464–67. Folena's count is erroneous, however, since several names appear twice in the signature section of the document.

[10] Folena, "Gli antichi nomi," pp. 468–73. The list is based on *Deliberazioni del Maggior Consiglio di Venezia*, ed. Roberto Cessi, 1 (Bologna, 1950).

[11] Alain Birolini, "Étude d'anthroponymie génoise," *Mélanges de l'École Française de Rome* 107 (1995), 467–96; Benjamin Z. Kedar, "Noms de saints et mentalité populaire à Gênes au XIVe siècle," *Le Moyen Age* 73 (1967), 431–46; Benjamin Z. Kedar, *Merchants in Crisis* (New Haven, 1976), pp. 98–101.

[12] The affinity between the names from Frankish Acre and the Italian preferences is evident in various Italian studies. See, for example, Sante Bortolami, "Il sistema onomastico in una quasi-città del Veneto medioevale," *Mélanges de l'École Française de Rome* 106 (1994), 343–80; François Menant, "L'Italie centro-septentrionale," in *L'Anthroponymie. Document de l'histoire sociale des mondes méditerranéens médiévaux. Actes du colloque international "Genèse médiévale de l'anthroponymie moderne" (Rome, 6–8 octobre 1994)*, ed. Monique Bourin, Jean-Marie Martin and François Menant, Collection de L'École française de Rome 226 (Rome, 1996), pp. 19–28. An illustrative example of the difference between the preferences of the Latins of the East and their western European contemporaries can be illustrated in a list of most frequent names of Poitevin knights who sailed to the Holy Land in 1252: Raymundus, Arnaudus, Guillelmus, Petrus, Bernardus, Odo, Hugo, Berengarius and Augerius. All, except Peter, are Germanic names, and none is named after a universally popular saint. *Preuves de l'histoire de Languedoc*, ed. Auguste Molinier (Paris, 1875), doc. 432, pp. 1314–15.

greater similarity between the most dominant Frankish names and the dominant names of the Italian towns compared to other parts of Europe is also evident when looking at the names from Acre only, a similarity that may be ascribed to a growing level of cultural integration between these areas resulting from communications and trade between the Italian towns and the Levant, and from a greater number of Italian merchants settling permanently in Acre.[13]

Did Acre, the largest city of the Latin kingdom and its capital in the thirteenth century,[14] display the characteristics common to the larger urban areas in western Europe? Studies from France, England and, especially, from Italy have documented a typical difference between urban and semi-urban areas during the thirteenth century.

Based on three case studies in central Italy, Etienne Hubert suggested that the bigger cities in the central Middle Ages (eleventh to thirteenth centuries) exhibited more evolution in their naming system (such as the addition of a by-name, renewal of the name-stock) than did their rural surroundings.[15] Kedar found that the *contadini* of the Genoese countryside also exhibited an onomastic conservatism compared to the citizens of Genoa itself, by continuing to use some Germanic names that were already outmoded in the city.[16] These findings are corroborated by findings from Tuscany and Emilia-Romagna, as well as by findings from Languedoc, where Jean-Louis Biget found that in terms of naming Toulouse presented "a specific cultural milieu."[17] This specific milieu, and the role of the great urban area as a source of innovation, was usually reflected, especially in the thirteenth century, in high frequencies of the name John and those other major saints' names which were on the rise in the thirteenth century, like James and Nicholas; in a relatively early and rapid renovation, essentially a "Christianization," of the name-stock; in higher concentration levels on the dominant names;[18] and in the contraction of the name-stock.

For the purpose of this study I compared the city of Venice with a smaller town in the Veneto area, Padua, for which data are available from 1254 and 1275. The

---

[13] Joshua Prawer, *Crusader Institutions* (Oxford, 1980), p. 221.

[14] Prawer estimated the city's population at around 40,000. *Crusader Institutions*, p. 182, n. 159.

[15] Étienne Hubert, "Structure urbaine et système anthroponymique," *L'anthroponymie* (above, note 12), p. 313.

[16] Kedar, *Merchants in Crisis*, p. 98. The conservatism of the peasantry was also noted in an earlier period in England, where the post-conquest peasant population clung to traditional Anglo-Saxon personal names. See Cecily Clark, "*Willelmus rex? Vel alius Willelmus?*", in Peter Jackson, ed., *Words, Names and History* (Woodbridge, 1995), pp. 281, 284 n. 22.

[17] Jean-Louis Biget, "L'évolution des noms de baptême en Languedoc au moyen âge," *Cahiers de Fanjeaux* 17 (1982), 297–341, esp. p. 322.

[18] Concentration is the accumulated frequency of a defined number of the top choices. It is represented in percentages, and reveals the intensity of the shared element in naming preferences. A trend of increasing concentration reflects the clustering of commonly shared preferences. As a social phenomenon, greater homonymity may reflect greater socio-cultural cohesion, prevalent fashion and imitation.

difference between the great urban centre and its provincial town is evident. The level of saints' names in Venice is 86 per cent (in 1261) and in Padua (in 1254) 37 per cent. The ever-decreasing rate of Germanic names in Venice was 4 per cent and 15 per cent in Padua. The stock of names was considerably larger in Padua than in Venice (on average 53 names per 100 individuals in Padua, 13 in Venice), and the concentration, or clustering, on the top choices, was much stronger in Venice (73 per cent of people held the ten top choices in Venice, 40 per cent in Padua). A similar pattern is confirmed in Vicenza, a smaller town in the Veneto.[19] These phenomena seem to be characteristic of the difference between large urban areas and their surroundings in most of Catholic Europe.

The data from Acre, as compared to the rest of the Latin kingdom, give a similar, though not as robust, impression. In the thirteenth century the residents of Acre presented the lowest rate of Germanic names, 35 per cent, while in the rest of the kingdom the rate was 44 per cent and among the people who lived in places other than Acre 45 per cent. The rate of saints' names in the thirteenth century was higher in Acre (56 per cent) than in the rest of the kingdom (46 per cent) and was also higher than among those people who lived in places other than Acre (51 per cent). So far, then, the patterns accord with the expected characteristics of a larger town. Yet, the difference between those who lived in Acre and those who did not is not to be found in other parameters. The preference for John, the leading name, was slightly higher among those who definitely did not live in Acre (16 per cent) than among those from Acre (14 per cent). The linked phenomenon of greater concentration on the top choices displays a similarly complex picture, as the ten top choices in Acre are held by 43 per cent of the population (Fig. 2), compared with 40 per cent in the rest of the kingdom, but among those living in places other than Acre the concentration rate is higher (45 per cent) than in Acre. In addition, the number of names in the name-stock presents a mixed picture: there are no significant differences between the groups. These results blur the expected difference between Acre, as the largest city, and other places in the kingdom. On the one hand, the results produced by the statistical measures do not support the urban pattern shown in various western European studies: there is a relatively high number of names in circulation in Acre, and the concentration level is not particularly high compared to the other groups. This may be explained by the diversity of the population within the city and by the inhabitants of Acre being less distinctive, compared to the rest of the kingdom; indeed, most of the people who lived in places other than Acre lived in other towns, since the size of the non-urban settler population was insignificant in the thirteenth century. On the other hand, a

---

[19] Based on the chronicle of Battista Pagliarini it has been suggested that in the thirteenth century augural and descriptive names (such as Bonagente, Brutofante, Senzabriga) were much more current among the Vicentine *estimi* than later on. Indeed, among the Venetian *estimi* of the 1254 list, such names were almost non-existent. For later patterns of Vicentine popular names see James S. Grubb, *Provincial Families of the Renaissance. Private and Public Life in the Veneto* (Baltimore, 1996), p. 225.

difference between Acre and the rest of the kingdom is to be found in the levels of Latin, Germanic and saints' names in a way that corresponds to the general urban phenomenon. This suggests a more innovative naming behaviour, one that rejects the older Germanic names and names of weak devotional significance in favour of the names of major saints.

Conclusion

The findings on the naming patterns in the Latin kingdom of Jerusalem show that the naming practices followed the major trends prevalent in twelfth- and thirteenth-century Catholic Europe, but also incorporated elements from the naming practices of Eastern Christianity. This reinforces the notion that immigrant groups in new areas of settlement rarely form insulated cultural units, even within what is considered a hostile environment. The religiously-oriented profile of the Frankish name-stock is reflected in the trends of abandoning names of no Christian significance and favouring the names of major saints that were dominant in eastern Christian name-stocks for centuries. These trends are characteristic of the whole kingdom, but are even more pronounced in its capital in the thirteenth century. This finding underscores the role of Acre, with its dense and diverse population, in the promotion of interaction between Catholics and non-Catholics. The encounter needs naturally to be seen within the wider context of the impact of the Greek Orthodox naming tradition in the Mediterranean region, where a preference for saints' names was a centuries-long legacy. The comparison between Acre, Venice and Genoa demonstrates the extent of the shared element and general affinity between them, and thus places Acre distinctly in this world. The comparison between naming patterns of the residents of Acre and others suggests that unlike the observed phenomena in other towns, Acre does not demonstrate a trend of greater concentration and shrinkage of the name-stock when compared to the rest of the kingdom. This may result from a greater extent of similarity between the inhabitants of Acre and those of the rest of the kingdom in the thirteenth century. Yet the city presents important characteristics of a greater urban area, especially in being on the avant-garde of the vogue of popularity of major saints' names, which was to be the dominant western European trend for centuries.

Vassal and Faṣal: The Evidence of the Farkhah Inscription from 608/1210[*]

Moshe Sharon

The Hebrew University of Jerusalem

Farkhah (Farkhā) is a small village built on a steep hilltop 500 m above sea level in the heart of Samaria, south-west of the small town of Salfīt (Israel Grid 164 164 = NIG 214 664). Samaritans populated it until the Arab conquest, and probably throughout the Umayyad period. Under the crusaders its name is not mentioned, but its location suggests that it was included in the royal domain of the kingdom of Jerusalem.[1] In 1187, after the battle of Ḥiṭṭīn, it came under Ayyūbid rule. In Islamic literature its name appears in connection with the Muslim scholar 'Abdallah b. Abū 'Abdallah al-Farkhāwī (d. 818/1415). In his biography, as-Sakhāwī remarks that the *nisbah* al-Farkhāwī refers to the village of Farkhā, which he spells with a long "ā", adding that it was a village in the district of Nābulus.[2] I have found no other mention of it in the literary sources. This fact grants particular significance to the present Ayyūbid inscription, found in the village and mentioning its name.

The Inscription

In November 1937, D.C. Baramki, surveying the village for the Department of Antiquities of the British Government of Palestine, discovered in the village mosque four fragments of an inscription dating from 15 Shawwāl 606/12 April 1210, originally engraved on a slab of limestone measuring 0.52 × 0.42 m. A squeeze copy was prepared from the four available fragments; a part on the bottom left, containing the end of lines 7–10 of the inscription, was missing. Baramki was the first to read the inscription in November 1937 (see Fig. 1);[3] later it was transcribed by Sukenik and Ben-Horin.[4] All of them used the squeeze copy of four out of the five fragments

---

[*] This article forms part of the research on the Arabic inscriptions in Palestine supported by the Israel Science Foundation. A study of the inscription from Farkhah is included in M. Sharon, *Corpus Inscriptionum Arabicarum Palaestinae* (*CIAP*), 3 vols. to date (Leiden, 1997–), 3.188–200.

[1] Jonathan Riley-Smith, ed., *The Atlas of the Crusades* (London, 1991), pp. 36–37.

[2] Shams ad-Dīn Muḥammad b. 'Abd ar-Raḥmān as-Sakhāwī, *Aḍ-Ḍaw' al-Lāmi' li-Ahl al-Qarn at-Tāsi'* (Beirut, n.d.), 5.29. See also Victor Guérin, *Description géographique, historique et archéologique de la Palestine*: II. *Samarie*, 2 vols. (Paris, 1874), 2, ch. 50.

[3] See File Palestine Antiquities Museum (PAM) ATQ/165 in the archives of the Israel Antiquities Authority (IAA), housed in the Rockefeller Museum, Jerusalem.

[4] Yigael Sukenik (Yadin), unpublished (and lost?) M.A. thesis on some of the squeeze copies of the Arabic inscriptions in PAM, p. 24; Uri Ben-Horin, manuscript of a private file, including copies of

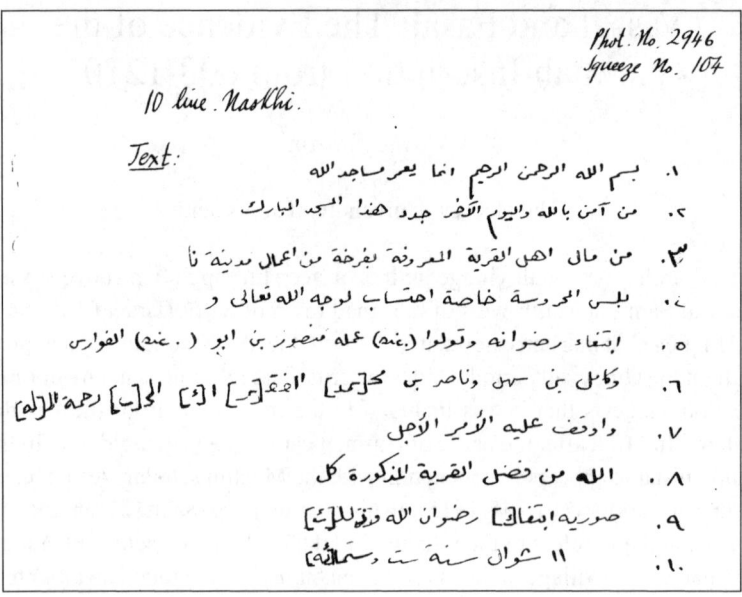

Fig. 1   Farkhah. D.C. Baramki's original reading (courtesy IAA)

of the inscription. I found the photograph of the lost fifth fragment in the archives of the Israel Antiquities Authority (IAA)[5] and, bringing it to the same scale as that of the existing photograph of the squeeze, I was able to reconstruct the inscription in its entirety (see Fig. 2).

The inscription deals with the reconstruction of a mosque and an endowment dedicated to it. It consists of ten lines, incised in monumental, typical Ayyūbid *naskhī* script furnished with diacritical points and many vowels. What follows is the first publication of the whole inscription (Fig. 2):

١)بسم الله الرحمن الرحيم انما يَعْمر مساجد الله ٢) من آمن بالله واليوْم الآخر جدّدَ هذا المسجد المبارك ٣)مِنْ مَال اهل القرية المعروف[ة] بفرخة من اعمال مدينة نا ٤) بُلس المـحروسة خاصة احتساب(!) لوجه الله تعالى و ٥)ابتغاء رضوانه وتولوا(!) عمله منصور بن ابو(!) الفوارس ٦)وكامل بن سنان وناصر بن محـ[مد] الفقراء الـى رحمة الـ[لّه] ٧) واوقف عَليه الامير الاجل الكبير بـهـ[ـا الـ]دين الوداخر(؟) بن عبد ٨)الله مِنْ فضلّ القرية المذكورة كل سنة ثلاث دنانير ٩) صوريّة ابتغاء رضوان الله وملك دار الآخرة وذلك لا ١٠)ستقبال شوال سنة ست وستمائة وصلى الله على محمد.

---

the published inscriptions in Palestine and Trans-Jordan and inscriptions dealt with by Sukenik, p. 26 (without translation).

[5] See PAM S 104.

Fig. 2 Farkhā 606/1210 (courtesy IAA)

Basmalah. They only shall manage [visit, perform the *'umrah* to] Allah's places of worship who have believed in Allah and the Last Day.[6] This blessed mosque was renewed particularly by the funds of the inhabitants of the village known [by the name of] Farkhah that belongs to the subdistrict of the divinely protected town of Nābulus, as a pious deed for the sake of Allah – the exalted – and seeking His approval. Those who assumed charge of the work were Manṣūr b. Abū al-Fawāris and Kāmil b. Sinān [or Sayyār] and Nāṣir b. Muḥammad who are all in need for Allah's compassion. And the most exalted, the great Amīr Bahā' ad-Dīn Alūdākh(?) b. 'Abd Allah has endowed for it, from the [income of the] *faṣal* of the aforementioned village, three Tyrian dīnārs every year, seeking the approval of Allah and [hoping to] gain the abode of the world to come. And this took place on the full moon of the month of Shawwāl the year 606 [=12 April 1210].

---

[6] *The Qur'ān*, trans. (with a critical rearrangement of the Sūrahs) Richard Bell (Edinburgh, 1937), 9.18.

General Notes

This is definitely a monumental inscription, produced by a skillful hand representing all characteristics of the Ayyūbid script from the time of al-'Ādil (596/1200 – 615/1218) and al-Mu'aẓẓam 'Īsā (615/1218 – 624/1227). Its provinciality might be detected, if one wishes, in three grammatical errors: in line 4 the word *iḥtisāb* in the nominative instead of *iḥtisāban* in the accusative (*maf'ūl li'ajlihi*); in line 5 the verb *tawallaw* in the plural instead of *tawalla* in the singular; and the patronymic *Abū al-Fawāris* in the nominative instead of *Abī al-Fawāris* in the genitive.[7]

The Amīr Bahā' ad-Dīn in our inscription (l. 7) was a first generation Mamlūk and therefore had a Turkish name; as a convert to Islam, his father's name was the fictional 'Abdallah ("the servant of Allah"). The name Alūdākh could well just be another way of transcribing the Turkish Ulūdāgh ("high mountain").[8]

The common title Bahā' ad-Dīn appears in the late medieval literature attached to many names: Aṣlam,[9] Bughdī,[10] Raslān,[11] Qarāraslān,[12] Qarāqūsh,[13] Quṭlūshāh (Quṭlījāh).[14] I could, however, find nothing in the literature about him or about the other persons mentioned in the inscription (ll. 5–6).

Tyrian dīnārs – *danānīr ṣūriyyah*

The inhabitants of Farkhah financed the renovation of the mosque and they made sure to indicate very clearly in the inscription their sole contribution to the project (ll. 2–3). The mosque had expenses, too: the oil for lighting, the floor mats and the salaries of the *imām* and the muezzin.[15] Most probably, these were covered by income from various endowments (*waqfs*), to which another one was added by the Amīr Bahā' ad-Dīn. It consisted of three Tyrian dīnārs (*danānīr ṣūriyyah*) paid annually from the *faṣal* of the village, *the fixed annual amount that the village paid the amīr* (ll. 8–9). This reading was made possible only because of the discovery of the inscription's missing part.

---

[7] For further analysis of the inscription see Sharon, *CIAP*, *s.v.* "Farkhah," 3.188–200.
[8] Contribution of my colleague Reuven Amitai.
[9] Karl V. Zettersteen, *Beiträge zur Geschichte der Mamlukensultane* (Leiden, 1919), pp. 171–72, 178, 187, 219.
[10] Ibid., p. 24.
[11] Ibid., pp. 108, 130, 131, 133, 134, 166.
[12] Ibid., p. 53.
[13] Ibid., pp. 28, 52; Ibn Khallikān, Shams ad-Dīn Aḥmad b. Muḥammad, *Wafayāt al-A'yān wa-Anbā' Abnā' az-Zamān*, ed. Iḥsān 'Abbās (Beirut, 1971), 4.91–92; Ibn Taghrī Birdī, Jamāl ad-Dīn Abū al Maḥāsin Yūsuf al Atābibkī, *An-Nujūm az-Zāhira fī Mulūk Miṣr wa-al-Qāhirah* (Cairo, 1970), 13.29; 14.79; Maqrīzī, Taqī ad-Dīn Aḥmad b. 'Alī, *Kitāb as-Sulūk li-Ma'rifat Duwal al-Mulūk*. ed. Muḥammad Muṣṭafā Ziyādah and Sa'īd 'Abd al-Fattāḥ 'Āshūr (Cairo, 1956–72), 1/1.158.
[14] Zettersteen, pp. 75–77.
[15] *Cf.* Sharon, *CIAP*, 1.189; 2.xvi.

It appears that the dīnārs of Tyre (*danānīr ṣūriyyah*) were used as reliable currency, although they did not retain their value over time. However, on the whole, European gold currency was sought after, until modern times, as the best money because of its exact weight, especially since the equivalent Muslim coins fluctuated in weight even from province to province and were sometimes devalued by cutting away their edges with the purpose of using the metal (gold or silver) for minting more coins. For this reason Qalqashandī as late as the fifteenth century emphasized that "commercial transactions take place in Egyptian or similar dīnārs by weight, and in Frankish dīnārs by tale" (*al-muʿāmalah bi-ad-danānīr al-miṣriyyah wa-naḥwihā waznan wa-ad-danānīr al-ifrantiyyah ʿaddan*).[16] What he meant was that since the Muslim dīnārs were of different weight, the value of any number of coins could be decided only by weight, but in the case of the Frankish dīnārs (*ad-danānīr al-ifrantiyyah*) counting or telling was enough. Qalqashandī further explained this issue, writing:

> Currency used in trade by tale (*mā yutaʿāmal bihi muʿāddatan*) are dīnārs imported from the lands of the Franks and from Byzantium. They have a fixed weight (*maʿlūmat al-awzān*). Every such dīnār weighs nineteen and a half Egyptian *qīrāṭ*.[17]

The determination of the gold-coin value by weight rather than by tale was a common practice in the East, which makes Qalqashandī's report about the passing of the "Frankish dīnārs" by tale quite important. It is clear that Qalqashandī did not speak about Tyrian dīnārs, but about European money in general – Venetian, Genoese and similar currency – which was respected by the Muslim merchants.

Tyre was famous from ancient times for producing currency of exact weight and its name became a model for reliable currency even after such currency ceased to be produced there; it was used particularly when an exact amount had to be established in contracts and commercial transactions. In many places in the Talmud (the *Mishnah* and the *Gemarah*) we find mention of the Tyrian currency in cases discussing accurate amounts of money, which attests to a documented usage of the term for over 600 years.[18]

The term "Tyrian dīnār" probably referred in general to the gold coin of the classical world, but more specifically to the *solidus*, the Byzantine gold coin which the Arabs knew from before Islam, since it was mentioned in the Qurʾān as a unit of a small but well-known weight:

---

[16] Qalqashandī, Abū al-ʿAbbās Aḥmad b. ʿAlī, *Ṣubḥ al-Aʿshā fī Ṣināʿat al-Inshā* (Cairo, 1963), 4.180.

[17] Ibid., 3.437.

[18] Babylonian Talmud, *Kiddūshīn*, 11a: "Every money mentioned in the Torah is Tyrian money"; 11b: "Every accurate amount of money mentioned in the Torah means Tyrian money." *B. Qama*, 366, 90b; *ʿAbodah zarah*, 11a; *Bekhorot*, 9b, 49b, 50b.

> Among the people of the Book there are those who, if you entrust them with a talent, will pay it back, but among them are others who if one entrusts them with a dīnār, will not pay it back, except so long as one remains standing over them.[19]

The first Islamic dīnārs struck after the reforms of ʿAbd al-Malik in 77/696 had the same weight as the Byzantine *solidus*, 4.25 g. On the basis of glass weights and coins, Hinz established the weight of 4.231 g for the classical Muslim gold dīnār in most of the major provinces of the East around the year 780.[20] When Qalqashandī defined the Frankish gold coins (*ifrantiyyah*) as weighing 19½ Egyptian *qirāt*, short of the full weight of 24 *qirāt* for the gold dīnār (= *mithqāl*), he wished to explain that this weight, being constant, enabled the passing of the Frankish (European) dīnārs, including the Byzantine bezant, by tale. This was important for carrying out quickly and accurately not only commercial transactions but also all other payments which involved accurate sums of money determined by counting and not by weight, which in many cases could not be precisely established. Qalqashandī wrote on the whole about his own time, that is, the late fourteenth and the beginning of the fifteenth century. But there are many examples from the literature of the time of our inscription in which payment by Tyrian gold coins was specified.

In the crusader period the "Tyrian dīnār" was a common name for the Frankish gold coin that retained the name "bezant" or "besant." This was not, however, modelled on the Byzantine gold coin bearing this name but on a Fāṭimid coin. Tyre was one of the few places where the Franks minted their bezants imitating the dīnār of the Fāṭimid caliph al-Āmir (495/1101 – 524/1130), although only a small quantity of the "Tyrian" dīnārs was actually minted in Tyre. The details concerning the Frankish minting activity, which throughout most of the existence of the Latin kingdom produced gold coins displaying (corrupt) Arabic epigraphy and clear Islamic formulae, are well documented.[21] The term *dīnār ṣūrī* "was the generic Arabic term for crusader Arabic gold coins, but only a small proportion of these imitations actually bear the mint-name Ṣūr."[22] In other words, whether these coins were minted in Tyre or not they were called Tyrian dīnārs. It must be remembered that Fāṭimid minting of gold coins steadily continued in the coastal towns of Syria, particularly Tripoli, Tyre and Acre, while minting in the inland towns was frequently interrupted. According to a Muslim source, the Franks continued to mint at Tyre imitation Fāṭimid coins, bearing the name of al-Āmir, for three years after its capture.[23]

---

[19] *The Qurʾān*, trans. Bell, 3.68.
[20] Walther Hinz, *Islamische Masse und Gewichte, umgerechnet ins metrische System* (Leiden, 1955), p. 2.
[21] D. Michael Metcalf, *Coinage of the Crusades and the Latin East in the Ashmolean Museum Oxford*, 2nd edn (London, 1995), pp. 43–45.
[22] Michael L. Bates and D. Michael Metcalf, "Crusader Coinage with Arabic Inscriptions," in Setton, *Crusades*, 6.429.
[23] Ibn Khallikān, 5.301; Bates and Metcalf, "Crusader Coinage," p. 429.

The fact that Tyrian dīnārs were regarded as standard currency can be learnt from the following examples. When Saladīn conquered Jerusalem in 1187, the Christian inhabitants could ransom themselves by paying "ten Tyrian dīnārs for every man, five Tyrian dīnārs for every woman, and one Tyrian dīnār for every child, whether boy or girl."[24] In a report about the release of Raymond III of Tripoli from Muslim prison in 570/1175, Ibn al-Athīr (d. 630/1233) wrote that after having been imprisoned since 559/1163, Sa'd ad-Dīn agreed to let Raymond go for "150,000 Tyrian dīnārs, and one thousand [Muslim] captives."[25] Ibn Jubayr, in his description of the grand mosque of Damascus which he visited on 11 April 1184, indicated that its annual income reached the sum of "8,000 Tyrian dīnārs, which are equivalent to about 15,000 mu'miniyyah dīnārs." The latter were the Muslim dīnārs used in the Maghrib of his time. This gold dīnār issued by the Almohad 'Abd al-Mu'min (524/1130 – 558/1163) – hence its name – weighed 2.28 g. Ibn Jubayr estimated an exchange rate of 8:15 (or 1:1.875) of the Tyrian dīnār to the Mu'min dīnār.[26] Knowing exactly the weight of the Mu'min dīnār from well-known existing specimens,[27] the Tyrian dīnār accordingly weighed 4.275 g, which is essentially the weight of the classical Byzantine gold coin.[28]

An example for the usage of Tyrian dīnārs even in an inter-Islamic conflict appears in an agreement between al-Malik az-Ẓāhir of Aleppo and al-Malik al-Manṣūr of Ḥamāh. The former agreed to lift a long siege over the latter's city in 597/1201, "provided he paid a certain sum of money said to have amounted to 30,000 Tyrian dīnārs."[29] There are many other examples for the usage of Tyrian dīnārs among Muslims. Thus the waqf established by Nūr ad-Dīn (d. 569/1174) yielded 9,000 Tyrian dīnārs a month.[30] Ṣafadī, in his biography of ad-Dakhwār aṭ-Ṭabīb, reports that the salary of this physician was 100 Tyrian dīnārs a month.[31] Bates and Metcalf are right to assume that crusader gold coins were regularly used by the Muslims "since it is known that crusader bezants came into the Moslem

---

[24] Ibn Taghrī Birdī, 6.37 (ll. 12–13), quoting Bahā' ad-Dīn Ibn Shaddād's description of the conquest of Jerusalem in 583/1187 in his an-Nawādir as-Sulṭāniyyah, ed. Gamal ad-Din ash-Shayyal (Cairo, 1964), p. 82 and n. 2. For an English translation see Bahā' al-Dīn Ibn Shaddād, The Rare and Excellent History of Saladin, trans. Donald S. Richards (Aldershot, 2001), p. 78.

[25] Ibn al-Athīr, 'Izz ad-Dīn 'Alī b. Muḥammad ash-Shaybānī, al-Kāmil fī at-Ta'rīkh (Beirut, 1982), 11.419. Cf. Steven Runciman, A History of the Crusades, 3 vols. (Cambridge, 1951–54), 2.395.

[26] Ibn Jubayr, Abū al-Ḥasan Muḥammad b. Aḥmad, Riḥlah (The Travels of Ibn Jubayr), ed. W. Wright (Leiden, 1907), p. 267.

[27] David Wasserstein, "Notes on Spanish and North African Coins in the Paul Balog Collection in the Israel Museum Jerusalem," Israel Numismatic Journal 10 (1988–89), 98–112.

[28] The difference of 25 mg between 4.275 and the 4.25 of the Byzantine coin is too small to be taken into account, especially since Ibn Jubayr himself takes such small discrepancy into account in his report ("aw naḥwihā").

[29] Abū al-Fidā' 'Imād ad-Dīn Ismā'īl, al-Mukhtaṣar fī Akhbār al-Bashar (Cairo, 1325/1907), 3.99.

[30] Ibn al-Athīr, 11.404. See also an-Nu'aymī, 'Abd al-Qadir b. Muḥammad ad-Dimashqī, ad-Dāris fī Ta'rīkh al-Madāris, ed. Ja'far al-Ḥasanī (Cairo, 1988), 1.609; Bates and Metcalf, "Crusader Coinage," p. 430 n. 25, and additional references there.

[31] aṣ-Ṣafadī, al-Wāfī bi-al-Wafāyāt.

territories as tribute, indemnities, and perhaps even trade payments, it can only be assumed that these bezants were used by Moslems in further transactions among themselves."[32] The rich evidence from the literature and the Farkhah inscription make it clear that the coin named *dīnār ṣūrī* gained respect as a reliable gold coin in spite of its inferior gold contents,[33] and passed in trade by tale, which facilitated commercial and other transactions considerably since weighing was a rather laborious procedure.

Moshe Gil drew attention to an interesting report about the Tyrian dīnār in medieval Rabbinic sources. In his commentary to the tractate Bekhorot (49b) in the Babylonian Talmud, Rashi (Rabbi Solomon b. Isaac, 1040–1105) remarks: "A Tyrian *selaʿ* means an Arab (Ishmaelite) dīnār. Its value was not clear to me; then, in the responsa of the Babylonian *Geonim*, I found that seven dīnārs were worth ten Arab ones." "In other words," says Gil, "the Arab dīnār was considered to be worth 7/10 of the Roman-Byzantine *nomisma*. Rashi further mentions that in Arabic such [Arab] dīnārs are called *migrʿot*, which is probably *mujarraʿa*. I did not find this term elsewhere, but the Hebrew meaning of 'reduced' [*migraʿot*, M.S.] may underlie it."[34]

Rashi, who lived in France, was not sure what the Tyrian dīnār really was and thought that it was an "Arab (Ishmaelite)" currency. As he died about six years after the crusader conquest of Jerusalem and almost twenty years before the crusader capture of Tyre, all Tyrian dīnārs he could have heard about were either the Fāṭimid gold coins or the Byzantine *nomisma*. It is questionable, however, whether he actually saw any of them. It is also clear that he sought more accurate information about this Tyrian currency and found it in a most reliable source: the authoritative *responsa* of the *Geonim*, the heads of the Talmudic Academies of Iraq from the end of the sixth to the beginning of the eleventh century, the last of whom had died in 1038. The *Geonim* who lived under Islamic rule were deeply involved in the economic, social and even political life of the Jewish communities as well as of the Muslim empire at large and their *responsa* constitute therefore reliable sources for economic and financial matters. According to Rashi, they differentiated between the Tyrian dīnār and the Arab coin, reporting a ratio of 7/10 between the two. This ratio is interesting because it reflects a weight of about 3.0 g of the Arab dīnār at the time (compared to 2.28 g of the Muʾmin dīnār in Ibn Jubayr's report).

It is therefore not surprising that, wishing to establish the exact value of the funds allotted to the mosque in Farkhah, the amount of three dīnārs a year was specifically fixed in Tyrian dīnārs.[35]

---

[32] Bates and Metcalf, "Crusader Coinage," p. 430 n. 25.

[33] On the reduced alloy-standard of the Frankish bezants see Metcalf, *Coinage of the Crusades* (above, n. 21), p. 44.

[34] Moshe Gil, "Additions to *Islamische Masse und Gewichte*," in *Occident and Orient. A Tribute to the Memory of Alexander Scheiber* (Leiden, 1988), p. 167.

[35] On this subject see also *Encyclopaedia of Islam* (1st and 2nd edns.), *s.v.* "Dīnār;" Maqrīzī, *Nuqūd*,

faṣal – vassal

In line 8 of the inscription appears the term *faṣal al-qaryah* – that is, the *faṣal* of the village. The previous readers of the inscription did not provide a meaningful Arabic reading for the first word. Baramkī offered the most obvious possibility and read *faḍl*, but since he offered no translation I am not sure how he understood it. *faḍl* can mean "surplus, excess, redundance" as well as "benevolence, grace, benefit, bounty, excellence," none of which fits into our text. Sukenik and Ben-Horin read *faṣl*, which means "separation, division." This again does not make too much sense unless one is ready to indulge in complicated linguistic acrobatics. In fact, however, the word does not pose a problem at all, as it is very clearly vowelled in the inscription with a *fatḥah* over the *ṣād* and therefore must be read: *faṣal*. Evidently this is a term that signifies a certain status of the village and its land, either completely or partially. It is also clear that the Amīr Bahā' ad-Dīn derived income from this *faṣal*. The wording: "*wa-awqafa 'alayhi al-amīr ... min faṣal al-qarayh al-madhkūrah ...*" (the amīr has endowed for it [=the mosque] from the *faṣal* of the aforementioned village ...), suggests that *faṣal* was used here in a sense that denotes both the status of the land and the income derived from it.

The term *faṣal* has intrigued students of the crusades, especially those dealing with the feudal system of the Latin kingdom of Jerusalem and its land tenure rules. It has been observed that a special form of vassalage developed in the kingdom, different from the one existing in feudal Europe. It stemmed from the fact that in the kingdom there was no intermediary class between the lower knights and the lords simply because the country was too small. The larger estates, which the early conquerors received, became in time very rare. The higher seigneurial class absorbed the villages and large estates, and in subsequent generations the knights of the lower class received small fiefs or even money payments, money fiefs or "*fiefs de besants*."[36] A land fief could have amounted to a small village, given to one or more knights. It seems that in such case the status of the estate was defined, as we shall see, by a term that contained the word *vassal*.

At this point we have to turn to the well known passage of Nuwayrī in which he speaks about the status of "certain areas" in Syria where the remnants of Frankish customs were still in force in his time. Shihāb ad-Dīn Aḥmad an-Nuwayrī (d. 733/1333) was a professional bureaucrat in the Mamlūk service in Syria, well acquainted with the land categories, ownership rules and regulations of the country as well as with taxation laws and various mechanisms of extortion. He

---

1968:60; N.D. Nicol, "Islamic coinage in imitation of Faṭimid types," *Israel Numismatic Journal* 10 (1988–89), 61–67.

[36] Joshua Prawer, *Histoire du royaume latin de Jérusalem*, trans. Gérard Nahon, 2 vols. (Paris, 1969–70), 1.371 n. 13; Robert Kool, "Coins at Vadum Jacob: New Evidence on the Circulation of Money in the Latin Kingdom of Jerusalem during the Second Half of the Twelfth Century," *Crusades* 1 (2002), 76. Cf. Sharon, *CIAP*, 1.179.

wrote a multi-volume work[37] summarizing the knowledge of his time in the various branches of science, language and history; it amounts to an encyclopaedic manual for the learned scribe or secretary.[38]

The passage relating to the term *faṣal* runs as follows:[39]

وفي بعض الأعمال الشامية نواح مفصولة ومضمّنة على أربابها بشيء معلوم يؤخذ منهم عند إدراك المُغَلّ من غير توكيل ولا مقاسمة، وهي نظير المتأجرات بالديار المصرية؛ ولفظ الفصَل بالشام كلّه كلمة فرَنْجية ، واستمرّ استعمالها في البلاد الساحلية التي ارتجعت من أيدي القرَنْج جريا على عادتهم.

> In some of the districts of Syria there are areas that are "*mafṣūlah*" and leased out to their holders/occupants against a fixed sum, which is taken from them when the crop is collected without [the employment of] an inspector or crop-sharing. This [method of land tenure] is similar to the "*muta'ajjarāt*" ["rented out" lands] in Egypt. Throughout Syria the term *faṣal* is a Frankish word that continued to be used in the coastal areas, which had been repossessed from the hands of the Franks, in accordance with their custom.

This passage was discussed by scholars who studied "feudal" practices in the Islamic world.[40] In June 1999 it was freshly examined by Reuven Amitai in a workshop on the governance of the Frankish Kingdom held at the Institute for Advanced Studies at the Hebrew University of Jerusalem.

The passage is clear and straightforward. Nuwayrī knew well the hierarchy of the Mamlūk socio-military system and the mechanisms by which this system derived income, preserved loyalties and paid for them. Having been part of the administration that dealt directly with the various kinds of taxation, he is a first-hand authority on land tenure, land status and land taxation. His usage of terms and terminologies connected with his profession gives the impression of accuracy and confidence. It is therefore very difficult to question his testimony that a Frankish term characterizing a special type of land tenure and land taxation continued to be used under the Mamlūks "according to their [the Franks'] custom (*'ādah*)." The term that denotes this system or "custom" is "*faṣal*." Nuwayrī made sure to indicate

---

[37] 30 volumes appearing in 33 printed ones. Cf. Ibn Ḥajar, Shihāb ad-Dīn Abū al-Faḍl Aḥmad b. ʿAlī al-ʿAsqalānī, *ad-Durar al-Kāminah fī Aʿyān al-Miʾah ath-Thāminah* (Hayderabad, AH 1348–50), 1.197 no. 506; Ibn Kathīr, Abū al-Fidāʾ Ismāʿīl, *al-Bidāyah wa-an-Nihāyah*, ed. Yūsuf ash-Shaykh and Muḥammad al-Buqāʿī (Beirut, 1996), 9.417.

[38] See *Encyclopaedia of Islam* (1st and 2nd edns.), *s.v.* "al-Nuwairī;" Ziriklī, Khayr ad-Dīn, *al-Aʿlām, Qāmūs Trājim* (Beirut, 1986), 1.165.

[39] Nuwayrī, Shihāb ad-Dīn Aḥmad b. ʿAbd al-Wahhāb, *Nihāyat al-Arab fī Funūn al-Adab*, vol. 8 (Cairo, 1931), 260–61.

[40] Claude Cahen, "Aperçu sur les impôts du sol en Syrie au moyen âge," *Journal of the Economic and Social History of the Orient* 18 (1975), 238; Joshua Prawer, *Crusader Institutions* (Oxford, 1980), p. 195; Linda S. Northrup, *From Slave to Sultan: The Career of al-Manṣūr Qalāwūn and the Consolidation of Mamlūk Rule in Egypt and Syria (678–689 A.H./1279–1290 A.D.)* (Wiesbaden, 1998), pp. 269, 276; Yehoshua Frenkel, "The Impact of the Crusades on Rural Society and Religious Endowments: The Case of Medieval Syria (Bilad al-Sham)," in Yaacov Lev, ed., *War and Society in the Eastern Mediterranean, 7th–15th Centuries* (Leiden, 1997), pp. 242–43.

that this term (*lafẓ*), which was used all over the province of ash-Shām, was a "Frankish word" (*kalimah faranjiyyah*). Aḥmad Zakī Pāshā (1867–1934), who initiated the publication of Nuwayrī's *magnum opus* within his larger project of the Revival of the Arabic Book, and edited its early volumes, was the first to identify the word *faṣal* as the Arabic form, or pronunciation, of vassal. Having explained that originally the term described a subordinate person holding land under the obligation of rendering service (military or its equivalent) to his superior, he goes on to clarify that "the people of Syria used it as a verbal noun depicting subordination (*wa-'arādū bihi al-ma'nā al-maṣdarī ayy at-taba'iyyah*); then, because of constraints of their Arabic pronunciation, they corrupted it into *faṣal*, as it is written here, from which they derived the term '*mafṣūlah*'."[41] The corruption in pronunciation of the Latin "s" or the Greek sigma to ṣād is common (for example, *qayṣar, ṣanjīl, ṣābūn, ṣandal, qunṣul*), but Aḥmad Zakī Pāshā, who was an accomplished linguist, made sure to confirm the obvious. Yet the term "*mafṣūlah*," defining the status of the land given to a person in the status of *faṣal*, has already all the features of pure Arabic; it is the passive participle of the root f-ṣ-l which, not surprisingly, could easily be understood to form the basis of (the foreign) *faṣal* as well. Nuwayrī, therefore, makes a point to emphasize that the origin of the word is Frankish and that it denoted a Frankish custom.

Had the present inscription not been found, scholars questioning Nuwayrī's credibility and arguing that his testimony is uncorroborated, could have had a case. However, information supplied by an inscription is, on the whole, as solid as the material on which it was incised, especially when the information is offered in passing. Our inscription speaks about a *faṣal* in a village that until 1187, merely 23 years before its incision, was under Frankish rule. Since Nuwayrī describes a state of affairs in Syria, where he himself was employed at the beginning of the fourteenth century,[42] it is clear that we are facing here a well-entrenched institution, which had been already in practice since the early Ayyūbid rule, that is, for at least a century. It must have served its purpose very well if it endured for so long a period.

Before analysing Nuwayrī's passage, let us go back to the inscription. It says that a high-ranking officer, an amīr, a first-generation Muslim of Turkish origin who must have been in the service of an Ayyūbid superior (Saladin or al-Malik al-'Ādil?), endowed annually the rather modest amount of three dīnārs for the mosque of the village. This sum came from the money which the village paid him, because the endowment is defined as deriving from "the *faṣal* of the aforementioned village." Evidently the amīr received this income from the village in return for some service which he had to render to his Ayyūbid superior, but the payments by the village were clearly defined as *faṣal*, namely a fixed sum unrelated to the size of the crops and, one may add, with no need for supervising and registering the size of the cultivated land, the olive groves or the harvest. Because it was a fixed

---

[41] Aḥmad Zakī Pāshā in Nuwayrī, *Nihāyat al-Arab fī Funūn al-Adab*, 8.261 n. 1.
[42] See *Encyclopaedia of Islam*, 2nd edn, 8.156–60.

payment, the amīr could define his endowment in an exact sum as well, specified in the most accurate currency of the time: "Tyrian dīnārs." Is not this what Nuwayrī tells us?

There are areas in some of the Syrian districts, he says, which are administered according to the *faṣal* custom that continued from the time of the Frankish rule. According to this system the land is leased out to its occupants, or holders, against a determined payment (*muḍammanah 'alā arbābihā bishay' ma'lūm*), which they have (collectively) to pay at harvest time to the amīr who, in Frankish terms, would be the vassal of the lord who granted him this income. This system of payment is not crop-sharing (*muqāsamah*), which means that it is not dependent on the size of the produce (be it large or small), and that it does not involve the appointment (*tawkīl*) of an inspector-agent (*wakīl*) to supervise the size of the cultivated land and the crops so as to prevent cheating. In the previous passage Nuwayrī explains exactly the function of the *wakīl*, saying that he closely supervised the process of harvesting (especially of cotton, rice, almonds, olives, pistachio, walnuts and the like) until the produce reached its gathering places (*ilā an yaṣīr fī bayādirihi*), where its proper sharing out or division (*maqāsamah*) could take place, setting aside the percentage of the crop as tax (*ḍarībah*) or payment to whom it was due.[43] This system of crop-sharing, which meant payments made in kind, is clearly distinguished from the *faṣal* custom, to which Nuwayrī brings a parallel from Egypt where a similar arrangement called *muta'ajjarāt* existed. The term suggests leasing or renting out land against fixed payment, exactly as any other property (houses, shops) was leased or rented out. From my personal experience I can vouch that both systems – of crop-sharing, and of renting cultivable land against fixed payment – have survived in the country until the present.

The *faṣal* custom which, as we have just learnt from the Farkhah inscription, existed in Muslim Syria under the Ayyūbids, continued to be employed, following the Frankish feudal system, in some parts of the lands reconquered from the Franks. Under the Ayyūbids, the custom was employed in parts of the country's interior, the first to come under their rule after Ḥiṭṭīn. When the Mamlūks finally occupied the coastal areas, the *faṣal* was used also there, as Nuwayrī confirms speaking about his own time, that is, some twenty years after the conquest of Acre that marked the end of Frankish presence in Syria.

It would be far fetched to conclude, on the basis of Nuwayrī's information and the Farkhah inscription, that the *faṣal* method was similar to a variant of the already mentioned money fief (*fief de besants*) of the Franks.[44] Money fiefs (Lat. *feodum de bursa*; Fr. *fief de bourse, fief de chambre*; Ger. *Kammerlehen*) existed also in Europe. The earliest example dates from 1087 and comes from Flanders, but the most extensive use of this kind of fief was made by the English kings after Henry I

---

[43] Nuwayrī, *Nihāyat al-Arab fī Funūn al-Adab*, 8.260.
[44] Prawer, *Histoire du royaume latin de Jérusalem*, 1.371–72.

(1100–35). In France the first to make a money grant was Louis VII in 1155/56.⁴⁵ The difference between the *faṣal* and the "money fief" is that in the latter the "fief" involved only money and was not connected with any land property whatsoever. In the case of the *faṣal*, both the inscription and Nuwayrī's report speak about the income derived from land property granted to the amīr-vassal; he *rented it out* to its actual holders for a fixed payment that did not take into consideration the peasants' income from it.

Neither is this arrangement, which Nuwayrī compares to the *mut'ajjarāt* in Egypt, similar to the extraordinary tax which the general council of the Latin Kingdom imposed early in 1183. On that occasion, described in detail by William of Tyre, the lords of each village had to pay one bezant for each hearth in their possession and then collect this sum from their peasants.⁴⁶ The decree of 1183 spoke about an actual tax imposed on everybody: churches, monasteries, barons, vassals and mercenaries. The imposition of one bezant on each hearth was probably an easy way of establishing the amount of money due from owners of *casalia*, but it was a tax which the lords had first to pay and then to reimburse themselves by extracting it from the peasants in addition to their usual income from the produce of the land. It is also very possible that the edict of 1183 was a one-off tax imposed to meet emergency circumstances. In the case of our *faṣal* the situation described was totally different. Here the money due to the lord was related neither to the number of households nor to the quantity of the produce. It was a known sum of money paid by the cultivators for renting the land as one pays rent for any other property. The income which the lord usually received from his land as a percentage of the produce (*muqāsamah*) was transformed in the *faṣal* system into a fixed rental.

The Date

The way the date is given in the inscription (ll. 9–10) is also unusual. One rarely finds the day of the month defined as *li-'istiqbāl*.⁴⁷ The word *istiqbāl* denotes the full moon of every month just as *hilāl* (crescent) means the month's first day. The word signifies the opposition of two heavenly bodies and in this case the moon on the fifteenth of the lunar month is in direct opposition to the sun. I calculated the date as the fifteenth of the Muslim month which begins on the evening of the following day.

---

⁴⁵ Marc Bloch, *Feudal Society*, trans. L.A. Manyon, 2 vols. (London, 1962), 1.174; François-Louis Ganshof, *Feudalism*, trans. Philip Grierson (New York, 1961), pp. 114–15.

⁴⁶ WT 22.24, p. 1045. Cf. Benjamin Z. Kedar, "The General Tax of 1183 in the Crusading Kingdom of Jerusalem: Innovation or Adaptation?", *English Historical Review* 89 (1974), 339; repr. in his *The Franks in the Levant, 11th to 14th Centuries* (Aldershot, 1993), no. VII.

⁴⁷ It is not surprising that Baramki did not recognize this usage and instead placed two lines that look like the number 11 (١١) before the month.

Conclusion

The discovery of the term *faṣal* in an inscription from the Ayyūbīd period, and its use in a matter-of-fact manner, proves that Nuwayrī was indeed accurate in his report. The term and the customs accompanying it continued to be employed in some territories that had been under Frankish rule for a long time after their return to Muslim hands. With his keen sensitivity for important details the Muslim encyclopaedist could not miss the peculiarity of a Frankish land tenure custom followed by Muslims. The fact that a similar system of *muta'jjarāt* existed also in Muslim lands (Nuwayrī mentions Egypt), must not be taken as the reason for the acceptance of the foreign term and the foreign custom by the Muslims. It was rather the effective system of land tenure which the *faṣal* offered that tipped the scale in favour of the perpetuation of its usage.

Inventio Patriarcharum

R.B.C. Huygens

University of Leiden

This article forms the first part of a project undertaken jointly by the author and Benjamin Z. Kedar; Kedar's commentary will appear in a forthcoming issue of *Crusades*.

Introduction

The two texts published here[1] have never been edited critically before. Parts of nr. I, about one-third of it, were first printed in the *Acta Sanctorum* (AA SS) (October 9, vol. IV, 1780, pp. 688–90, nrs. 533–43), then, unabridged, by Count Paul Riant in a posthumous contribution to the *Recueil des Historiens des Croisades* 5, 1895, pp. 302–14. Text nr. II was printed in the *Revue de l'Orient latin* 4, 1896, pp. 496–502, by Ch. Kohler, who had already seen Riant's text through the printing. Kohler had stumbled upon a bad manuscript in Avranches: unfortunately, I have been unable to find any more copies and thus enlarge the manuscript basis of this otherwise interesting account: in spite of quite a few corrections made by both Kohler and myself, its textual quality is still far from satisfactory. A third version of the events leading up to and including the discovery of the patriarchs' remains (BHL 10) was edited by Riant under the title *Tractatus eiusdem* (= I) *Breviarium* (l.c., pp. 314–16), but since it is only an abridgment of the first text, I have used it as just another manuscript, of which the readings are listed in the critical apparatus under the siglum B.

Text I: the oldest, and by far the most important manuscript of this text had remained unknown to both Riant and Kohler. It was discovered by Albert Poncelet,[2] who mentioned it in the *Analecta Bollandiana* (AB) 20, 1901, p. 406 and printed its final lines (412–22), which are lacking in all other manuscripts (p. 464). This manuscript is Douai 851, written in a beautiful hand shortly after 1200, f. 93v–103v (Catalogue général 6, p. 598), which came from Anchin and contains two more hagiographical texts. I list its readings under the siglum D. The manuscript Riant reproduced is my L: Leiden, Vossianus *lat.* 4° 125, f. 195–205v, of the 14th century (catalogue 2, 1975, pp. 273–74). This manuscript also contains the *Historia*

---

[1] Bibliotheca hagiographica latina (BHL) (1898–99), nrs. 9 and 11. For BHL 10, see below.

[2] As a token of respect for this learned Jesuit, and for all Bollandists his successors, I'd like to mention that Father Poncelet's obituary, with a portrait and a bibliography, appeared in the *Analecta Bollandiana*, (AB) 31 (1912), pp. 129–41.

Orientalis and *Occidentalis* of James of Vitry, as well as his Letter VIa (Huygens, *Serta mediaevalia* I, 2000, p. 505). Riant also used a complete copy of a (now lost?) manuscript of Saint-Martin of Tournai,[3] made in 1671 by the Carmelite Father Joseph-Ignace de Saint-Antoine for the Bollandist Daniel Papebroch, and which served to print the above-mentioned chapters in the *Acta Sanctorum*. I call this copy (in the Library of the Bollandists in Brussels: *Collectanea Bollandiana* 162, f. 53–60): T^1. Unbeknown to Riant (but not to Kohler) another copy exists (T^2), which was made by the same Carmelite for another priest, Charles du Molinet, and now is in Paris in the library of Sainte-Geneviève – of which Kohler happened to be the librarian (ms. nr. 693, just 5 ff.). Both T^1 and T^2, although written by the same man, are independently made copies of the Tournai manuscript, and their consensus is listed here under the siglum T. But where T^1 and T^2 disagree among each other, one of them quite frequently agrees with D, the other with (one of) the other manuscripts – a fact I'm unable to explain. Unfortunately, we are in the dark about its date, but its text certainly was better than that of L, with which it belongs to the same branch of the manuscript tradition – quite apart from the fact that T ends with exactly the same words as L. The original manuscript of Riant's "Breviarium" (= B), of which text Riant/Kohler used another copy in the Bollandists' library, actually still exists: it is now Lille 450, of the second half of the 13th century, from Loos-Notre-Dame. It counts two foliations, of which the second f. 57–58v contain the abridged text. The Catalogue général (26, p. 300) does mention the text, but in the Index one has to look for it on p. 837 under the heading "Saints." B lacks the Prologue (27 lines) as well as the last 16 lines, and in between, apart from numerous short omissions, there are several longer ones, such as 30–38, 40–57, 73–83, 117–34, 159–230, 232–44 and 271–82. And two more notable omissions, viz. of the epitheton *impios* before *Iudeos* (85) and of lines 402–403, where B leaves out the criticism of the patriarch of Jerusalem and restricts itself to writing *Prior autem* instead. Except for line 270, where B supports the spelling of the name *Rainerius* in D, and in 337: *fer(m)e* (B+DT^1), the Lille manuscript presents the same readings as T, L or TL, so that we can safely divide the manuscript tradition of text I into two groups: D, which forms the basis of this edition, on the one hand, and the three remaining witnesses TLB on the other. This being established, I have judged it unnecessary, and even undesirable, to overburden the critical apparatus beyond all proportion by reproducing all of B's readings and omissions: they add nothing and serve merely *ad implendas paginas*. So only in a few relevant cases have these variants been added to those of the other manuscripts.

---

[3] A large number of manuscripts from this Benedictine abbey still exist. The catalogue of the Tournai manuscripts (1950) does not mention the text, and I have to thank Mesdames De Smet and Favier for checking the manuscripts of the Bibliothèque Municipale, and M. l'abbé Dubois those in the library of the Séminaire. See also L. Delisle, *Le cabinet des manuscrits* 1 (1868), pp. 305–307 and 2 (1874), pp. 487–92, and *The Phillipps Manuscripts* ... with an introduction by A.N.L. Munby (London 1968), pp. 23–25, nrs. 2011–156, and, by the same author, *Phillipps Studies*, nr. 3 (1954), p. 22, note, and *Portrait of an Obsession: the Life of Sir Thomas Phillipps* (1967), pp. 17–18.

The use, and the adoption into the text, of two words requires an explanation. As a rule, *illic/illuc* and *consilium/concilium* are used correctly. *Illic* instead of *illuc* occurs frequently in more than one text, and *illuc* can often be explained by an idea of movement. But in I,399 (*patriarche*) *qui tunc temporis illic* (TL, *illuc* D) *preerat*, I have adopted the reading of TL, and the same applies to lines 98 and 344, where D presents *concilio inter se habito* and *accersito fratrum concilio*, but TL *consilio* (cf. 114 *initoque cum sapientibus regni sui consilio*). I'm perfectly aware of the fact that these confusions are quite common, but we should also take into account that in the present case we are dealing with a well-written, usually correctly spelled 12th c. text, and that D, however good in general, is still only a copy, and not an altogether faultless one at that. Therefore, in the above-mentioned cases, I have adopted the correct spellings and grammatically correct forms: *malo errare cum ratione*.

Text II: the manuscript Avranches 130, second half of the 13th century, f. 79v–81v, comes from the Mont-Saint-Michel, as do so many other manuscripts in that library (Catalogue général (4, p. 491 and) 10, p. 59).The first lines are corrupt already (actually, even the very first word!), and the scribe either did not understand much of the text he copied, or (and?) his model was also a bad one. Kohler corrected a few obvious mistakes, but left more than enough for this editor: my own corrections have all been identified as such.

The orthography of text I is that of manuscript D, in which the name of the central figure is always spelled *Arnulfus* (*Arnulphus* TLB), and one of the patriarchs both *Isaac* and *Ysaac*. The orthography of II is that of the only known (Avranches) manuscript. This last text presents also two words which after considerable hesitation I have maintained, since (or rather: although) they are little or not at all attested elsewhere: 133 *contentus* ("its contents") and 137 *illibare* (= *infundere*, "communicate," "impart"), and I have added a cautioning note on each of these passages.

Text I

Karitate vestra me compellente, immo sancto Spiritu stimulante, fratres karissimi qui Cariatarbe estis, vestris volens parere iussionibus opus michi iniunctum incipere nequaquam distuli, sed statim acceptis tabulis iuxta preceptum vestrum quomodo sanctorum patriarcharum, Abraham videlicet, Isaac et Iacob corpora inventa fuerint
5 describere satis timide temptavi: grave quidem opus, sed dignum memorie commendandum. Unde, licet ad hoc explanandum meis meritis me non posse sufficere non ignorem, vestris tamen confisus precibus que hortati estis aggressus sum, et satis cum periculo. Cum enim in quantis deliquerim recordor et hoc quanta extollendum sit laude perpendo, peccatum super peccatum apponere valde
10 pertimesco, cum dominus sub interrogatione peccatori prohibeat, dicens: *Quare tu enarras iustitias meas et assumis testamentum meum per os tuum? Tu vero odisti disciplinam et proiecisti sermones meos retrorsum*. Sed tamen contra hec omnia de eiusdem misericordia non diffido, dicentis: *Peccator quacumque hora ad me conversus fuerit, omnium offensionum eius non recordabor*. In illo itaque totam
15 spem meam pono, ad ipsum totis visceribus confugio, ipsi soli mee timide navis vela omni devotione committo, qui surdos fecit audire et mutos loqui. Scio namque qui dixit: *Aperi os tuum, et ego adimplebo illud*. Sed absit quod me tanti meriti esse pronuntiem, potens est tamen dominus etiam de lapidibus suscitare filios Abrahe. Vos ergo, fratres karissimi, quia tantum opus me subire voluistis, pulsate deum
20 precibus, interpellate misericordiam Redemptoris nostri, ut qui sanctorum corpora vobis revelare dignatus est, dignetur etiam in ore meo ponere sermonem rectum et benesonantem, quo sanctorum inventionem digne declarare queam ad laudem et gloriam ipsorum. Ego vero sicut ab ipsis inventoribus, religiosis scilicet viris

---

1 = 190–191.   **5** *satis timide* = 301, cf. 15.—opus] See the critical apparatus.   **8** Cf. Marc. 15, 4: *Vide in quantis te accusant.*   **9** Eccli. 5, 5: *neque adicias peccatum super peccatum.*   **10–12** Ps. 49, 16–17.   **13–14** Dan. 3, 15: *quacumque hora.*—Ezech. 33, 12. 16 and 18, 21–22; Is. 43, 25, Hebr. 10, 17.   **14–15** (= 205–6) Ps. 72, 28 (77, 7): *ponere in domino deo spem meam.*   **15** *totis visceribus*: Hieronymus *in prophetas minores*, Habacuc 2, 3, 14–16, CC 76A, p. 643, 937–938; Gregory the Great, *Ep.* 5, 44, CC 140, p. 331, 43–44 and *Moralia in Iob* 33, 5, 11, CC 143B, p. 1679, 20.   **15** *timide* cf. 5. 301.   **16** Marc. 7, 37.   **17** Ezech. 2, 8; Ps. 80, 11.   **18** Matth. 3, 9; Luc. 3, 8. **22–23** Philipp. 1, 11: *in gloriam et laudem dei.*   **23–24** Cf. 275.

1–27 *om.*B   **1** Raritate (!) L   spiritu sancto TL   **4** videlicet DT², et *add.* L, *om.*T¹   fuerunt TL   **5** timide temptavi] timui TL   opus] *an* onus (*Ps. 37, 5*)? *cf.* 2.19. **7** tamen *om.* TL   que] quod T   **9** quantum L   sit extollendum TL   **10** peccatori D *et ut vid.* L, peccatorem T   **11** Tu ... 12 retrorsum *om.*L   **15** visceribus DT², viribus T¹L   mee timidus T², timidus mee T¹   **16** qui ... loqui *om.*T   et *om.*L   qui DT², quod T¹L   **17** ego *om.*T   **18** tamen est dominus T, est deus tamen L   et de T, de tantum L   **19** igitur T   quia] qui T   **21** nobis L   etiam] et T   **23** sicut *om.*L   inventoribus ipsis T   viris scilicet TL

Arnulfo et Odone, sub canonica regula ibi deo militantibus, michi relatum est, que etiam a quodam greco montis Synay monacho sub Theodosio imperatore facta didici, diligenter in unum colligens nichilque de meo apponens, licet rusticano stilo, tamen veracissimo, deo adiuvante patefaciam.

Beatos igitur patriarchas Abraham, Isaac et Iacob in Ebron civitate Iudee, que nomine alio Arbe antea dicta est, sepultos fuisse cum uxoribus suis nullus fidelium ambigit qui plene et studiose librum Geneseos legerit. Legitur namque in fine eiusdem libri quia cum Iacob infirmaretur in Egypto vocavit duodecim filios suos, quibus singulis singulas benedictiones dedit, precepitque eis dicens: *Ego congredior ad populum meum*, tollite me hinc et portate in Ebron ibique *me sepelite cum patribus meis in spelunca duplici, quam emit Abraham cum agro ab Ephron Etheo in possessionem sepulcri. Ibi sepelierunt eum cum Sara coniuge, ibi sepultus est Ysaac et Rebecca, ibi et Lia condita iacet.* Mortuo itaque Iacob fecerunt filii eius sicut preceperat eis et conditum aromatibus tulerunt in Ebron posueruntque eum in sepulcro patrum suorum. Ibi etiam ferunt prothoplastum Adam fuisse sepultum, quod bene ex libro Iosue intelligi potest, ubi scriptum est: *Dedit Iosue Caleph filio Iephone Ebron, ubi Adam maximus situs est*. De hoc testatur beatus Ambrosius, in libro de creatione Ade dicens: *In valle Ebron formatus est Adam primus omnium et de eodem loco in paradysum assumptus, unde propter inobedientiam expulsus deiectus est in valle lacrimarum, de qua assumptus fuerat, ibique mortuus sepultus est a filiis suis in spelunca duplici*. Non inconvenienter ergo veteres locum illum Cariatarbe, id est 'Sepulcrum quatuor', appellare voluerunt, cum isti quatuor

---

24 2 Tim. 2, 4: *nemo militans deo* ...   **25** Cf. 235.—*Theodosio* (II) *imperatore* (408–450) = 106–107.   **28–29** Gen. 23, 2: *in civitate Arbee, quae est Hebron*.   **30–36** (cf. 182–183) Gen. 48, 1 and 49, 1. 29–31, cf. 50, 24.   **32** *singulis singulas* cf. 387. **37** *conditum aromatibus*: Gen. 50, 2 and 25; Ex. 13, 19 and Ios. 24, 32.   **39–40** Ios. 14, 14–15.   **41–44** I have been unable to trace this quotation. Maybe one should even print: *in libro <De ... > de creatione Ade dicens* ...   **45–46** Cf. Hieronymus, *Hebraicae quaestiones* (Gen. 23, 2, *cf.* ad 28–29), CC 72, p. 28, 27–29: ... *dicitur arbee, hoc est quatuor, quia ibi Abraham et Isaac et Iacob conditus est et ipse princeps humani generis Adam*, or *Ep.* 108, 11, CSEL 55, p. 319, 8–11: *Chebron, haec est Chariatharbe, id est "oppidum virorum quattuor," Abraham, Isaac et Iacob et Adam magni, quem ibi conditum ... Hebraei autumant* (I'm unaware of any variant reading *sepulc(h)rum*).

---

24 que] qui TL   **25** etiam] et T   factam T   **27** patefaciam] Qui vi(vit) et reg(nat) *add.* L, qui vivit et regnat in saecula saeculorum. Amen *add.* Riant (!)   **28** Iudee *om.*T   **29** alio nomine TB   **30** Legitur ... 38 suorum *om.*B   **31** quia] quod TL **32** Ego *om.*TL   **33** egredior TL   **34** meis] nostris L   **34–35** ab Ephron Etheo cum agro T   **35** sepulture T   Ibi ... ibi] Ibi ... ibique T¹, ibique ... ibi L, ibique ... ibique T²   coniuge] sua *add.* TL   **36** et Rebecca DT², cum Rebecca LT¹   Mortuo itaque] Mortuoque T², Mortuo T¹   fecerant L   **40** maximus Adam TL   De ... 57 testatur *om.* B, *cf. adn. ad 41–44*.   De] et T   sanctus T   **41** omnium *om.*L **42** assumptus est in paradisum TL   **43** vallem T   mortuus *om.*T

viri ibidem sepulti referantur. Illa eadem etiam vallis 'Vallis plorationis' et
'benedictionis' dicta est, plorationis eo quod ibi fleverit Adam propter filium suum
quem occiderat Cain, benedictionis autem quia in ea benedixit deus Abraham,
dicens: *Benedicens benedicam tibi et multiplicabo te*, et iterum: *in semine,* inquit,
50   *tuo benedicentur omnes gentes*. Hec, fratres karissimi, ideo satis prolixe sed tamen
congrue replicavimus, ne quis forte, quod absit, ita esse ut diximus hesitet; sed quia
sunt nonnulli qui nominare quidem speluncam duplicem sciunt, sed cuiusmodi
locus sit penitus ignorant, dignum, prout vidimus, duximus explanandum, ut cum
mirificam difficultatem ipsius audierint, beatos patriarchas non sine divino miraculo
55   repertos esse fateantur.

Venerandus ille locus, in quo sanctorum corpora requiescunt, quante auctoritatis
quanteque reverentie et excellentie apud veteres fuerit ipsius edificii fabrica testatur.
Circumcludit namque eum murus altus et fortis aspectuque mirabilis, ex magnis
quadratisque atque politis lapidibus miro modo compositus, habens intrinsecus X et
60   VIII cubitos altitudinis, nonaginta IIII longitudinis, XLVIII latitudinis. Pavimentum
etiam cernitur intus similiter ex magnis quadratisque lapidibus pulcre et mirabiliter
constructum, adeo solidum et forte, ut quelibet magna fabrica firmiter super illud
fundari queat. Durities vero lapidum utriusque edificii omne genus marmoris
excedit. Totum autem opus ita compaginatum et inter se conexum est, ut minimus
65   qui interest lapis non sine laboriosa gravedine tolli possit. Continentur preterea intus
VI piramides, in honore sanctorum Abraham, Isaac et Iacob et uxorum eorum
fabricate sibique alternatim opposite, id est piramides virorum contra piramidas
feminarum, uniuscuiusque contra comparem suam, sed que sub nomine sancti
Abrahe et beate Sare dicuntur in medio sunt, que autem Isaac et Rebecce ad plagam
70   orientalem, ille quidem que Iacob et Lie nomine vocantur ad occidentalem.
Spelunca vero duplex sub piramide sancti Abrahe in profundum sita est, a
pavimento habens cubitos ferme XIIII. Huius tam mirandi operis constructores

---

46–47 Gen. 4, 8 (*vallis benedictionis*: 2 Paral. 20, 26).   **49–50** (cf. 313) Gen. 22, 17–18 and 26, 4.   **58–59** Cf. 61. 329.   **59–60** A *cubitus* being 1½ *pes* = 45 cm., these measures are: 8 m. 10 high, 42 m. 30 long, and 21 m. 60 wide.   **61** Cf. 58–59. 329. **72** (cf. 59–60) *Ca.* 6 m. 30.

---

46 eadem *om*.TL   **47** suum *om*.T   **48** dominus T   **49** alt. et *om*.T   inquit *om*. TL   **50** Hoc T   ideo *om*.T   sed tamen] si tamen T², sed satis T¹   **52** quidem *et* duplicem *om*.TL   **53** enarrandum T   **54** eius T   beatos] bonos (*cf. 165. 167*) T   **58** aspectu L   **59** quadratis TLB, *cf. 61*.   (*cf. 329*) impolitis T   habens] Huius T   **60** nonaginta IIII longitudinis *om*.TLB   quadraginta (et *add*. B) novem TLB   **61** similiter] scilicet T   (*cf. 59*) quadratis TLB   laudabiliter T   **62** magna] mag̃ (= magis) D   firmiter *om*.TLB   super illud *om*.D   **64** inter] in T   **65** non h. l. *om*.TL (tolli non possit T), haut B   **66** sanctorum patriarcharum TLB, *cf. 377*. **67** piramidas] piramides TLB   **68** sed] scilicet T   **69** autem *om*.TLB   sancti Isaac T

quidam Esau et Iacob autumant, sed periculosum est valde affirmare quod ex veritate nescitur: hoc unum profecto scimus, quod ob reverentiam sanctorum factum sit. Sciendum quoque est quod civitas illa Cariatarbe, que et Ebron, a tempore quo sorte divisa est terra repromissionis filiis Israel, sacerdotum semper fuisse memoratur. Sic enim in libro Iosue scriptum est: *Dedit Iosue filiis Aaron sacerdotis Cariatarbe, que vocatur Ebron, in monte Iuda, et suburbana eius per circuitum, agros quoque et villas eius, que dederat Chaleph filio Iephone ad possidendum.* Dignum quippe erat ut de quibus summus sacerdos, id est Christus, nasciturus erat, eos sacerdotes venerarentur et colerent, sicque sacerdotes Levitici generis usque ad adventum Christi ibidem extitisse et post usque ad tempus Titi et Vespasiani Romanorum principum credimus consedisse.

Predictis autem principibus regnantibus orta est non minima persecutio adversos impios Iudeos, in tantum, ut aut vix aut nullus in tota terra repromissionis posset inveniri Iudeus qui vel alienigenis turpiter non venderetur vel ab illis gladio violenter trucidaretur, sicque factum est ut omnis Iudea redigeretur in solitudinem nec esset qui habitaret in ea, exceptis paucis fidelibus, qui propter metum incredulorum in montibus latitantes de radicibus erbarum vitam sustentabant, pauperes facti propter deum, ut ab ipso eternaliter ditari mererentur. Hi, videntes quod factum fuerat et totam terram habitatore vacuam, exeuntes de speluncis sancta loca, que de se ipso dominus sanctificaverat, tantummodo occupaverunt, in ipsis die noctuque ei servientes, vigilando, ieiunando, orando ob amorem patrie celestis sua corpora afficientes deoque preces assiduas fundentes, ut sine timore, de manu inimicorum suorum liberati, servirent illi in sanctitate et iustitia. Et convenerunt ad eos diversi ordinis multi Christiani, episcopi, presbiteri, diacones, subdiacones, a domino consolationem expectantes, parati etiam corpora sua tradere propter deum ad supplicia, et consilio inter se habito in singulis in quibus habitabant civitatibus episcopos, archiepiscopos constituerunt, Cesaree videlicet, Ierosolimis et Bethsan et multis aliis. In Ebron quoque archipresulem et cum eo sacri ordinis ministros

---

73 Cf. Gregory the Great, *Ep.* 5, 51, CC 140, p. 345, 3, and *Hom.in Hiezech.* 1, 11, CC 142, p. 176, 283: *valde periculosum est ...*   **73–74** ex veritate] Ioh. 18, 37; 1 Ioh. 2, 21 and 3, 19.   **77–79** Ios. 21, 9–12.   **80** *Dignum* cf. 173.   **81** sacerdotes Levitici generis] Ios. 21, 10.   **84** Act. 8, 1: *Facta est autem in illa die persecutio magna.*   **87** Cf. Ier. 2, 15.   **88–89** Ioh. 7, 13 and 19, 38: *propter metum Iudaeorum.*   **90** *propter deum* (= 97.271): 1 Petr. 2, 13.   **94–95** Luc. 1, 74–75: *ut sine timore, de manu inimicorum nostrorum liberati, serviamus illi in sanctitate et iustitia.*   **96–97** Iudith 8, 20: *Exspectemus ... consolationem eius.*   **97** *propter deum* = 90.

---

73 sed ... 83 consedisse *om*.B   **75** fuerit TL   que est L   **76** semper *om*.TL   esse T   **77** sacerdotibus TL   **79** agrosque L   quas T   Caleph TL   **81** Davitici (!) Riant   **85** impios *om*.B   Iudeos *om*.L   nullus] nullum T   possit T   **88** habitasset L, in ea habitaret B   **89** de ... 90 mererentur *om*.B   **90** facti] sunt *add.* TL   **92** se *om*.L   **93** patie (*sic*) D, patriae T², patris T¹ L   **95** liberarentur et (ut T¹) TL   **96** multi *om*.TL   **98** (114. 344) concilio D   **99** episcopos] et *add.* T

destinaverunt, confirmantes et multorum testimonio approbantes quod aliquando metropolis Philistinorum civitas fuerit: hoc ipsum autem Iosephus et Eusebius Cesariensis necnon Ieronimus affirmant. Et ex ipsis episcopis et presbiteris multi ab infidelibus rapiebantur diversisque penis excruciati ad ultimum miserabiliter
105 detruncabantur.

Multorum vero annorum labente termino, piissimo imperatore Theodosio regnante, aperte sunt ecclesie Christi, pullulavit fides evangelii, crevit christiani populi numerus, fidelibus ministris per universum mundum divini verbi semina rudibus populis spargentibus. Hic conglobata ad se multa credentium turba cepit
110 sanctorum martyrum inquirere corpora, qui ab iniquis predecessoribus suis imperatoribus vel eorum satellitibus in diversis mundi partibus, et maxime in Oriente, interempti fuerant, et Constantinopolim transferre et in honore ipsorum basilicas edificare. Facta est etiam non parva inquisitio de beatis patriarchis Abraham, Isaac et Iacob, initoque cum sapientibus regni sui consilio copiosam
115 multitudinem cum episcopis et clericis direxit in Iudeam, qui sanctorum patriarcharum sacrosancta ossa diligenti cura inquirerent et, si ullomodo posset, honorifice ad eum Constantinopolim deferrent, mandans insuper beato archipresuli, qui tunc temporis Cariatarbe preerat, ut eos summo studio iuvaret. Ipse enim christianissimus princeps in Oriente usque in Alexandriam et ultra principabatur,
120 nec erat qui eo tempore Christianos perturbaret: per omnem enim terram illam erant Greci christiani. O pia presumptio! Tantum enim pia illa mens de dei misericordia presumebat, ut se posse impetrare crederet quod adhuc non merebatur, et pie inscius voluntati domini contraire conabatur. Putas quantis afflictionibus se macerabat qui tantum thesaurum habere cupiebat: pernoctans siquidem in orationibus flebat
125 ubertim et sanctarum illarum reliquiarum ardenti desiderio estuans, inter preces, quas sepius domino fundebat, hoc summum et precipuum postulabat, ut suum deus desiderium implere dignaretur. Aut non sufficiebant ei tot et tam sancte reliquie, VII

102–103 = 241–242. I have found no such identification in any of the authors mentioned, neither in the original texts nor in Latin translations.　　**106** *piissimo* = 231.244.
106–107 Cf. 25.　　**107** Rom. 16, 16: *ecclesiae Christi*.　　**108** 2 Macch. 3, 12: *per universum mundum*.　　**121–122** Iudith 9, 17: *de tua misericordia praesumentem*.
124 Luc. 6, 12: *pernoctans in oratione*.

---

102 civitas *om*.T　　ipsum autem] et (etiam L) ipse TL　　**103** affirmavit L　　et *om*.T　　**107–108** populi christiani T　　**108** fidelibus] Christi *add*. TL　　sermonis L　　**109** Sic T　　conglomerata L, *cf.* 376.　　**110** corpora inquirere TL　　**111** imperatoribus ... satellitibus *om*.T　　diversi L　　**112** ipsorum] eorum B, episcoporum T　　**113** etiam] et T　　**116** ossa sacrosancta TL　　possent TL　　**117** mandans ... 134 declarabunt *om*.B　　**120** eo tempore qui TL　　conturbaret T　　**121** pia ... pia] pia ... tua TL　　**122** posse *om*.D　　imperare T, *corr*. T²　　non *om*.L　　**123** se macerabat afflictionibus T¹, se afflictionibus macerabat T²　　**124–125** ubertim flebat T　　**127** sufficiebat L　　VII] sex TL

videlicet apostolorum et beati Luce evangeliste, beati etiam protomartyris Stephani et aliorum plurimorum tam martyrum quam confessorum et virginum corpora, que beata Elena in basilica sua digno honore collocaverat? Non utique! Dicebat enim: 'Non sufficit michi, nisi sanctorum patriarcharum corpora habeam.' Sed fraudatus est a desiderio suo. Verumtamen, quia nolebat deus preces eius remanere vacuas, dedit illi thesaurum preciosum, corpus scilicet beati Ioseph filii Israel, quemadmodum sequentia declarabunt.

   Venientes igitur cum apparatu multo qui missi a Theodosio erant in Iudeam, sciscitati sunt Ebron ubi esset; quo cum pervenissent, locuti sunt ad archiepiscopum loci eiusdem, pacifice ex parte Theodosii eum salutantes causamque vie innotescentes et suppliciter rogantes ut illis speluncam duplicem demonstraret. Quo audito sacerdos, ut erat vir columbine simplicitatis, prorumpens in lacrimas satis consulte respondit eis, dicens: 'Gravissimum est, filii, quod requiritis: speluncam quidem duplicem aspectu non novi, ubi tamen sanctorum corpora sepulta perhibentur nequaquam ignoro: en habetur intra muros' – muros enim ostenderat eis–, atque subiunxit: 'Manete ergo apud me aliquantis diebus et requiescite, longi enim itineris labore fatigati estis, et interim deo humiliter votiva precamina offeramus, ut ipse occultum thesaurum nobis aperire dignetur, et eius voluntas fiat: absque nutu enim eius non poterimus quicquam facere.' Acquieverunt itaque ei suscepitque eos benigne in domum suam, ministrans eis que necessaria erant. Illi vero interim paraverunt palos ferreos fortes ad sustollendos lapides pavimenti, ligones ad fodiendam terram, operarios qui eos iuvarent mercede conducentes, et statuto die ad portam claustri venerunt. Quo cum intrare presumerent, ita eos dominus cecitate percussit, ut apertis oculis nichil viderent nec ullomodo portam contingere valerent. Sed qui etiam murum palpare temptarent et sic ingredi, adherebant manus eorum muro nec ulterius proficisci poterant: regredi quidem leviter quibant, sed antea ire nequibant, et si aliquando regrederentur, luci statim pristine reddebantur. Angebantur nimis rubore pariter et stupore, et intra se quod

---

132 Ps. 77, 30: *non sunt fraudati a desiderio suo.*   **135** 1 Macch. 9, 39: *apparatus multus.*   **137** 1 Reg. 30, 21: *salutavit eos pacifice*; 1 Macch. 7, 29: *salutaverunt se invicem pacifice.*   **139** Matth. 10, 16: *estote simplices sicut columbae.*   **145** Cf. Act. 21, 14: *Domini voluntas fiat* (Matth. 6, 10).   **147** Iudith 6, 19: *suscepit eum in domum suam.*—Matth. 27, 55: *ministrantes ei.*   (= 297) Act. 28, 10: *quae necessaria erant.*   **148** *palos ferreos* = 194.   **149** Matth. 20, 1: *conducere operarios.* **150–151** Gen. 19, 11: *percusserunt caecitate.*   Act. 9, 8: *apertisque oculis nihil videbat.*

---

128 beati et T[1], et beati T[2]   Stephani prothomartyris TL   **130** Helena TL   **132** suo desiderio T, suo *om*.L   **137** ipsum T   **140** eis respondit T   Gravissimum ... requiritis *om*.TB   **142** infra L   **143** illis T   **144** interim] in terra L   humiliter *om*.T   **146** enim *om*.L   **147** que eis (ei T[2]) T[2] L   **148** vero *om*.TL   interim] enim T[1], autem T[2]   paraverunt *om*.T   sustollendum TL   **149** mercedem L   **152** qui et T, cum etiam L   temptaverant T[1], temptaverunt T[2]

sic eis contigisset mirabantur. Quibus ad hospicium regressis et existimantibus ne forte peccatis suis exigentibus hoc eis eveniret, presbiteris qui cum ipsis venerant confitebantur delicta sua, sicque ad ceptum opus recurrebant, sed nichilominus omnipotens deus sua in illis miracula operabatur. Quod videntes loci illius habitatores laudabant et glorificabant Viventem in secula, qui solus facit mirabilia. O quantus erat luctus eorum, quantas inter ipsos singultuosos gemitus preces universali domino fundebant! Timebant enim ne forte secundum preceptum regis a tantis patronis desolarentur.

Comparemus, si placet, quamvis dispariliter, quod factum est illi antiquo miraculo quod fecit dominus in Sodomitis beato Loth, angelis hospicio receptis. Vallaverunt viri civitatis illius domum eius ut intrarent et exercerent execranda scelera sua, sed isti beatorum patriarcharum claustrum intrare voluerunt ut pie et honorifice eorum tollerent corpora. Obcecati sunt illi ad malum ut omnino perirent, obcecati sunt et isti ad bonum, ut de malefactis suis penitentes salvi fierent, illi cum magno fetore et orrore trusi sunt in infernum, isti cum summo gaudio preciosissimam margaritam secum, et si non quam vellent, deferentes, in melius de tanto miraculo profuturi ad sua reversi sunt. Nec hoc ut puto sine causa factum est: indignum namque esset ut quibus viventibus deus terram Chanaan dono concesserat, ab ea, licet cum digna veneratione, exularent. O mira dei providencia: futurum quippe erat quandoque ut in quo humati fuerant loco a fidelibus Christianis reperirentur, a quibus ibidem, sicut et nunc, laudibus eximiis extollerentur.

His ita gestis, considerantes predicti nuncii quod factum fuerat, flentes et nimis tristes ad prefatum archiepiscopum venerunt. Cui et dixerunt: 'Scimus, pater beatissime, quia quod volebamus merita nostra adipisci non possunt, saltem, si nosti ubi corpus sancti Ioseph filii Iacob sepultum sit, indica nobis.' Quibus episcopus: 'Recordamini', inquit, 'filii, verborum eius, que ipse moriens in Egipto dixit fratribus suis: *Post mortem meam visitabit vos deus et introducet in terram quam*

158–159 *nichi*lominus ... <non> operabatur] Ellipsis of a negation, cf. Stotz, *Handbuch* IV, 9, 98.   **160** Dan. 6, 26: *deus vivens et aeternus in saecula*; Apoc. 1, 18: *vivens in saecula saeculorum*.—Ps. 71, 18 and 135, 4: *qui facit mirabilia solus.*   **162** Ex. 1, 17: *iuxta praeceptum regis.*   **164ff.** Gen. 19, 3–24.   **171** Cf. 412–413.   **173** *indignum* cf. 80.   **182–183** (cf. 30–36) Gen. 50, 23; Ex. 13, 5 and 11.

---

156 sic *om.*TL   **157** evenerit T   venerant *om.*L   **159** in illis sua L, in illis *om.*T. *Cf. adn.*   **159** Quod ... 230 cum gaudio *om.*B   **161** quantas DT^2, quantos L, quanta T^1 **163** patrociniis TL   **164** dispariliter] displiceat T   **165** Sodomis TL   beato] bono T, *cf. ad 54. 167.*   **165–166** angelis ... Vallaverunt: *sic distinxi cum* DL, Angelis ... vallaverunt T   **167** (= *165*) bonorum T   nolebant T   **169** et *om.*TL   peccatis TL   **170** fetore et orrore] horrore *tantum* TL   **171** secum margaritam TL   quod TL   **172–173** Nec ... est *om.*T^2 ut *om.*L   sine causa puto T^1 **173** qui L   deus viventibus T   **174** condigna T   **175** quandoque erat TL   **177** itaque T   quod ... flentes et] quod tantus fuerat fletus T   **178** pater] Presbiter T   **181** que] quomodo T, quoniam L   **182** fratribus] filiis T

dedit patribus nostris; tollite ergo hinc ossa mea et ferte vobiscum et sepelite illuc.
Post multum vero temporis filiis Israel a deo visitatis et in terram promissam introductis, asportantes secum ossa Ioseph sepelierunt in Luza, que nunc est Neapolis: ite illuc et eum diligenter inquirite.' Qui dixerunt: 'Ita esse ut ais, pater, non dubitamus, sed tuam sanctitatem exoramus ne nobiscum venire pigriteris, ut nobis locum ostendas: credimus enim quod tuis precibus impetrantibus non patietur deus laborem nostrum esse inanem.' Et ille: 'Locum quidem, karissimi, determinatum nescio, sed campum, in quo humatus fertur, karitate vestra me cogente vobiscum veniens demonstrabo.' Nec mora, a sanctis patriarchis venia pro tanta presumptione postulata, simul cum archiepiscopo Neapolim profecti sunt; quos assumens vir sanctus, ad campum, quem se ostensurum predixerat, duxit, nulloque sepulture signo in eo viso, assumptis innumeris palis ferreis, ceperunt illos passim in terram figere, ut sic quod querebant possent invenire. Quibus per aliquos dies laborantibus et pre nimio labore pene deficientibus, tandem dei miserante clementia unus ex eis, cui forsitan mens iustior inerat, accipiens palum fixit in terram, quem cum malleo desuper percuteret, contigit ut super vas quoddam lapideum palus descenderet. At ille vocatis sociis suis quod senserat retulit: tunc illi, sumptis sarculis et ligonibus, ceperunt ubi palus fixus manebat viriliter fodere, et fodientes cum lacrimis deum orare ut ipse opus suum bono fine cito consummaret. Igitur dum illi fodiendo anxiati desudarent, vas quoddam magnum lapideum invenerunt. Existimantes autem ibi esse quod optabant, gaudio magno gavisi sunt. Quod cum aperuissent nichilque in eo repperissent, unde prius letati fuerant inde postea contristati sunt. Hortantes tamen sese mutuo et totam spem suam in deo ponentes illud inde eiecerunt, sub quo etiam aliud mire pulcritudinis marmoreum invenerunt; ad quod accedentes cum aperire voluissent, subito terremotus factus est magnus, quem tanta lucis coruscatio secuta est, ut solis claritatem lux illa excederet. Celum quoque apertum est et VII planete de celo visi sunt descendere, et quasi

---

184 Ex. 2, 23: *post multum vero temporis.* visitatis = 182. **185–186** Not *Neapolis* (Nablus) but *Bethel*: Iud. 1, 22–23. **188–189** 1 Cor. 15, 58: *scientes quod labor vester non est inanis in domino.* **190–191** = 1. **194** *palis ferreis* = 148. **203** Matth. 2, 10. **205–206** = 14–15. **207–208** Matth. 28, 2 and Apoc. 11, 13. **209** Apoc. 19, 11.

---

183 fratribus meis T   ergo *om*.TL   **184** tempus D   domino T   **185** asportaverunt T   Ioseph] et *add*. T   **186** illuc ite TL   diligenter eum T, eum *om*.L   pater ais TL   **189** dominus T^1, *om*.T^2 **190** humatum TL   **190–191** vestra cogente me L, me *om*.T   cogente] ego *add*. T   **192** Neapolim *om*.T   **193** ostensurum se TL   **195** ut scilicet quod T^1, scilicet ut quod T^2 invenire possent TL   aliquot TL   **196** pene] fere TL   dei miserante DT^1, miserante dei T^2L   **198** percussisset T   **201** deum cum lacrimis T   cito *om*.L   **205** contristati DT^1, tristati T^2L   et] ut T   suam *om*.TL   **206** inde *om*.T^1, vas T^2 aliud etiam (et T) TL   **208** quos T   coruscatio lucis TL   excluderet T   **209** planete ... visi sunt D, stelle ... vise sunt L, septem stelle vise sunt de celo T

210 sancto corpori obsequium prestantes circa eius tumulum in aere per aliquantum
spacium consedere. Illi autem, videntes quod factum est signum, nimio terrore
perculsi ceciderunt in terram, ubi tam diu exanimes iacuerunt, quam diu lux illa
divinitus emissa ibidem consedit; qua discedente surrexerunt etiam ipsi, sed ubi
essent nescientes stabant stupefacti, et ecce illis audientibus vox de celo facta
215 est, dicens ad archiepiscopum, quem secum de Ebron adduxerant: 'Tuis meritis
optinentibus isti quidem thesaurum tam desideratum secum cum gaudio deferent, tu
vero, quacumque hora de loco suo tolletur, scias te moriturum.' Quo audito vir dei
protinus se in orationem dedit, cumque surrexisset, vocatis ad se viris illis, dixit eis:
'Vos audistis quod deus minatus est michi, sed nolite timere: accipite quod vobis
220 deus largiri dignatus est. Non enim timeo mortem, tantum ipse animam meam
accipiat in pace.' Qui dixerunt ei: 'Non sumus ausi, pater sanctissime, ulterius ad
sanctum tumulum accedere, sed de manu tua donum dei accipiemus.' Pergens itaque
sacerdos cum psalmis et ymnis accessit ad sepulcrum; quo aperto tanta suavissimi
odoris fraglantia ab eodem exiit, ac si omnium pigmentorum genera et aromatum
225 in eo sparsa fuissent. Voces insuper angelice de celo audite sunt, laudantes et
benedicentes deum, qui dedit potestatem talem hominibus. Accipiens autem
venerabilis pontifex sacratissima ossa, cum magna reverentia involvit in panno
mundo et optimo, et cum tradidisset nuntiis, iuxta celestem vocem terre corpus
commendans, celo spiritum reddidit. Illo vero sepulto recesserunt viri cum thesauro
230 sibi divinitus concesso et deo gratias agentes cum gaudio ad propria repedaverunt,
tradentes preciosissimam glebam piissimo principi Theodosio, qui eos miserat, et
ei referentes quam magna et terribilia eis fecisset dominus. Quam ille gaudenter
suscipiens, ut decuit honorifice in basilica sua collocavit.

211–212 Gen. 45, 3: *nimio terrore perterriti*.   **214–215** Act. 9, 7: *stabant stupefacti, audientes quidem vocem (neminem autem videntes)*.—(cf. 225) Ier. 31, 15: *Vox in excelso audita est*.   **219** Gen. 43, 23 (and *passim*): *nolite timere*.   **220–221** Cf. Ps. 54, 19: *Redimet in pace animam meam*.   **222** Ioh. 4, 10 and Act. 8, 20: *donum dei*.   **223** Ephes. 5, 19: *in psalmis et hymnis*.   **223–225** Cf. Text II, 153–154.   **225** Cf. 214–215.
225–226 Luc. 24, 53: *laudantes et benedicentes deum*.   **226** Matth. 9, 8 (cf. 385–386): *qui dedit potestatem talem hominibus*.   **228** mundo] Cf. Deut. 12, 15: *mundum, hoc est integrum et sine macula*.   **230** = 411–412.   **231** piissimo = 106.244.   **232** Cf. Deut. 10, 21: *magnalia et terribilia*.   **232–233** Cf. 313.

---

210 in aere *om*.D   aliquantulum L, aliquot T[2]   **212** percussi T, *om*.L   **213** recedente T   etiam] et T   ubi] ut TL   **214** ecce *om*.TL   **214–215** vox facta est de celo T   **215** dicens *om*.T   de] ad (*sic*) L   **218** in orationem se T   illis *om*.TL
219 minatus est michi dominus TL   **219–220** deus vobis T   **220–221** accipiat animam meam L   **222** sed *om*.TL   accipiemus donum dei TL   **223** psalmis] ipsis T
224 fragrantia T, flagrancia L   **225** in ipso TL   **226** enim TL   **227** mirabilis T
228–229 corpus commendans terre L   **229** tradidit T   viri *om*.TL   **232** Quam … 244 temporis *om*.B   **232** gaudens TL   **233** sua basilica T

Hec, fratres karissimi, que sub Theodosio imperatore facta memoravimus, a quodam Iohanne montis Synai monacho et a quodam Siro sacerdote, religiosis ut 235 videbantur viris, nobis sub veritate testificata sunt. Que ideo huic operi inseruimus, ut cum patriarcharum ossa, que a tantis et tam religiosis viris, immo a C iam transactis generationibus non potuerunt inveniri, a Latinis inventa esse audieritis, aperte intelligatis quantam benivolentiam creator omnium deus eis plus quam ceteris gentibus exibuerit, et insuper ut resipiscant et peniteant qui dicunt civitatem 240 Ebron metropolim non esse. Qui si Eusebio Cesariensi et Christi confessori Ieronimo Iosephoque credere nolunt, his saltem, que in grecis voluminibus, ut scripsimus, continentur assentiant.

Post aliquantum vero temporis, mortuo piissimo principe iam dicto, peccatis christiani populi exigentibus ebullierunt Sarraceni de finibus suis direxeruntque 245 acies suas contra Iudeam. Quo comperto Greci, maxima pars eorum fugit Constantinopolim habitavitque in ea et in finibus eius. Quidam autem, quos Christi caritas artius copulaverat, ad eius sancta loca excolenda sub tributo barbarorum ibi remanserunt, sed qui Cariatarbe habitabant cum aliis fugerunt, illius sanctissimi claustri introitum ita obturantes, ut porta in eo nunquam fuisse arbitraretur. 250 Irrumpentes igitur barbari obtinuerunt totam regionem illam et Ierusalem civitatem quam elegit dominus, sacerdotes quoque eorum possederunt templum domini, quod erat in ea, et civitatem Ebron. Sed qui Ebron venerunt dum mirarentur murorum fortem et pulchram compositionem, et quia nullus ad ingrediendum pateret aditus, supervenerunt quidam Iudei, qui sub Grecorum ditione circa regionem illam 255 morati fuerant, et dixerunt eis: 'Reddite nos securos ut simul inter vos habitemus concedaturque nobis ante introitum sinagogam construere, et sic ubi portam facere debeatis vobis ostendemus.' Sicque factum est. Sed quia enarrare longum est quam honorifice gens illa, licet infidelis, locum illum tenuerit, quod nullus eorum nisi

---

235 Cf. 25.   **235–236** = 237.   **237** = 235–236.   **239**(262) 2 Macch. 1, 24: (*Domine*) *deus creator omnium* (Ambrose, *Hymn.* 2, 1).   **239–240** Cf. 278.409–410.   **241–242** = 102–103.   **244** *piissimo* = 231.106.   **245** 2 Macch. 1, 12: *ebullire fecit de Perside eos qui pugnaverunt contra nos et sanctam civitatem.*   **245–246** 1 Reg. 17, 2: *direxerunt aciem ... contra ...*   **247** Ios. 19, 50: *habitavitque in ea.*   **247–248** 2 Cor. 5, 14: *caritas ... Christi.*   **251–252** 3 Reg. 14, 21: *in Ierusalem civitate quam elegit dominus.*   **258** = 346.

---

234 facta *om*.T², gesta T¹   **235–236** ut videbantur *om*.TL   **236** relata TL   **237** (= *400. 406*) sanctorum patriarcharum TL   **238** transgressis TL   esse *om*.TL   **240** exhibuit T   **241** si *om*.TL   **242** noluerunt L   **244** iam dicto principe piissimo T, iam piissimo dicto principe L, (–246) Mortuo Theodosio imperatore piissimo venerunt Saraceni (*sic*), totam Iudeam obtinentes (*cf. 251–252*) B   **245** populi christiani T   **246** eorum *om*.L   **247–248** quos ... copulaverat] Christiani B, caritas artius copulaverat TL, (copulaverat caritas sibi (*om*.artius) , *ss*. c, a, b =) caritas sibi copulaverat D   **248** sancta *om*.T, loca sancta L (B)   **249** qui] quia D   **251** illam] eorum T   **252** sacerdotesque L   **257** et *om*.TL   **258** quam] quod TL

discalciatis et lotis pedibus in eo intrare presumpserit et quod intus oratorium miro opere fabricaverit quodque etiam auro et argento sericisque pannis illud mirabiliter decoraverit, et quomodo creator omnium et Redemptor universam regionem illam post multos annos predictis incredulis abstulerit et Latinis christianis reddiderit, vel qualiter Appamiensis archiepiscopus post Ierusalem a Francis dei virtute captam sanctorum patriarcharum locum omnino spoliaverit, quomodo etiam conventus clericorum sub apostolica regula ad serviendum deo in eodem loco a Latinis constitutus fuerit, ad rem gestam, quam sua gratia deus nostris temporibus manifestare dignatus est, sicut polliciti sumus stilum vertamus.

Anno igitur vicesimo primo regni Francorum preerat in Cariatarbe quidam pie memorie nomine Rainerius, prior Latinorum primus, virtute venerabilis et per cuncta laudabilis et propter deum apud se tantum despectus, ut, quamvis super alios prelatione fungi putaretur, sibi subditorum tamen minister esse videbatur, pium scilicet imitans magistrum, qui dixit: *Non veni ministrari sed ministrare*. Nonnulli itaque confluebant ad eum, sub eius magisterio deo servire cupientes, inter quos erant Odo et Arnulfus domini sacerdotes, quorum relatione didici quod narro. Hi tres, predictus videlicet prior et duo nominati viri, orationibus nocturnisque vigiliis pre ceteris insistebant et lacrimosis suspiriis sese iugiter affligentes omnipotentem deum exorabant, quatinus eis concederet quod retro tot et tantis gentibus negaverat. Tandem exaudivit illos deus et quod ab eo postulaverant dedit. Videte, fratres, quantum valeat deprecatio iusti assidua: iusti enim erant et quod iustum erat postulabant, et datum est eis: si enim iusti non essent, utique quod volebant non impetrassent. Quadam vero die in mense Iunio, sicut mos est Regularium canonicis post meridiem in lectulis suis quiescentibus, quidam eiusdem ecclesie frater, arte scriba, estivum calorem devitans intravit in ecclesiam et iuxta piramidem, que sancti Ysaac nomine dicitur, super pavimentum accubuit: ibi namque inter duos magnos

---

262 = 239.   **264** Peter of Narbonne.   **269** Anno ... *regni* Francorum] 1119, counted from the election of Godfrey of Bouillon, 23 July 1099.   **270** Rainerius] See RRH 68 (a. 1112).   **271** *propter deum* = 90.   **271** ut ... 272 videbatur] ut *c. ind.*!   **273** Matth. 20, 28.   **275** Is. 61, 6: *sacerdotes domini vocabimini*.   Cf. 23–24.   **278** Cf. 239–240. 409–410.   **280** Ier. 37, 19: *valeat deprecatio mea in conspectu tuo*.

---

260 discalciatus L, discalceatus T   et lotis *om*.B   in eum T   oratorium intus T
261 etiam] et T   illud] illico T   mirabiliter *om*.T   **263** predictis incredulis DL *et ex illis incredulis corr*. T², incredulis illis predictis T¹   vel] ut T¹, et T²   **265** etiam] et T   **267** dominus T   **268** sicut *om*.L   **269** in *om*.T   **270** Rainerius DB, Rainerus L, Raynerus T   **271** et propter ... 282 impetrassent *om*.B   **271** apud se *om*.T
272 fungi prelatione TL   sibi tamen subditorum T, sibi subditorum (*om*. tamen) L
274 domino T   **275** erat L   narratione T   **276** predicti TL   prenominati TL
278 dominum TL   gemitibus (!) T   **280** quantum] multum *add*. L   valet TL
282 Quadam die mense Iunio B   sicut ... Regularium *om*.B   **283** eiusdem (eius T²) ecclesie DT, ecclesie eiusdem L   **284** devitans calorem TL   in *om*.TL   **285** ibi namque DT², ibi autem T¹, ibique L   magnos *om*.T (B)

lapides pavimenti quedam rimula erat, de qua tenuis ventus et suavis, frigidus
tamen, per subterraneum meatum egrediebatur, ideoque ille in loco illo accubuerat,
ut a vento refrigeraretur. Dum ergo ibi esset et auram desubtus procedentem aperto
sinu exciperet, cepit per rimulam illam minutos lapillos intus quasi ludens iacere,
quos audiens in profundum cadere illic cisternam vel antrum aliquod esse arbitratus   290
est; et assumens virgulam quandam ligavit in summitate eius filum longum et forte
et in capite fili plumbatam parvam, et intromittens mensus est cubitos XI in
profundum. Prior tunc forte aberat, quibusdam enim negotiis impeditus ierat
Ierosolimis. Expergefactis autem a somno fratribus et Hora Nona decantata, narravit
frater ille quod invenerat. Quod illi audientes duplicis spelunce introitum suspicati   295
sunt, et expectantes duobus aut tribus diebus deumque assidue orantes ut laborem
suum in bonum dirigeret, interim que necessaria erant ad secandos lapides
ferramenta paraverunt: duri quippe erant et pene omni ferro invincibiles. Evoluto
itaque bidui aut tridui spacio, communi omnium fratrum consilio et tribuni assensu,
qui eodem tempore ibidem principabatur, nomine Balduini, illud laboriosum opus   300
in nomine sancte Trinitatis, satis tamen timide, arripuerunt. Timebant enim ne forte
propter sua peccata nollet eos celorum dominus et orbis iuvare, ideoque se magis
affligebant, sacerdotes missarum sollempnia celebrando, alii clerici psalteria
legendo, laici quoque nichilominus universe creature dominatorem orando, ut
iniquitatibus suis propiciaretur et eorum supplicationibus placatus quod inceperant   305
secundum preces suas ad effectum ducere dignaretur. Sed qui secabant dum in
secando per plures dies nimia fatigatione gravarentur, tandem sectis sublatisque
lapidibus apparuit os spelunce introitus, quo aperto omnes, ut erant ardenti
desiderio, intrare unanimiter volebant. Sed quia locus ille omnes simul capere non
poterat, voluerunt ut iam memoratus Odo, quia senior omnibus videbatur et primus   310
post priorem eiusdem loci canonicus fuerat, primus omnium introiret, dignum
iudicantes ut, si fors tulisset, ab antiquiore et eorum secundum etatem patre
multarum gentium patres invenirentur. Quod ille gratanter accipiens, ab eis cum

---

289 Gen. 19, 14: *quasi ludens.*   **292** (cf. 59–60) 4 m. 95.   **293–294** Cf. 340.
294 = 345.   **297** = 147.   **299–300** (= 366 and Text II, 70) Balduinus] See RRH 80. 90.
115. 120. 133. 134 and 164 (a. 1115–1136).   **300** Eccli. 7, 16: *laboriosa opera.*
301 *satis ... timide* = 5, cf. 15.   **304** Cf. Zach. 4, 14: *dominatori universae terrae.*
305 Ps. 102, 3: *qui propitiatur omnibus iniquitatibus tuis.*   **313** *multarum gentium patres*
cf. 49–50.   Cf. 232–233.

---

287 ideoque ... **288** refrigeraretur *om*.B *et Riant*   **289** intus minutos lapides T, minutos
intus lapides L   **290** ibi T   **292** parvam] paratam L   **294** autem *om*.TL   **296** et
expectantes] Expectantis, *ss*. que L, Exspectantibus (*corr. AA SS*) T   **298** pene] fere
T   **300** Baldoini T, Baldewini L, *cf. ad 366*   **301** forte *om*.T   **302** peccata sua
TL   magis ac magis se (sese T¹) TL   **307** nimia] intima T   **308** os spelunce
introitus D, os spelunce et introitus TL, spelunce introitus *tantum* B   ut erant omnes
TL   **309** simul omnes T   **310** qui T (B)   primus] prior T   **312** sors attulisset
TL   **313** suscipiens TL

fune submissus est; qui pervium quo ulterius posset ingredi iter non inveniens,
315 ut eum foras traherent clamavit. Illo vero abstracto, sequenti die Arnulfum
submiserunt, et dato ei lumine – caliginosus enim erat locus – cepit intra se mirari
quid hoc esse potuisset: videbat enim utrumque parietem ita unitum, ut de uno
lapide factum putares et totum opus illud muro superiori consimile. Iam quid
ageret nesciebat et animi dolore incredibili vexabatur, presertim cum nullus ei ad
320 ingrediendum aditus pateret. Tandem resumpto animo, ut erat vir gnarus, accepto
martello ferreo cepit utrimque percutere, si vacuum aliquid audiret; percutiens
autem illum qui ad Occidentem respicit parietem, audivit sonum quasi concavum
deintus resonantem. Tunc aliquantulum spe recuperata iussit summitti qui lapidem
magnum, quo subterraneum iter claudebatur, tollerent; quibus summissis vix per
325 IIII dierum spacium potuerunt eum movere. Sublato demum lapide apparuit quasi
conductus aque magnus, siccus tamen, duos habens altitudinis cubitos, viginti octo
longitudinis et unum latitudinis; quem intrantes et diligentius intuentes sed nichil
prorsus invenientes, mirabantur opus et gravi merore afficiebantur. Mira res,
uterque murus a dextra et leva ex quadratis politisque lapidibus est compositus et
330 superiori equipollens. Igitur qui presentes aderant plus animi langore quam corporis
dolore deficiebant. Sed Arnulfus, cuius mens sanctorum reliquias inveniendi iam
quasi conscia erat, assumpto martello ut supra cepit huc illucque percutere, si forte
audiret quod superius audierat, et ante se sono concavitatis audito hortatus est qui
secum erant quia illic laborare debuissent, alium quem tollerent lapidem ostendens.
335 Cumque ut eum quoque ammoverent per alios quatuor dies desudarent, aspicientes
per foramen quod fecerant viderunt domunculam in modum basilice, opere
ammirabili et rotundo fabricatam, homines ferme triginta capientem, quam desuper
unus lapis continuus claudit. Qua visa, pre nimia leticia flentes deo gloriam
dederunt, sed intrare minime presumpserunt. Putabant enim ibi sanctorum esse
340 reliquias, ideoque donec a Ierosolimis prelatus eorum rediret expectaverunt. Quo

---

316 2 Petr. 1, 19: *in caliginoso loco*.   318 Cf. 330.   326–327 (cf. 59–60) According to the adopted text (= D) , the corridor measured 90 cm. high by 12 m. 60 long by 45 cm. wide.   329 Cf. 58–59. 61.   330 Cf. 318.   338 = 409.   340 Cf. 293–294.

---

314 ingredi DT¹, progredi L, progredi posset ingredi *sed* progredi *del*.T²   316 enim] quippe TL   intus se T   318 illud opus TL   319 ei nullus T   319–320 ad ingrediendum *om*.T   321 cepit *om*.T   utrumque T, percutere utrumque parietem B   322 respicit ad occidentem L   323 sonantem L   326–327 duos habens altitudinis cubitos D, habens altitudinem (huius altitudinis T) cubitos XI (undecim L) TL, habens altitudinis cubitos decem B—viginti octo longitudinis (longitudinis viginti et octo B) DB, et XVII longitudinis TL—et unum latitudinis (latitudinis vero unum B) *codd. omnes*   328 dolore T   329 leva] parte *add*.TL   330 aderant] ad *ss.m²*D (B)   332 accepto (= *320*) T   ut supra martello TL   333 et ante] trans T   est] eos *add*.L   334 quia illic] quatinus ibi T, quater (?) L, quantum gnaviter (!) *Riant*   deberent TL   337 ferme DT¹B, fere T²L   quam] quod TL   339 illic L

regresso, ei que facta fuerant intimaverunt. O quanta cordis exultatione repletus est audito quod volebat, sed quia principio geste rei non interfuerat dolens se miserum clamabat.

Eadem itaque die accersito fratrum consilio statuerunt ut ipsa die, omnibus a somno post Nonam excitatis, ingrederentur illuc et, diligenter inquisito si quid ibi esset, scirent quid postea facere deberent. Et factum est ita. Statuta namque hora venientes ad locum ammotoque ab hostio invente basilice lapide intraverunt, sed quod putabant minime repererunt. Unde quamplurimum stupefacti mansiunculam illam mirabantur, miranda quippe adhuc est, cum aliqua talis aut vix aut nunquam, presertim sub terra, possit inveniri. Illi vero qui cum priore illic ingressi fuerant, sed et ipse prior, dum considerarent si alicubi duplicis spelunce aditum possent cognoscere, reversus Arnulfus ad hostium basilice et studiosius intuens, in ipsius aditu non magnum lapidem animadvertit, in saxo nativo in modum cunei insertum, quem ammoveri iussit; quo ammoto, spelunce tam desiderate ingressus apparuit. Tunc omnes cum lacrimis deo gratias egerunt, ipsum obnixius deprecantes ut eis quod intus erat revelare dignaretur, similes facti mulieri sapienti, que perdita dragma accendit lucernam, domum everrit et querit diligenter donec inveniat illam. Subverterunt namque domum, sepulcrum illud sanctorum, accenderunt lucernam orationum et afflictionum, deo accepta munera offerentes, et quod in nomine eius petierunt ab ipso consecuti sunt. O vera dei promissio, que neminem fallit! Ait enim: *Si quid petieritis patrem in nomine meo, dabit vobis*. Aperta igitur spelunca VII Kal. Iulii, prior sub nomine obediencie et penitentie Arnulfo iniunxit ut ipse, qui plus omnibus laborarat, intraret sicque laborem suum ad finem usque perduceret. Nec mora acceptis ille cereis in manibus, signo sancte crucis se muniens, altissona voce *Kirieleyson* cantando, non tamen sine timore, ingressus est, et secum cogitans ne forte Balduinus, eiusdem loci defensor, illuc thesaurum auri vel argenti esse suspicaretur, hortatus est priorem ut eum commoneret secum intrare, et deprecatus est eum. Cuius precibus ille acquiescens intravit, sed timore correptus confestim exiit. Arnulfus vero querens circuibat speluncam, si ossa sanctorum inveniret, et

---

341 Ps. 118, 111: *exultatio cordis mei.*   **345** *Nonam* = 294.   **346** = 258. **356–357** Luc. 15, 8.   **358** Tit. 1, 11: *universas domos subverterunt.*   **361** Ioh. 15, 16 and 16, 23.   **361–362** 25 June.   **362–363** 1 Cor. 15, 10: *abundantius illis omnibus laboravi.*   **364** = 405.   **366** = 299–300.   **368** Act. 10, 4: *timore correptus.*

---

342 rei geste TL   dolens *om*.T   **344** concilio D, *cf. 98.*   **349** adhuc *om*.T **350** "*lege* illuc" *AA SS*   **351** consideraret TL   **352** cognoscere] agnoscere T studiose L   **355** obnixius *om*.TL   **357** everrit *optime* T *cum textu biblico,* evertit (*cf. 358*) DL   **358** illud D, videlicet TL   **359** munera deo offerentes accepta T   in eius nomine TL   **360** O vera] quia T   **361** igitur *om*.L   XVII° B   **363** omnibus *om*.TL   laboraverat TL   usque ad finem L   **364** (= *405*) altissima T   **366** (= *300*) Baldoinus T, Baldewinus L   illic *corr. AA SS*   vel] aut T   **367** secum] illuc (= *366*) *add*.TL   **368** quiescens D   confestim L, confestit (*sic*) D, statim T   **369** et] in *add*.T

370 illa hora nichil invenit nisi terram quasi sanguine aspersam, et reversus nuntiavit his qui eum foris expectabant; quod illi audientes omnes exierunt foras, tristicia magna repleti. Sequenti autem die prior Arnulfum ammonuit ut iterum speluncam ingrederetur et cum summa diligentia terram fodiens circumquaque inquireret. Ille vero, magistri sui iussa exequens, assumpto in manu baculo introivit, cumque cum
375 baculo terram foderet ossa sancti Iacob invenit et, nesciens adhuc cuius essent, ea in unum conglobavit. Deinde ultra progrediens et diligentius intuens, vidit ad caput sancti Iacob spelunce alterius hostium, in qua beatorum Abraham et Isaac ossa erant, sed tamen clausum; quod cum aperuisset intuitus est caveam, et ingressus in eam repperit in ipsius fundo sacratissimum corpus sancti Abrahe patriarche
380 signatum et ad pedes eius ossa beati Ysaac filii sui. Non enim, sicut nonnulli autumant, omnes in una spelunca conditi fuerunt, sed in interiore Abraham et Isaac, in exteriore vero Iacob. Arnulfus vero, qui hunc summum et incomparabilem thesaurum reppererat, egressus de spelunca nuntiavit priori et fratribus se beatorum patriarcharum reliquias invenisse. At illi, quod tam diu cum summo desiderio
385 expectaverant audientes, in hymnis et canticis animis exultantibus glorificaverunt deum. Accipiens autem Arnulfus aquam et vinum, lavit sanctarum reliquiarum ossa posuitque uniuscuiusque patris reliquias singillatim super singulas tabulas ligneas, quas ad hoc forte preparaverat, dimisitque ibi et recessit. Tunc prior omnibus egressis diligenter introitum signavit, ne aliquis sine sui licencia ingrederetur. Altera
390 siquidem die quidam eorum illuc orationis causa intrantes, a dextra sicut intratur quasi elementa literarum in quodam lapide sculpta viderunt, quod aliis ostenderunt, sed quid exprimerent scire non potuerunt. Tollentes ergo lapidem illum, sed nichil nisi terram invenientes et cogitantes quod ibi litere sculpte sine causa non fuissent, econtra a leva scilicet intrantis murum perforantes, invenerunt VI Kal. Augusti
395 vasa testea ferme quindecim plena pulvere et ossibus mortuorum, sed quorum essent

---

371–372 1 Macch. 6, 13: *tristitia magna*.   **372** 26 June.   **373** 2 Paral. 11, 12: *summa diligentia*.   **385** 1 Macch. 13, 51: *cum ... hymnis et canticis*.   **385–386** Matth. 9, 8 (cf. 225–226): *glorificaverunt deum*.   **387** Cf. 32.   **388** 2 Reg. 3, 24: *quare dimisisti eum et ... recessit?*   **389–390** 27 June.   **394** 27 July.   **395** Cf. Iob 20, 11: *ossa eius ... cum eo in pulvere dormient*.   **395–397** See Text II, 100–101.

---

371 foras T, foris *corr. AA SS*   **372** iterum] item D   **374** sui *om*.L   intravit L   **376** Dein T   **378** aperuissēt D   est *om*.T   et *om*.L   **379** ipsius] eiusdem T   sacratissimum *om*.T   **380** signatum TL, *om*.D, *sed cf.* II, 123: sancti Habrahe *declaratur* sepulcrum.   filii sui (eius D) *om*.B   **381** in una spelunca omnes L   **383** beatorum] horum T   **385** expectabant L   animis exultantibus] laudantes (*cf. Luc.* 2, 20) T   **386** sacrarum T, sanctorum LB   **387** singillatim DT¹, sigillatim T²LB   singulas *om*.LB   **388** paraverat T, paraverant L   **390** eorum] illorum T   causa orationis illuc L, orationis caussa (*sic, om.* illuc) T¹, orationis gratia T²   ad dexteram TL   **392** sed] tunc *add*. L, tamen *add*.T   igitur T   lapidem illum] ibi unum lapidem TL   **393** non sine caussa (*sic*) non T, *pr.* non *del*.T²   **395** pulvere et *om*.TLB veraciter nescierunt. Credendum tamen est illa aliquorum primatum filiorum Israel esse reliquias.

His ita gestis profectus est prior Ierusalem, inventionem sanctorum sancte recordationis Guarmundo patriarche, qui tunc temporis illic preerat, manifestaturus eumque ut ad sublevanda patriarcharum corpora Cariatarbe veniret deprecaturus.   400
Quid multa? Se venturum benigno animo promisit, sed non bono usus consilio eum, cui se venturum promiserat, fefellit. Videns itaque prior se a patriarcha delusum esse, presente magna multitudine populi, qui de Ierusalem et de vicinis civitatibus ad sollempnitatem sanctorum convenerat, pridie Nonas Octobris, clericis vocibus altissonis modulantibus et *Te deum laudamus* decantantibus, cum decenti   405
honorificentia preciosas patriarcharum reliquias protulit, claustroque pompatice lustrato desiderantibus populis ad videndum ostendit. Benedictus es, domine deus, qui abscondisti hec a sapientibus et prudentibus et revelasti ea parvulis! O quanta fuit omnium exultatio, quantus pre nimia letitia fletus, dum illa beata ossa, quod nunquam genti alteri licuit, deoscularentur! Omnibus igitur rite peractis, omnes   410
se beatorum patriarcharum patrociniis commendantes ad propria cum gaudio remearunt. Reverendus vero prior et qui cum eo erant fratres illas III incomparabiles margaritas prout decentius potuerunt in ecclesia sua collocaverunt, ubi etiam fuerunt per biennium. Sed sicut mos est malorum bonorum successibus invidere, adeuntes quidam supra memoratum Ierosolimitanum patriarcham instigaverunt   415
eum, ut que Cariatarbe invente fuerant reliquias unde sublate fuerant iuberet remitti. Quorum ille verbis nimium credulus, ammonuit sepe nominatum priorem ut in hoc voluntati sue parere voluisset. Sicque prior, ne velut inobediens iudicaretur, sanctorum corpora in eo loco, unde ea substulerat, licet tristis, honorifice reposuit, ubi adhuc ab universis gentibus pia devotione requiruntur et devota veneratione   420
glorificantur, et per eos omnipotens deus, cui est honor et gloria per infinita secula seculorum. Amen.

---

404 6 October.   **405** *vocibus altissonis* = 364.   **407** Dan. 3, 26 and 52: *Benedictus es, domine deus patrum nostrorum.*   **408** Matth. 11, 25 and Luc. 10, 21.   **409** = 338.   **409–410** Cf. 239–240 and 278.   **411** = Text II, 47–48.   **411–412** = 230.   **412–413** Cf. 171.   **417** Gen. 39, 19: *nimium credulus (verbis coniugis).*

---

396 aliquorum] antiquorum T   **398** itaque L   profectus est *om*.L   **399** Gaurmundo D   illuc D   **400** sublimanda TL   **402–403** Videns ... delusum esse (esse delusum TL) : Prior autem B   **405** altissimis (*cf. 364*) T   cantantibus L   **406** (= *400.237*) sanctorum patriarcharum TLB   **407** ostendit] *Hinc desinit* B   es *om*.T   **408** a TL, *om*.D   **410** alteri] alii TL   **412** remearunt] *Hinc desinunt* TL: *quae sequuntur solus* D *habet*

Text II

Gloriosissimorum patriarcharum Abrahe, Ysaac atque Iacob veteris testamenti †
obumbrantia <ne> inter catholicos in terris ebesceret memoria quociens renatos
sancta veneratur ac colit ecclesia, imo ut ad eorum merita inenarrabilia, typum
nostre redemptionis prefigurantia, excelsi patris declarentur magnalia, apud quem
5 nulla transmutatio vicissitudinis seu oblivionis obumbratio, anno incarnationis
domini nostri Iesu Christi M°. C° XX° eorum dignatus est revelare corpora,
multimoda virtutum prodigia in eorum laudibus divina cooperante gratia, ut
Ebronica testatur ecclesia, in qua rerum quas prelibavimus manifeste prepollet
historia revelatione precipua, ut in sequentibus reperietur sic habita: Contigit
10 clericum quemdam, Gallie parcium, Turonice regionis, indigenam, compunctione
salutifera a sinistra declinando ad dexteram, quibus habunde pollebat spretis opibus
rerum temporalium atque fluxarum et fragilium, sui sectatores ad ima trahentium,
gloriosissimum domini nostri Iesu Christi adisse sepulcrum. Ubi cum humillima
devotione suorum implorando veniam delictorum, habita oratione Ebron gressum
15 direxit ut sanctos invocaret patriarchas sue peticionis intercessores, quos apud
deum fide ac meritis noverat prestantiores. His vero in locis venerabilibus biennio
conversatus, quin etiam inspectis ac perfectis que optaverat exhilaratus, tam
affinium quam parentum visitatione titillatus, ut quos mestos devotus eius liquerat
abscessus opido optatus refoveret accessus ad natale solum Turonice regionis
20 regressus est. Hic autem dum non multo post reditum in ecclesia Beati Martini
antistitis Turonice civitatis ex consuetudine continuis orationibus, psalmorum
inflexis modulationibus, nocte quadam incomberet <et> prolixe noctis vigiliis
paulisper afflixus inter verba orationis paulum obdormisset, innumerabilium
sanctorum multitudinem contemplatur coram se pretereuntem. Quorum quedam
25 veneranda effigies, cui prelucida inerat canicies, manu eum apprehendens paululum
excussit atque quis esset, cum taliter inibi obdormisset, scrutatus est. Ille autem,
terribili visione tremefactus, miserum atque peccatorem se confessus ac prenimia
inbecillitate corporis vim inferente vigiliis sic se temere obdormisse ibidem, tandem

---

1 Cf. 144.   **4** Cf. 126.   **4–5** Iac. 1, 17.   **8** rerum quas prelibavimus] Apparently a reference to words missing from the first lines.   **10** = 19.   **11** Deut. 17, 20: *neque declinet (cor) in partem dexteram vel sinistram*; 1 Macch. 5, 46: *non erat declinare ab ea dextera vel sinistra*.   **19** = 10.   **23** *obdormisset*: apparently a rather frequent occurrence, cf. (48–49), 54 (= 68), 74, 84.   **23–24** = 85.   **25** (cf. 30) = 34–35.

---

1 Gloriossimorum   **2** obumbrata *coni. Kohler*: obumbrantia (*cf.* 4 prefigurantia *et* 5 obumbratio): *exciderunt quaedam, cf. adn. ad 8*.   ne *correxi*   quociens] quare *coni. Kohler*   **5** vicissituditis   obumbratio. Anno *Kohler*   **6** M°.C°.XX° *correxi*, M°.CC°.XX° *codicem secutus Kohler*   **8** maniste   **10** *post* parcium *deletum est* et (? esse?)   **17** inspectis que a perfectis optaverat, *corr. Kohler*   **18** ut quos *Kohler*: utque   **22** et *correxi*   **23** afflixus *retinui, cf.* affixus, *et Stotz, Handbuch III, 182:9.*

exorsus est: 'Quis es, domine, qui me miserum tam inepto sopori deditum ac tante visionis illustratione indignum excitando alloqueris?' Cui reverenda effigies 30 inquit: 'Ego sum Abraham, pater multitudinis gentium, quem in Ebron peregre profectus requisisti cuique famulatum orationibus continuisque laudibus propensius exhibuisti. Surge ergo nunc, celerius ad eundem depositionis mee locum rediturus, ibidem mei patrocinii ac consolationis alloquium habiturus.' His dictis veneranda effigies cum multitudine precedentium nusquam comparuit. Surgens autem 35 quantotius, quasi in extasi positus utpote tante visionis illustratione attonitus, certus tamen ex his que fuerat ammonitus, primo diei qui iam aderat, noctis abeunte caligine, imminente crepusculo, nullorum propinquorum fultus solatio, ut fuerat edoctus in sompno iter arripuit, solo comitante baculo quem secum tulerat pro sustentaculo, valedictis tamen amicis quos obviam tulerat casus itineris. 40

Adveniens autem Ierosolimam rerum necessariarum quamplurimam passus est inediam. Adorato reparationis nostre sepulcro progrediens Sanctum repetiit Abraham. Ubi a priore eiusdem ecclesie supra memorato commorationis eius aditu ac precipue religionis optentu prius agnitus, digne ac laudabiliter receptus est, ceteris fratribus confaventibus, quibus plurimum eius placebat adventus multo 45 ampliusque qui innotuerat inibi remansionis affectus. Professus autem cum aliis canonicam sortitus est vitam. Quid multis moror? Sanctorum patriarcharum patrocinia obnixius implorabat, oratione nunquam vacabat nisi quando rarus ac brevis sompnus occupabat, vigiliis indefessus hanelabat, pauperum inedias quibus poterat elemosinis sublevabat, ecclesie vero, nisi cum necessitas inevitabilis 50 evocaret, raro aberat. Clerus eum diligebat pro reverentia et equitate, populus autem collaudabat pro maxima caritate. Nocte vero quadam dominica, matutinis decantatis laudibus ad cubilia sua iam regressis fratribus, in ecclesia remansit solitarius, ubi intra psalmorum obdormiens decantatione, denuo venerabilem sancti Habrahe videre meruit visionem, talem ab eo suscipiens ammonitionem: 'Surge, 55 frater, surge, adiens regem Balduinum pariterque patriarcham Warmundum defer legationis mee sacramentum, videlicet ut advenientes huius ecclesie aperiant pavimentum, ubi inferius, quo difficiles <reddit> aditus compages artificiosa lapidum, Abraham, Ysaac atque Iacob eorundemque uxorum corpora clausum

---

30 Cf. 25.   **31** Gen. 17, 4–5 (Rom. 4, 16–17): *erisque pater multarum gentium. Nec ultra vocabitur nomen tuum Abram, sed appellaberis Abraham, quia patrem multarum gentium constitui te.*   **34–35** = 25.   **35** (cf. 66) Plautus, *Aul.* 629 (4, 4, 2): *qui modo nusquam comparebas ...*   **40** Cf. 102–103.   **42** Cf. 129.   **47** Terentius, *Andria* 114 (1, 1, 87): *quid multis moror?*   **47–48** = 81 and Text I, 411.   **48** Cf. 1 Cor. 7, 5: *ut vacetis orationi* (but see the critical apparatus!)   **48–49** See the note to line 23.   **54** See the note to line 23.   **56** Cf. 135.   **58** Ovid, *Rem.amoris* 120: *difficiles aditus*.

---

32 propensius *correxi*: perpensius   **40** tamen ... itineris *in margine*   **43** commorationis *correxi*: commemorationis   **46** qui (= affectus) *correxi*: quam (*cf.* ampliusque)   **48** oratione *correxi*: orationi   **49** hanelabat] ba *ss*.   **54** intra *c. abl.* ("during") : *ThLL 7, 2, 43:25–48, cf. Stotz, Handbuch IV, 9, 18:4.*   **58** reddit *Kohler*   **59** eorundumque

60 continet venerabile testimonium, temporibus suis revelandum, ut amodo plebs
christiana salutis sue contra paganos suscipiat incrementum. Multi enim tam
Grecorum quam Turcorum, Surianorum ac Sarracenorum generumque diversorum
homines, a tempore depositionis nostre locum istum obtinentes, obsequium
reverentiamque cum hostiis pro ritu exhibentes, corpora nostra videre exobtabant,
65 sortibus suis omnia perlustrantes, muros locatim suffodientes, superiorum
sepulcrorum cassatis inspectionibus: nulli tamen eorum adhuc comparuimus.' His
ita prolatis recessit effigies tam graciose felicitatis.

Excitatus tanquam dormiens canonicus, tante visionis illustratione parumper
attonitus, psalterium, quod ante obdormitionem incoaverat, attentius decantabat.
70 Cuncta vero que audierat ac viderat tantum Balduino, eiusdem loci patrono,
enucleans, preterea tacitus observabat. Haut multo post, adveniente Paschali
tempore, canonicum eundem, haut ab incepto psalmocinandi opere desistentem,
hora matutinali iuxta superiora patriarcharum sepulcra in eadem accumbentem
ecclesia, aliquantisper obdormientem iam tercio religiosa corripuit visio, inquiens:
75 'Usquequo, frater, dormis tacendo? Usquequo negligis precepta mea? Cur que
audieras ac videras quibus iusseram non manifestabas? Que si tacueris ulterius, ex
inobtemperantia corripieris ut meritus.' Nec plura inferens divina visio recessit.
Canonicus autem, pertimescens se vidisse sompnium, cum paucis huiusce rei
habens consilium, quibus precipue iussum fuerat nullum patefecit indicium,
80 psalmorum tamen decantationibus, ieiuniorum afflictionibus, vigiliarum curis
pocioribus, sanctorum patriarcharum patrocini<or>um invocationibus studium
inpendebat. Preterito autem Paschali tempore, Pentecosten quarte ferie hora nona
propinquante, eiusdem pagi clero ac populo una Quatuor Temporum ieiunia
celebrante, canonico supradicto, in eadem ecclesia inter orationum verba sopito,
85 apparuit quarto sanctorum patriarcharum cum innumerabili sanctorum multitudine
visio tremebunda, dormientem quasi excitando taliterque obiurgando: 'Quid,
desidiose, soporas? Utquid clausos totiens monitus non reseras? Cur quos pre
omnibus orationibus tuis invocas manifestare iam cessas?' Canonicus quidem ad
hec perterritus, aditum quem ignorabat ostendi poscit enucleatius, adiciens quod
90 ob hoc formidaverat adire imperii principatus, ne, post manifestationem si alio

---

60 *venerabile testimonium* (see the critical apparatus) ... *revelandum*: cf. 1 Tim. 2, 6: *testimonium temporibus suis*; cf. 2 Thess. 2, 6: *ut reveletur in suo tempore*.   Num. 23, 23 and 1 Tim. 2, 6: *temporibus suis*.   **65** *sortibus* = *sortilegiis*: 'tricks'.   **65–66** Cf. 73.   **66** Cf. 35.   **68** = 54. 101.   **70** (= 105–106 and 75–76) Luc. 2, 20: *quae audierant et viderant*.   **70** Balduino] See Text I, 299–300 and 366.   **71–72** In 1120 (line 6) Easter fell on 18 April.   **73** Cf. 65–66.   **74** See the note to line 23.   **75–76** Cf. *ad* 70.   **79** *quibus ... iussum fuerat*] 56.   **81** = 47–48.   **82** 9 June.   **84** See the note to line 23.   **85** = 23–24.

---

60 *testimonium correxi*: testamentum   **73** *superiora (cf.65–66) correxi*: superiorum   **74** *visio inquiens correxi*: inquiens visio   **76** non] tamen (tñ)   **79** *iussum correxi*: visum   **81** *patrociniorum correxi coll. 47–48 (= I, 411)*.   **89** *aditum correxi*: ad eum

cassaretur conatus, contumeliosos sibi ac meritos rependerent cruciatus: quis igitur alius quam ignorantie sermo contemplanti † potius fieri posset excusatoris? Summus ad hec patriarcha: 'Sequere, fili, sequere nos contemplando, aditus intuere ignorantiam declinando.' In angulo quidem orientali, ad dexteram eius ecclesie, mira sollercia lapis superpositus spelonce ultro revolvitur, quam   95
Abraham patriarcha summus ingreditur, superius memorata multitudo tam gloriosa prosequitur. Transeuntes vero septem portas marmoreas ultro reclusas, unam ingrediuntur basilicam, in cuius introitu, lapide revoluto, per quosdam ad inferiora descensus dimittuntur, ubi infra mausolea una sanctorum patriarcharum corpora habebantur inclusa multorumque preterea sanctorum, quorum revelationis indicium   100
nundum divinitus ostensum est. Canonicus igitur excitatus, tam propalata visione illustratus et ut cercior fieret ex his que fuerat contemplatus, ferro quodam, quod ibidem casus obtulerat, lapidem revolvit facillime quem ultro revolutum viderat in visione, speluncam deorsum reperiens, quam, funi affixo lumine et inferius demisso, visu tantum perlustravit undique. Dein lapide spelunce revoluto, que   105
audierat et viderat fratribus enuntiavit continuo. Hora autem diei erat quasi nona. Audito tante tamque obtate salutis desiderio irruunt ecclesiam affectu nimio, omni oblito cibario quo iam refici parabant. Res miranda: lapis, quem paulo ante solus revolutum advolverat, vix a bis senis iam revolvi poterat. Inferius intuentes speluncam una collaudant dei clementiam. Fama extimplo diffusa per totam   110
provintiam, ad hoc spectandum ad eandem omnes concurrunt ecclesiam. Inmissis vero fune fratribus, cum lucerna speluncam perlustrabant interius, cuius ad modum quinque cubitorum computabatur profundum. In qua vix reperitur aditus ulterior, quem prepediebat lapis marmoreus: multis enim diebus vix a macerie solutus – tanta vero fuerat soliditate coniunctus – artus hinc reperitur aditus, macerie undique   115
munitus, in quo alter post alterum pre angustia, tantum dimissis humeris a capite, vix poterat incedere. Quinque adhuc prioribus similes in aditu restabant lapidum

---

91–92 According to Kohler, "l'auteur ... dans cette phrase un peu contournée, veut dire probablement ceci: "Quel langage, sinon celui de l'ignorance, pourrait être tenu à celui qui viendrait contempler la prétendue découverte par le révélateur cherchant à excuser sa déconvenue?" That may have been the idea, but I consider the passage corrupt.   **95** Ioh. 11, 38: ... *venit ad monumentum. Erat autem spelunca, et lapis superpositus erat ei.*— Cf. 98.   **96** = 85.   **98** (105. 120) Marc. 16, 4: *revolutum lapidem*, Luc. 24, 2: *lapidem revolutum*.   **99** (cf. 110 = 126. 150) *una*: 'in one and the same place,' 'together.'
100–101 Cf. Text I, 395–397.   **101** = 68.   **102–103** Cf. 40.   **103–104** = 95.
105–106 = 98 and 70.   **110** (99) = 126. Act. 2, 47: *collaudantes deum*.   **114** solutus, *sc.* lapis] Nominative absolute.   **116** (cf. Terence, *Eun.* 314 (2, 3, 23): *demissis umeris*): *tantum ... a capite*: 'only by practically dislocating their shoulders.'

---

91 contumuliosos   **91–92** Cf. adn.   **95** spelonce *sic*   **99** descensus] et *add.* cod.   **100** indicium *correxi*: iudicium   **105** revolunto   **108** refici *e* reficit *corr.* cod.   **109** intuens   **112** ad modum *correxi*: admodum   **113** In qua vix *conieci*: Inqua vis   **114** mamoreus

obstructiones, quibus miro ac diuturno molimine a macerie dissolutis reperiunt
quandam basilicam XXIX lapidibus circumseptam et desuper solo contectam,
120 centum hominum experimento capacem. In cuius vero introitu revoluto lapide,
pavimento paululum eminentiore ebraicis litteris Ysaac atque Iacob inscripto
nomine, ipsorum gloriosa emicuere mausolea, haut longeque remotum, reclusa
porta marmorea, sancti Habrahe declaratur sepulcrum. Ex quo tanta tamque
suavis processit odoris flagrantia, quanta nullus hominum perlustratus est antea,
125 quinimmo in superiori sursum expectantes ecclesia, rati dulcedine perlustrari
paradisiaca, una collaudant dei magnalia, alternantes quis umquam sensit talia.
Revelatio vero tante exultationis contigit in vigilia beatissime virginis Marie
assumptionis, in qua etiam, adveniens de celo, Ierosolimis rutilans ignis effulsit
in templo ac super sanctissimum redemptionis nostre sepulcrum. O admiranda
130 dei dispensatio, o inenarranda dei exultatio, in qua in celum nostre salutis mater
assumitur, gloriosus in terris patriarcharum thesaurus aperitur, in qua celitus
adveniens rutilans ignis declaratur! O felix Ebron populus, quem ditavit thesaurus, o
spelunca admirabilis, cui nulla contentu similis, nulla artificio equiperabilis, nulla
tam copiosa tamque laudabilis! Ebronicus ergo clerus ac populus, tante revelationis
135 non ultra incredulus, una mittunt Ierosolimam consulere regem ac patriarcham,
ut qui preerant cultui christiane religionis diem constituerent et afforent tante
revelationi. Quorum communi consilio divinitus orantibus illibato pridie Nonas
Octobris ad translationem dies pronunciatur omnibus circummanentibus, ut qui
luctuosus extiterat exequiis patris Abrahe depositionis, gloriosus appareret
140 compendio eiusdem translationis. Cuius vero die per circuitum prenotata viritimque
Babiloniam usque delata, Ebron confluebant undique tam gentiles quam
Christicole, eorum pariter optantes cernere translationem, utrinque implorantes
eorum interventionem. O viri per omnia laudabiles, in quibus tam diversorum non
discrepat fides: alii venerantur per veteris testamenti successionem, alii per novi ac
145 veteris agnitionem, alii ut patres ac sue secte priores, alii agnitionis filii dei primos
doctores ac trium personarum in unitate predicatores. Ieiunio quidem septem
dierum in commune prius ab omnibus cum devotione celebrato, pridie Nonas
Octobris sanctorum patriarcharum corpora extracta mauseolis ac capsis inposita

---

120 = 98.   **126** Cf. 4.   **127–128** 14 August.   **129** Cf. 42.   **133** *contentu*: 'its contents'—apparently a newly formed substantive (cf. *continere*), cf. Stotz, *Handbuch* II, 6, 56: 1.   **135** Cf. 56.   **137** illibato] An extremely rare word (= *infuso*: 'communicated,' 'imparted'), cf. Latham, *Dictionary of Medieval Latin*, p. 1211; cf. Stotz, *Handbuch* II, 6, 101.   **137–138** (cf. 147–148) 6 October.   **142** *utrinque* = 141–142 *tam gentiles quam Christicole*.   **144** Cf. 1.   **147–148** = 137–138.   **148** mauseolis] See the critical apparatus.

---

119 et ... contectam *in margine*   **132** ditavit *e* dicavit *corr. cod.*   **141** delata *correxi* (*cf.* prenotata): delato (delato ebron. Confluebant *cod.*)   **144** *post* discrepat *deletum est* increpat   **148** mauseolis *(cf. 122) non corrigendum (cf. Stotz, Handbuch III, 296)!*

competentibus in superiorem transferuntur ecclesiam, tribus presulibus incoantibus
Te deum laudamus, ceteris idem una concinentibus. O quanta resultant laudum 150
preconia, o quanta gentilium ac Christicolarum exultatio, o quanta in utroque
populo sue peticionis devocio, o quanta omnium in ostensione corporum cunctorum
lacrimatio! Ex quibus tanta processit odoris fragrantia, ac si omnia aromata adessent
in presentia. O quanta et quam magnifica utrimque preparantur infirmantibus
beneficia, eorum affectuose poscentibus suffragia! Quorum nos translationis sacra 155
celebrantes sollempnia, ad ea quo precessere gaudia eorum nos perducant suffragia,
prestante domino nostro Iesu Christo, cui honor et gloria in eternum et ultra. Amen.

---

150 = 99.   **153–154** Cf. Text I, 223–225.   **154** *in presentia*: 'at/on hand,' 'on the spot:' *ThLL* X, 2, col. 856, 52ff. (64–67).

---

149 cumpetentibus   **152** ostensione *correxi*: ostensiones   **154** preparantur *correxi*: prerantur (parantur *sed coni.* procurantur *Kohler*)

REPORTS ON RECENT EXCAVATIONS

The Church of St John in Acre

Eliezer Stern

Israel Antiquities Authority

In 1995 a trial excavation was conducted in the courtyard of the Ottoman Serai. Part of a floor composed of marble tiles in different colours, three fallen marble columns and two marble capitals were uncovered. One of the capitals, covered by a coloured fresco, was in the Corinthian style; the second, also with a coloured fresco, bears a Maltese cross painted in red on a black background. In addition many stained-glass window fragments in various colours were found strewn on the floor. These elements apparently comprise parts of the nave of the church of St John.

Another excavation was carried out in the Serai in 2003. Two trenches were excavated in the western part of the building. The trenches exposed features associated with the principal west door of the church, among which was a threshold stone of black granite, 4 m wide, with two hewn door sockets. Bases of the pilasters that supported the ribs of a cross-vault were unearthed in two corners of the room.

Two additional trenches, excavated in the eastern part of the Serai, uncovered remains of a chancel screen. The northern face of the screen was exposed to a length of 4 m and a height of 0.60 m. The screen was carved in relief on slabs of hard *nari* limestone within a carved defining border. The slabs were positioned in a row, one adjacent to the other.

Remains of the church floor were found in all the excavated areas. The floor was composed of marble and glazed tiles in a variety of colours. Few of the tiles were found in their original setting, most having been robbed, leaving only their negative impressions in the floor make-up.

Latrun

Adrian Boas

Haifa University

In August 2003 clearance work and a surface survey were carried out at the site of the Templar castle Toron des Chevaliers (Latrun), near the Tel-Aviv–Jerusalem highway. The Israel Antiquities Authority with the support of the Armoured Corps Association organized the project, which was directed by Rafael Lewis, advised by Adrian Boas. It took place over a period of three weeks, employing about 65 workers. Clearance of the accumulated surface debris and vegetation exposed parts of the castle which had long been hidden from view and certain elements which were not previously recorded.

This castle has never been excavated, with the exception of limited investigations carried out within the grounds of the Trappist monastery to the north of the site by M. Louhivuori (for the University of Karlsruhe, Germany) in 1995. However, a number of surveys have been carried out in the past. The plans of an unpublished survey by D. Bellamy are located in the Palestine Exploration Fund offices in London. M. Ben Dov's survey was published in Hebrew in 1974.[1] D. Pringle carried out the survey for the British School of Archaeology in Jerusalem in 1989 (with a plan drawn by M. Pease).[2] Z. Greenhut's survey was conducted for an internal publication of the Israel Antiquities Authority in 2001. These examinations provided detailed plans of the site and the present survey aimed at clarifying certain discrepancies in these plans and providing new information.

The castle, which is located on an ancient tell, appears to consist of three main elements: a tower keep, a rectangular enclosure and an outer ward consisting of curtain walls, vaults and towers. The castle chapel is believed to have been located on the eastern side of the inner ward and a group of remarkably fine Romanesque capitals, found at the site in the early twentieth century and now in Istanbul, probably originated in it.

Discoveries made by the present survey include all four faces of the inner ward with its steep external talus (on the north this wall was exposed for almost its entire length). A portal in the barrel-vaulted hall on the northern side of this ward, which did not appear in the plans published by Bellamy and Pringle, was exposed and other elements in the southern groin-vaulted range were defined. Several architectural elements scattered around the site were photographed and measured, and masons'

---

[1] "The Fortress of Latrun," *Qadmoniot* 7.3/4.117–20.
[2] Denys Pringle, *Secular Buildings in the Crusader Kingdom of Jerusalem: An Archaeological Gazetteer* (Cambridge, 1997), pp. 64–65; *The Churches of the Crusader Kingdom of Jerusalem: An Archaeological Gazetteer* 2 (Cambridge, 1998), pp. 5–9; "Templar Castles between Jaffa and Jerusalem," *MO*, 2.89–109.

marks were recorded. Through the generous aid of Boaz Peleg and Ehud Heffer aerial photographs were taken of the site after the clearance was completed.

A paper describing these finds and discussing the history and architecture of the castle is being prepared and it is hoped that the present work will aid in providing funding for badly needed restoration and conservation work and for the future excavation of this important site.

REVIEWS

Thomas S. Asbridge, *The Creation of the Principality of Antioch, 1098–1130*. Woodbridge: The Boydell Press, 2000. Pp. xii, 233. ISBN 0 85115 661 4.

This is a book in the best tradition of advanced military history. It provides a meticulous framework of the early history of the crusader principality of Antioch. The primary focus is on the changeful territorial history of the principality, and, indeed, the frequency with which cities and fortresses change hands may at times appear confusing. But the territorial gains and losses are the key to understanding the strategic and political context of its early history, which is at the heart of this volume. Other major topics covered are the evolution of the secular government and its various institutions and offices (quite different from those in the kingdom of Jerusalem), relations with the neighboring Christian and Muslim lordships and states, and the status of the prince of Antioch. In the latter section it is argued that use of the title "prince" was intended as a political statement aimed at asserting the political autonomy of Antioch vis-à-vis both the Byzantine empire and the kingdom of Jerusalem (pp. 132–33). The final chapter on the ecclesiastical history includes a highly readable and stimulating section on Bernard of Valence, the first Latin patriarch of Antioch (1100–35). His long term of office at a time when the lay rule changed hands so frequently enabled him to exert considerable influence on the history of the principality. This may serve as a good example of the complex interplay between secular and ecclesiastical authorities in the administration of the Latin East.

Our knowledge of the principality is based on meagre sources, the most significant of which, as the author argues, is the previously underrated Walter the Chancellor's *Bella Antiochena* (pp. 5–7). The lack of sources is necessarily reflected in the text of the book which frequently, if clearly, informs the reader that the author is about to leave the *terra firma* of the original sources and must venture into the realm of conjecture, however reasonable. But the author makes the most of the incomplete sources. For example, he quite convincingly argues that the fateful Battle of the Field of Blood in 1119 was the result of an opportunistic decision by Il-Ghazi to forego the planned attack on al-Atharib when he realized that the Latin army was camped in a vulnerable position (pp. 75–76).

Several line-drawn maps (which, unfortunately, lack topographical information) are essential for understanding the narrative, which is also augmented by a prosopographical study and table of lay landholders in the principality, a comprehensive index, and several concise summaries. The style of writing is terse, however, and indeed the book would not have been the worse for some amplifications of the dry facts: for example, after Bohemond's departure for the West in 1104/05, the key figure in the history of Antioch was Tancred. The reader may understandably be curious about the cause of the death in 1112 of this ambitious and indeed outstanding Antiochene ruler: did he succumb to an enemy in battle, to illness or debauchery?

The strength of the book is the overriding concern for understanding the strategic situation in northern Syria in the broadest sense, and how it influenced the policy decisions of the Antiochene leadership. Occasional truces and revenue-sharing notwithstanding, Antioch and Aleppo were the principal antagonists in this region, and for the most part, Antiochene policy aimed at the eventual capture of the Muslim city. It is well worth keeping in mind that in the period under discussion, or at the least until 1119, the continued Muslim success in resisting the Frankish pressure on Aleppo was anything but a foregone conclusion. The importance of Antioch for the Latin East should not be underestimated, and Thomas Asbridge's book makes this authoritatively clear.

MARTIN HOCH
KONRAD-ADENAUER-FOUNDATION, SANKT AUGUSTIN, GERMANY

The Canso d'Antioca*: An Occitan Epic Chronicle of the First Crusade*, ed. and trans. Carol Sweetenham and Linda M. Paterson. Aldershot: Ashgate, 2003. Pp. xi, 363. ISBN 0 7546 0410 1.

The Old French Crusade Cycle Volume IV: La Chanson d'Antioche, ed. Jan A. Nelson. Tuscaloosa and London: University of Alabama Press, 2003. Pp. 865. ISBN 0 8173 1294 3.

The *Canso d'Antioca* edited by Sweetenham and Paterson is no more than a surviving fragment of a copy of a version of a putative work written in Occitan by Gregory Bechada in the first half of the twelfth century. It occupies forty-six pages: twenty-three each of Occitan edition and facing translation (pp. 192–237). The publishers as well as the writers are to be commended for presenting the restored Occitan text alongside the very readable translation. This editon definitively replaces that of Paul Meyer in the *Archives de l'Orient latin* (1884).

The text is preceded by four closely argued chapters. The first examines the evidence for Bechada's "verse chronicle" of the First Crusade and argues for the development of a *Canso d'Antioca* tradition based upon it. The "Madrid fragment" which contains the extant *Canso* is described, and there is an exhaustive discussion of its relationship with the Spanish poem, the *Gran Conquista de Ultramar*. The editors conclude that the latter preserves further fragments of the *Canso* tradition. In Chapter 2 there is an equally searching investigation of the relationship between the *Canso* and the Old French tradition of the First Crusade, in particular the *Chanson d'Antioche*. Since the *Antioche* has been the subject of much scrutiny, this is of exceptional interest. While giving full weight to the arguments for and against a "primitive *chanson*" of Richard the Pilgrim, the editors conclude, fairly enough, that there is a relationship between the French and the Occitan traditions, but that each poem is too distant from its lost antecedent for the precise nature of the relationship to be established.

The *Canso* is then examined as a historical source, which entails a survey of the eye-witness and other early accounts of the First Crusade. As others have done, the editors conclude that relationships are complex, and that legendary material is to be found in all the sources. Their conclusion is that: "There is no reason to accord the *Canso* tradition any less credence than any other source for the crusade – nor any more." In view of its distance from events and the lack of antecedent texts, this might be considered an over-generous assessment. An interesting aspect of the historical discussion is the exact content of the fragment, which is a description of the battle of Antioch; it begins, apparently at the start of a *laisse*, with the drawing up of the battle lines, but ends abruptly in the midst of the fray. The preservation of this fragment, and no other, of the *Canso* reflects the centrality of the battle of Antioch in the whole campaign which was the First Crusade, as the editors rightly observe.

The fourth and longest introductory chapter looks at the *Canso* as literature, and its place in epic tradition. The discussion of vernacular historiography is wide-ranging, encompassing Anglo-Norman as well as Latin and Old French texts. Much of it focuses on the lost composition of Gregory Bechada, and is necessarily speculative. It is likely to be of more interest to literary scholars than to historians. There follows a short exposition of editorial principles and practices before the text and translation. The editors have provided a full critical apparatus, including rejected readings as footnotes; explanatory notes keyed by line; glossary; bibliography, and index of proper names. Without wishing to detract from their considerable achievement, there are one major and a couple of minor quibbles. The first is, no doubt, the consequence of providing camera-ready copy: at the very beginning, as one turns from page 1 to 2, something has dropped out of the text. It may be no more than a couple of lines, but it introduces the Madrid fragment and without it the initial line of argument collapses. More subjectively, the close arguments of the introductory chapters involve rather a lot of repetition, and provision of translations of Latin extracts but not of the various medieval vernaculars seems odd.

By coincidence, 2003 also saw the publication of the final volume (of ten) in the Alabama Press edition of the Old French Crusade Cycle, *La Chanson d'Antioche*. This volume presents a striking contrast to the *Canso* edition. The *Antioche* is, of course, a much longer text, and in this edition it occupies just over 300 pages, not counting the appendices and without a translation. The introductory material is, by comparison with the *Canso* at least, exiguous: a note of the two previous editions; a summary of the narrative; a short explanation of how the *Antioche* fits into the Cycle; a description and discussion of the manuscripts, and a bibliography occupy altogether 32 pages. The main text is followed by 9 appendices which are passages not in the main manuscript tradition; 400 pages of variants keyed by line, and an index of proper names.

There are no historical notes, nor is there any discussion of the historical value of the text. The editor believed – correctly – that the 1977 edition of Suzanne Duparc-Quioc has rendered such a discussion superfluous. One could, rather unkindly, say the same for the edition as a whole. In order not to replicate the previous edition, Nelson chose a different base manuscript, which he shows to be the most inclusive. He also recorded variants from all extant manuscripts. However, for the historian who will wish to use Duparc's extensive notes, it is a great inconvenience that the two editions early part company as to line and *laisse* and there is no concordance. For example, the famous battalion of women is *laisse* 327, lines 8295–320 in Duparc; *laisse* 342, lines 10093–118 in Nelson. From the historian's point of view (again) one would wish for a different approach. Nevertheless, this volume marks the culmination of a worthy enterprise, conceived nearly forty years ago, which has made available in definitive editions the whole of the Crusade cycle, from *La Naissance du Chevalier au Cygne* to *Godefroi de Buillon*. The series also stands as a fitting tribute to Jan Nelson, who saw its completion before his recent death.

SUSAN B. EDGINGTON
QUEEN MARY, UNIVERSITY OF LONDON

The Assizes of the Lusignan Kingdom of Cyprus, trans. Nicholas Coureas (Cyprus Research Centre Texts and Studies in the History of Cyprus, 42.) Nicosia: Cyprus Research Centre, 2002. Pp. 404. ISBN 9963 0 8074 X.

The original French text of the *Livre des Assises des Bourgeois* was written in Acre and has been dated to about 1250. In the 1530s the Venetian authorities in Cyprus arranged for it to be translated into Italian, but by that date there already existed at least two Greek versions. Indeed, two Greek manuscripts survive, one dated to 1512 and the other to 1469, each preserving the text of a different translation. Precisely when these translations were made is unclear, and, although the 1512 manuscript would seem to contain linguistic traits that suggest that its version is earlier, the evidence for determining which of the two texts came first is not entirely clear cut. Sathas edited these manuscripts in 1877, and it is his edition that Dr Coureas has now translated into English. It appears that two other manuscript copies of Greek versions of the *Assises* were once extant. C.E. Zachariae von Lingenthal published 61 chapters from one of them in his *Historiae Juris graeco-romani Delineatio* (Heidelberg, 1839). This manuscript appears to have contained preferable readings to those in the extant 1512 manuscript, but Coureas admits that he has not been able to consult Zachariae von Lingenthal's work and has had to content himself with Sathas's references to it.

The *Livre des Assises des Bourgeois* provides an account of the law as administered in the burgess court at Acre. In other words, it deals with civil, commercial and criminal matters as they affected the non-noble population. Clearly the law applied in the burgess courts in Cyprus was sufficiently similar for the

French text to be copied and preserved there and also for it to be translated into both Greek and Italian. The Greek versions both approximate most closely to the version of the French text to be found in a manuscript now in Munich. This manuscript, a characteristic of which is the presence of a number of sentences and sometimes longer passages in Latin, was used by E.H. Kausler as the base for his edition which appeared in 1839, and it is the version preserved there that modern scholars generally consider superior to the other French texts. What is striking is that both Greek translations contain statements that specifically relate to circumstances obtaining in Acre, evidence that the translators were reluctant to adapt the text to suit their Cypriot context. The importance of the *Livre des Assises des Bourgeois*, however, is not in doubt. Among the many topics discussed are claims for medical malpractice, merchandise lost through wreck, the ordeal to exonerate a man accused of rape, and the rights and obligations of the man who manages to catch an escaped falcon, as well as more mundane matters such as debt, theft and homicide. The Greek texts both include the long lists of tariffs on imported merchandise, although much of this apparently related specifically to Acre and so was presumably irrelevant in Cyprus.

There is therefore much here that is of interest, and Dr Coureas has done well to make the Greek texts more readily available to researchers. It is inevitable that a reviewer will have quibbles. Although Coureas rightly discusses how much of the Latin portions of the text that are to be found in the Munich manuscript was omitted from both Greek translations, it is a pity that he does not identify or analyse those sections which were derived ultimately from the Provençal text known as *Lo Codi* nor examine how they fared at the hands of the translators. (Half a century ago Joshua Prawer demonstrated that the anonymous author of the *Livre* used *Lo Codi*, thereby allowing his construction of the law in the kingdom of Jerusalem to be influenced by the western European tradition of Roman Law.) At page 14 Coureas offers a definition of the word "assizes". Here he follows Maurice Grandclaude in claiming that one meaning of the word was "the whole *corpus* of legislation" and that this definition had become "the most prevalent by the beginning of the thirteenth century." I fear that Grandclaude, writing in 1923, was wrong, and that, when "*assises*" does not refer explicitly to enacted legislation, it is employed simply as a shorthand term for "*assises et usages*" (as used for example in the heading for the table of rubrics in the printed editions of the *Livre des Assises des Bourgeois*). This is not the only place where Coureas has been misled by Grandclaude. At page 29 he repeats Grandclaude's idiosyncratic view based on a misunderstanding of Philip of Novara's account of the Cypriot civil war of 1229–33 that it was only from 1233 onwards that kings and his vassals in Cyprus had sworn to uphold the *assises* of Jerusalem. Also the idea (p. 31) that Famagusta only acquired a burgess court of its own in the early years of the reign of King Henry II (1285–1324) is strange. Certainly there are no references to it before that period, but then the town is very poorly documented for most of the thirteenth century. Famagusta had, however, been important enough to be the seat of a Latin bishopric since the 1190s, and it is more likely that its burgess court similarly dated from the early years of Frankish rule. These criticisms, however, do not affect the value of Coureas's work which will undoubtedly provide a useful took for students of medieval law and society in Cyprus and the Latin East and of medieval law in general.

PETER EDBURY
CARDIFF UNIVERSITY

La Commanderie: Institution des ordres militaires dans l'Occident médiévale, ed. Anthony Luttrell and Léon Pressouyre (Archéologie et histoire de l'art, 14). Paris, Comité des travaux historiques et scientifiques, 2002. Pp. 361. ISBN 2 7355 0485 9 (paperback).

Die Kommende war in allen Ritterorden die kleinste Einheit, auf der Ordensstruktur und Besitzverwaltung beruhten. Sie bestimmte zudem den Rahmen, in dem sich das alltägliche Leben der Ordensbrüder entfaltete. In allen Fallstudien zur regionalen oder lokalen Entwicklung eines Ritterordens spielen die Kommenden daher eine zentrale Rolle. Als Institution ist die Kommende jedoch bislang kaum vergleichend in den Blick genommen worden. Diese Lücke schließt der vorliegende Sammelband mit einigen grundlegenden Beiträgen, zu denen zahlreiche weitere Einzeluntersuchungen treten.

Jonathan Riley-Smith ("The Origins of the Commandery in the Temple and the Hospital," S. 9–18), zeigt auf, dass die Johanniter ihre Besitzungen im Abendland zunächst von St-Gilles und Messina aus verwalteten, während die Templer von Anfang an eigenständige Häuser auf den ihnen übertragenen Besitzkomplexen einrichteten. Die Entwicklung lief jedoch in beiden Orden auf die Ausbildung einer mittleren Ebene hinaus, vermutlich eine pragmatische Lösung des sich beiden Orden stellenden Problems, dass sie die Verwaltung ihrer Besitzungen im Westen vom Heiligen Land aus nicht unmittelbar überwachen konnten, andererseits aber die Geber Wert darauf legten, dass ihre Schenkungen dem Heiligen Land zu gute kamen. Jean Marie Carbasse ("Les commanderies: aspects juridiques et institutionnels," S. 19–27), betont den unterschiedlichen Status der Kommenden im kirchlichen und weltlichen Recht. Kirchenrechtlich nichts weiter als einfache "maisons religieuses," wurden sie durch ihre Ausstattung mit weltlichen Herrschaftsrechten zu eigenständigen "seigneuries." Ausführlich untersucht Jean-Marc Roger, ("Les différents types de commanderies du prieuré de Champagne au XVe siècle," S. 29–56), die Unterschiede der Johanniterkommenden in der Champagne: Einkünfte, Stellung in der Hierarchie, wirtschaftliche Funktion. Besondere Beachtung verdient seine Darstellung der "partition" durch die die Verteilung der Kommenden auf die Gruppen der Ritter, Priester und *sergents* ausgehandelt wurde. Luis García-Guijarro Ramos ("The Development of a System of Commanderies in the Early Years of the Order of Montesa, 1319–1330," S. 57–73) zeigt auf, wie sich in dem kleinen, unter unmittelbarer Aufsicht der Krone stehenden Orden, der 1319 aus den Niederlassungen der Templer und Johanniter im Königreich Valencia hervorging, bis 1330 eine Struktur eigenständiger Kommenden ausbildete, obwohl der Anteil der zentral verwalteten Mittel weiterhin hoch blieb. Carlos de Ayala Martínez ("Les commanderies des ordres militaires en Castille et León au Moyen Âge. Étapes d'une évolution," S. 75–90) weist nach, wie in den Jahren 1175–1225 (*phase de formation*) Niederlassungen der Ritterorden entstehen, die noch kein Netzwerk bilden und daher oft instabil sind, wie in den Jahren 1225–75 diese Niederlassungen zu einem strukturierten System von Kommenden ausgebaut werden (*phase de territorialisation*) und wie schließlich im 14. und 15. Jahrhundert durch Lockerung der Gelübde der Armut und der Ehelosigkeit die Kommenden zum persönlichen Besitz der Ordensritter werden, denen sie übertragen worden sind (*phase de patrimonialisation*).

Eine Reihe von Beiträgen ist der Personalstruktur der Kommenden gewidmet. Von grundlegender Bedeutung ist der Beitrag von Helen Nicholson ("Women in Templar and Hospitaller Commanderies," S. 125–34). Sie hebt hervor, daß alle großen Ritterorden, auch wenn dies in ihren Statuten nicht vorgesehen war, Frauen aufnahmen, und zwar zum Dienst in den Kommenden der Männer ebenso wie zur Bildung eigener Frauenkonvente. Ebenso wichtig ist der Beitrag von Alan Forey ("Provision for the Aged in Templar Commanderies," S. 175–85), der aufzeigt, daß es nur in England erkennbare Ansätze zur Bildung eigener Häuser gab, in denen alt und gebrechlich gewordene Ordensbrüder versorgt wurden, im allgemeinen jedoch (und meist auch in England) alterende Brüder in dem Haus blieben, in dem sie zuletzt gedient hatten. Wegweisend ist ferner der Beitrag von Anthony Luttrell ("The Finances of the Commander in the Hospital after 1306," S. 277–83), der eindrucksvoll darstellt, in welchem Ausmass das Privateigentum der Ordensbrüder im 14. Jahrhundert verbreitet war (mit weitreichenden Auswirkungen für die Aussagekraft der Rechnungen der einzelnen Kommenden als wirtschaftsgeschichtliche Quellen). Alain Demurger untersucht in knapper Form die Größe der Templerkommenden (S. 135–43). Karl Borchardt (S. 297–305) analysiert für Deutschland die Auswirkung der Niederlassung der Ritterorden in Städten auf die Sozialstruktur der Konvente. Michel Miguet (S. 93–105), untersucht anhand der Akten des Templerprozesses und der päpstlichen Untersuchung des Jahres 1373 über den Besitz der Johanniter Zahl, Stellung und Mobilität des Personals in den einzelnen Häusern, doch sind die Ergebnisse beider Teile seiner Untersuchung aufgrund der Unterschiede in Zeit und Quellenlage nicht vergleichbar.

Die Wirtschaft einzelner Kommenden ist Gegenstand zahlreicher Beiträge: Benoît Beaucage (S. 107–23), analysiert anhand der Protokolle der Generalvisitation von 1338 die Wirtschaftsführung der provenzalischen Kommenden. Die auch von Miguet herangezogenen *interrogatoires du procès des Templiers* und die *enquête pontificale* des Johanniterbesitzes von 1373 bilden die Grundlage weiterer Beiträge: Jean Delmas (S. 319–27) skizziert für das Jahr 1308 die Besitzverwaltung der Templerkommende Ste-Eulalie du Larzac (zu deren Befestigung durch die Johanniter im 14.–16. Jahrhundert vgl. den Beitrag von Jacques Miquel, S. 329–58).

Noël Coulet wertet die Angaben für die südfranzösischen Johanniter unter alltagsgeschichtlichem Aspekt aus (S. 147–57). Robert Favreau (S. 261–76) analysiert die Angaben von 1373 für die Diözese Saintes und zeigt die wirtschaftlichen Auswirkungen des Hundertjährigen Krieges auf (*une économie ruinée par la guerre*). Vergleichend untersucht Michael Gervers (S. 245–60) die wirtschaftliche Entwicklung der Templer und Johanniter in London und Essex und zeigt auf, daß die Templer den Johannitern an Geldeinkünften weit überlegen waren. Der aufgrund der schlechten Quellenlage wenig behandelten Frage der Schiffahrt der Templer widmet sich am Beispiel La Rochelles Jean-Claude Bonnin (S. 307–15).

Den Deutschen Orden behandelt der Beitrag von Dieter Weiß über das "spirituelle Leben" der Deutschordensbrüder, das sich als im wesentlichen durch das niederadlige Umfeld der einzelnen Kommenden bestimmt erweist, in dem aber neben der Erinnerung an das Heilige Land besonders die Verehrung des hl. Georg und der Gottesmutter, in Franken außerdem der hl. Elisabeth gepflegt wurde (S. 159–73). Ausführlich behandelt Sven Ekdahl ("The Strategic Organization of the Commanderies in Prussia and Livonia," S. 219–42).

Zsolt Hunyadi (S. 285–96) untersucht die privilegierte Stellung der ungarischen Johanniterkommenden als *loci credibiles*, die mit ihrem Siegel Rechtsgeschäfte beglaubigen konnten. Joan Fuguet Sans (S. 187–217) beschreibt die Befestigungsanlagen der Templer in Aragón (Barberá, Miravet, Gardeny, Peníscola, Xivert, Monzón, Castellote).

Das Thema Kommende hat die Bearbeiter der Beiträge teils zu vergleichenden Untersuchungen, zu Einzelfragen, teils zu detaillierten Untersuchungen einzelner oder mehrerer Häuser veranlaßt und insofern stimulierend gewirkt. Der Zusammenhang der einzelnen Beiträge mit dem Thema des Bandes ist allerdings oft nur schwer erkennbar. Gleichwohl ist die Publikation des Bandes durch die hohe Qualität der meisten Beiträge mehr als gerechtfertigt.

KLAUS VAN EICKELS
OTTO-FRIEDRICH-UNIVERSITÄT BAMBERG

The Crusades from the Perspective of Byzantium and the Muslim World, ed. Angeliki E. Laiou and Roy Parviz Mottahedeh. Washington, D.C.: Dumbarton Oaks Research Library and Collection, 2001. Pp. viii, 297. ISBN 0 88402 277 3.

Der vorliegende Band vereinigt insgesamt 15 Beiträge, die auf einer aus Anlass des 900. Jahrestags der Belagerung Nikaias durch die Ritter des 1. Kreuzzugs veranstalteten Tagung vom 2. bis 4. Mai 1997 gehalten wurden. Allerdings findet dieses Ereignis nirgends einen besonderen Niederschlag, so daß dieses Jubiläum eher beliebig erscheint. Gegenstand der Tagung war, wie der Titel aussagt, die Haltung der Byzantiner und Muslime gegenüber den Kreuzzügen. Diese Perspektive gewinnt in der Forschung zunehmend an Raum, wie auch die ähnlich gelagerten Tagungen in Huesca und Binghamton (beide 1999) zeigen, deren Akten gleichfalls zur Veröffentlichung anstehen.

Die Beiträge selbst sind inhaltlich weiter gestreut, als der Titel vermuten läßt. Als Einführung gibt Giles Constable ("The Historiography of the Crusades," S. 1–22) einen souveränen Überblick über die Kreuzzugsforschung von ihren Anfängen bis in die jüngste Zeit: Notwendigerweise nicht vollständig, aber sinnvoll vor allem wegen der von Constable sichtbar gemachten Tendenzen.

Den "ideologischen" Entsprechungen der Kreuzzüge im Islam und in Byzanz widmen sich Roy Parviz Mottahedeh / Ridwan al-Sayyid und George T. Dennis. Mottahedeh und al-Sayyid ("The Idea of the Jihad in Islam before the Crusades," S. 23–29) beschäftigen sich vor allem mit den Verhältnissen im frühen Islam und weisen darauf hin, dass es kein einheitliches Konzept des Jihad gibt. Die in dieser Zeit entwickelten Konzepte wurden zum Teil auch während der Epoche der Kreuzzüge benutzt, aber man kann nicht davon sprechen, dass "Jihad" ausschließlich als "Heiliger Krieg gegen alle Ungläubigen" verstanden worden ist. Demgegenüber hat laut Dennis ("Defenders of the Christian People: Holy War in Byzantium," S. 31–39) in Byzanz ein solches Konzept überhaupt nicht existiert, da die Byzantiner den Krieg als ein grundsätzliches Übel abgelehnt hätten. Auch wenn dies theoretisch zutrifft, scheint die nahezu völlige Ablehnung von Gewalt, wie Dennis sie aufgrund der programmatischen Aussagen in verschiedenen byzantinischen Kriegshandbüchern unterstellt, doch etwas überzogen. In der Praxis haben auch die Byzantiner Angriffskriege geführt und diese durchaus nicht immer als "Verteidigung der Christenheit und der Christen" begriffen. Natürlich lehnte man die Kreuzzüge ab, da man sie auch als Angriff auf byzantinisches oder zumindest von Byzanz beanpsruchtes Gebiet begriff, aber es bleibt doch zu fragen, ob die rhetorische Überhöhung dieser Ablehnung bei Anna Komnene oder anderen byzantinischen Schriftstellern nicht doch in erster Linie literarisches Stilmittel gewesen ist. Zumindest begriffen die Byzantiner das mit den Kreuzzügen verbundene Konzept so weit, dass Manuel I. Komnenos 1175 selbst einen Kreuzzug anregen konnte, auch wenn er selbst ihn sicherlich als einen "imperial war" im Sinn von Dennis betrachtet haben dürfte.

Am interessantesten dürften wohl die Beiträge sein, die sich mit der Wahrnehmung der Kreuzzüge bzw. des lateinischen Europa im Orient befassen. So untersucht M.C. Lyons ("The Land of War: Europe in the Arab Hero Cycles," S. 41–51) das Europabild in den arabischen Epen, Robert W. Thomson ("The Crusaders through Armenian Eyes," S. 71–82) befaßt sich mit der Sicht der armenischen Quellen auf die Kreuzzüge. Alexander Kazhdan ("Latins and Franks in Byzantium: Perception and Reality from the Eleventh to the Twelfth Century," S. 83–100) analysiert das Verhältnis von Lateinern und Byzantinern in der Romania während des 11. und 12. Jahrhunderts und die Einstellung zueinander. Elizabeth und Michael Jeffreys ("The 'Wild Beast from the West': Immediate Literary Reactions in Byzantium to the Second Crusade," S. 101–16) konzentrieren sich auf den Niederschlag des Zweiten Kreuzzugs in byzantinischen rhetorischen Texten während und kurz nach dem Unternehmen. Auffällig ist hier insbesondere die negative Charakterisierung selbst bei solchen Personen, mit denen Byzanz positive Verbindungen unterhielt, wie etwa Heinrich Jasomirgott, dessen Braut Theodora Komnene anläßlich ihrer Heirat mit Heinrich bedauert wird, dass sie "das wilde Tier aus dem Westen" heiraten muß. Gerade dieser Beitrag ergänzt in erfreulicher Weise die 1987 erschienene Studie von Herbert Hunger über die gegenseitige Wahrnehmung von Griechen und Lateinern (Herbert Hunger, *Graeculus perfidus – Italos itamos. Il senso dell' alterità nei rapporti Greco-Romani ed Italo-Bizantini.* Rome, 1987). Komplettiert wird diese Sektion durch Tia M. Kolbaba ("Byzantine Perceptions of Latin Religious 'Errors': Themes and Changes from 850 to 1350," S. 117–43), die die "Irrtümer" der lateinischen Theologie, wie sie von den Byzantinern zwischen dem 9. und 14. Jahrhundert aufgefaßt wurden, darstellt. Kolbaba hat sich dieses Themas wenig später in einer eigenen Monographie noch einmal ausführlich angenommen (Tia M. Kolbaba, *The Byzantine Lists. Errors of the Latins.* Urbana und Chicago, 2000). Thematisch etwas aus dem Rahmen der Tagung fällt Nadia Maria El-Cheikh ("Byzantium through the Islamic Prism from the Twelfth to the Thirteenth Century," S. 53–69), die Byzanz aus der islamischen Perspektive des 12. und 13. Jahrhunderts untersucht. Man vermisst eine ähnliche Analyse zu den Kreuzzügen in den arabischen Quellen, die bisher in der Forschung – schon aus sprachlichen Gründen – viel zu sehr vernachlässigt worden sind. Ebenso fehlen leider die syrischen Quellen, obwohl die Chroniken Michaels des Syrers aus dem 12. und Abulfaradjs aus dem 13. Jahrhundert sowie die anonyme Chronik von 1234 mit zu den wichtigsten Quellen des christlichen Orients über die Kreuzzüge zählen.

Die ökonomischen Veränderungen in Byzanz infolge der Kreuzzüge werden von Angeliki E. Laiou und David Jacoby untersucht. Laiou ("Byzantine Trade with Christians and Muslims and the Crusades," S. 157–96) konzentriert sich hierbei auf den rechtlichen Status vor allem der italienischen Kaufleute im 12. Jahrhundert, auf die Versorgung der durch die Romania marschierenden Kreuzfahrerheere und auf die Relationen der byzantinischen Währung zu verschiedenen westlichen (zu letzterem hat Cécile Morrisson im Rahmen dieses Beitrags einen eigenen Appendix beigesteuert, S. 192–96). Im Zusammenhang mit dem hierbei behandelten Dritten Kreuzzug wäre ein Blick auf die Arbeit von Rudolf Hiestand ("'Precipua tocius christianismi columpna.' Barbarossa und der Kreuzzug," in: Alfred Haverkamp (Hrsg.), *Friedrich Barbarossa. Handlungsspielräume.* Sigmaringen, 1992, S. 51–108) nützlich gewesen, der ebenfalls auf diese Probleme eingeht.

David Jacoby ("Changing Economic Patterns in Latin Romania: The Impact of the West," S. 197–233) widmet sich den Verhältnissen in der lateinischen Romania nach 1204 und liefert dabei im wesentlichen eine nützliche Zusammenfassung seiner eigenen, früheren Forschungen auf diesem Gebiet. Den christlichen Fernhandel im islamischen Raum untersucht Olivia Remie Constable ("Funduq, Fondaco, and Khan in the Wake of Christian Commerce and Crusade," S. 145–56), indem sie die Institutionen und ihre Bezeichnungen vergleicht, die der Unterbringung auswärtiger Händler und Reisender dienten. Auch wenn hier durchaus interessante Beobachtungen zu finden sind, vermisst man doch eine Untersuchung zu dem Fernhandel selbst, zu den Handelswaren und zu den möglichen Veränderungen im islamischen Orient durch die verstärkte Handelsintensität zur Zeit der Kreuzzüge.

Der Band wird abgeschlossen durch die Sektion "Kunst und Architektur." Oleg Grabar ("The Crusades and the Development of Islamic Art," S. 235–45) gibt einen kurzen Überblick über den Einfluss der Kreuzzüge auf die Entwicklung der islamischen Kunst. Er sieht – mit einigen wenigen Ausnahmen im Bereich der Architektur – keinen direkten Einfluss. Ebensowenig hatte die islamische Kunst ihrerseits direkte Auswirkungen auf das lateinische Europa, abgesehen vielleicht von dem normannischen Unteritalien und Sizilien. In ähnlicher Weise verneint Charalambos Bouras ("The Impact of Frankish Architecture on Thirteenth-Century Byzantine Architecture," S. 247–62) einen größeren Einfluß der lateinischen Architektur auf auf die byzantinische im 13. Jahrhundert und später. Lateinischer Baustil fand eigentlich nur in den Regionen Eingang, die unter fränkischer Herrschaft standen, während die Byzantiner ihn eher ablehnten. Demgegenüber sieht Sharon E.J. Gestel ("Art and Identity in the Medieval Morea," S. 263–85), die sich in ihrem Artikel vorwiegend auf die Darstellung berittener Soldatenheiliger auf dem Peloponnes konzentriert, bei allen Unterschieden doch eine gewisse wechselseitige Befruchtung.

Wenn man bei diesem Band etwas vermisst, dann den religiösen und den literarischen Bereich. Die Trennung der beiden Kirchen führte, auch über die von Kolbaba behandelten "Irrtümer" hinaus, zu einer intensiven Auseinandersetzung um die Unterschiede in dogmatischen und liturgischen Fragen, über die man gerne etwas mehr erfahren hätte (siehe z. B. Jannis Spiteris O.F.M., *La Critica Bizantina del Primato Romano nel secolo XII*. Rome, 1979), und im literarischen Bereich begegnen in Byzanz seit dem 12. Jahrhundert neue Werke, in denen der westliche Einfluss unverkennbar ist (siehe dazu beispielsweise jetzt P.A. Agapitos und D.R. Reinsch [Hrsg.], *Der Roman im Byzanz der Komnenenzeit*. Frankfurt am Main, 2000). Allerdings sollte man vielleicht von einer Tagung keine vollständige Behandlung aller Aspekte eines so umfangreichen Themas erwarten. In jedem Fall haben wir hier eine Reihe hochinformativer, niveauvoller Beiträge, die dem interessierten Leser einen guten Überblick über den derzeitigen Forschungsstand geben. Und das ist mehr, als man von vielen anderen Sammelbänden der jüngeren Zeit sagen kann.

RALPH-JOHANNES LILIE
BERLIN-BRANDENBURGISCHE AKADEMIE DER WISSENSCHAFTEN, BERLIN

Yvonne Friedman, *Encounter between Enemies: Captivity and Ransom in the Latin Kingdom of Jerusalem* (Cultures, Beliefs and Traditions: Medieval and Early Modern Peoples, 10). Leiden: Brill, 2002. Pp. xx, 295. ISBN 90 04 11706 7.

Given that captivity was a perennial danger for crusaders and their opponents in the course of all crusading expeditions as well as in the frontier warfare of Outremer, Spain and the Baltic lands, it is remarkable that until now there has been no full-length general treatment of the subject. While important aspects have been dealt with in articles by Richard, Friedman, Cipollone, Forey and others, most monographic treatments of captivity in connection with the crusades have tended to focus on the activities of the redemptionist orders, primarily in the Western Mediterranean. This situation has now at last been rectified with the publication of this fine study by Yvonne Friedman herself, which builds on several relevant articles already published by her. The scope of the book is actually far more wide-ranging than its subtitle indicates, since it also investigates Byzantine and Muslim practices with regard to captivity before the First Crusade, and includes treatment of warfare in northern Syria and in Iberia during the crusading period.

The core of the book consists of Chapters I–IV, which provide a diachronic analysis of the development of attitudes to captivity on the part of the Franks and their Muslim enemies, taking in the ideological background as well as actual practice. Friedman argues that while the liberation of Jerusalem from captivity was a major theme in early crusade preaching, there was no mention of the real possibility of captivity, despite a great stress on sacrifice and tribulation. This meant, she reasons, that the participants of the First Crusade were conceptually unprepared for captivity, and equally, did not expect to take prisoners themselves, an attitude which easily led to the massacres of captives at Ma'arrat al-Numan and Jerusalem. She then outlines a gradual process of changes of attitude: in the early years of the kingdom of Jerusalem the Franks were unwilling to ransom captives, although they would often undertake quite daring rescue attempts. However, by around 1105 ransoms – often of around 1,000 bezants per noble prisoner – had become an important part of the income of the Frankish rulers and warrior classes, who would often prefer to obtain ransom money than secure release of their co-religionists by exchange. While prisoner exchange had been commonplace between Byzantium and the Arabs, with accepted mechanisms and tariffs, it was only during the second and third generations of the Frankish settlement that the ransom of captives became regular; and, even then, a ransom remained the responsibility of an individual captive, his family and vassals, rather than of his king, lord or commander. It was only after the battle of Hattin and the vast numbers of Frankish prisoners taken in 1187, that the Christian side was obliged to institutionalize the ransom of captives through the involvement of the military orders and the foundation of new orders with a dedicated redemptionist mission.

Chapters V–VI form a thematic discussion of life in captivity and escape from it, taking in the mechanics of surrender, the setting and levels of ransoms, conditions of imprisonment, torture and mutilation of captives, and means of escape and its consequences. This section is a fascinating piece of social history and is the most original and interesting part of the book. The remainder of the narrative deals with the experience of women (ch. VII), the role of the military orders (ch. VIII), literary images (ch. IX) and, finally, ransom in Spain (ch. X). While this final chapter provides some useful comparisons with Outremer, its inclusion was perhaps less necessary, given that captivity in Iberia has been treated in some detail by Brodman and others; it might have been more profitable to have used the space devoted to this chapter to enlarge on some important issues relating to the kingdom of Jerusalem, particularly economic matters. Thus, for example, there is very useful discussion of the levels of ransoms and of how they were arrived at, with a table comparing prices at pp. 158–61. However, there are other interesting cases, such as those of Walter of Beirut, John Gotmann, and others, which do not figure in the table and which could have been discussed at greater length. In particular, such cases raise the important question as to the long-term effects on landholding structures of captivity and ransom on nobles who could often only raise the large sums required by alienation of property. There certainly seems to be a prima facie case for a correlation between the increasing consequences of such ransoms and the acquisition of territory in Outremer by the military orders, institutions which usually seem to have had ready supplies of cash available for purchase.

The book is illustrated with 10 colour plates and 4 black-and-white illustrations. Errors are minimal in number; one might mention the statement that Baldwin I was the uncle of Baldwin of Bourcq (p. 31) – they were in fact fairly distant cousins. *Encounter between Enemies* is an excellent, wide-ranging study which draws on a wide variety of Latin, Greek, Arabic, Hebrew, Syriac and Old French sources to give us not only an account of the development of attitudes to captivity, but – perhaps more importantly – a detailed picture of the realities of captivity on the Frankish-Muslim frontier in the twelfth and thirteenth centuries. As such it constitutes a very welcome addition to the scholarly literature not only on the crusades but on the practice of medieval warfare in general.

ALAN V. MURRAY
INTERNATIONAL MEDIEVAL INSTITUTE, UNIVERSITY OF LEEDS

Thomas A. Fudge, *The Crusade against Heretics in Bohemia, 1418–1437: Sources and Documents for the Hussite Crusades* (Crusade Texts in Translation, 9). Aldershot: Ashgate, 2002. Pp. xix, 419. ISBN 0 7546 0801 8.

The later crusades have not conquered the lecture theatres of universities to the same extent as the "classical" crusades of the twelfth and thirteenth centuries, which have gained a firm place within undergraduate syllabi at many English-speaking universities. In part, the neglect of the later crusades has been due to the lack of available sources in translation for studying the crusades of the fourteenth and fifteenth centuries from primary texts. This situation is now beginning to be remedied. A few years ago Norman Housley published a valuable collection of sources in translation covering the period of the late thirteenth to the sixteenth centuries (*Documents of the Later Crusades, 1274–1580*. New York, 1996). On Housley's instigation, as one of the editors of Ashgate's Crusade Texts in Translations series, Thomas Fudge has now published 209 documents, or excerpts of documents, relating to the crusades against the Hussite heretics of Bohemia between 1418 and 1437. The texts are translated from seven different languages: Czech, Latin, German, French, Middle English, Polish and Hebrew, which indicates the formidable task Fudge took upon himself. He selected excerpts of different types of sources, from chronicles, papal bulls, letters, sermons and poetry to all sorts of administrative documents representing the points of view of both sides of the conflict, that is, the crusaders sponsored by the papacy and their Hussite opponents.

Fudge chose to arrange his material in chronological order, dividing it into seven sections representing the five crusade campaigns as well as the preparations before 1430 and the aftermath of the campaigns after 1431. This means that some works, mainly chronicles, appear several times at different points of the collection, but it has the advantage that the primary texts can almost be read as a chronological narrative of the events that made up the crusades against the Hussites. This is facilitated by the short and lucid introductions to each text, in which Fudge explains the historical context of each document. Unfortunately, he does not always give detailed information about authors and addressees or the way the texts were made, used and preserved, all questions very much at the forefront of modern scholarship. Where the texts themselves are not self-explanatory on these points, this can lead to confusion. Thus, for example, in document no. 164, a letter somewhat erratically entitled "City of Basel appraised of crusade strength," we have no idea who was addressing whom. There is also the rather dubious technique of leaving out apparently insignificant passages of some documents, like for example the rather important papal bull *Inter cunctos* (doc. no. 18). Whilst this is understandable from the point of view of saving space, it leaves the attentive reader with the kind of dissatisfaction and frustration experienced by many historians using the hagiographical texts published in the MGH. Who says what is insignificant?

In fairness to the author, however, it must be pointed out that Fudge did not intend his collection of translated sources as a tool for research. Being aware of the difficulties of producing accurate translations across such a wealth of languages and documentary styles, he explicitly warns "scholars *au fait* with the late medieval texts in their original language" that "this volume was not prepared for [them]" (p. xvi). This reviewer, for one, is not in a position to check the accuracy of the translations of most of the documents included in this collection. But if such a warning is issued by the author himself, it should be taken seriously!

Fudge's collection must be judged against the aims he set himself: "I am confident this volume will prove to be an asset in helping to open the curtain a little wider on the story of the crusade against heretics in Bohemia and at the same time on the larger fascinating Hussite world" (p. xvii). There is no doubt that Fudge has done a great service in providing university teachers with an exceptional tool for presenting an important field of crusade studies to their undergraduate students. At the same time, the collection will serve researchers whose linguistic competence does not stretch to languages such as Polish, Czech or Hebrew, of which there are many, to acquire a taste and gain an insight into the wealth of different sources available for the history of the crusades against the Hussites.

CHRISTOPH T. MAIER
UNIVERSITÄT ZÜRICH

Norman Housley, *Religious Warfare in Europe, 1400–1536*. Oxford: Oxford University Press, 2003. Pp. ix, 238. ISBN 0 19 820811 1.

Das vorliegende Buch stellt sowohl eine Erweiterung als auch eine Vertiefung der vorherigen Arbeit von N. Housley zu den "Later Crusades" aus dem Jahre 1992 dar. Gleichzeitig eröffnet es neue Perspektiven zur Debatte, wie sich die Kriegführung im Spätmittelalter und in der Frühen Neuzeit veränderte. Die Darstellung behandelt das Phänomen innerhalb der ganzen europäischen "christianitas", wobei das Schwergewicht auf den Randgebieten liegt (Ungarn, Böhmen, Spanien). Besonders hervorzuheben ist die Breite und Vielsprachigkeit der herangezogenen Sekundärliteratur.

N. Housley geht es bei seiner Untersuchung von "warfare" nicht um die Aspekte von Professionalisierung und Söldnerwesen, Auflösung des Lehensaufgebotes usf., sondern sein Hauptaugenmerk richtet sich auf die Religion, welche die Intentionen und Legitimationen der spätmittelalterlichen Kriegführung prägte. Damit verbindet sich eine Absage an einseitige funktionalistische Deutungen (S. 7f.); die Akteure – gemäss Quellenlage mehrheitlich Männer – werden vielmehr beim Wort und somit ernst genommen.

Das erste Kapitel belegt, dass bereits das Alte Testament eine Reihe von Urszenen und Argumenten zur Verfügung stellte, auf welche die christlichen Heerführer seit jeher zurückgreifen konnten. Hinzu kommt, dass die Kriege, die nach dem Fall Akkons geführt wurden, immer wieder die typischen Muster von Kreuzzügen (Gelübde, Kreuz und Ablass) aufwiesen, ohne eigentliche "cruciatae" zu sein: "Crusading, and religious war in the non-crusading sense, incessantly crisscrossed" (S. 12).

Das zweite Kapitel illustriert am Beispiel der Hussiten, was der Verfasser unter "religious warfare" versteht. Die eingehende Analyse der Ereignisse in Böhmen während der ersten Hälfte des 15. Jahrhunderts gehört zu einer der vielen Qualitäten des vorliegenden Buches, denn die Auswirkungen der hussitischen Revolution auf die europäische Geschichte werden immer noch unterschätzt. Housley bettet anschliessend die Kriegszüge der "böhmischen Ketzer" in den gesamteuropäischen

Kontext ein und zeigt, dass die "christianitas" von inneren Konflikten bedroht war, welche letztlich zur Glaubensspaltung führten.

Das vierte Kapitel beschreibt die Erscheinungs- und Verlaufsformen von "religious warfare." Berufung auf die Heilige Schrift, messianisch auftretende Anführer und die Schaffung von Symbolen zwecks Selbstrepräsentation lassen sich als wiederkehrende Grundmuster nachweisen. Housley schildert eingehend das Auftreten verschiedener Gruppierungen und die medialen Mittel (Bilder, Erkennungszeichen, Lieder), die zum Einsatz kommen; damit gelingt es ihm, die selbstsichere Aggressivität, welche die religiös geprägte Kriegführung des Spätmittelalters begleitete, kenntlich zu machen.

Anschliessend wendet sich der Autor den echten und imaginären Bedrohungen zu, welche die damaligen Menschen umtrieben. Er geht dabei metaphorisch von "three Turks" aus. Gemeint sind damit zuerst die Osmanen, dann aber auch die "Türken" innerhalb der Christenheit, d. h. politische Gegner, auf die das osmanische Feindbild angewandt wird. Karl der Kühne und die Burgunder, die Eidgenossen, spanische Söldner, Franzosen, Katholiken usf. mussten erfahren, dass die feindliche Propaganda sie als Personen bezeichnete, die "Türken" oder sogar noch schlimmer als Türken seien. Der dritte Türke aber befand sich für die Zeitgenossen, wie Housley anhand der Schriften des Erasmus und anderer belegt, in der Seele jedes Christenmenschen. Dieser "dritte Türke" stand für individuelle moralische Verkommenheit, die zuerst von jedem einzelnen Gläubigen überwunden werden musste, bevor überhaupt an eine reale Auseinandersetzung mit den Osmanen gedacht werden konnte. Es war Thomas Morus vorbehalten, in seinen Schriften alle drei "Türken" zu erwähnen und deren Bedrohung miteinander zu verknüpfen. Für Morus galt es Osmanen, Ketzerei und persönliches Versagen gleichzeitig zu bekämpfen.

Das vorletzte Kapitel weist nach, dass im behandelten Zeitabschnitt die erwähnten Religionskriege ebenfalls auf Kritik stiessen. Gerade die religiösen Revolutionäre des Hussitentums, die mit ihren Gegnern ja nicht zimperlich umgingen, diskutierten die Rechtmässigkeit ihres Vorgehens; Peter Chelčický verurteilte grundsätzlich jede Gewalttat, die im Namen der Religion begangen wurde. Seine Einwände und auch diejenigen anderer Autoren (Erasmus, Michael Sattler, einzelne Täufer) verhallten aber ungehört.

Das Schlusskapitel erweitert das eingangs aufgeworfene Problem: Was ist unter "religious warfare 1400–1536" zu verstehen, und wie wirkte sich "religious warfare" auf die Religionskriege aus? Housley geht es darum, eine Beziehung zwischen den Kreuzzügen und den konfessionellen Kriegen der Frühen Neuzeit herzustellen, wobei er dieses Bindeglied als "religious warfare" bezeichnet. Die Eigenschaften dieses Bindeglieds lassen sich dank Housleys Buch deutlicher fassen: Übernahme von Kreuzzugsmustern durch Gruppierungen, die weder vom Papst eine entsprechende Erlaubnis haben noch im Einverständnis mit der kirchlichen Lehre handelten; eigenständige Interpretation der Heiligen Schrift durch neu sich konstituierende Glaubensgemeinschaften, die damit gleichzeitig ihre Kriegführung legitimierten; wachsender Druck von aussen und innen auf das christliche Europa; Brutalisierung der Auseinandersetzungen, die von frommen Rebellen ausgelöst wurden.

Wie lassen sich diese Vorgänge auf einen Begriff bringen? "Religious warfare" waren bereits die Kreuzzüge, und auch die Kriege während der Glaubensspaltung lassen sich füglich so bezeichnen. Offensichtlich gibt es aber im Zeitabschnitt, der hier zur Diskussion steht, viele "Kriege von selbsternannten Gläubigen," so dass eher "faith" als "religion" für die Definition der Epoche herangezogen werden sollte; N. Housley erwähnt selber auf S. 2 den deutschen Begriff "Glaubenskrieg."

Religious warfare eröffnet eine neue Diskussion und bestätigt gleichzeitig aus der Perspektive der Kriegführung die Eigentümlichkeiten des Spätmittelalters. Es handelt sich um eine "Sattelzeit" (R. Koselleck), die weder dem Mittelalter noch der Neuzeit angehört. Sie weist Züge einer Krise im Sinne von "heikler Entscheidung" auf, wobei die Menschen nicht nur in demographischer und wirtschaftlicher Hinsicht schmerzhafte Veränderungen erdulden mussten, sondern auch während des Grossen Schismas eine tiefe Verunsicherung ihres Glaubens erfuhren. Sie reagierten darauf mit gesteigerter Frömmigkeit, oder sie beschlossen, sich selber einen neuen Glauben zu schaffen und dafür Krieg zu führen. Dass diese Denk- und Handlungsweise von höchster Aktualität ist, bedarf keiner weiteren Erklärung und lädt ein, im Spiegel von Housleys Buch die Ereignisse der Gegenwart zu überdenken.

CLAUDIUS SIEBER-LEHMANN
UNIVERSITÄT BASEL

Nikolas Jaspert, *Die Kreuzzüge*. (Geschichte kompakt.) Darmstadt: Wissenschaftliche Buchgemeinschaft, 2003. Pp. ix, 180. ISBN 3 534 15129 1.

For decades Hans Eberhard Mayer's *Geschichte der Kreuzzüge*, first published in 1965 and by now in its ninth revised edition, has critically shaped the perception of the crusades in German-speaking countries at universities and beyond. Mayer's handbook no doubt represents sound scholarship of the highest order based on the author's outstanding expertise, which has made him one of the leading crusade historians of our time. The problematic side of Mayer's *Geschichte* and the concept of the crusade it sets out has to do with all those elements of the history of the medieval crusades which the author chose to ignore. By excluding all aspects of the crusading movement which fell outside the crusades to the Holy Land of the twelfth and thirteenth centuries and the crusader states of the Latin East, Mayer has stubbornly refused to integrate a wealth of scholarly work, primarily done in Britain and the United States, which puts forward the now predominant view of the medieval crusade movement as consisting of numerous crusades launched against supposed enemies of the Church both within and on the peripheries of Christendom throughout the later Middle Ages and into the modern era. With Nikolas Jaspert's

Die Kreuzzüge teachers and students of medieval history in German-speaking universities are now for the first time given a concise and competent introduction to the history of the medieval crusade movement which acknowledges and represents the enormous advances of crusade studies over the past four decades.

Jaspert's book is part of a new series of handbooks aimed primarily at undergraduate students and budding researchers. The series editors have opted for an attractive uniform layout which includes chronological tables at the beginning of each chapter, occasional quotations from sources and frequent explanations of technical terms and sub-themes set into the main text. For those readers coming to the crusades as a fresh topic these are welcome aids for understanding the complexities of the scholarly narrative. The main challenge to the author must have been the length, or, better, the shortness of the book, as his brief was not to exceed 160 pages of main text. Jaspert has done admirably well trying to fit in as many aspects of the crusade movement as possible, even though he was at times forced to reduce the history of centuries to only a few paragraphs of text. He chose to concentrate on five major aspects of the crusade movement: the origins of the crusades, the crusades to the Levant, the crusader states of the Latin East, the "European" crusades (that is, all crusades outside the Levant), and the military orders. Having done so, Jaspert manages to recount the main events of crusade history as well as discuss themes such as crusade ideology, colonialism, criticism of crusading and so on. His scholarship is up-to-date and reliable and his style very readable as befits a good handbook.

The shortness of the book, however, means that it can be no more than a first introduction to the medieval crusade movement, and a brief one at that. This in a way is a pity. Given another 50 to 100 pages, Jaspert, I am sure, would have been able to expand and give greater depth and substance to all those aspects he was forced to treat all too briefly. It also would have allowed him to expand the bibliography which largely concentrates on monographs and leaves out many important articles in journals and essay collections. More, and more-detailed, maps would also have been welcome. But these are none of Jaspert's faults given the constraints put upon him by the series editors.

With Jaspert's *Die Kreuzzüge* teachers and students at German-speaking universities finally have a competent up-to-date guide in their own language to the thematic breadth of the scholarly discussion about the medieval crusade movement. The story told by Jaspert is different, more modern and ultimately much more complex than the one available in Mayer's *Geschichte der Kreuzzüge*.

CHRISTOPH T. MAIER
UNIVERSITÄT ZÜRICH

Amnon Linder, *Raising Arms: Liturgy in the Struggle to Liberate Jerusalem in the Late Middle Ages*. (Cultural Encounters in Late Antiquity and the Middle Ages, 2.) Turnhout: Brepols, 2003. Pp. xx, 423. ISBN 2 502 51092 2.

The Christian defeat at the Battle of Hattin and the subsequent loss of Jerusalem struck at the very heart of the Catholic soul. Bewildered and profoundly alarmed, clergy, religious and, following them, the lay faithful perceived the twin disasters as an issue of faith and they turned, therefore, to supplicate God for help, raising their corporate voice in a liturgical clamour of psalms, versicles and prayers. But, this would not be the only time that God would be supplicated on the matter of crusading. In the course of the next three centuries, crusading armies would continue to have an appalling record of military defeats and these, together with "the long, protracted agony of Latin Outremer" (p. 3), maintained a context of crisis in which the liturgy of what Linder terms the Holy Land clamour continued to be voiced.

The clamour was not, however, the sole liturgical channel through which the Church supplicated God on the matter of the Holy Land and crusading. If the evidence of the numerous liturgical manuscripts and incunabula presented here constitutes an accurate reflection, the picture that emerges is one of liturgical frenzy as diocesan, religious, and curial liturgists worked feverishly until well into the sixteenth century, composing, copying and transmitting more clamours, Holy Land masses, dedicated war masses for crusading, Holy Land bidding prayers, and, in England, the Gregorian Trental, which, by the fifteenth century, joined supplications for the Holy Land with those for souls in Purgatory.

Linder approaches these liturgies mainly as texts requiring dating, identification, semantic analysis and classification. There is the jargon ("polysemy," "variability matrix") that goes with this, but, mainly, his discussion of methodology and of the problems of identification and dating reflects an impressive command of the material. Aided by a data-processing programme, he dissects the language, grammar, and phraseology of the prayers and mass texts, noting all variants, however minor, and collates the results to establish critically edited versions for which readers will be most grateful. There is, however, little in the way of translation.

This taxonomic approach to the sources reveals much that is new and interesting about the liturgical creative process and about the ideas of crusade that underpinned it. The textual affinities, which Linder detects, for instance, between the earliest Holy Land clamour and older clamours, particularly the eleventh-century clamour *Contra invasores*, highlight their inherent adaptability. The *Contra invasores*, according to Linder, petitioned God for aid against "generic" enemies. In the wake of Hattin and the fall of Jerusalem liturgists made the enemy "specific." Such easy movement from "generic" to "specific" was made possible, he suggests, by a fundamental affinity of ideas that Christians had about their enemies, regardless of their identity. Thus, the crises that gave rise to both clamours were viewed by the liturgists, and, it is assumed, by the lay faithful, as essentially similar. The same movement from "generic" to "specific" is apparent too in the dedicated war mass. With its focus upon the infidel, namely Muslims, Turks and heretics, this mass, a mature adaptation of the transportable triple prayer sets (collect, secret, postcommunion), represents, Linder says, "the final stage in the evolution of war liturgy from the generic to the specific" (p. 175). Pope Calixtus III's war mass of 1456 is a telling example. Linder's construct of the generic/specific at times seems forced. It does, however, bear interesting implications both for the continued broad appeal of the crusade as Christian defensive war and an imperative of faith, as well as for the propagandistic effectiveness of the clamour and dedicated war mass specifically. Regrettably, however, Linder does not explore these possibilities in detail.

Textual adaptation, associated closely with the generic/specific dynamic, is a thematic mainstay of this study. Linder shows in exhaustive detail, for instance, that not even papal prayer sets and masses for the Holy Land and crusading were immune from adaptation. Indeed, the great collect prayer *Deus qui admirabili*, composed almost certainly by Pope Innocent III around 1213 as a clamour and disseminated in *Quia maior*, was spare. But, as Linder shows, its history is one of change and expansion as liturgists, popes included, heedless of any need for co-ordinated effort, added, altered, omitted, replaced and rearranged Innocent's materials to suit their own crusading projects. The Carthusians built an office clamour around it, and in 1333 Pope John XXII adapted it as the collect to anchor the text of his own great mass for the Holy Land.

Recounting the liturgical history of the crusading movement in one volume has obliged Linder to focus more upon details of manuscript transmission than upon broader historical issues. Not all readers will find this consistently satisfying. With respect to Clement V's liturgical initiatives, for instance, we learn only that there is a relationship between these and contemporary crusade sermons. This, manifestly, is an important point, but it is undeveloped. Linder's examination of John XXII's Holy Land triple set of 1331–33 is equally tantalizing. John used Innocent III's *Deus qui admirabili* as his collect. Linder assembles the manuscript variants in the versions of the collect (Table 2.B), most of which, he says are minor and attributable to "the usual scribal inaccuracies, omissions and additions" (p. 149). What he passes over is the omission in John's text of Innocent's reference to the "vows of the faithful" (*vota fidelium*). In light of the fact that crusade vows were at this time a source of considerable tension between the papacy and members of the French nobility, it is, surely, more reasonable to suppose that John deliberately had the potentially troublesome reference to vows edited out of the collect than it is to attribute the omission to scribal negligence.

If anything undermines this invaluable study, it lies in its presentation and expression. First, a thorough editorial overhaul is essential. There is excessive repetition. Typographical carelessness is rampant. There are errors: *Quia maior* was an encyclical, not a bull, and its date was 1213 (cf. p. 399). The notes are often cumbersome, obscure and misplaced: p. 101, n. 19 simply directs the reader to pp. 78–79; nn. 39–41 on p. 106 belong on p. 105; n. 635 belongs on p. 265, not p. 266; and n. 66, p. 286 should be on p. 285. On p. 188 n. 41 the reader is told to see "above" when manifestly "below" is meant. There are figures of reproductions of folio pages of prayers, but the reproductions are of poor quality and some of the accompanying descriptions confusing. What purports to be a description of fig. 6 makes sense only if applied to fig. 7, and vice versa. And, the interpolated *Preces pro ecclesia*, which Linder claims can be seen in fig. 2, are utterly obscured by the reproduction's fuzziness. This is irritating. So, too, is this book's inconsistency in citing manuscripts and incunabula. On pp. 326–30 nn. 370–88 the manuscripts are said to be in Graz, Munich, Paris, Oxford and Vienna: there is no identification of repository; a manuscript in Oxford – one assumes the Bodleian Library is meant – lacks a number. Incunabula seem to be cited mainly by shelf number, and not, as is conventional, by publisher and date, and it is odd that, while an index of consulted manuscripts is provided, there is no equivalent index of incunabula.

Secondly, the opaqueness of some expressions and passages obscures essential meaning. What is to be made of the designation of "popes and the cardinals, patriarchs" as "semi-abstract institutions" (p. 356)? The language may be arresting, but it denotes little. Equally baffling, theologically speaking, is Linder's statement about a mass text "reminding God of His passion" (p. 277), and for sheer convoluted verbiage, there is this description of the medieval liturgists' working method: "They produced such emphases by means of unequivocal rubrics and texts that imposed their specific meaning on other polysemic components, through the accumulation of particular components to the extent that they coloured the entire complex (in this case the whole Mass) of which they formed parts, and, finally, through the perceived correspondence and hence relevance of that complex to a given historical situation" (p. 181). It is to be hoped that in a revised edition these difficulties will be addressed.

Raising Arms explodes the prejudice that liturgy was, and is, ossified. Liturgy is by nature authoritative and conservative, but, paradoxically, it was these characteristics that provided liturgists, working in the centuries after Hattin, with the texts that they adapted and transmitted, supplicating God on behalf of the faithful for aid to liberate the Holy Land and defend western Christianity against its multifarious enemies.

PENNY J. COLE
TRINITY COLLEGE, UNIVERSITY OF TORONTO

David Marcombe, *Leper Knights: The Order of St Lazarus of Jerusalem in England, 1150–1544*. (Studies in the History of Medieval Religion, 20.) Woodbridge: The Boydell Press, 2003. Pp. xx, 320. ISBN 0 85115 893 5.

One consequence of the growth in crusading studies since the 1980s has been the recognition that what might once have been regarded as the purely "domestic" history of institutions in the West is in fact inseparable from crusading interests.

Historians of the military orders in particular can exploit the surviving records from the orders' landholdings in the West. This book falls into the same tradition. The Order of St Lazarus was founded in Jerusalem in the mid-twelfth century, probably as a means of exploiting the military potential of knights who had contracted leprosy and, because of the prevailing belief that all forms of the disease were infectious, had to be kept separate, yet who were still – initially at least – able to fight. The brothers, who are characterized by Marcombe as being comparable in their social origins to monastic lay brothers, adopted the Rule of St Augustine, but they seem to have been run on similar lines to the Templars. After 1187 they settled in Acre, and by 1253 were already recruiting able-bodied as well as sick knights. Since the reign of Louis VII, an important early patron, the Order had its western headquarters at Boigny, near Orléans. By the end of the century there were also houses in the Empire, Hungary, Italy and England. In 1291 the Order was forced to withdraw to its western possessions, and this also brought about a shift in its recruitment strategies and identity.

In his discussion of the Order's early years in the Holy Land, Marcombe largely accepts the conclusions drawn by Malcolm Barber ("The Order of Saint Lazarus and the Crusades," *Catholic Historical Review*, 80 [1994]). Once he is firmly entrenched back in the Order's English heartland of the East Midlands, however, Marcombe draws on the cumulative work of the Burton Lazars Research Group to plot and evaluate the role and function of the Order as a landowning charitable institution in English society. The financial resources of the Lazarites, like those of other military orders, stemmed partly from their spiritual privileges. They received tithes from the parishes of which they had the livings, and claimed exemption from clerical taxation. They also, Marcombe argues, located many of their houses near main roads and bridge chapels so as to solicit regular alms. Their landed resources, which by 1291 already amounted to more than 5,000 acres, rose by the mid-sixteenth century to over 9,000 acres. The majority of grants, in keeping with the Order's own presumed membership, came from prosperous "peasant farmers." Because these estates were collected piecemeal, a variety of agricultural practices are found, and the archaeological evidence Marcombe discusses also indicates some light industry, such as the manufacture of juniper wine.

With the exception of the somewhat anomalous hospital of St Giles in London, gifted to the Order in 1299, most of the estates were grouped in Leicestershire and Lincolnshire. The Lazarites were rather haphazard when it came to internal government, however, and there is little evidence of centralized control over the internal affairs of the English houses from the main house at Burton Lazars, let alone from Boigny. Marcombe tends to be sceptical about the extent to which the Lazarites' English houses ever functioned as leper hospitals – there is no trace in the documentary or archaeological evidence of lepers at Burton Lazars, for instance. This may be because the need was no longer there once leprosy itself declined from the fourteenth century onward. St Giles, which was originally a hospital, gradually diversified so that by the fifteenth century it largely functioned as an old people's home by providing accommodation for corrodians. But changes in function may also follow the shifting pattern of the Order's own self-perception. By the last quarter of the fifteenth century, the Order was attracting more aristocratic members, and doubtless wished to shed its original associations with infectious disease.

All military orders, as Marcombe notes, found recruitment difficult in the fourteenth century. The Lazarites shifted the focus of their attention, buying into the chivalric memorialization of crusading and trading on their historical links with the Holy Land so as to attract a different class of patron. Judging from their continued ability to acquire landed estates, they appear to have succeeded not only in surviving the changing winds but even to have prospered. By the 1470s, when the first aristocratic grand master was elected, the English Lazarites had become independent of the French mother-house. Charitable work was now supported by lay confraternities, and the Lazarites seem to have found a place in the spirituality of the later medieval laity. The key elements in attracting patronage were family loyalty and associations with local gentry.

David Marcombe's emphasis throughout the book rests on the thorough reading and interpretation of cartularies and local records. He is not a crusader historian, and there are a few oddities – "Marsuna" for "Mansura," a bishop instead of a patriarch of Jerusalem – that ought to have been picked up in the editorial process. On the whole, however, the book succeeds in presenting the Lazarites as an example of the continuing importance of "passive crusading": devotion to the ideal and practice of crusading on the part of patrons who were themselves unable to take up arms. This study never loses sight of the original purpose for which the Order was founded, and the assessment of the Order's performance in the later Middle Ages allows Marcombe to view the Leper Knights through the wider lens of a cultural shift in knightly ideals from the twelfth to the fifteenth centuries.

ANDREW JOTISCHKY
LANCASTER UNIVERSITY

David Nicolle, *Warriors and their Weapons around the Time of the Crusades*. (Variorum Collected Studies Series CS756.) Aldershot: Ashgate, 2002. Pp. xiv, 324. ISBN 0 86078 898 9.

David Nicolle is a chiefly known for his remarkable studies of medieval weaponry, and his *Arms and Armour of the Crusading Era, 1050–1350*, 2 vols (New York, 1988) is a majestic study of the greatest value to those interested in the history of war. This is a collection of essays written by him since 1980 and includes a new piece as Essay XI. This kind of book has become something of a speciality of Ashgate. They have evolved a standardized format. The pagination of the original is retained, but it is possible to find your way about because the articles are numbered in the Table of Contents and in the headers. In addition, there is a helpful index.

The justification for such volumes is that they conveniently bring together some of the otherwise scattered articles produced by scholars. Essay I, "Medieval Warfare: the Unfriendly Interface" (1999), introduces us to the unifying theme of this volume – the influence of changes in military technology in one culture upon another to which it is unfriendly, and includes some useful translations of Byzantine and Arab source-material. This very general essay asserts the importance of cultural exchange in military matters. Although Nicolle accepts that interchange is imperfect, the emphasis here is upon cross-cultural influences and there is not much about the possibility of parallel developments. Thus he suggests that the late-medieval "coat of plates" came to Europe from the east in the thirteenth century – however, such armour is referred to as worn by the Norse in their attack on Dublin in 1171. The counterweight trebuchet appears in our sources almost simultaneously in Europe and the Arab world at the very end of the twelfth century. Again, pragmatic solutions to military problems can produce similar results in different cultures. Twelfth-century crusader Saone is a ridge-castle with a famous rock-cut ditch defending its vulnerable approach: I do not believe the similar (probably thirteenth-century) structure at Shaizar is a cultural influence. Essays II, "Byzantine and Islamic Arms and Armour: Evidence for Mutual Influence" (1991), and III, "No way overland? Evidence for Byzantine Arms and Armour on the 10th–11th Century Taurus Frontier" (1995), explore this theme in the specific context of Byzantine-Islamic warfare. Here Nicolle's sharp eye for detail and encyclopaedic knowledge show at their very best. He brings out the very powerful influence of Central Asian military cultures on these two areas. Of course these cultures were in very long-term contact with one another, and Turks were found in armies on both sides. In Essay IV, "The Impact of the European Couched Lance on Muslim Military Tradition" (1980), Nicolle ventures into a highly controversial field. At the time this was a very bold and radical article, expressing scepticism about the then accepted orthodoxy that the couched lance, used in mass cavalry charges, was the secret of the success of the European knights. It remains a highly valuable study of the diverse military uses of cavalry in Islam and Europe. Usamah, writing about his first fight with Franks explains the technique involved, but significantly in the context of one-to-one skirmishing: "That he who is on the point of striking with his lance should hold his lance as tightly as possible with his hand and under his arm, close to his side, and should let his horse run and effect the required thrust; for if he should move his hand while holding the lance or stretch out his arm with the lance, then his thrust would have no effect whatsoever and would result in no harm" (Usamah, *Memoirs* ed. P.K. Hitti, pp. 69–70). The European settlers in the Holy Lands rapidly developed this into a mass technique for their "famous charge," but they were unusual in having the discipline to deliver such a coherent shock. Essays V, "Armes et Armures dans les Épopées des Croisades" (1987); VI, "Arms and Armour Illustrated in the Art of the Latin East" (1992); IX, "The Monreale Capitals and the Military Equipment of Later Norman Sicily" (1980); X, "The Capella Palatina Ceiling and the Muslim Military Inheritance of Norman Sicily" (1983); and XI, "Arms, Armour and Horse Harnesses in the Parma Baptistery Painted Ceiling" (2002), focus on discussion and analysis of illustrations of arms and armour, very much in the tradition of *Arms and Armour of the Crusading Era*. The last of these was written specially for this volume. The panels in the Parma Baptistery date from the mid-thirteenth century, but the analysis shows Nicolle's admirable perception of detail and his wide knowledge of eastern and western artefacts. Nicolle draws out their full importance by his detailed exploration and cross-references. Essays VII, "Wounds, Military Surgery and the Reality in Crusading Warfare: The Evidence of Usamah's Memoires" (1993), and VIII, "Ain al Habis. The Cave de Sueth" (1988) stand somewhat apart from the others in this volume and serve to remind us that Nicolle is not just a specialist in arms and armour. The study of Ain al Habis is clear and painstaking with excellent drawings and photographs. There has been recent work on cave-fortresses in North Syria which, it is to be hoped, will give more comparison and context to this remarkable place. The study of military surgery based on Usamah is fascinating though, of course, much has been done on this subject more recently by Piers Mitchell. This is a very useful volume whose central worth derives from Nicolle's amazing knowledge of the arms and armour of Asia, the Middle East and Europe. This has been deployed here to assert the theme of cross-cultural influences. One might have some reservations about the conclusions, but there can be none about the scholarship.

JOHN FRANCE
UNIVERSITY OF WALES SWANSEA

Johannes Pahlitzsch, *Graeci und Suriani im Palästina der Kreuzfahrerzeit. Beiträge und Quellen zur Geschichte des griechisch-orthodoxen Patriarchats von Jerusalem.* (Berliner Historische Studien, 33. Ordensstudien, XV.) Berlin: Duncker & Humblot, 2001, Pp. 452. ISBN 3 428 09884 6.

Während die lateinische Kirche und ihre Hierarchie im Kreuzfahrerkönigreich Jerusalem sowohl in Gesamtdarstellungen als auch in Einzeluntersuchungen vergleichweise gut untersucht sind (siehe etwa die Arbeiten von B. Hamilton, K.-P. Kirstein, M. Matzke und anderen), sind die Bedingungen, unter denen die griechisch-orthodoxe "melkitische" Kirche während der lateinischen Herrschaft (und auch später) existierte, nur wenig bekannt. Diese Lücke ist nun durch diese Dissertation, die in Berlin unter der Anleitung von Kaspar Elm entstanden ist, so weit möglich geschlossen worden. Freilich sollte man jetzt keine umfassende Geschichte des griechisch-orthodoxen Patriarchats erwarten, da dazu die Quellenbasis nicht ausreicht. Aber die vorhandenen Nachrichten sind von Johannes Pahlitzsch sorgfältig zusammengetragen worden, so daß sich doch ein, wenngleich lückenhaftes Gesamtbild ergibt. Die Schwerpunkte des Buches sind hierbei durch die Quellensituation bedingt. So werden die Patriarchen Symeon II., Johannes VIII., Leontios II. und, im 13. Jahrhundert, Anastasios II. relativ ausführlich behandelt, während über die anderen Patriarchen vergleichweise wenig bekannt ist, in Einzelfällen kaum mehr als nur der Name.

Pahlitzsch beschränkt sich nicht nur auf die griechisch-orthodoxen Patriarchen von Jerusalem, sondern stellt in einer ausführlichen Einleitung, die den Forschungsstand bequem zusammenfasst, auch die theologische und politische Entwicklung zwischen dem Schisma von 1054 und dem Ersten Kreuzzug dar, insbesondere den Azymenstreit (zu dem Schisma siehe zuletzt die Dissertation von Axel Bayer, *Spaltung der Christenheit. Das sogenannte Morgenländische Schisma von 1054*. Köln – Weimar – Wien, 2002), in dem die Auseinandersetzung zwischen Lateinern und Orthodoxen im Heiligen Land sozusagen symbolisch ihren Ausdruck fand. Im folgenden werden die Gründung der lateinischen Kirchenorganisation nach dem Ersten Kreuzzug, die Unterwerfung bzw. Vertreibung des griechischen Klerus und dessen vergebliche Versuche, im Königreich wieder Fuß zu fassen, behandelt.

Von großer Bedeutung ist laut Pahlitzsch, daß die Kreuzfahrer bewusst eine römisch orientierte Kirchenorganisation mit einem "lateinischen" Patriarchen an der Spitze schufen, um sich von der griechisch-orthodoxen Kirche, die nach wie vor unter byzantinischem Einfluss stand, unabhängig zu machen und damit auch die byzantinischen Ansprüche auf das Heilige Land abzuwehren. Man könnte diese Beobachtung wohl noch dadurch ergänzen, daß die von den Kreuzfahrern geschaffenen Herrschaften, deren ganze Strukturen in jeder Hinsicht denjenigen des lateinischen Europa entsprachen, zwingend entsprechend angepasste kirchliche Institutionen brauchten. Da die griechisch-orthodoxe Kirche solches weder wollte noch konnte, war die Schaffung der lateinischen Patriarchate von Antiocheia und Jerusalem letztendlich eine logische Folge der Errichtung der Kreuzfahrerstaaten überhaupt.

Die "neue" lateinische Kirche akzeptierte zwar die Existenz des orthodoxen Klerus, solange dieser sich ihr unterwarf, verhinderte aber, selbst in Zeiten der politischen Zusammenarbeit zwischen Konstantinopel und Jerusalem, die Wiederetablierung der orthodoxen Patriarchen. Da diese Patriarchen während des 12. Jahrhunderts im Exil in Konstantinopel weiterhin amtierten, bedeutete dies das erste faktische Schisma zwischen Ost- und Westkirche, denn es beanspruchten jetzt für dasselbe Gebiet zwei verschiedene klerikale Organisationen die alleinige Zuständigkeit. Die griechischen Kleriker in den Kreuzfahrerstaaten, bei denen es sich in der Regel um die Mönche der orthdoxen Klöster, wie etwa des Sabasklosters, oder um einfache Kleriker unterhalb des Bischofsranges handelte, erkannten notgedrungen und nur nach außen die lateinischen Bischöfe und Patriarchen an, tatsächlich betrachteten sie deren Ansprüche als illegitim und sahen in den in Konstantinopel im Exil amtierenden Patriarchen ihre eigentlichen Vorgesetzten.

Damit gewann das, bis dahin eher als nicht so schwerwiegend empfundene Schisma von 1054 auch im allgemeinen Bewußtsein eine immer stärkere Bedeutung, die auch durch die politischen Diskrepanzen zwischen Byzanz und dem lateinischen Europa weiter verstärkt wurde und schließlich in der Eroberung

Konstantinopels durch den Vierten Kreuzzug 1203/04 und die Errichtung eines lateinischen Patriarchats dortselbst kulminierte. Vielleicht wäre es günstig gewesen, wenn der Autor, um diese Entwicklung zu illustrieren, auch einen Blick auf die parallelen Entwicklungen in Antiocheia und, ab dem Dritten Kreuzzug, auf Zypern geworfen hätte, jedoch muß man seine Begründung akzeptieren, daß eine solche Ausweitung wohl den Rahmen der Untersuchung gesprengt hätte, zumal für beide Regionen eigene neuere Untersuchungen existieren.

Pahlitzsch ergänzt seine Arbeit durch einen Katalog der griechischen Handschriften aus Palästina, die dort während des 12. und 13. Jahrhunderts entstanden sind, sowie durch die Analyse und zum Teil auch Edition von Werken, die von griechischen Patriarchen von Jerusalem verfaßt worden sind oder die man ihnen zugeschrieben hat. Ein besonderer Wert der Untersuchung liegt zweifelsohne darin, dass er diese Werke zugleich auswertet, um den persönlichen Hintergrund der jeweiligen Verfasser besser auszuleuchten. Eine Liste der griechischen Patriarchen von Jerusalem, ein ausführliches Literaturverzeichnis und ein Personen- und Ortsnamenregister runden diese wichtige Veröffentlichung ab.

Insgesamt gesehen haben wir mit der Dissertation von J. Pahlitzsch jetzt einen verlässlichen Leitfaden für die Beziehungen zwischen den lateinischen und den griechisch-orthodoxen Christen im Kreuzfahrerkönigreich Jerusalem während des 12. und 13. Jahrhunderts.

RALPH-JOHANNES LILIE
BERLIN-BRANDENBURGISCHE AKADEMIE DER WISSENSCHAFTEN, BERLIN

Jonathan Phillips, *The Crusades, 1095–1197*. Harlow: Longman, 2002. Pp. xx, 226. ISBN 0 582 32822 5 (paperback).

Phillips's highly accessible textbook on the first century of the crusading movement continues the best older traditions of crusade historiography while adding some useful innovations. He aims at contemporary classrooms, and he hits the bull's-eye in his level of detail, well-chosen primary sources, and broad array of learning aids. Instructors and students alike will enjoy the combination of clear narrative and thoughtful discussions of research. Yet, for all its strengths, Phillips's book also reflects some of the faults of traditional crusading historiography – most noticeably, a narrow definition of the movement that downplays or bypasses a broader range of research questions.

Though Phillips discusses the origins of crusading and thirteenth-century campaigns, he concentrates (as the title indicates) on the immediate circumstances of the First, Second, and Third Crusades. Teachers seeking a new comprehensive treatment of the entire movement may initially be disappointed. But when they look at Phillips's text a second time, they will see that this seeming weakness is actually a strength. Phillips has been able to focus on his specialty – the pivotal first century of crusading. Thus the book does not overwhelm with detail or spread itself too thin, as several older treatments do. Phillips's introduction sets the stage nicely by explaining why students might wish to study the crusades, referring to recent world events and the West's interest in this topic since the nineteenth century. The other twelve chapters cover the First Crusade, political and social developments in the early Crusader States, the military orders, the Second Crusade, military strategies, trends after the Second Crusade throughout the Mediterranean, religious life, the build-up and aftermath of Hattin, the Third Crusade, and new directions for thirteenth-century crusades. This mixture of narrative and thematic chapters allows teachers to select topics as they choose. The chapters' brevity will also permit instructors to assign multiple chapters at once and add additional readings without overburdening students.

Phillips shows further sensitivity to classroom requirements by adding chronologies, genealogies, maps, and a who's who, so that students have reference materials at their fingertips. His bibliography comments on seminal reference works and various topics within crusades studies, then lists the primary and secondary sources most accessible to students. The primary sources included in the text portray Latin, Byzantine, Jewish, and Muslim perspectives over a century, arranged in twenty-one categories. None is overly long, and given the size of this volume they cover the period very well. This text could easily be combined with Madden's *The Crusades: The Essential Readings* (Oxford, 2002) and/or Allen and Amt's source reader *The Crusades: A Reader* (Peterborough, 2003) for a crusades course, or it could be incorporated into a survey of medieval Europe.

Specialized courses on medieval crusading typically attract students who are interested in military history (medieval or contemporary) and Christian–Muslim interaction. Phillips serves such students well. He also incorporates the latest research on Jews, Greeks, and indigenous peoples of the Levant, and he does so in a way that shows how historians do their work.

However, for all intents and purposes, this is still a boys' story about battles and high politics. Few women are named in the entire book, and they are all royals or nobles. Moreover, the bibliography appears just as gender-biased on the surface. Undoubtedly Phillips chose to make the most of his limited space by listing overviews of topics such as the military orders, and undoubtedly he intended students to rely on the overviews' extensive bibliographies. Yet his citations give the unintended and unfortunate impression that only male historians work in this field. Helen Nicholson's extensive research on the military orders could have been noted in the annotated section, as could newly emerging work on gender in the crusades. To my mind, the most creative and exciting research on the Middle Ages has inserted political narratives into the larger context of the social order and medieval world view. Crusades historians have typically lagged behind in this regard. We cannot catch up if we keep using narrow definitions and repeating them to our students. Crusading affected the entire Mediterranean; it shaped all sorts of policies and popular attitudes back in Europe as well as in the East; it touched people of both sexes from all walks of life.

This is where Phillips's text may provide a useful starting point. Hopefully Longman has plans for a series of compact textbooks on various aspects of crusading. Thirteenth-century developments in the Levant, the Baltic crusades, the *Reconquista*, crusades against heretics, and the impact of crusading in Europe, would all be suitable topics. Byzantine- and Muslim-centred volumes would enhance the series even more. A collection like this would allow instructors to work in more social and gender history or provide less Eurocentric perspectives as they chose by combining volumes in their classes.

Phillips has delivered a great deal in this slim text; teachers and students will find the combination of features highly convenient. Although his work emphasizes holes in the field, instructors can fill these gaps by supplementing the text with appropriate readings or by directing students towards untapped areas of research.

DEBORAH GERISH
EMPORIA STATE UNIVERSITY

Jonathan Riley-Smith, *What Were the Crusades?* 3rd edition. Basingstoke: Palgrave Macmillan, 2002. Pp. xiii, 114. ISBN 0 333 94904 8.

Historians of the crusades have often found it difficult to agree about just what it is that they are historians of. Giles Constable in a recent essay on "The Historiography of the Crusades" (2001) proposed a helpful scheme to sort out various approaches to crusading history. He distinguished four schools of thought about the subject, which he labelled the popularist, the traditionalist, the generalist, and the pluralist.

Adherents of the popularist school champion a concept of crusading that resembles Walter Ullmann's "ascending thesis" in the realm of political theory. For popularist historians, the armed expeditions to the Holy Land that began in the late eleventh century and that we call crusades originated with the Christian faithful. Popular enthusiasm, stirred up and channelled by preachers who espoused prophetic, eschatological beliefs, provided the motive force that brought crusades into being. The crusades, according to advocates of this view, were essentially powered by spiritual beliefs and values. Popes, beginning with Urban II, encouraged that enthusiasm by blessing the expeditions and bestowing privileges upon their participants, but theirs was a second-level role in the whole enterprise. Popes, as popularist historians see things, responded to the movement but did not inaugurate it.

Traditionalist historians, in contrast, assign a top-down explanation, reminiscent of Ullmann's "descending thesis," to account for the origins of the crusading movement. For traditionalist crusade historians, the papacy provided the initial impetus for military expeditions whose goal was to capture Jerusalem, together with the circumjacent regions associated with the life of Jesus and His early followers, and to bring them permanently under Latin control. Traditionalists espouse a narrow construction of the crusades. They reject the label "crusade" for any and all other military enterprises sanctioned by the pope, such as those against heretics or the papacy's political enemies in Europe. They likewise regard campaigns in regions outside of the Holy Land, such as Spain or the Baltic, as something other than crusades, despite the fact that popes proclaimed them, and even though participants used the insignia and enjoyed the privileges accorded to crusaders. For traditionalists, the crusades are also bound within a two-century-long time frame. They hold that the crusades began with Urban II's sermon at Clermont in 1095 and ended with the fall of Acre in 1291.

Generalists are the nihilists of crusading history. They regard the whole enterprise of trying to distinguish crusades from other wars motivated by Christian zeal as anachronistic, artificial, and fundamentally pointless. Generalist historians deny that the armed pilgrimages to Palestine and Syria during the late eleventh and twelfth centuries were crusades at all. They argue that the idea of the crusade was a thirteenth-century fabrication. Later generations of historians, according to the generalist view, retroactively imposed this label on the deeds of their eleventh- and twelfth-century ancestors.

Pluralist historians agree with the traditionalists that papal authorization was the basic defining element of a crusade. Unlike traditionalists, however, pluralists adopt a broad construction of the term. Members of this camp are prepared to apply the term "crusade" to any military campaign, regardless of its theatre of operations, so long as it was proclaimed by the pope and its participants enjoyed the right to the indulgence and other privileges accorded to those who fought to secure Latin Christian control of the Holy Land. Pluralists are likewise prepared to extend the time range of crusading far beyond the fall of Acre, since popes continued to call for military campaigns and to fortify them with crusading privileges well into the eighteenth century.

Although Professor Riley-Smith certainly did not invent the pluralist view of crusading history, his *What Were the Crusades?*, which first appeared in 1977, has become the classic manifesto of the pluralist school of thought. It has been far more successful than most intellectual manifestos. In this book Riley-Smith delineates the basic premises of the pluralist approach to the history of the crusades and does so vigorously (one might even say passionately) and persuasively.

Adherents to the other viewpoints that feature in Professor Constable's classification seem not to have been moved to produce a similar coherent and systematic theoretical justification for their approach to the subject. They have, for the most part, either confined themselves to describing their approach in a few sentences or else left it to their readers to deduce the premises on which that approach is grounded. This seems a pity. A detailed explanation of the rationale that underlies the premises for one or another of these alternative approaches might not only be intrinsically interesting and enlightening for readers of crusading history, but might perhaps persuade others of the merits of adopting that point of view.

As things currently stand, Riley-Smith's eloquent advocacy of pluralism has enjoyed an extraordinary success, as is demonstrated by the appearance of the book's third edition a quarter of a century after its original publication. As promised in the publisher's announcement, Riley-Smith had revised this new edition and brought both its arguments and its bibliography up to date. Historians who share his view of the crusades have largely come to dominate this field of historical study during the past generation. *What Were the Crusades?* remains essential reading for anyone seriously interested in the problems that crusading history and historiography present.

JAMES A. BRUNDAGE
THE UNIVERSITY OF KANSAS

Jürgen Sarnowsky, *Macht und Herrschaft im Johanniterorden des 15. Jahrhunderts. Verfassung und Verwaltung der Johanniter auf Rhodos (1421–1522).* (Vita Regularis. Ordnungen und Deutungen religiösen Lebens im Mittelalter 14.) Münster: Lit Verlag, 2001. Pp. x, 750. ISBN 3 8258 5481 7 (paperback).

After the dissolution of the Templars in 1312, the Hospitallers were the only military order with possessions in almost all countries and regions of Latin Christianity, from Portugal to Sweden, from Ireland to Sicily. This fact had important consequences for the central headquarters of the Hospitallers on Rhodes and later on Malta. Whilst the Teutonic Order and the various military orders on the Iberian Peninsula were embedded in their particular regional or national societies and policies respectively, the Hospitallers can be seen as some kind of European Community *avant la lettre*, because their headquarters relied on men and money from all over Europe and their officers represented social and political groups from almost all European countries. The quarrels resulting from their rivalries are studied by Sarnowsky during the fifteenth century, a period for which an ever-increasing number of sources – especially cartularies, registers and accounts – from Rhodes survive. For the fourteenth century the documentation is more incomplete, and for the earlier period, the Hospitallers in the Holy Land up to the fall of Acre in 1291, it is almost non-existent, so that similar studies are not possible, although Jochen Burgtorf's thesis (*Führungsstrukturen und Funktionsträger in der Zentrale der Templer und Johanniter von den Anfängen bis zum frühen 14. Jahrhundert*, Düsseldorf, 2001) on the higher officers of the military orders in the Holy Land does give some insights into networks and pressure-groups. Sarnowsky is primarily interested in the Hospitaller Convent on Rhodes and its possessions in the Aegean, that is, the *partes* on the Eastern side of the sea, not the priories on the Western side of the sea. In 1466 the Convent was supposed to have 350 brethren, that is 300 knights, 30 chaplains and 20 *servientes*; there should be 166 brethren from France, 89 from Spain, 47 from Italy, 28 from England, and 20 from Germany. The twenty-five Western priories paid about 30,000–40,000 florins to the Convent, and in the early sixteenth century this increased to about 100,000 florins each year (54 per cent from France, 17 per cent from Spain, 12 per cent from Italy, 14 per cent from England, 3 per cent from Central Europe).

After an introduction about the state of the research the book is arranged into six main chapters: (I) about the rule, the statutes, and the laws, that is, the general prescriptive regulations for all brethren living in the order, including the reform chapter convoked by Pope Eugenius IV at Rome in 1446 and the codex printed by the vice-chancellor Guillaume Caoursin in 1489; (II) about the general constitutional framework, the Master, his council, the priories, the Convent with its tongues, the general and provincial chapters, the relationship with the Supreme Pontiff and the Roman curia; (III) about the typical careers of the Masters and of the grand officers in the Convent, among others the Conventual Prior, who supervised the chaplains, and the four old offices of the Grand Preceptor, the Marshal, the Hospitaller and the Drapier; (IV) about the administration of Rhodes and the adjacent islands, with special emphasis on the relations with non-Latin groups, the Greek majority and the Jewish minority; (V) about the revenues and the expenditures of the order, that is, the regular payments from the Western houses, their transfer to Rhodes with the help of Western merchants or banks, trade, shipping and piracy, and finally the loans needed to fortify Rhodes against Mamlukes and Ottomans, with twelve tables; (VI) about the struggle of the Italian and Spanish brethren against French domination on Rhodes. The numerical strength of the three French tongues – *Francia*, Auvergne and Provence – was countered by voting according to tongues and by regulations reserving certain posts for the three other important tongues, giving Italy the Admiral, Spain the Drapier and England the Turcopolier. The weakness of the French monarchy after Agincourt and the importance of the Italian hinterland for Rhodes permitted and provoked attempts to secure a non-French majority of tongues. As a first step, the tongue of Germany was revived in 1422, and in 1428 it got the Grand Commander as its Conventual officer. As a second step, in 1462 Spain was formally divided into two tongues, Aragón-Catalunya-Navarre with the Drapier and Castile-Portugal with the Chancellor as their Conventual officers respectively.

The book describes in detail the struggle on Rhodes between brethren from different tongues as well as between brethren from different priories, for example from Castile and Portugal, within the same tongue. As a guideline for settling such conflicts the Hospitallers developed the principle of seniority (*ancianitas*) which gave precedence to brethren according to their time and quality of service. The quarrels on Rhodes, however, were always correlated with the political and social situation in the West. Therefore the book furnishes invaluable information about fifteenth-century Europe in general. Invaluable for future research are the lists of offices and officers both on Rhodes and in the West, the glossary of technical terms in the sources concerning the Hospitallers and the edition of 31 documents from the National Library of Malta in Valletta. These texts include appointments, administrative and financial affairs as well as decisions concerning the Greek clergy on Rhodes. Sarnowsky could, of course, not identify all Hospitaller brethren mentioned in his sources; this has to be done by regional studies. But his book is a great step forward and an indispensable research tool for everyone who wants to understand the fifteenth-century Latin colony on Rhodes or the Hospitaller position regarding fifteenth-century reform debates among churchmen and politicians in Latin Europe.

KARL BORCHARDT
UNIVERSITÄT WÜRZBURG

William Urban, *The Teutonic Knights: A Military History*. London: Greenhill Books and Mechanicsburg, PA: Stackpole Books, 2003. Pp. xiii, 290. ISBN 1 85367 535 0.

Dieses Buch ist eine hervorragende Leistung des amerikanischen Historikers William Urban, Professor für Geschichte und Internationale Studien am Monmouth College in Monmouth, Illinois. In einer Zeit, wo sich fast jeder interessierte Laie berufen fühlt, Sachbücher zu historischen Themen zu schreiben, ist es wohltuend, wenn ein ausgewiesener Fachmann Ergebnisse von fast 40 Forschungsjahren in leicht verständlicher Form zusammenfasst und damit zugleich eine Wissenslücke schließt. Sowohl die Fachkollegen als auch die interessierten Laien werden ihm für dieses Buch dankbar sein.

Urban hat viele Arbeiten über die Kreuzzüge im Baltikum und über Baltische Geschichte geschrieben, wobei sich Titel und Inhalte manchmal überschneiden: *The Samogitian Crusade* (Chicago, 1989), *The Baltic Crusade* (Chicago, 1975 und 1994), *The Prussian Crusade* (Chicago, 1980 und 2000), *The Livonian Crusade* (Chicago, 1981 und 2004). Er ist auch Mitherausgeber von vier livländischen Chroniken in englischer Übersetzung und hat ein umfangreiches Buch über die Schlacht bei Tannenberg 1410 verfasst (*Tannenberg and After. Lithuania, Poland, and the Teutonic Order in Search of Immortality*, Chicago, revised edition 2003). Hinzu kommen viele Aufsätze zu diesem Themenkreis und auch zur Geschichte des Baltikums nach dem Zerfall des Sowjetimperiums.

Der Untertitel seines hier zu besprechenden neuen Buches hätte ergänzt werden und lauten können "A Political and Military History," denn Militärgeschichte lässt sich nur vor dem Hintergrund der politischen Entwicklung schildern, wie es Urban auch tut. Er beginnt mit den bekannten historischen Vorgängen bei der Gründung der Ritterorden im Heiligen Land und widmet sich dann der Geschichte des Deutschen Ordens. Wir werden mit verschiedenen Aspekten des Ordenslebens und der Kriegsführung im Heiligen Land bekannt gemacht, folgen dann den Deutschordensrittern nach Siebenbürgen und nach ihrer Vertreibung von dort nach Preußen, wo sie dem polnischen Fürsten Konrad von Masowien im Kampf gegen die heidnischen Prußen beistehen sollten. Sie erfüllten diese Aufgabe so effektiv, dass sie gegen Ende des 13. Jahrhunderts einen eigenen mächtigen Territorialstaat in Preußen besaßen und außerdem als "Erben" des Schwertbrüderordens in

Livland (nach 1237) auch dort die wichtigste politische und militärische Kraft darstellten. Die Kriege gegen heidnische Gegner in Preußen, Livland und Litauen sowie gegen orthodoxe Russen und römisch-katholische Polen werden alle unter Berücksichtigung politischer, strategischer, taktischer, kriegstechnischer und vieler anderer Aspekte dargestellt. Die Schilderung erstreckt sich bis zum Ende der beiden Ordensstaaten, d.h. bis 1525 in Preußen und 1561 in Livland.

Der Verfasser schildert Tatsachen, die in Teilbereichen bereits von sehr vielen Historikern abgehandelt worden sind, aber es gelingt ihm mit pädagogischem Geschick, die mehr als dreihundertjährige Geschichte in kurzen und nie ermüdenden Kapiteln und Abschnitten zusammenzufassen und die Quintessenz seiner Forschungen in gut lesbarer Form zu gestalten. Etwas Vergleichbares gab es bisher nicht. Immer wieder überrascht der Verfasser mit zum Teil sehr realistischen Beobachtungen und scheut sich dabei auch nicht, hier und dort seine eigene Lebenserfahrung in Form von amüsanten psychologischen Deutungen von Menschen und Ereignissen einzubringen. Insofern ist die Darstellung durch die persönliche Note typisch "Urban'sch" und wohl für kühl-sachliche Historiker manchmal etwas gewöhnungsbedürftig. Der Verfasser ist allerdings in diesem jüngsten Werk zurückhaltender als sonst. Aber immer noch kann man Sätze wie diese lesen (wobei es um die Entbehrungen der Ordensritter im Vergleich mit dem Leben weltlicher Ritter geht): "Secular knights who preferred a hot drink and a warm woman (or the other way around) were not eager to patrol dark paths in the forest or endure the freezing winds atop a lookout tower above lonely ramparts" (S. 57). Mit dieser Äußerung hat Urban vermutlich recht – und der Laie freut sich über das Bonmot – aber mancher Fachkollege wird wohl weniger tolerant urteilen. Das angeführte Beispiel soll nicht darüber hinwegtäuschen, dass Urban ein seriöser und belesener Historiker ist. Wer sich selbst mit ähnlichen Fragestellungen beschäftigt hat, weiß, wie viel Forschermühe sich oft hinter der flüssigen Darstellung verbirgt.

Man tut Urban sicher nicht unrecht, wenn man ihn als einen Apologeten des Deutschen Ordens bezeichnet, denn er macht selbst kein Hehl daraus. Diese Tendenz kommt bei der Lektüre immer wieder zum Vorschein. Urban sieht sich nämlich nicht nur als Historiker, sondern auch als Anwalt, ja Botschafter des christlichen Kreuzzugsideals des Abendlandes, des "Latin Europe," und damit auch des Deutschen Ordens. Zwar heißt es an einer Stelle, dass "nicht jeder Ordensritter ein Heiliger war," aber Urban neigt grundsätzlich dazu, die seit dem Mittelalter geäußerte Kritik an dem Orden als zumeist unberechtigt, unhistorisch und anachronistisch abzuwehren ("… at the hands of propagandists, nationalists, Protestants and secularists") (S. xii). Er hat damit zweifellos in vielem recht – man braucht nur an den Missbrauch des Ordens in der Propaganda des "Dritten Reichs" zu denken – aber auch die strikte Gegenposition lässt sich nicht immer verteidigen. Die Behauptung, Hitler "had nothing good to say about the Teutonic Order" (S. xii), ist allzu pauschal ausgedrückt (vgl. Sven Ekdahl, "Tannenberg/Grunwald – ein politisches Symbol in Deutschland und Polen," *Journal of Baltic Studies*, 22 [1991], 271–324, speziell S. 287). Gerade hierin sieht der Rezensent eine Schwachstelle der

Darstellung. Urban vertritt Ansichten, die er schon in den Aufsätzen "Victims of the Baltic Crusade" (*Journal of Baltic Studies*, 29 [1998], S. 195–212) und "Rethinking the Crusades" (*Perspectives*, 36 [1998], S. 25–29) zum Ausdruck gebracht hat und die zwar in den USA und teilweise auch in Deutschland, aber auch nach dem Zerfall der Sowjetunion in den ehemaligen "Target countries" kaum begrüßt werden (vgl. Sven Ekdahl, "Crusades and Colonialism in the Baltic," in *The Palgrave Guide to the Crusades*, ed. Helen Nicholson, London, 2005).

Das Thema des Buches ist aber die Militärgeschichte des Deutschen Ordens, weshalb die historiographischen Aspekte hier beiseite gelassen werden können. Es ist eine erstaunliche Fülle von wertvollen Informationen und Analysen, die geboten werden und vom Rezensenten dankbar zur Kenntnis genommen worden sind. Abschließend ein paar Korrekturen. Auf S. 94 soll es nicht "Karl Birger," sondern "Jarl Birger" oder "Birger Jarl" heißen, denn "Jarl" (d. h. Earl) war ein Titel und kein Vorname. Der erste Thorner Frieden wurde nicht 1422, wie es auf S. 229 heißt, sondern 1411 geschlossen – sicherlich ein Flüchtigkeitsfehler. Und die Unterscheidung in der Bibliografie am Ende des Buches zwischen "Secondary Sources" für die englischsprachige und "Secondary Accounts" für die Literatur in anderen Sprachen will nicht ganz einleuchten.

Kurzum: William Urbans Buch ist sehr empfehlenswert nicht nur für den Kriegshistoriker, sondern für jeden, der sich für die Geschichte der Deutschordensritter und deren Nachbarn interessiert. Es dürfte bald zum Standardwerk in vielen Sprachen werden und dabei auch eine lebhafte Diskussion auslösen.

SVEN EKDAHL
POLISH-SCANDINAVIAN RESEARCH INSTITUTE, COPENHAGEN

The Templars: Selected Sources, trans. and annotated by Malcolm Barber and Keith Bate (Manchester Medieval Sources Series). Manchester and New York: Manchester University Press, 2002. Pp. xiv, 350. ISBN 0 7190 5109 6 (hardback), 0 7190 5110 X (paperback).

Given the perennial interest generated by the Templars, it is surprising that no volume of translated sources relating to the Order has appeared before now in English. That there has been none is perhaps an indication of the degree to which the popular obsession with the Templars has frequently been unconcerned with hard evidence, evidence that is too often left to the province of specialists with command of the requisite – and demanding – languages. One may hope that the publication of this collection will in some small way help to steer the popular imagination fact-ward. In any case, the collection is most welcome and long overdue.

The book is divided into seven parts – a 16-page historical introduction, which provides a context for the subsequent documentary evidence and which is historiographically up-to-date, and six sections of documents: Foundation and Privileges, Warfare and Politics, Religious and Charitable Functions, Human and

Material Resources, Attitudes towards the Templars, and (necessarily in its own section) The Trial. A short but well-crafted bibliography and a 16-page index complete the book.

Virtually all of the important surviving documents from Templar history are here: elements of the Latin and French Rules, the papal bulls *Omne datum optimum*, *Milites Templi* and *Militia Dei*, a host of letters by or about the Templars, excerpts from relevant historical writings and from Bernard of Clairvaux's *De laude novae militiae*, the odd and intriguing will of Alfonso I of Aragon, a host of charters and other legal documents, the anonymous "*De constructione castri Saphet*," a Templar obituary from Reims, the bitter poem of Ricaut Bonomel, the treatises of Jacques de Molay on crusading and on military order union, and a great deal more. The section on the trial, about 85 pages long, contains a satisfying and fairly thorough selection from the plethora of documentation available, including the arrest order, a version of the charges, various depositions and letters, the questions of King Philip IV to the University of Paris and the masters' reply, the papal bulls *Vox in excelso* and *Ad providam*, and a pair of letters from the Hospitallers to Philip IV and Louis X on the subject of that order's absorption of Templar properties after the suppression.

Altogether this is an admirable achievement. As with any collection of this sort, one may find ways in which this one might have been profitably augmented. It would have been useful to have included *Pastoralis praeeminentiae* and *Faciens misericordiam* in the trial section for completeness' sake, if nothing else. Inclusion of Jacques de Molay's 1301 letter to the king of Aragon, describing efforts to recover the Holy Land made by the Templars around 1300, would have helped illustrate the fact that the Templars did not wallow in idleness or indecision after the fall of Acre in 1291 (a point which the collection does not make entirely clear). And – stretching the mandate of the volume a bit – inclusion of the letters exchanged by Philip IV and Hospitaller Master Fulk de Villaret in early 1309 would have driven home the danger to that order too. Although Philip failed to bring it down or to incorporate it into a mega-order controlled by a member of the French royal family, and it is easy to underestimate the threat from a distance of some 700 years, the danger to the Hospital was quite real at the time.

But these are mere perfectionist niggles, and do not detract from the success of the project. The primary audience intended for books in this series ("students and teachers of medieval history") will find this to be a remarkably useful and illuminating collection. More advanced scholars will find it to be helpful to have these documents together in one place (and, truth to tell, many people may find it helpful to have an English version with which to compare their own translations – some of the documents included here are defective or otherwise quite challenging in the original). In sum (if one may be permitted a sound bite): no one with an interest in the Templars can afford to be without this volume!

PAUL CRAWFORD
ALMA COLLEGE

SOCIETY FOR THE STUDY OF THE CRUSADES AND THE LATIN EAST

BULLETIN No. 25, 2005

Editorial

Our new treasurer is James D. Ryan, Professor Emeritus of the City University of New York, 100 West 94th St. #26M, New York, NY 10025 U.S.A.; Summer Mailing Address (mid-June to mid-September): P.O. Box 17, St. Regis Falls, NY 12980 U.S.A. We apologize for all confusions, problems or delays. James Ryan will now try to answer all questions concerning membership fees and subscriptions.

Our journal entitled *Crusades*, now 4 (2005), allows the Society to publish articles and texts; encourages research in neglected subfields; invites a number of authors to deal with a specific problem within a comparative framework; initiates and reports on joint programmes; and offers reviews of books and articles. Editors: Benjamin Z. Kedar and Jonathan Riley-Smith; associate editors: Michael Evans and Jonathan Phillips; reviews editor: Christoph Maier; archaeology editor: Denys R. Pringle.

Colleagues may submit papers for consideration to either of the editors, Professor Benjamin Z. Kedar or Professor Jonathan S.C. Riley-Smith. A copy of the style sheet may be obtained either from one of the two editors or online at: http://freespace.virgin.net/nigel.nicholson/SSCLE/sscleguidelines.htm

The journal includes a section of book reviews. In order to facilitate the reviews editor's work, could members please ask their publishers to send copies to: **Dr Christoph T. Maier, Reviews editor,** *Crusades*, **Sommergasse 20, CH-4056 Basel, Switzerland**. Please note that *Crusades* reviews books concerned with any aspect(s) of the history of the crusades and the crusade movement, the military orders and the Latin settlements in the Eastern Mediterranean, but not books which fall outside this range.

The cost of the journal to individual members is £20, $30 or €33; the cost to institutions and non-members is £65, $95 or €105. Cheques should be made payable to SSCLE.

Members may opt to receive the Bulletin alone at the current membership price (single £11, $15 or €17; student £6, $9 or €10; joint £15, $23 or €25). Those members who do not subscibe to the journal will receive the Bulletin from the Bulletin editor to whom the publisher of *Crusades* sends the copies.

The Bulletin editor would like to remind you that, in order to avoid delays, he needs to have information for the Bulletin each year at an early date, usually in January: stadtarchiv@rothenburg.de. Since most members now use e-mail, we think that we can save time and money by stopping to distribute the former 'pink' sheets. Postal address: Prof. Karl Borchardt, c/o Stadtarchiv, Milchmarkt 2, D-91541 Rothenburg, Germany.

Zsolt Hunyadi has been appointed to run our formal website: http://www.sscle.org. There is another website set up by Michael Markowski: http://people.westminstercollege.edu/faculty/mmarkowski/mmpage.html

Karl Borchardt

Message from the President

Dear Member,

As many of you know, one great event for our Society this July will be the meeting in Sydney (Australia), first for a symposium, organized by John Pryor, and then for the conference of the International Congress of Historical Sciences. I hope that many of you will be able to take part in these two events, whose programme you can get from John Pryor, john.pryor@arts.usyd.edu.au Our secretary Sophia Menache sent an early version of the programme to you in March this year.

Our conference in Istanbul, 25–30 August 2004, was a great success with ninety-five papers delivered by our members in the Bosphorus University. I should like to thank professors Nevra Necipoglu and Sophia Menache, who prepared everything for the welcome of our members. We all enjoyed the warm hospitality. A three-day trip to historical sites in North-Western Turkey closed the conference. The papers are to be sent to Thomas Madden. If they deal with the Fourth Crusade itself, they will be published in a special issue by Ashgate. If they deal with other subjects, they can be published in our periodical 'Crusades'. The information is available at http://sscle.slu.edu

Michel Balard

Contents

List of abbreviations		202
1.	Recent publications	202
2.	Recently completed theses	217
3.	Papers read by members of the Society and others	217
4.	Forthcoming publications	225
5.	Work in progress	231
6.	Theses in progress	234
7.	Fieldwork planned or undertaken recently	234
8.	News of interest to members:	
	a) Conferences and seminars	235
	b) Other news	235
9.	Members' queries	236
10.	Officers of the Society	236
11.	Income and expenditure account	236
12.	List of members and their addresses	236

List of abbreviations

Chemins d'outre-mer: Études d'histoire sur la Méditerranée médiévale offertes à Michel Balard, 2 vols, ed. Damien Coulon, Catherine Otten-Froux, Paule Pagès and Dominique Valérian, Byzantina Sorbonensia 20 (Paris: Publications de la Sorbonne, 2004), 857pp.

CLE-Seminar: The Crusades and the Latin East Seminar, Institute of Historical Research and Emmanuel College, Cambridge or London.

EI: The Encyclopedia of Islam, 2nd edition (Leiden: Brill).

EncycCru: Encyclopedia of the Crusades, ed. Alan V. Murray (ABC-Clio, 2005).

HES: International colloquium on the History of Egypt and Syria in the Fatimid, Ayyubid and Mamluk Eras, Katholieke Universiteit Leuven.

IMC: International Medieval Congress, Kalamazoo or Leeds.

MO3: The Military Orders, vol. 3: Their History and Heritage, ed. William G. Zajac (Aldershot: Ashgate).

MO4: The Military Orders on Land and by Sea, The Fourth International Conference of the London Centre for the Study of the Crusades, the Military Religious Orders and the Latin East, Clerkenwell, London, 8–11 September 2005.

OM 2003: Selbstbild und Selbstverständnis der geistlichen Ritterorden, Self-Image and Self-Perception of the Military Orders, Toruń, 26–28 September 2003.

OM 2005: Die Ritterorden als Träger von Herrschaft: Territorien, Grundbesitz und Kirchen, Ordines militares – Colloquia Torunensia Historica XIII, Toruń, 23–25 September 2005.

OTM: L'Ordine Teutonico nel Mediterraneo, Atti del Convegno internazionale di studi Torre Alemanna (Cernigola) – Mesagne – Lecce 16–18 ottobre 2003, ed. Hubert Houben, Acta Theutonica 1 (Galatina: Congedo, 2004), xi, 321pp.

Runciman-Conference: Terceras Jornadas Internacionales: Medio siglo de estudios sobre las Cruzadas y las Órdenes Militares, 1951–2001, A Tribute to Sir Steven Runciman, Universidad de Zaragoza y Ayuntamiento de Teruel, Teruel (Aragon), 19–25 July 2001, ed. Luis García-Guijarro Ramos (Madrid: Castelló d'Impressió SL).

SSCLE-Istanbul: The Sixth Conference of the Society for the Study of the Crusades and the Latin East, Istanbul, 25–30 August 2004.

SSCLE-Sydney1: From the West to the Holy Land in the Age of the Crusades, Symposium at the Centre for Medieval Studies, Sydney, 1 July 2005.

SSCLE-Sydney2: Peoples and Cultures of the Levant in the Age of the Crusades, CISH, 20th International Congress of Historical Sciences, Sydney, 4 July 2005.

1. Recent publications

AIRALDI, Gabriella, Je suis Bertrand de Gibelet, in: Chemins 25–30.

ANDENNA, Giancarlo, Città padane e carità verso i poveri e i pellegrini, in: OTM 17–32.

ARBEL, Benjamin, Les listes de chargement de navires vénitiens (XVe–début du XVIe siècle): un essai de typologie, in: Chemins 31–50.

BAHAT, Dan, with A. M. Maeir, Excavations at Kikar Safra (City Hall) Jerusalem 1989, in: Atiqot 47 (2004), 169–192 [the probable site of St. Lazar's hospital of crusader Jerusalem].

BALARD, Michel, Genoese Naval Forces in the Mediterranean during the Fifteenth and Sixteenth Centuries, in: War at Sea in the Middle Ages and the Renaissance, ed. John B. Hattendorf and Richard W. Unger (Woodbridge, 2003), 137–149; La circulation monétaire à

Péra dans la seconde moitié du XIVe siècle, in: Money and Markets in the Palaiologian Era, ed. Nikolaos G. Moschonas (Athens, 2003), 365–371; Mélisende, reine de Jérusalem, in: Retour aux sources: textes, études et documents d'histoire médiévale offerts à Michel Parisse (Paris, 2004), 449–455; Clarence, escale génoise aux XIIIe–XIVe siècles, in: Byzance et ses périphéries: hommage à Alain Ducellier (Toulouse, 2004), 185–203; Comercio local y comercio internacional: las mercancias, in: Mediterraneum: el esplendor del Mediterraneo medieval (Barcelona, 2004), xiii–xv, 269–287; La puissance maritime en Méditerranée au Moyen Âge, in: La puissance maritime, ed. C. Buchet, J. Meyer and J.-P. Poussou (Paris, 2004), 39–48; Carlo I° d'Angiò e lo spazio mediterraneo, in: Le eredità normanno-sveve nell'età angioina, ed. Giosuè Musca, Atti delle quindicesime giornate normanno-sveve, Bari, 22–25 ottobre 2002 (Bari, 2004), 85–100; Vendere nel dominio e fuori: botteghe di città e colonie mercantili, in: Storia della cultura ligure, ed. Dino Puncuh, vol. 2 (Gênes, 2004), 99–116; Costantinopoli nella prima metà del Quattrocento, in: Medio Evo Greco 4 (2004), 7–17.

BALLETTO, Laura, La storia medievale, in: Tra i palazzi di via Balbi: storia della Facoltà di Lettere e Filosofia dell'Università degli Studi di Genova, ed. Giovanni Assereto, Atti della Società Ligure di Storia Patria n.s. 43 (117) e Fonti e Studi per la Storia dell'Università di Genova 5 (Genova, 2003 [2004]), 455–522; Commerci e rotte commerciali nel Mediterraneo orientale alla metà del Quattrocento: l'importanza dell'isola di Chio, in: Money and Markets in the Palaiologian Era, ed. Nikolaos G. Moschonas, The National Hellenic Research Foundation, Institute for Byzantine Research 4, Byzantium today (Athens, 2003 [2004]), 97–112; Il Mar Nero nei notai genovesi: un *excursus* tra atti editi ed inediti, in: Nuova Rivista Storica 87 (2003), 669–692; Uomini e merci dalla Krämerthal sulla via del mare, in: Walser, mercanti e notai: il passato di Ayas e Gressoney attraverso i suoi protagonisti: Atti, ed. Gabriella Morchio (Comune di Ayas, 2004), 31–50; L'isola di Andros in atti notarili genovesi redatti a Chio nel XV secolo, in: Αγκυρα 2 (2004), 89–120; Tra Genova e Chio nel tempo di Cristoforo Colombo, in: Chemins 51–61.

BARBÉ, Hervé, with Emanuel Damati, La forteresse médiévale de Safed: Données récentes de l'archéologie, in: Crusades 3 (2004), 171–178.

BASSO, Enrico, I Gattilusio tra Genova e Bisanzio: Nuovi documenti d'archivio, in: Chemins 63–74.

BEREND, Nora, History and Identity: Mediaeval Frontiers and the Formation of Europe, in: Humanities: Essential Research for Europe, Danish Research Council for the Humanities (2003), 33–49.

BIRD, Jessalynn, The 'Historia Orientalis' of Jacques de Vitry: Visual and Written Commentaries as Evidence of a Text's Audience, Reception and Utilization, in: Essays in Medieval Studies: Proceedings of the Illinois Medieval Association 20 (2003), 56–74; The Victorines, Peter the Chanter's Circle, and the Crusades: Two Unpublished Crusading Appeals in Paris, Bibliothèque nationale, Ms. Latin 14470, in: Medieval Sermon Studies 48 (2004), 5–28.

BOMBI, Barbara, L'Ordine Teutonico nell'Italia centrale: la casa romana dell'Ordine e l'ufficio del procuratore generale, in: OTM 197–216.

BONNEAUD, Pierre, Le prieuré de Catalogne, le couvent de Rhodes et la couronne d'Aragon, 1415–1447 (Millau: Conservatoire Larzac Templier et Hospitalier, coll. Milites Christi, 2004), 439pp.

BORCHARDT, Karl, Kurie und Orden: Johanniter in den päpstlichen Supplikenregistern 1342–1352, in: Kurie und Region, Festschrift für Brigide Schwarz zum 65. Geburtstag, ed.

Brigitte Flug, Michael Matheus and Andreas Rehberg, Geschichtliche Landeskunde 59 (Stuttgart: Steiner, 2005), 17–39.

BRESC, Henri, Les territoires de la grâce: l'évêché de Mazara (1430–1450), in: Chemins 75–85.

BYSTED, Ane, with John H. Lind, Carsten Selch Jensen, Kurt Villads Jensen, Danske korstog: Krig og mission i Østersøen [Danish Crusades: War and Mission in the Baltic] (Copenhagen, 2004).

CARDINI, Franco, Il pellegrino assente: l'enigma di una mancata partenza per Gerusalemme (Firenze, agosto 1384), in: Chemins 87–97.

CARLSSON, Christer, Årsta: en medeltida gård med anor från järnåldern?, in: Tankar om Ting och Text, ed. Per Lekberg (Växjö, 2005) [commandery Årsta of the Teutonic Order on the eastern coast of Sweden].

CAROFF, Fanny, L'affrontement entre chrétiens et musulmans: le rôle de la vraie Croix dans les images de croisade (XIIIe–XVe siècle), in: Chemins 99–114.

CARR, Annemarie Weyl, ten entries in: Pilgrimage to Sinai: Treasures from the Holy Monastery of St. Catherine, Catalogue of exhibition at the Benaki Museum, Athens, 20 July–26 September 204 (Athens: Benaki Museum, 2004); Reflections on the Life of an Icon: the Eleousa of Kykkos, in: Epetirida Kentrou Kykkou 6 (2004), 103–162; The Holy Icon: a Lusignan Asset?, in: France and the Holy Land: Frankish Culture at the End of the Crusades, ed. Daniel H. Weiss and Lisa Mahoney (Baltimore – London: Johns Hopkins UP, 2004), 315–335; Images: Expressions of Faith and Power, in: Byzantium: Faith and Power (1261–1557), ed. Helen C. Evans, Catalogue of exhibition at the Metropolitan Museum of Art, New York, 23 March–4 July 2004 (New Haven – London: Yale UP, 2004), 143–152 and twelve catalogue entries.

CHEYNET, Jean-Claude, Byzance et l'Orient latin: le legs de Manuel Comnène, in: Chemins 115–125.

CIERZNIAKOWSKI, Piotr, L'Ordine Teutonico nell'Italia settentrionale, in: OTM 217–235.

CLAVERIE, Pierre-Vincent, La dévotion envers les lieux saints dans la Catalogne médiévale, in: Chemins 127–137.

COLLARD, Franck, *Timeas Danaos et dona ferentes*: Remarques à propos d'un épisode méconnu de la troisième croisade, in: Chemins 139–147.

CONGDON, Eleanor A., Protectionist Legislation and Italians in Aragon/Catalonia 1398–1404, in: Journal of Medieval Encounters – Special Issue: Law and Trade 9/2 (2003), 214–235.

CONTAMINE, Philippe, De Chypre à la Prusse et à la Flandre: les aventures d'un chevalier poitevin: Perceval de Couloigne, seigneur de Pugny, du Breuil-Bernard et de Pierrefitte (133.–141.), in: Chemins 149–157.

COULON, Damien, Du nouveau sur Emmanuel Piloti et son témoignage à la lumière de documents d'archives occidentaux, in: Chemins 159–170.

COUREAS, Nicolas S., Commercial Relations between Cyprus and the Genoese Colonies of Pera and Caffa, 1297–1459, in: Epetirida tou Kentrou Epestimonikon Ereunon 30 (Nicosia, 2004); The Place to be: Migrations to Lusignan and Venetian Cyprus, in: Kypriakai Spoudai 67 (2002 [Nicosia, 2004]).

CRAWFORD, Paul, reprint of excerpts from The Templar of Tyre: Part III of the Deeds of the Cypriots in: An Eyewitness History of the Crusades, ed. Christopher Tyerman, 4 vols.

(London: Folio Society, 2004); The Military Orders in Italy, in: Medieval Italy: An Encyclopedia, ed. Christopher Kleinhenz, John Barker et al. (Routledge, 2004), 720–722.

DALENA, Pietro, Gli insediamenti dell'Ordine Teutonico e la rete viaria nell'Italia meridionale, in: OTM 161–174.

DANSETTE, Béatrice, Le voyage d'outre-mer à la fin du XVe siècle: essai de définition de l'identité pèlerine occidentale à travers le récit de Nicole Le Huen, in: Chemins 171–182.

DÉDÉYAN, Gérard, De la prise de Thessalonique par les Normands (1185) à la croisade de Frédéric Barberousse (1189–1190): le revirement politico-religieux des pouvoirs arméniens, in: Chemins 183–196.

DELACROIX-BESNIER, Claudine, Les couvents des sœurs dominicaines de Nin et de Zadar (XIIIe–XIVe siècle), in: Chemins 197–215.

DEMEL, Bernhard, Der Deutsche Orden im Spiegel seiner Besitzungen und Beziehungen in Europa, Europäische Hochschulschriften III/961 (Frankfurt/Main et al.: Lang, 2004), 742 pp., 16 plates; Die Deutschordensballei Sachsen vom 13.–19. Jahrhundert: Ein Überblick, in: ibid. 7–189; Die Rekuperationsbemühungen des Deutschen Ordens um Livland von 1558/62 bis zum Ende des 18. Jahrhunderts, in: ibid. 190–258; Bausteine zur Deutschordensgeschichte vom 15. bis zum 20. Jahrhundert, in: ibid. 259–378; Der Deutsche Orden in Schlesien und Mähren in den Jahren 1742–1918, in: ibid. 379–472; Zur Geschichte des Piaristen- und späteren Staatsrealgymnasiums in Freudenthal (1730–1945), in: ibid. 472–537; Hoch- und Deutschmeister Leopold Wilhelm von Österreich (1641–1662), in: ibid. 538–603; Die Reichstagsgesandten des Deutschen Ordens von 1495 bis Ende 1805, in: ibid. 604–656.

DEMURGER, Alain, Outre-mer: Le passage des Templiers en Orient d'après les dépositions du procès, in: Chemins 217–230; Les Templiers, une chevalerie chrétienne au Moyen Âge (Paris: Editions du Seuil, 2005).

DONDI, Christina, Hospitaller Liturgical Manuscripts and Early Printed Books, in: Revue Mabillon 75 = n.s. 14 (2003), 225–256; The Liturgy of the Canons Regular of the Holy Sepulchre of Jerusalem: A Study and a Catalogue of the Manuscript Sources, Bibliotheca Victorina 16 (Turnhout: Brepols, 2004).

DOUMERC, Bernard, *Novus rerum nascitur ordo*: Venise et la fin d'un monde (1495–1511), in: Chemins 231–246.

DRORY, Joseph, Some Observations During a Visit to Palestine by Ibn al-'Arabī of Seville in 1092–1095, in: Crusades 3 (2004), 101–124.

DUCELLIER, Alain, Du Levant à Rhodes, Chio, Gallipoli et Palerme: démêlés et connivences entre chrétiens et musumlans à bord d'un vaisseau génois (octobre–décembre 1408–avril 1411), in: Chemins 247–283.

EDBURY, Peter, Women and the customs of the High Court of Jerusalem according to John of Ibelin, in: Chemins 285–292.

EDGINGTON, Susan B., Medicine and Surgery in the *Livre des Assises de la Cour des Bourgeois de Jérusalem*, in: Al-Masāq 17 (2005), 89–97.

EKDAHL, Sven, Tannenberg-Grunwald-Žalgiris: Eine mittelalterliche Schlacht im Spiegel deutscher, polnischer und litauischer Denkmäler, in: Zeitschrift für Geschichtswissenschaft 50/2 (2002), 103–118; Crusades and Colonisation in the Baltic: A Historiographic Analysis, in: XIX Rocznik Instytutu Polsko-Skandynawskiego 2003/2004 (Copenhagen, 2004), 1–42; Soldtruppen des Deutschen Ordens im Krieg gegen Polen 1409, in: Le convoi militaire, ed.

Tadeusz Poklewski-Kozieł, Fasciculi Archaeologiae Historicae 15 (Łódź, 2002 [2003]), 47–64.

ELIOPOULOU, Mary, Colonisation latine en Romanie: le cas de la principauté franque de Morée (XIIIe–XVe siècle), influences et survivances, in: Byzantinische Forschungen 28 (2004), 119–130; The Structure of Frankish Society in Romania: The Example of Corfu and the Principality of Achaea, in: Proceedings of the 7th Panionian Congress, Leucas, 26–30 May 2002, vol. 2 (Athens, 2004), 435–443; The Knights of Saint John and the Principality of Achaea, in: Proceedings of the Monasticism in the Peloponnese (4th–15th cent.), 14th International Symposium of the Institute for Byzantine Research, National Hellenic Research Foundation (Athens, 2004), 309–318.

FAVREAU-LILIE, Marie-Luise, Die italienischen Seestädte und die Kreuzzüge, in: Kein Krieg ist heilig: Die Kreuzzüge, Essay- und Katalogband zur Ausstellung Mainz, Bischöfliches Dom- und Diözesanmuseum, 2 April–30 Juli 2004, ed. Hans-Jürgen Kotzur, Brigitte Klein and Winfried Wilhelmy (Mainz, 2004), 193–203; L'Ordine Teutonico in Terrasanta (1198–1291), in: OTM 55–72; 1099: Die Eroberung Jerusalems, in: Höhepunkte des Mittelalters, ed. Georg Scheibelreiter (Darmstadt, 2004), 108–122; Welf IV. und der Kreuzzug von 1101, in: Welf IV. Schlüsselfigur einer Wendezeit, regionale und europäische Perspektiven, ed. Dieter Bauer and Mathias Becher (München, 2004), 420–447.

FEJIČ, Nenad, La *Chronique Ragusaine* de Junije Rastić et la politique de Venise dans la mémoire collective de Dubrovnik, in: Chemins 293–310.

FERRER I MALLOL, Maria Teresa, La reina Leonor de Chipre y los Catalanes de su entorno, in: Chemins 311–332.

FLORI, Jean, Il cammino verso la guerra santa, in: KOS 214 (2003), 26–29; Jihad and Holy War, in: Queen's Quarterly 110/3 (2003), 339–345; Violence et religion: La "guerre sainte" dans le christianisme et l'islam, in: Comprendre la violence et surmonter la haine en Méditerranée, Rencontres d'Averroès 9 (Marseille, 2003), 11–23; La peur de l'islam au Moyen Âge, in: L'Histoire 285 (March 2004), 1–6; Aliénor d'Aquitaine, la reine insoumise (Paris: éd. Payot, 2004), 543pp.; Aliénor l'insoumise: le rôle de la personalité d'Aliénor dans l'histoire de son temps, in: Aliénor d'Aquitaine 303, Art, recherche et création (2004), 53–57; Les "cours d'amour" d'Aliénor d'Aquitaine, in: L'Histoire 288 (June 2004), 76–80; Amour courtois ou amours de cour? Sur le rôle des sentiments dans la politique des rois de France au XIIe siècle, in: Les Temps médiévaux 5 (2003), 7–14; Knightly Society, in: New Cambridge Medieval History 4/1 (1024–1198), ed. David E. Luscombe and Jonathan Riley-Smith (Cambridge, 2004), 148–184; Sacre milizie e guerra santa: Lo spirito degli ordini militari, in: Monachi in armi: gli ordini religioso-militari dai Templari alla battaglia di Lepanto, storia ed arte, ed. Franco Cardini (Roma, 2004), 41–51; Pour une redéfinition de la crusade, in: Cahiers de civilisation médiévale 47 (2004), 329–350; Quelques aspects de la propagande antibyzantine dans les sources occidentales de la première croisade, in: Chemins 333–344.

FOLDA, Jaroslav, eight entries for crusader icons from the Monastery of St. Catherine on Mount Sinai, in: Byzantium: Faith and Power, 1261–1557 (New York: Metropolitan Museum of Art, 2004), 355–356, 357–358, 366–367, 374, 374–375, 376, 379–381; Pilgrimage to Sinai: Treasures from the Holy Monastery of St. Catherine, ed. Anastasis Drandakis (Athens: Benaki Museum, 2004), 88–90, 91–93, 108–111, 121–123, 124–127, 128–133, 134–138, 139–143; Trésors du Monastère Sainte-Catherine, Mont Sinaï, Egypte, ed. Helen C. Evans (Martigny/Switzerland: Fondacion Pierre Gianadda, 2005), 64–66, 67–69, 84–87, 97–99, 100–103, 104–106, 110–114, 115–119.

FONSECA, Cosimo Damiano, L'Ordine Teutonico nel Mediterraneo: una pista di lettura, in: OTM 277–289.

FOREY, Alan, The Siege of Lisbon and the Second Crusade, in: Portuguese Studies 20 (2004), 1–13; Templar Knights and Sergeants in the *Corona de Aragón* at the Turn of the Thirteenth and Fourteenth Centuries, in: As Ordens Militares e as Ordens de Cavalaria na Construcao do Mundo Ocidental, Actas do IV Encontro sobre Ordens Militares, ed. I.C.F. Fernandes (2005), 631–642.

FRANCE, John, The Crusades and Military History, in: Chemins 345–352.

FRANKOPAN, Peter, Co-operation between Constantinople and Rome before the First Crusade: a Study of the Convergence of Interests in Croatia in the late Eleventh Century, in: Crusades 3 (2004), 1–13.

GANCHOU, Thierry, Autonomie locale et relations avec les Latins à Byzance au XIVe siècle: Iôannès Limpidarios / Libadarios, Ainos et les Draperio de Péra, in: Chemins 353–374.

GARCÍA-GUIJARRO, Luis, La reforma eclesiástica romana en el desarrollo de formaciones politicas: el caso de los condados catalanes, *ca*.1060–*ca*.1100, in: Chemins 375–385.

GAUVARD, Claude, De la difficulté d'être étranger au royaume de France: les avatars de Colard le Lombard en 1413–1416, in: Chemins 387–399.

GENET, Jean-Philippe, Qu'allaient-ils faire dans ces galères?, in: Chemins 401–410.

GERTWAGEN, Ruthy, ed. with A. Zemer, Pirates: The Skull and Crossbones (Haifa, 2002); Piracy in the Middle Ages, in: ibid. 25–29 [Hebrew], 234–238 [English]; Pirate and Regular Vessels in the Mediterranean – Characteristics, Weaponry and Battle Tactics (8th Century BC–16th Century CE), in: ibid. 69–90 [Hebrew], 160–178 [English]; Pirates – Facts and Fiction, in: ibid. 99–103 [Hebrew], 148–152 [English]; with E. Blechman and S. Nudel, Life among the Pirates, in: ibid. 91–98 [Hebrew], 154–158 [English]; Characteristics of Mediterranean Ships in the Late Medieval Period (13th–15th Centuries CE), in: Splendour of the Medieval Mediterranean: Art, Culture, Politics, Navigation and Commerce in the Mediterranean Martime Cities (13th–15th Centuries), ed. Xavier Barral i Altet and Joan Alemany (Barcelona, 2004), 543–561; Maritime History in Israel, in: New Directions in Mediterranean Maritime History, ed. V. Carmelo and G. Harlafakis, Research in Maritime History 28 (2005), 171–188; Does Naval Activity – Military and Commercial – Need Artificial Ports? The Case of Venetian Harbours and Ports in the Ionian and Aegean till 1500, in: Graeco Arabica, Festschrift for Professor Christides (2005).

GILLINGHAM, John, Richard I, in: Oxford Dictionary of National Biography (Oxford UP, 2004).

GOURON, Philippe, Pour un réévaluation des phénomènes de colonisation en Méditerranée occidentale et au Maghreb pendant le Moyen Âge et le début des Temps Modernes, in: Chemins 411–423.

GUGLIELMI, Nilda, Miradas de viajeros sobre Oriente (siglos XII–XIV), in: Chemins 425–437.

GUTH, Klaus, Die Frühzeit des Zisterzienser-Klosters Ebrach unter Abt Adam (1127–*ca*.1167), in: Festschrift Ebrach, 200 Jahre nach der Säkularisation, hg. Wolfgang Werner (Ebrach, 2004), 15–36.

HARARI, Yuval N., Eyewitnessing in Accounts of the First Crusades: the *Gesta Francorum* and Other Contemporary Narratives, in: Crusades 3 (2004), 77–99.

HARRIS, Jonathan, Byzantium and the Crusades (London: Hambledon & London, 2003), Greek translation by Leonidas Karatzas (Athens: Oceanida, 2004); The Last Crusades: The

Ottoman Threat, in: Crusades: The Illustrated History, ed. Thomas F. Madden (London: Duncan Baird – Ann Arbor: Univ. of Michigan Press, 2004), 172–199.

HEULLANT-DONAT, Isabelle, Les martyrs franciscains de Jérusalem (1391), entre mémoire et manipulation, in: Chemins 439–459.

HIESTAND, Rudolf, The Papacy and the Second Crusade, in: The Second Crusade: Scope and Consequences, ed. Jonathan Philips and Martin Hoch (Manchester, 2001), 32–53; Die Göttinger Akademie als Trägerin eines internationalen Forschungsunternehmens: Das Papsturkundenwerk, in: Die Wissenschaften in der Akademie, ed. R. Smend and H.-H. Voigt (Göttingen, 2002), 321–341; Das Papsttum und die Welt des östlichen Mittelmeers, in: Das Papsttum in der Welt des 12. Jahrhunderts, ed. Ernst-Dieter Hehl, Ingrid Heike Ringel and Hubertus Seibert, Mittelalterforschungen 6 (Stuttgart, 2002), 185–206; with Hans Eberhard Mayer, Ein Bischof von Odense bei den Tataren, in: Deutsches Archiv 58 (2002), 219–227; Boemondo I e la prima Crociata, in: Il Mezzogiorno normanno-svevo e le Crociate, ed. Giosuè Musca (Bari, 2002), 65–94; Vom Himmel hoch da komm ich her …: Himmelsbriefe und ihre Funktion, in: Botschaften aus dem Jenseits, ed. H. Körner, Studia Humaniora 35 (Düsseldorf, 2002), 59–88; Gaufridus abbas Templi Domini: An Underestimated Figure in the Early History of the Kingdom of Jerusalem, in: The Experience of Crusading, vol. 2, ed. Peter Edbury and Jonathan Phillips (Cambridge, 2003), 48–59; Ein Zimmer mit Blick auf das Meer: Einige wenig beachtete Aspekte der Pilgerreisen ins Hl. Land im 12. und 13. Jahrhundert, in: East and West in the Crusader States, Context – Contacts – Confrontations, vol. 3, ed. Krijnie N. Ciggaar and Herman G. B. Teule (Leuven: Peeters, 2003), 139–164; Ed., 100 Jahre Papsturkunden: Ergebnisse – Methoden – Ziele (Göttingen, 2004); 100 Jahre Papsturkundenwerk, in: ibid. 11–44; Die unvollendete Italia Pontificia, in: ibid. 47–57; Methodische und sachliche Probleme des Oriens Pontificius, in: ibid. 245–263; Die Frau als Missionarin, in: Die Macht der Frauen, ed. Heinz Finger, Studia Humaniora 36 (Düsseldorf, 2004), 21–48; *crucem secreto accepit*: Zur Frage heimlicher Kreuzzugsgelübde, in: Frömmigkeitsformen in Mittelalter und Renaissance, ed. Johannes Laudage, Studia Humaniora 37 (Düsseldorf, 2004), 180–206; Die Kreuzzugsarmeen, in: Armeen in Europa – Europäische Armeen: Von den Kreuzzügen bis ins 21. Jahrhundert, ed. M. Salewski and H. Timmermann, Dokumente und Schriften der Europäischen Akademie Otzenhausen 111 (Münster/Westfalen, 2004), 13–39.

HOUBEN, Hubert, Neuentdeckte Papsturkunden für den Deutschen Orden (1219–1261) aus dem Staatsarchiv Neapel, in: Quellen und Forschungen aus italienischen Archiven und Bibliotheken 83 (2003), 41–82; Der Deutsche Orden im Mittelmeerraum, in: Der Deutsche Orden in Europa, Schriften zur staufischen Geschichte und Kunst 23 (Göppingen, 2004), 29–48; ed., OTM, xi, 321pp.; Nuovi orientamenti nelle ricerche sull'Ordine Teutonico, in: ibid. 3–16; L'Ordine Teutonico, in: Monaci in armi: gli ordini religioso-militari dai Templari alla battaglia di Lepanto, storia ed arte, ed. Franco Cardini (Roma, 2004), 101–112.

HOUSLEY, Norman J., Crusading in the Fifteenth Century: Message and Impact (Palgrave Macmillan, 2004).

JACOBY, David, Foreigners and the Urban Economy in Thessalonike, *c*.1150–*c*.1430, in: Dumbarton Oaks Papers 57 (2003), 85–132; Society, Culture and the Arts in Crusader Acre, in: France and the Holy Land: Frankish Culture at the End of the Crusades, ed. Daniel H. Weiss and Lisa Mahoney (Baltimore – London: Johns Hopkins UP, 2004), 97–137; Seide und seidene Textilien im arabischen und normannischen Sizilien: der wirtschaftliche Kontext, in: Nobiles Officinae: Die königlichen Hofwerkstätten zu Palermo zur Zeit der Normannen und Staufer im 12. und 13. Jahrhundert, ed. Wilfried Seipel, Catalogue of the Kunsthistorisches Museum, Wien (Milano: Skira, 2004), 61–73; The Silk Trade of Late Byzantine

Constantinople, in: 550th Anniversary of the Istanbul University, International Byzantine and Ottoman Symposium (15th Century), 30–31 May 2003, ed. Sümer Atasoy (Istanbul, 2004), 129–144; Dall'oriente all'Italia: commerci di stoffe preziose nel Duecento e nel primo Trecento, in: Cangrande della Scala: la morte e il corredo di un principe nel medioevo europeo, ed. Paola Marini, Ettore Napione, Gian Maria Varanini, catalogue of exhibition Museo di Castelvecchio (Verona Venezia: Marisilio, 2004), 141–153; Le consulat vénitien d'Alexandrie d'après un document inédit de 1284, in: Chemins 461–474.

JASPERT, Nikolas, Im Bann des "Wahren Kreuzes", in: Damals 4/2004, 42–46; Ein Polymythos: Die Kreuzzüge, in: Mythen in der Geschichte, ed. Helmut Altrichter, Klaus Herbers and Helmut Neuhaus, Rombach Wissenschaften Reihe Historiae 16 (Freiburg im Breisgau: Rombach, 2004), 202–235; "Wo seine Füsse einst standen" (Ubi steterunt pedes eius) – Jerusalemsehnsucht und andere Motivationen mittelalterlicher Kreuzfahrer, in: Kein Krieg ist heilig: Die Kreuzzüge, Ausstellungskatalog, ed. Hans-Jürgen Kotzur, Brigitte Klein and Winfried Wilhelmy (Mainz: Zabern, 2004), 173–185; L'Ordine Teutonico nella penisola iberica: limiti e possibilità di una provincia periferica, in: OTM 109–132.

JENSEN, Janus Møller, Denmark and the Holy War: A Redefinition of a Traditional Pattern of Conflict in the Baltic in the Twelfth Century, in: Scandinavians and Europe 800–1350: Contact, Conflict, and Coexistence, ed. Jonathan Adams and Katherine Holman, Medieval Texts and Cultures of Northern Europe 4 (Turnhout: Brepols, 2004), 219–236; Vejen til Jerusalem: Danmark og pilgrimsvejen til det Hellige Land i det 12. århundrede: En islandsk vejviser, in: Ett annat 1100-tal: Individ, kollektiv och kulturella mönster i medeltidens Danmark, ed. Peter Carelli, Lars Hermanson and Hanne Sanders, Centrum för Danmarksstudier 3 (Göteborg: Makadam, 2004), 284–337; Den glemte periferi og de glemte korstog, Grønland og korstogene 1400–1536, in: Historie 1 (2004), 109–145; Die Bezwinger der Slawen: Kreuzzug, Königsideologie und Wende im 12. Jahrhundert, in: Freunde und Feinde: Alltagsleben an der Ostsee 700–1200, ed. Palle Birk Hansen, Anna-Elisabeth Jensen, Manfred Gläser and Ingrid Sudhoff, Ausstellungen zur Archäologie in Lübeck 7 (Lübeck: Schmidt-Römhild, 2004), 33–45; Fra korstog til religionskrig? Korstogstanken i Skandinavien, 1400–1600, in: Konge, adel og militærmakt, 1400–1600, ed. Knut P.L. Arstad, Forsvarsmuseets Småskrift 39 (Oslo: Forsvarsmuseet, 2004), 34–78.

JORDAN, William C., Unceasing Strife, Unending Fear: Jacques de Therines and the Freedom of the Church in the Age of the Last Capetians (Princeton: UP, 2005).

JOTISCHKY, Andrew, Penance and Reconciliation in the Crusade States: Matthew Paris, Jacques de Vitry and the Eastern Christians, in: Retribution, Repentance and Reconciliation, ed. Kate Cooper and Jeremy Gregory, Studies in Church History 40 (Woodbridge: Boydell, 2002), 74–83; Ethnographic Attitudes in the Crusader States: The Franks and the Indigenous Orthodox Peoples, in: East and West in the Crusader States: Context, Contacts, Confrontations, vol. 3, ed. Krijnie N. Ciggaar and Herman G.B. Teule (Leuven: Peeters, 2003), 1–19; The Mendicants as Missionaries and Travellers in the Near East in the 13th and 14th Centuries, in: Eastward Bound: Travel and Travellers 1050–1550, ed. Rosamund Allen (Manchester: UP, 2004), 88–106.

KAPLAN, Michel, Un patriarche byzantin dans le royaume latin de Jérusalem: Léontios, in: Chemins 475–488.

KARPOV, Sergej P., Les empereurs de Trébizonde, débiteurs des Génois, in: Chemins 489–494.

KEDAR, Benjamin Z., A Second Incarnation in Frankish Jerusalem, in: The Experience of Crusading, vol. 2: Defining the Crusader Kingdom of Jerusalem, ed. Peter Edbury and Jonathan Phillips (Cambridge, 2003), 79–92; The Jerusalem Massacre of July 1099 in the

Western Historiography of the Crusades, in: Crusades 3 (2004), 15–75; Again: Genoa's Golden Inscription and King Baldwin I's Privilege of 1104, in: Chemins 495–502.

KIESEWETTER, Andreas, Documenti vecchi e nuovi sulla vita di Marino da Caramanico, in: Studi per Marcello Gigante, ed. S. Palmieri (Napoli, 2003), 347–370; L'Ordine Teutonico in Grecia e in Armenia, in: OTM 73–107; La diocesi di Martina Franca: un progretto fallito ancora di nascere, in: Cenacolo: Rivista storica di Taranto n.s. 15 (2003), 43–50; Il governo e l'amministrazione centrale del Regno, in: Le eredità normanno-sveve nell'età angioina: perisistenze e mutamenti nel Mezzogiorno, Atti delle quindicesime Giornate normanno-sveve Bari, 22–25 ottobre 2002, ed. Giosuè Musca (Bari, 2004), 25–68; Tre privilegi originali inediti di Roberto II di Basunvilla, conte di Conversano e di Loretello (*ca*.1140–1182), in: Mediterraneo, Mezzogiorno, Europa: Studi in onore di Cosimo Damiano Fonseca, ed. Giancarlo Andenna and Hubert Houben, vol. 2 (Bari, 2004), 593–620; Jamvilla (Joinville-Briquenay), Niccolò di Giovanni, in: Dizionario biografico degli Italiani 62 (2004), 136–137; Ladislao d'Angiò-Durazzo, re di Sicilia, in: ibid. 63 (2004), 39–51.

KRÄMER, Thomas, Der Deutsche Orden in Frankreich – Ein Beitrag zur Ordensgeschichte im Königreich Frankreich und im Midi, in: OTM 237–276.

KREKIČ, Bariša, Trois documents concernant les marchands vénitiens à Tana au début du XVe siècle, in: Chemins 503–509.

KRÜGER, Jürgen, Die Loca Sancta in Jerusalem zur Zeit Karls des Großen, in: Ex Oriente, Isaak und der weiße Elefant, Bagdad – Jerusalem – Aachen, Eine Reise durch drei Kulturen um 800 und heute, 3 vols. (Mainz, 2003), vol. 2, 18–31; entries in exhibition catalogue Kein Krieg ist heilig: Die Kreuzzüge, Ausstellungskatalog, ed. Hans-Jürgen Kotzur, Brigitte Klein and Winfried Wilhelmy (Mainz: Zabern, 2004).

LAIOU, Angeliki E., Monopoly and Privileged Free Trade in the Eastern Mediterranean (8th–14th Century), in: Chemins 511–526.

LAURIOUX, Bruno, Quelques remarques sur la découverte du sucre par les premiers croisés d'Orient, in: Chemins 527–536.

LICINIO, Raffaele, Teutonici e masserie nella Capitanata dei secoli XIII–XV, in: OTM 175–195.

LIGATO, Giuseppe, Le tombe dei re di Gerusalemme, in: La Terra Santa (settembre–ottobre 2004), 4–10.

LILIE, Ralph-Johannes, Byzanz und die Kreuzzüge, Urban-Taschenbuch 595 (Stuttgart: Kohlhammer, 2004), 280pp.

LIMOR, Ora, In the Palace of Barcelona and the Market of Majorca – Towards a New Typology of Religious Disputations in the Middle Ages, in: Pe'amim 94/95 (2003), 105–134 [Hebrew]; with Israel I. Yuval, Scepticism and Conversion: Jews, Christians and Doubters in Sepher ha-Nizzahon, in: Hebraica Veritas? Christian Hebraists and the Study of Judaism in Early Modern Europe, ed. Allison Coudert and Jeffrey Shoulson (Philadelphia: Pennsylvania UP, 2004), 159–180; Pilgrims and Authors: Adomnán's *De locis sanctis* and Hugeburc's *Hodoeporicon Sancti Willibaldi*, in: Revue Bénédictine 114 (2004), 253–275; Charlemagne's Holy Land, in: Zmanim 89 (2004) [Hebrew].

LOUD, Graham, with Prescott Dunbar, The History of the Normans by Amatus of Montecassino (Woodbridge: Boydell & Brewer, 2004), xxi, 220pp.; Southern Italy in the Eleventh Century, in: New Cambridge Medieval History 4/2, ed. David E. Luscombe and Jonathan Riley-Smith (Cambridge: UP, 2004), 94–119; Norman Sicily in the Twelfth Century, in: ibid. 442–474.

LUTTRELL, Anthony, I Cavalieri di San Giovanni di Gerusalemme, Rodi e Malta, in: Monaci in armi: gli ordini religioso-militari dai Templari alla battaglia di Lepanto, storia ed arte, ed. Franco Cardini (Roma, 2004), 53–62.

MADDEN, Thomas F., ed., Crusades: The Illustrated History (Ann Arbor: Univ. of Michigan Press, 2004); Venice, the Papacy, and the Crusades before 1204, in: The Medieval Crusade, ed. Susan J. Ridyard (Woodbridge: Boydell & Brewer, 2004), 85–95; The Enduring Myths of the Fourth Crusade, in: World History Bulletin 20 (2004), 11–14.

MAIER, Christoph T., The Roles of Women in the Crusade Movement: A Survey, in: Journal of Medieval History 30 (2004), 61–82; Die Rolle der Frauen in der Kreuzzugsbewegung, in: Päpste, Pilger, Pönitentiarie, Festschrift für Ludwig Schmugge zum 65. Geburtstag, ed. Andreas Meyer, C. Redtel, M. Wittmer-Butsch (Tübingen, 2004), 253–281.

MALTÉZOU, Chryssa, Un artisan verrier crétois à Venise, in: Chemins 537–541.

MANSOURI, Mohamed Tahar, Tissus et costumes dans les relations islamo-byzantines (IXe–Xe siècle), in: Chemins 543–551.

MAYER, Hans Eberhard, Die porta nova de Belcayra im Jerusalem der Kreuzfahrer, in: Zeitschrift des Deutschen Palästina-Vereins 119 (2003 [2004]), 183–190.

MESCHINI, Marco, 1204: l'incompiuta: la quarta crociata e le conquiste di Costantinopoli (Milano:Àncora, 2004); "Diabolus ... illos ad mutuas inimicitias acuebat": divisions et dissensions dans le camp des croisés au cours de la première croisade albigeoise (1207–1215), in: La Croisade albigeoise, Actes du colloque du Centre d'Études Cathares, Carcassonne, 4–6 octobre 2002 (Carcassonne, 2004), 171–196; L'evoluzione della normativa antiereticale di Innocenzo III dalla *Vergentis in senium* (1199) al IV concilio lateranense (1215), in: Bollettino dell'Istituto Storico Italiano per il Medio Evo 106/2 (2004), 207–231.

MICHEAU, Françoise, Les croisades dans la Chronique universelle de Bar Hebraeus, in: Chemins 553–572.

MITCHELL, Piers D., Medicine in the Crusades: Warfare, Wounds and the Medieval Surgeon (Cambridge: UP, 2004); The Palaeopathology of Skulls Recovered from a Medieval Cave Cemetery at Safed, Israel, in: Levant 36 (2004), 243–250; Evidence for Elective Surgery in the Frankish States of the Near East in the Crusader Period (12th–13th Centuries), in: Gesundheit – Krankheit: Kulturtransfer medizinischen Wissens von der Spätantike bis in die frühe Neuzeit, ed. Kay Peter Jankrift and Florian Steger (Köln – Weimar – Wien: Böhlau, 2004), 121–138.

MÖHRING, Hannes, Warum verlor die islamische Kultur ihre führende Stellung?, in: Historische Zeitschrift 277 (2003), 655–666; König der Könige: Der Bamberger Reiter in neuer Interpretation (Königstein im Taunus, 2004); Der Traum von der "Großen Revanche" in populären Weissagungen des mittelalterlichen Orients und Okzidents, in: Kriegsniederlagen: Erfahrungen und Erinnerungen, ed. Horst Carl, Hans-Henning Kortüm, Dieter Langewiesche and Friedrich Lenger (Berlin, 2004), 213–231.

MUTAFIAN, Claude, L'Église arménienne et les chrétientés d'Orient (XIIe–XIVe siècle), in: Chemins 573–588.

NICOLAOU-KONNARI, Angel, Ethnic Names and the Construction of Group Identity in Medieval and Early Modern Cyprus: The Case of *Kypriotis*, in: Kypriologia: Studies Presented to Theodoros Papadopoullos, Kypriakai Spoudai 64/65 (2000/01 [Nicosia, 2003]), 259–275.

NICOLLE, David, Poitiers 1356, Osprey Campaign 138 (Oxford, 2004); Crusader Castles in the Holy Land 1097–1192, Osprey Fortress 21 (Oxford, 2004); Silah: The Islamic Period, in: EI Supplement 11/12 (2004), 736–746; Kriegstechnologie und Waffenherstellung, in: Kein Krieg ist heilig: Die Kreuzzüge, Ausstellungskatalog, ed. Hans-Jürgen Kotzur, Brigitte Klein and Winfried Wilhelmy (Mainz: Zabern, 2004), 97–115; The Vocabulary of Medieval Warfare: Arms, Armour and Siege Weapons Terminology in the *Excidium Aconis*, in: The Fall of Acre 1291: Excidii Aconis gestorum collectio, Ystoria de desolatione et conculcatione civitatis Acconensis et tocius Terre Sancte, ed. Robert B. C. Huygens (Turnhout, 2004), 165–187; Gibraltar: A Medieval Military Base, in: Medieval History 12 (August 2004), 40–45; with Helen Nicholson, God's Warriors: Crusaders, Saracens and the Battle for Jerusalem (Oxford, 2005).

NIELEN, Marie-Adélaïde, L'œuvre de Richard Cœur de Lion en Orient, in: Actes du colloque Richard Cœur de Lion, roi d'Angleterre, duc de Normandie, Caen, Archives départementales du Calvados, 6–8 avril 1999 (Conseil général du Calvados, Direction des Archives départementales, 2004), 26–37; Du comté de Champagne aux royaumes d'Orient: sceaux et armoiries des comtes de Brienne, in: Chemins 589–606.

NYSTAZOPOULOU-PÉLÉKIDOU, Marie, Mouvements de populations, migrations et colonisations en Serbie et en Bosnie (XIIe–XVe siècle), in: Chemins 607–618.

O'MALLEY, Gregory, Pilgrimage, Crusade, Trade and Embassy: Pre-Elizabethan English Contacts with the Ottoman Turks, in: Crusades 3 (2004), 153–170; articles on four English Hospitallers, Thomas Newport (d.1523), Thomas Dingley (d.1539), William Weston (d.1540) and Nicholas Upton (d.1551), for: Oxford Dictionary of National Biography (Oxford: UP, 2004).

ORIGONE, Sandra, Questioni tra Bizanzio e Genova intorno all'anno 1278, in: Chemins 619–631.

ORTALLI, Gherardo, Les *giorni uziagi*: hommes de mer vénitiens et jours néfastes, in: Chemins 633–638.

OTTEN-FROUX, Catherine, Un notaire vénitien à Famagouste au XIVe siècle: les actes de Simeone, prêtre de San Giacomo dell'Orio (1362–1371), in: Thesaurismata 33 (2003), 15–158; Contribution à l'étude de la procédure du *sindicamentum* en Méditerranée orientale (XIVe–XVe siècle), in: Chemins 639–650.

PAHLITZSCH, Johannes, Georgians and Greeks in Jerusalem (1099–1310), in: East and West in the Crusader States, Context – Contacts – Confrontations, vol. 3, ed. Krijnie N. Ciggaar and Herman G. B. Teule, Orientalia Lovaniensia Analecta 125 (Leuven – Dudley/MA: Peeters, 2003), 35–51; with Christian Müller, Sultan Baybars I and the Georgians – In the Light of New Documents related to the Monastery of the Holy Cross in Jerusalem, in: Arabica 51 (2004), 258–290; Ärzte ohne Grenzen: Melkitische, jüdische und samaritanische Ärzte in Ägypten und Syrien zur Zeit der Kreuzzüge, in: Gesundheit – Krankheit: Kulturtransfer medizinischen Wissens von der Spätantike bis in die Frühe Neuzeit, ed. Kay Peter Jankrift and Florian Steger (Köln – Weimar – Wien: Böhlau, 2004), 101–119; ed. with Lorenz Korn, Governing the Holy City: The Interaction of Social Groups in Medieval Jerusalem (Wiesbaden, 2004); The Transformation of Latin Religious Institutions into Islamic Endowments by Saladin in Jerusalem, in: ibid. 47–69.

PAPACOSTEA, Şerban, Les Génois et la Horde d'Or: le tournant de 1313, in: Chemins 651–659.

PARISSE, Michel, Des Lorrains en croisade: la maison de Bar, in: Chemins 661–670.

PAVIOT, Jacques, Les ducs de Bourgogne, la croisade e l'Orient (fin XIVe siècle–XVe siècle), Cultures et civilisations médiévales (Paris, 2003), 394pp.; Les cartes et leur utilisation à la fin du Moyen Âge: l'exemple des principautés bourguignonnes et angevins, in: Itineraria 2 (2003 [2004]), 201–228; Burgundy and the Crusade, in: Crusading in the Fifteenth Century: Message and Impact, ed. Norman Housley (London: Macmillan, 2004), 70–80; Marins et marchands portugais en Méditerranée à la fin du Moyen Âge, in: Chemins 671–679.

PETTI BALBI, Giovanna, La celebrazione del potere: l'apparato funebre per Battista Campofregoso (1442), in: Chemins 681–689.

PHILLIPS, Jonathan P., The Fourth Crusade and the Sack of Constantinople (UK: Jonathan Cape, USA: Viking, 2004), xxii, 374pp., to be translated into Greek and Spanish in 2005.

PICARD, Christophe, Les arsenaux musulmans de la Méditerranée et de l'océan Atlantique (VIIe–XVe siècle), in: Chemins 691–710.

PISTARINO, Geo, L'Europa dal particolarismo medievale e dall'Impero feudale agli orizzonti aperti, in: Chemins 711–722.

POWELL, James M., The Deeds of Pope Innocent III, translated with an introduction and notes (Washington/DC: Catholic Univ. of America Press, 2004); Innocent III and Alexius III: A Crusade Plan that Failed, in: The Experience of Crusading, vol. 1, ed. Marcus Bull and Norman Housley (Cambridge: UP, 2003), 96–102; The Fifth Crusade to 1291: The Loss of the Holy Land, in: Crusades: The Illustrated History, ed. Thomas F. Madden (London: Duncan Baird – Ann Arbor: Univ. of Michigan Press, 2004), 144–171.

PRINGLE, R. Denys, Castle Chapels in the Frankish East, in: La fortification au temps des croisades, ed. Nicholas Faucherre, Jean Mesqui and Nicholas Prouteau (Rennes: Presses Universitaires, 2004), 25–41 [14 figs.]; Crusader Inscriptions from Southern Lebanon, in: Crusades 3 (2004), 131–151 [14 figs.]; with Johnny De Meulemeester, The 'Aqaba Castle Project 2003, in: Newsletter of the Council for British Research in the Levant (2004), 26–27; A Crusader Chapel in the Hippodrome of Tyre, in: Archaeology and History in the Lebanon 20 (2004), 2–8.

PUNCUH, Dino, Associazionismo e ricerca a Genova, tra tradizione ed evoluzione, in: Chemins 723–731.

RACINE, Pierre, Lucques, Gênes et le trafic de la soie (v. 1250–v. 1340), in: Chemins 733–743.

RICHARD, Jean, Les Arméniens dans les états latins d'Orient: les lendemains de la croisade, in: L'Arménie dans l'Orient chrétien, ed. P. M. Mouradijan (Erevan, 2000), 169–174; L'esprit de la croisade, Japanese translation by Hironori Miyamatsu (Hosei Univ. Press, 2004), xi, 254pp.; The Eastern Churches (c.1024–c.1198), in: The New Cambridge Medieval History, vol. 4/1, ed. David E. Luscombe and Jonathan Riley-Smith (Cambridge: UP, 2004), 564–598, 849–855; Le système défensif des États latins: programme et évolution, in: La fortification au temps des croisades, Actes du colloque international de Parthenay, sept. 2002, ed. Nicholas Faucherre, Jean Mesqui and Nicholas Prouteau (Rennes: Presses Univ., 2004), 15–24; Zayton, un évêché au bout du monde, in: Chemins 745–751.

RILEY-SMITH, Jonathan, Der Aufruf von Clermont und seine Folgen, in: Kein Krieg ist heilig: Die Kreuzzüge, Ausstellungskatalog, ed. Hans-Jürgen Kotzur, Brigitte Klein and Winfried Wilhelmy (Mainz: Zabern, 2004), 51–63; The Crown of France and Acre, 1254–1291, in: France and the Holy Land, Frankish Culture at the End of the Crusades, ed. Daniel H. Weiss and Lisa Mahoney (Baltimore – London: Johns Hopkins UP, 2004), 45–62; ed. with David E. Luscombe, The New Cambridge Medieval History, vol. 4/2 (Cambridge: UP, 2004); Were the Templars Guilty?, in: The Medieval Crusade, ed. Susan J. Ridyard (Woodbridge: Boydell, 2004), 107–124; The Structures of the Orders of the Temple and the Hospital in c.1291, in: ibid. 125–143; Further thoughts on the layout of the Hospital in Acre, in: Chemins 753–764.

SAINT-GUILLAIN, Guillaume, L'Apocalypse et le sens des affaires: Les moines de Saint-Jean de Patmos, leurs activités économiques et leurs relations avec les Latins (XIIIe et XIVe siècles), in: Chemins 765–790.

SCHABEL, Christopher, Camille Enlart and the Cistercians in Cyprus, in: Report of the Department of Antiquities, Cyprus (2002), 401–406 [Greek]; The Greek Bishops of Cyprus, 1260–1340, and the *Synodicon Kyprion*, in: Kypriakai Spoudai 64/65 (2000/01), 217–234; Etienne de Lusignan's *Chorograffia* and the Ecclesiastical History of Frankish Cyprus, in: Modern Greek Studies Yearbook 18/19 (2002/03), 339–353; with James Schryver, The Graffiti in the 'Royal Chapel' of Pyrga, in: Report of the Department of Antiquities, Cyprus (2003), 327–334; The Latin Bishops of Cyprus, 1255–1313, with a Note on Bishop Neophytos of Solea, in: Epeterida tou Kentrou Epistemonikon Erevnon 29 (2004), 75–111; Hugh the Just: the Further Rehabilitation of King Hugh IV of Lusignan of Cyprus, in: ibid. 123–152.

STEPANSKY, Yosef, The Crusader Castle of Tiberias, in: Crusades 3 (2004), 179–181.

STONE, Michael E., A Notice about Patriarch Aimery of Antioch in an Armenian Colophon of 1181, in: Crusades 3 (2004), 125–129.

STÖCKLY, Doris, Une autre fonction des capitaines de galées du marché vénitiennes: le contrôle des officiers d'outre-mer, in: Chemins 791–799.

TESSERA, Miriam Rita, Memorie d'Oriente: la traslazione del braccio di San Filippo a Firenze nel 1205, in: Aevum 79 (2004), 531–540.

TOOMASPOEG, Kristjan, L'Ordine Teutonico in Puglia e in Sicilia, in: OTM 133–160.

TOUATI, François-Olivier, Entre Orient et Occident: les archives de Saint-Lazare de Jérusalem au Moyen Âge, in: La présence latine en Orient au Moyen Âge (Paris, 2000), 95–129; De Fontevraud à Jérusalem: Sainte-Lazare, une renaissance spirituelle et hospitalière à l'aube du XIIe siècle, in: Transversalités 80 (octobre–décembre 2001), 33–43; Saint Lazare, Fontevraud, Jérusalem, in: Robert d'Arbrissel et la vie religieuse dans l'Ouest de la France, Actes du colloque international de Fontevraud (déc. 2001), ed. J. Dalarun, Disciplina monastica 1 (Turnhout: Brepols, 2004), 199–238; *De prima origine Sancti Lazari Hierosolymitani*, in: Chemins 801–812.

TZAVARA, Angéliki, À propos du commerce vénitien des 'schienali' (schinalia) (première moitié du XVe siècle), in: Chemins 813–826.

UPTON-WARD, Judith M., The Catalan Rule of the Templars: A Critical Edition and English Translation from Barcelona, Archivo de la Corona de Aragón, Cartas Reales, MS 3344, Studies in the History of Medieval Religion 19 (Woodbridge: Boydell, 2003), xxviii, 113pp.

URBAN, William, Crusades in Europe, in: Crusades: The Illustrated History, ed. Thomas F. Madden (London: Duncan Baird – Ann Arbor: Univ. of Michigan Press, 2004), 128–141.

VALÉRIAN, Dominique, Gênes, l'Afrique et l'Orient: le Maghreb almohade dans la politique génoise en Méditerranée, in: Chemins 827–837.

VAUCHEZ, André, Saint Homebon (†1197), patron des marchands et des artisans drapiers à la fin du Moyen Âge et à l'époque moderne, in: Chemins 839–846.

VERGÉ-FRANCESCHI, Michel, Les Ornano: des seigneurs feudataires corso-génois (1498–1610), in: Chemins 847–857.

VETERE, Benedetto, L'ideologia degli Ordini religioso-templari (Templari e Cavalieri Teutonici), in: OTM 33–52.

VEY-MESTDAGH, J. H. de, with J. A. de Boo, Liber sigillorum: De zegels in het archief van de ridderlijke Duitsche Orde, balije von Utrecht, 1200–1811, part 1: Beschrijvingen, part 2: Afbeeldingen (Utrecht, 1995), 243 and 111pp.

2. Recently completed theses

BYSTED, Ane, In Merit As Well As in Reward: Indulgences, Spiritual Merit, and the Theology of the Crusades, c.1095–1216, Univ. of Southern Denmark.

TOUATI, François-Olivier, Saint-Lazare de Jérusalem, Orient-Occident, XIIe–XIIIe siècles, thèse d'habilitation à diriger des recherches en Histoire médiévale, Univ. de Paris I, 2001, 191pp., présentation et édition scientifique des sources. Actes et cartulaire de Saint-Lazare de Jérusalem (1124?–1291), 324pp. [sous presse].

3. Papers read by members of the Society and others

DALL'AGLIO, Francesco, Brothers in arms: the art of war according to Baldwin and Henry [Latin emperors of Constantinople], at: SSCLE-Istanbul.

AHN, Sang-Joon, Grundbesitz und Herrschaftsfunktion der Kommenden Wesel und Burgsteinfurt, at: OM 2005.

ALLEN, David, Grandmaster Laskaris and the Catholic reformation, at: Ritterorden und Reformation, Utrecht, 2 October 2004.

ALTAN, Ebru, Anatolia after the Fourth Crusade, at: SSCLE-Istanbul.

AMITAI, Reuven, Slowly but surely: Mamluk siege methods against the Franks, at: SSCLE-Istanbul.

ANDREA, Alfred J., 'What we have here is a failure of communication': Innocent III and Alexius III on the eve of the Fourth Crusade, at: SSCLE-Istanbul.

ANGOLD, Michael, The debate over the sack of Constantinople, at: SSCLE-Istanbul.

ARNOLD, Udo, Hochmeister Albrecht von Brandenburg-Ansbach und Landmeister Gotthard Ketteler – Ordensritter und Territorialherren am Scheideweg in Preußen und Livland, at: Ritterorden und Reformation, Utrecht, 30 September 2004.

ASLANOV, Cyril, Villehardouin and Robert de Clari on the conquest of Constantinople: the rise of a new historiography?, at: SSCLE-Istanbul.

EL-AZHARI, Taef, The Muslim chroniclers' perspective of the Fourth Crusade, at: SSCLE-Istanbul.

BALARD, Michel, L'historiographie occidentale de la Quatrième Croisade, at: The Fourth Crusade and its Consequences, Académie d'Athènes, 9–12 March 2004; Les flottes de la Quatrième Croisade, at: The Fourth Crusade, Andros, May 2004; Spezie e farmacopea nel Medioevo, at: Giornate della Scuola Medica Salernitana, May 2004; Il notaio e l'amministrazione della giustizia nell'Oltremare genovese, at: Hinc publica fides, Gênes, October 2004; Il banco di San Giorgio e le colonie d'Oltremare, at: Il banco di San Giorgio, Gênes, November 2004; Les ports du monde byzantin et des régions pontiques, at: Les ports dans le monde méditerranéen, Lattes – Montpellier, November 2004; Orientals in Cyprus at the beginning of the 14th century according to Genoese notaries, at: SSCLE-Sydney1.

BALLETTO, Laura, Hommes et marchandises entre Gênes et la Corse au XVe siècle, at: 128th Congrès des Sociétés Historiques Relations, échanges et coopération en Méditerranée, Bastia, 14–21 April 2003; L'impresa di Filippo Doria contro Tripoli (1355), at: La Libia nella storia del Mediterraneo, Roma, 10–12 May 2003; Brevi note su Caffa genovese nel XIV secolo, at: 8th International Symposium Bulgaria Pontica Medii Aevi, Nessebar, 11–12 September 2003; Echi genovesi della conquista turca di Costantinopoli, at: La conquête de Constantinople: l'événement, sa portée et ses échos (1453–2003), Tunis, 11–13 December 2003; Negroponte nei traffici commerciali genovesi nel Mediterraneo Orientale sulla fine del medioevo, at: Venice – Euboea: From Egripos to Negroponte, Chalkida, 12–14 November 2004.

BARBER, Malcolm, The reputation of Gerard of Ridefort, at: SSCLE-Istanbul.

BARKER, John W., Crusading and matrimony in the dynastic policies of Montferrat and Savoy, at: SSCLE-Istanbul.

BARTON, Simon F., The nobility and the Iberian crusades, at: SSCLE-Istanbul.

BARTOS, Sebastian, Gender and power in the Latin East: perceptions of female authority in the chronicle of William of Tyre, at: IMC Kalamazoo, 2004.

BEIHAMMER, Alexander, The phenomenon of defection in Byzantine-Seljuk relations during the 12th and 13th centuries, at: SSCLE-Sydney1.

BELLOMO, Elena, Barotius, crusader and Templar master of Lombardy and Italy, at: SSCLE-Istanbul.

BENNETT, Matthew, Why and how were the Fourth Crusaders able to capture Constantinople?, at: SSCLE-Istanbul.

BERNTSON, Martin, The dissolution of the Hospitaller houses in Denmark and Sweden, at: Ritterorden und Reformation, Utrecht, 30 September 2004.

BIRD, Jessalynn, Heretics or allies? Oliver of Paderborn and James of Vitry on eastern Christians, at: IMC Kalamazoo, 2003; Theology and law: the theory and practice of fama-based inquisition among Peter the Chanter's circle in Paris, at: 12th International Congress for Medieval Canon Law, August 2004; Paris masters and the justification of the Albigensian crusade, at: Crusading and Against Whom? Holy Violence in the Middle Ages, Middlebury College/VT, October 2004; Paris masters preach the crusades: the rhetoric of holy war in the 12th and 13th centuries, at: Rhetorics of Holy War, Berkeley/CA, February 2005.

BISKUP, Radosław, Der Deutsche Orden und die Bistümer in Preussen: Bemerkungen über den Einfluss der Ritterbrüder auf die Diözesanverwaltung im Mittelalter, at: OM 2005.

BOAS, Adrian J., Crusader and Armenian castles: architectural interchange and adaptation, at: SSCLE-Istanbul; Archaeological evidence for Frankish rural administration in the Holy Land, at: SSCLE-Sydney1; The changing role of castles in the 12th-century kingdom of Jerusalem, at: SSCLE-Sydney2.

BOLTON, Brenda, The thirteenth Apostle: Innocent III between East and West after 1204, at: SSCLE-Sydney2.

BONNEAUD, Pierre, Hospitaliers catalans en Méditerranée au cours du XVe siècle, at: 130ème congrès des sociétés historiques et scientifiques, La Rochelle, 18–23 April 2005; Regulations concerning the reception of Hospitaler *milites* in the first half of the 15th century, at: MO4.

BORCHARDT, Karl, 'Good heretics?' Western attitudes towards the Armenians in the 14th century, at: SSCLE-Istanbul; Die Johanniter in Deutschland und die Reformation, at: Ritterorden und Reformation, Utrecht, 30 September 2004; Gilbert d'Assailly – Die Militarisierung des Johanniterordens, at: Gesellschaft für Internationale Burgenkunde, Aachen, 12 May 2005; Germany, Poland, and the Crimea: a late medieval overland trade route between Europe and Asia, at: SSCLE-Sydney1; Western intolerance? Theory and practice between the 13th and 15th centuries, at: SSCLE-Sydney2; Competition between the military orders in Central Europe, *c*.1140–1270, at: MO4.

BOWLUS, Charles R., The origins of Byzantine-Latin animosities in east-central Europe, at: SSCLE-Istanbul.

BURGTORF, Jochen, Die Herrschaft der Johanniter in Margat im Heiligen Land, at: OM 2005.

BYSTED, Ane, Crusade indulgences in 12th century theology: the spirit of the spiritual privilege, at: SSCLE-Istanbul.

CARLSSON, Christer, The religious orders of knighthood in medieval Scandinavia: historical and archaeological approaches, at: SSCLE-Istanbul.

CARR, Annemarie Weyl, Orthodox monasteries and the issues and images of cultural interchange in early Lusignan Cyprus, at: Cultural Convergences in the Medieval Mediterranean, Univ. of Michigan, 11 September 2004; The Panagia Theoskepaste and the Eleousa tou Kykkou: the space of a sacred encounter, at: State Tretjakov Gallery, Moscow, 2004; Reflections on the program of St. Herakleidios, Kalopanagiotis, at: Pierides Foundation and the Municipality of Nicosia, Nicosia, 2005.

CHRISTOFORAKI, Ioanna, Circulating images, transmitting ideas: the Cultural economy of crusader Cyprus, at: SSCLE-Istanbul.

CIPOLLONE, Giulio, In the language of Innocent III: Christians are worse than Saracens, Jews and Pagans: the case of the Venetians, at: SSCLE-Istanbul.

COUREAS, Nicholas S., The economy of Lusignan Cyprus in the 13th and 14th centuries with special reference to the development of Nicosia and Famagusta, the Gothic monuments of Nicosia, Kyrenia and Famagusta in their historical context, at: The Cyprus Tourism Organisation, 12 January 2005; Punishment and imprecations in the Cypriot monastic rules and how they compare with those in other Orthodox monastic rules, at: Meeting of the Cyprus Society of Historical Studies, 25 February 2005.

CRAWFORD, Paul, The university of Paris and the trial of the Templars, at: IMC Kalamazoo 2004; Jacques de Thérines, the University of Paris and the trial of the Templars, at: SSCLE-Istanbul.

CZAJA, Roman, Der Deutsche Orden als Stadtherr in Preussen und Livland, at: OM 2005.

DEMEL, Bernhard, Die Deutschordensballei Utrecht von 1525 bis 1815 in der Reichs- und Ordensüberlieferung, at: Ritterorden und Reformation, Utrecht, 2 October 2004.

DIVALL, Richard, Two relics of the Order of St. John of the Hospital in Constantinople, at: SSCLE-Sydney1; Galley tactics and supply and the siege of Malta, at: SSCLE-Sydney2.

DONDI, Christina, The liturgy of the church of the Holy Sepulchre in Jerusalem, at: Sovereign Military Order of Malta, Grand Priory of England, London, St John's Wood, 13 December 2003.

DOUROU-ELIOPOULOU, Maria, Latin colonialism in the Eastern Mediterranean during the Crusades, at: SSCLE-Sydney2

DURAK, Koray, Byzantine imperial discourse on the crusaders in Anna Komnena's *Alexiad* as a mechanism of imperial control, at: SSCLE-Istanbul.

DYGO, Marian, Die Herrschaftsterminologie des Deutschen Ordens in Prussen (13.–15. Jahrhundert), at: OM 2005.

ECHEVARRIA, Ana, Muslim vassals of the military orders and their conversion, at: SSCLE-Istanbul.

EDGINGTON, Susan B., Advice for an elderly crusader: Guido da Vigevano, at: Open Univ., 8 July 2004; Pagans and 'others' in the *Chanson de Jérusalem*, at: IMC Leeds 2004; A female physician on the Fourth Crusade? Laurette de Saint-Valery, at: SSCLE-Istanbul; Sieges of the

First Crusade, at: Charterhouse, 11 November 2004; with M.R. Evans, Penthesilea and the bearded lady, at: IHR 13 December 2004.

ELIOPOULOU, Mary, Allusions to the Fourth Crusade in Angevin and Venetian sources of the 13th and 14th century, at: International Symposium on the Fourth Crusade, Andros, 27–30 May 2004; The Albanians in Romania according to Latin sources of the 13th and 14th century, at: 9th International Congress of South-East European Studies, Tirana, 30 August–3 September 2004; Western institutions in the principality of Achaea, at: The Peloponnese after the Fourth Crusade, Mistras, 1–3 October 2004.

ELLENBLUM, Ronnie, Crusader history and plate tectonics: Vadum Iacob and the earthquakes of 1202 and 1759, at: SSCLE-Istanbul; Crusader cities, Muslim cities, and the post-colonial debate, at: ibid.

FOLDA, Jaroslav, The impact of the Fourth Crusade on the art of the crusaders in the Holy Land: reflections and observations, at: SSCLE-Istanbul; The multiculturalism of crusader art in 12th century Jerusalem, at: New York Univ. Medieval and Renaissance Center, 4 November 2004; Crusader art and the East: interactions in the later 13th century, at: 4th Annual Medieval and Renaissance Studies Symposium Eurasian Contacts, Univ. of Tennessee, Knoxville, 24–25 February 2005.

FOREY, Alan, A Templar lordship in northern Valencia at the turn of the 13th and 14th centuries, at: OM 2005.

FRANCE, John, The papacy and its Byzantine strategy, at: SSCLE-Istanbul.

FRIEDMAN, Yvonne, Christian-Muslim peace endeavours and conflict resolution, at: SSCLE-Istanbul; Gestures of conciliation? Peacemaking endeavours and cultural consequences in the Latin East, at: SSCLE-Sydney1.

GARCÍA-GUIJARRO, Luis, with Manuel Rojas, Crusader historiography and reconquista: a Spanish view of existing clichés, at: SSCLE-Istanbul.

GARDETTE, Philippe, Jews and the capture of Constantinople in 1204 and in 1453: a parallel, at: SSCLE-Istanbul.

GARDNER, Christopher, Torture and the medieval city: evidence from the law code of Toulouse, at: American Society of Legal Historians annual conference, Austin/Texas.

GERTWAGEN, Ruthy, Corfu and its port in the Venetian policy in the Ionian and southern Adriatic in the early modern period (14th and 15th centuries), at: Ionian Univ. Maritime History conference, Corfu/Greece, June 2004; The maritime factor in the creation of the so-called Venetian maritime empire in 1204, at: SSCLE-Istanbul; workshop for the History of Marine Animal Populations project, Institut de Ciències del Mar, Barcelona/Spain, September 2004; Naval activity around the port of Acre in the medieval period and its impact on the town's layout, at: SSCLE-Sydney1; Crusader Caesarea: a port town or a coastal town?, at: SSCLE-Sydney2.

GILILAND WRIGHT, Diana, The parlement of Ravenika, at: SSCLE-Istanbul.

GOUGUENHEIM, Sylvain, Gregor IX., Wilhelm von Modena und die Herrschaftsbildung des Deutschen Ordens, at: OM 2005.

GRABOIS, Aryeh, The Fourth Crusade and the Holy Land, at: SSCLE-Istanbul.

GRIVAUD, Gilles, La place du clergé mineur grec dans la société des états francs après 1204, at: SSCLE-Istanbul.

HARRIS, Jonathan, Collusion with the infidel as a pretext for military action against Byzantium, at: The Fourth Crusade Revisited, Andros/Greece, 27–30 May 2004, also at:

IMC, Leeds, 2004, and at: SSCLE-Istanbul; London and the Byzantine world in the 15th century, at: Medieval Cultures in Contact, King's College, London, January 2005.

HECKMANN, Marie-Luise, Herrschaft im Spätmittelalter, at: OM 2005.

HOROWITZ, Jenny, 'By overturning the cross with the cross they bore sewn on their backs, the Latins rejected Christ': Niketas Choniates' testimony as a reflection of the Byzantine stance towards the Franks, at: SSCLE-Istanbul.

HOUBEN, Hubert, La quarta crociata e l'Ordine Teutonico in Grecia, at: The Fourth Crusade Revisited, Andros/Greece, 27–30 May 2004.

HUNYADI, Zsolt, Mediterranean personnel in the commanderies of the Hungarian Hospitaller priory, at: 7th International Congress of Mediterranean Studies Association, Catalonia and the Mediterranean, Barcelona/Spain, 26–29 May 2004; Hospitallers, Templars, and Teutonic Knights in the medieval kingdom of Hungary, at: SSCLE-Istanbul; A johannita lovagrend katonai tevékenysége a keresztes hadjáratok idején [The military activity of the Hospitallers in the age of the crusades], at: Medieval Military History 5th to 15th Centuries, Pécs/Hungary, 15–16 November 2004.

JACOBY, David, Demography and society in Latin Constantinople, 1204–1261, at: SSCLE-Istanbul.

JASPERT, Nikolas, Ausstattung und Besitz des Ordens von Montjoie, at: OM 2005.

JENSEN, Janus Møller, Crusade, ideology, liturgy: the Danish experience, 1187–1600, at: Dept. of Theology, Univ. of Copenhagen, 14 March 2004; Anselm of Canterbury and the First Crusade, at: IMC Leeds 2004; The forgotten periphery and the forgotten crusades: Greenland and the crusades, 1400–1536, at: SSCLE-Istanbul.

KANGAS, Sini, The image of the Greeks in the sources of the First Crusades, at: SSCLE-Istanbul.

KEDAR, Benjamin Z., The Fourth Crusade's second front, at: SSCLE-Istanbul; Mediterranean sea currents – recent oceanographic research and its implications for crusader studies, at: SSCLE-Sydney1; Frankish cultural contact with Oriental Christians and Muslims, at: SSCLE-Sydney2.

KENAAN-KEDAR, Nurith, Returning crusaders and the mural cycle of Saint-Chef (Dauphiné), at: SSCLE-Istanbul.

KIESEWETTER, Andreas, La consistenza territoriale del Principato di Taranto tra l'età sveva e quella angioina, at: Il recupero di una identità storica attraverso le fonti d'archivio, Taranto, 12 April 2003; L'intervento di Niccolò IV e Bonifacio VIII nella lotta per il trono ungherese, at: Bonifacio VIII, ideologia e azione politica, Città del Vaticano – Roma, 26–28 April 2004; Premesse ioniche alla Quarta Crociata, at: Quarta Crociata: la partecipazione europea, le razioni, la risonanza, Venezia, 5–6 May 2004; Margarito da Brindisi e la sua signoria mediterranea, at: Amici della Biblioteca pubblica arcivescovile 'Annibale de Leo', Brindisi, 13 October 2004; Francesco Petrarca e Roberto d'Angiò, at: Società Dante Aligheri, Sezione di Taranto, Taranto, 19 October 2004; Martina Franca nel principato di Taranto (1260–1463), at: Comune di Martina Franca, Martina Franca, 22 October 2004; Il Castello in età normanna e svevo-angioina, at: Dal Kastron bizantino al Castello aragonese, Seminario di studio organizzato del Comando in Capo del Dipartimento militare marittimo dello Jonio e del Canale di Otranto, Taranto, 17 November 2004.

KREEM, Juhan, Der Deutsche Orden in Livland und die Reformation, at: Ritterorden und Reformation, Utrecht, 30 September 2004; Der Gehorsam der Gebietiger gegenüber dem livländischen Meister im 16. Jahrhundert, at: OM 2005.

KRÜGER, Jürgen, Relics, spoils, and mosaics: St Mark in Venice and its relation to the churches of Constantinople and of the Holy Sepulchre in Jerusalem, at: SSCLE-Istanbul; Outremer – Architektur im Heiligen Land als Kolonialarchitektur?, at: Reiss-Engelhorn-Museen Mannheim, 4–5 November 2004.

KÜCÜKSIPAHIOGLU, Birsel, The western plans to capture Byzantium from the beginnings of the crusades to 1204, at: SSCLE-Istanbul.

KUHSE, Lucie, The conquest of Constantinople: a question of honour? [Robert de Clari on 1204], at: SSCLE-Istanbul.

LEONARD, Robert D., The effects of the Fourth Crusade on European gold coinage, at: SSCLE-Istanbul.

LEV, Yaacov, Greek fire in Muslim warfare during the crusades, at: SSCLE-Sydney1; Nur ad-Dīn: his personality and wars with the Franks, at: SSCLE-Sydney2.

LIGATO, Giuseppe, Bonifacio VIII, la Terra Santa e la crociata, at: Bonifacio VIII, ideologia e azione politica, Città del Vaticano – Roma, 26–28 April 2004; Islam e Cristianità: culture cavalleresche a confronto, at: Fedi a confronto: ebrei, cristiani e musulmani nel Mediterraneo orientale (secoli XI–XIII), Montaione, 22–24 September 2004; Il mosaico pavimentale dell'abbazia di San Colombano e le crociate: il ruolo dei mostri, at: Genova e Bobbio tra storia e cultura, Genova – Bobbio, 3–4 September 2004; Le profezie della IV crociata, at: IV crociata: rapporti tra Oriente e Occidente, Venezia, 4 November 2004.

LINARDOU, Kelly, with Titos Papanastorakis, Politics of looting and the formation of symbolic identities: the choice of Venetians and Franks and the distribution of Constantinopolitan booty after the conquest of 1204, at: SSCLE-Istanbul.

LOUD, Graham, Monastic chronicles in the twelfth-century Abruzzi, at: 27th Anglo-Norman Conference, Battle, July 2004; Reflections on the failure of the Second Crusade, at: SSCLE-Istanbul.

LOWER, Michael, Pope Gregory IX and the Latin Empire, at: SSCLE-Istanbul.

LUCHITSKAYA, Svetlana I., Russian medieval perceptions of the Fourth Crusade, at: SSCLE-Istanbul.

MACEVITT, Christopher, Matthew of Edessa and the problem of tolerance in the Latin East, at: SSCLE-Istanbul.

MACK, Merav, Commercial aspects of the Fourth Crusade, at: SSCLE-Istanbul.

MACKKAY, Pierre A., Walking the streets of Negropont, at: SSCLE-Istanbul.

MADDEN, Thomas F., 'A creature most treacherous': Enrico Dandolo and the myth of medieval Venice, at: European Studies Forum, Southern Illinois Univ., Carbondale, 29 October 2003; The enduring myths of the Fourth Crusade, at: American Historical Association Convention, 10 January 2004; Teaching the medieval Middle East in the post-9/11 world, at: Medieval Academy of America Meeting, 2 April 2004; Eastern and western perspectives on the fall of Constantinople in 1204, at: Univ. of Illinois Urbana-Champaign, 6 April 2004; The crusades and the modern world, at: Saint Louis Univ., 22 April 2004; 1204 and historical memory, at: SSCLE-Istanbul; 1204 and the eastern schism, at: 43rd Annual Midwest Medieval History Conference, 10 October 2004.

MAJOR, Balazs, Zu den Ergebnissen der Ausgrabungen in Margat, at: OM 2005.

MALLEK, Janusz, Polen und die Protestantisierung Preussens, at: Ritterorden und Reformation, Utrecht, 30 September 2004.

MARIN, Serban, The Venetian chronicles' viewpoint regarding the Fourth Crusade: between justification and glory, at: SSCLE-Istanbul.

MENACHE, Sophia, Don Alonso of Aragon, master of Calatrava: fighting for monarchy or against the infidel?, at: SSCLE-Istanbul, also at: OM 2005.

MERTENS, Jozef, Die Deutschordensballei Biesen in der zweiten Hälfte des 16. Jahrhunderts, at: Ritterorden und Reformation, Utrecht, 2 October 2004.

MESCHINI, Marco, Les quatre croisades de 1204, at: SSCLE-Istanbul.

MEUVISSEN, Daantje, The portraits of the Teutonic commanders of Utrecht, at: Ritterorden und Reformation, Utrecht, 2 October 2004.

MILITZER, Klaus, Grundherrschaft und Gerichtsherrschaft des Deutschen Ordens im Reich, at: OM 2005.

MITCHELL, Piers D., Weapon injuries in the Frankish garrison of Vadum Iacob castle, Galilee, at: SSCLE-Istanbul; Wounds in the crusader period, at: European Conference of the Paleopathology Association, Univ. of Durham, August 2004; Trauma in the castles, at: Conference of the British Association for Biological Anthropology and Osteoarchaeology, Univ. of Bristol, September 2004; Torture in the crusades, at: Institute of Historical Research, Univ. of London, October 2004.

MOL, Johannes A., Ritterordenshäuser und Reformation in den nördlichen Niederlanden, at: Ritterorden und Reformation, Utrecht, 2 October 2004.

NICHOLSON, Helen, The Hospitallers' and Templars' organization of their estates in Wales and the Welsh Borders, at: OM 2005.

NICOLLE, David, Two medieval Islamic arms finds, at: Tower of London, 2003; A medieval Islamic arms cache (finds from the citadel of Damascus), at: Cambridge Univ., 2004.

NIELSEN, Torben K., War and marriage: cultural encounters in the Baltic crusades, at: SSCLE-Istanbul.

O'MALLEY, Gregory, The British and Irish Hospitallers and the Reformation, at: Ritterorden und Reformation, Utrecht, 30 September 2004.

OTTEN-FROUX, Catherine, Les Italiens à Chypre aux XIIIe–XVe siècles, at: Identités croisés en un milieu méditerranéen: le cas de Chypre, Rouen, 11–12 March 2004; Les ports de Chypre sous les Lusignans, at: Les ports et la navigation méditerranéenne au Moyen Âge, Lattès, 12–14 November 2004.

PAGES, Montserrat, Ripoll and Taull, memory and patronage after the reconquista, at: SSCLE-Istanbul.

PALAGYI, Tivadar, Images byzantines et persanes de Constantinople dans des texts épiques de Georges de Piside et de Firdousi, at: SSCLE-Istanbul.

PAPAYIANNI, Aphrodite, The Byzantines' views on the events of 1204, 1204–1453, at: SSCLE-Istanbul.

PELEG, Peter S., Frederick II and the major military orders, at: SSCLE-Istanbul.

PERRY, David, The *Translatio Symonensis* and the seven thieves: a Venetian Fourth Crusade *furta sacra* narrative and the looting of Constantinople, at: SSCLE-Istanbul.

PHILLIPS, Jonathan P., The legacy of the First Crusade and the origins of the Second Crusade, at: Cardiff Univ., March 2004; Armenia and the Second Crusade, at: SSCLE-Istanbul.

PIANA, Mathias, The crusader castle of Toron: first results of its investigation, at: SSCLE-Istanbul.

POWELL, James M., An alternative view of the Fourth Crusade, at: Midwest Medieval History Conference, Univ. of Tennessee, Knoxville, October 2004; Medieval sources I have known, at: Medieval seminar, ibid.; Francis of Assisi's Way of Peace, at: IMC Kalamazoo 2005.

PRICE, Jennifer A., Legatine power and the crusade vow: Innocent III, Peter Capuano, and the conquest of Constantinople, at: SSCLE-Istanbul.

PRYOR, John H., The chain of the Golden Horn, at: SSCLE-Istanbul.

DE LA PUENTE, Cristina, Jihad and reconquista in al-Andalus, at: SSCLE-Istanbul.

PURKIS, William, Crusading as *imitatio Christi*, 1095–1149, at: CLE-Seminar, Cambridge, February 2004; Bernard of Clairvaux and the Preaching of the Second Crusade, at: SSCLE-Istanbul.

RACINE, Pierre, Venise et son arrière-pays continental à l'époque de la 4ème croisade, at: SSCLE-Istanbul.

RAPHAEL, Kate, Arrows and catapult stones: hard evidence from the siege of Arsuf (1265) and Acre (1291), at: SSCLE-Istanbul.

RICHARD, Jean, Les états latins du Levant face à la conquête de Constantinople, at: SSCLE-Istanbul.

RILEY-SMITH, Jonathan, An alternative approach to the Fourth Crusade, at: SSCLE-Istanbul.

ROCHÉ, Jason T., Conrad III and the Second Crusade, 1147–1148: retreat from Dorylaeum?, at: SSCLE-Istanbul.

RODRÍGUEZ GARCÍA, José Manuel, 1269–1271: the Spanish and St. Louis' second crusade, at: SSCLE-Istanbul.

SARNOWSKY, Jürgen, Herrschaftssymbolik auf Münzen und Siegeln: Ritterorden als Landesherren auf Rhodos und in Preußen, at: Lübeck, 24 February 2004; Vorgeschichte und Anfänge der Reformation in der Ballei Brandenburg des Johanniterordens, at: Ritterorden und Reformation, Utrecht, 30 September 2004; Buchbesitz, Bibliotheken und Schriftkultur im mittelalterlichen Preussen, at: Culture and Learning in Prussia under the Teutonic Knights, Malbork, 24 September 2004; Die Johanniter als Landes- und Stadtherrn in der Ägäis, at: OM 2005.

SCHABEL, Christopher, Latin monasticism in Cyprus, at: SSCLE-Sydney1; Greeks, Latins, and the quarrel over the Eucharist in Frankish Cyprus, at: SSCLE-Sydney2.

SCHENK, Jochen G., Templar support and the crusading tradition of noble French families, at: SSCLE-Istanbul.

SEILER, Jörg, Der Deutsche Orden im Deutschen Reich im Reformationszeitalter, at: Ritterorden und Reformation, Utrecht, 2 October 2004.

SIBERRY, Elizabeth, The Fourth Crusade: some later perspectives, at: SSCLE-Istanbul.

SIMPSON, Alicia J., Before and after 1204: the versions of Niketas Choniates' *Historia* and the collapse of Byzantium, at: SSCLE-Istanbul.

SIMPSON, B. Vasiliki A., The fires of the Fourth Crusade: a memoir of the architectural loss, at: SSCLE-Istanbul.

SMITH, Tracy, The crusades: a cultural anthropological study, at: SSCLE-Istanbul.

STARNAWSKA, Maria, Die Johanniter in der Kirchenprovinz Gnesen und im Bistum Kammin gegenüber der weltlichen Macht: Amtsträger, Berater der Herrscher, Landesherren, at: OM 2005.

TARAGAN, Hanna, Mamluk patronage and crusader memories, at: SSCLE-Istanbul.

TOOMASPOEG, Kristjan, Der Deutsche Orden als Grund- und Kirchherr in Italien, at: OM 2005.

DE LA TORRE, Ignacio, The Templars as papal bankers, at: SSCLE-Istanbul.

TOUATI, François-Olivier, Lapidation et jet de pierres au Proche Orient: une approche anthropologique et historique du présent, at: Université de Paris IV, séminare de C. Thomasset, La pierre au Moyen Âge, 12 March 2003; Malades et médicine dans les États latins d'Orient: de la confrontation des practiques à la confrontation des savoirs, at: Congrès de la Société française d'histoire des sciences et des techniques, Université de Poitiers, CESCM, 20–22 May 2004; Mourir à Jérusalem aux XIIe et XIIIe siècles, at: La mort dans les villes du Sud, Tours, 9 March 2005.

VANN, Theresa M., Eleventh- and twelfth-century vocabulary of holy war in the Mediterranean, at: SSCLE-Istanbul.

VERZAR, Christine, The artistic patronage of the returning crusader: the arm of St. George and Ferrara cathedral, at: SSCLE-Istanbul.

VILAR, Herminia, The control of churches by the military orders in Portugal, at: OM 2005.

VAN WINTER, Johanna Maria, The origins of the priest Godschalk the crusader, at: SSCLE-Istanbul; Sugar, spice of the crusaders, at: Ethnological Food Research Conference, Dubrovnik, 27 September–3 October 2004.

ZAFEIRIS, Konstantinos A., The *Synopsis Chronike* and its selective use of sources, at: SSCLE-Istanbul.

ZERNER, Monique, Ceux qui refusèrent le détournement de la croisade vers Constantinople, at: SSCLE-Istanbul.

4. Forthcoming publications

EL-AZHARI, Taef, The Muslim Chroniclers' Perspective of the Fourth Crusade, in: Crusades 5 (2006).

BAHAT, Dan, Final Archaeological Report on the Western Wall Tunnels, Jerusalem.

BALLETTO, Laura, Nuclei familiari da Genova a Chio nel Quattrocento, in: Due popoli – una storia: Studi di storia ellenica (Atene); Il Mar Nero nei notai genovesi: panoramica generale, stato degli studi, progetti di pubblicazione, in: The Black Sea Region in the Middle Ages, Historical Faculty Moscow State University; I Genovesi a Focea ed a Chio fra XIII e XIV secolo, in: Atti del convegno dei Bizantinisti (Paris); Il mondo del commercio nel *Codex Comanicus*: alcune riflessioni, in: Atti del colloquio internazionale Il Codice Cumanico e il suo mondo (Venezia); Da Pera a Genova dopo la conquista di Costantinopoli (1453), in: Miscellanea in onore di Carme Batlle (Barcelona); Greci a Genova dopo la conquista turca di Costantinopoli, in: Studi in onore dei proff. Henrich e Matschke (Leipzig); Battista di Felizzano e Domenico di Novara fra Genova ed il Vicino Oriente a metà del Quattrocento, in: Studi in onore di Nilda Guglielmi (Buenos Aires); I Genovesi e la caduta di Costantinopoli: riflessi negli atti notarili, in: Néa Rhòme 1 (2004) = Festschrift Vera von Falkenhausen.

BARKER, John W., Crusading and Matrimony in the Eastern Mediterranean: The Dynastic Policies of Montferrat and Savoy, in: Mediterranean Historical Review (2005 or 2006); Medieval Themes in Opera: The Crusades, in: Sewanee Medieval Colloquium Papers of 2002.

BEREND, Nora, The Expansion of Latin Christendom 1000–1300, in: Shorter Oxford History of Europe, ed. Daniel Power; Frontiers; in: The Palgrave Guide to the Crusades, ed. Helen Nicholson (Basingstoke: Palgrave Macmillan, 2005).

BIRD, Jessalynn, Crusade and Conversion after the Fourth Lateran Council (1215): Oliver of Paderborn's and James of Vitry's Missions to Muslims Reconsidered, in: Essays in Medieval Studies: Proceedings of the Illinois Medieval Association 21 (2004); Paris Masters and the

Justification of the Albigensian Crusade; The Wheat and the Tares: Peter the Chanter's Circle and the Fama-Based Inquest against Heresy and Criminal Sins, c.1198–c.1235, in: Proceedings of the 12th International Congress for Medieval Canon Law.

BOMBI, Barbara, Innocenzo III e la relazione sulle condizioni del Medio Oriente coevo, in: Fedi a confronto: ebrei, cristiani e musulmani fra X e XIII secolo, Montaione, 22–24 September 2004 (Florence, 2006); Celestine III and the Conversion of the Heathen on the Baltic Sea, in: Celestine III in the Light of Europe, ed. J. Doran and D. Smith (Aldershot: Ashgate, 2006); see Bulletin 24 (2004), 24.

BONNEAUD, Pierre, Catalan Hospitallers in Rhodes in the First Half of the Fifteenth Century, in: International Mobility in the Military Orders (12th to 15th Centuries), ed. Jochen Burgtorf and Helen Nicholson (Cardiff: University of Wales Press, 2005).

BORCHARDT, Karl, entries on Bohemia-Moravia and the crusades, Hussites, crusades against, John of Luxembourg, king of Bohemia 1310–1346, Ottokar II, king of Bohemia 1253–1278, Mergentheim, for: EncycCru.

CARR, Annemarie Weyl, Cyprus and the Devotional Arts of Byzantium in the Era of the Crusades (Aldershot: Ashgate, 2005); Visual Art in Lusignan Cyprus, in: Managing Multiplicity in Medieval Cyprus, 1191–1373, ed. Angel Konnari and Christopher Schabel (Leiden: Brill, 2005); Cypriot Funerary Icons: Questions of Convergence in a Complex Land, in: Festschrift for Jeremy Adams, ed. Stephanie Hayes; The Virgin Mary East and West, in: Images of the Mother of God: Perceptions of the Theotokos in Byzantium, ed. Maria Vassilaki (Aldershot: Ashgate).

CONGDON, Eleanor A., The Venetian Mercantile Presence in the Western Mediterranean, c.1400 (Leiden: Brill).

COUREAS, Nicholas S., Controlled Contacts: The Papacy, the Latin Church of Cyprus and Mamluk Egypt, in: Egypt and Syria in the Fatimid, Ayyubid and Mamluk Eras, Proceedings of the 9th, 10th and 11th HES, ed. U. Vermeulen (Leuven: Peters, 2004); The Role of Cyprus in Provisioning the Latin Churches of the Holy Land in the 13th and early 14th Centuries, in: ibid.; Commercial Relations between Cyprus and Mamluk Eygpt and Syria, with special reference to Nicosia and Famagusta, in the 15th and 16th Centuries, in ibid., 12th HES; The Copts in Cyprus during the 15th and 16th Centuries, in: ibid., 13th HES; with Gilles Grivaud and Christopher Schabel, The Capital of the Sweet Land of Cyprus: Frankish and Venetian Nicosia, in: A History of Nicosia, ed. Demetrios Michaelides (Nicosia, 2005); Commercial Relations between Cyprus and Euboea, 1300–1362, in: Symmeikta tou Ethnikou Idrymatos Ereunon (Athens); Economy and Commerce of Lusignan Cyprus, in: A Social and Cultural History of Early Lusignan Cyprus, 1192–1369 (Leiden: Brill, 2005); Apple of Concord: The Great Powers and Cyprus from 400 AD onwards, in: Kypriakai Spoudai 68 (2003/04) [Nicosia 2005)]; entries on Sinai, Cyprus, Catherine Cornaro, Nicosia, Limassol, Paphos and Kyrenia, for: EncycCru.

CRAWFORD, Paul, The Trial of the Templars and the University of Paris, in: MO3; Imagination and the Templars: The Development of the Order-State in the early Fourteenth Century, in: Annual Review [Epetirida] of the Cyprus Research Centre 30 (2004); entries on Alexandria, capture of, Foulques de Villaret, Poulains, Guillaume de Machaut, St. Thomas, knights of, for: EncycCru; entries on Crusades, Hospitallers, Templars, Children's Crusade, Military Religious Orders, in: New Westminster Dictionary of Church History, ed. Christopher Ocker et al. (Westminster: John Knox Press, 2006).

DEMURGER, Alain, La croisade au Moyen Âge, Collection 'Champs' (Paris: Editions Flammarion, 2006).

DONDI, Christina, Liturgical Policies of the Hospitallers between the Invention of Printing and the Council of Trent: the Evidence of the Early Printed Breviaries and Missals, in: MO3.

EDBURY, Peter, Ramla: The Crusader Town and Lordship (1099–1268), in: The City of Ramla AD c.715–1917, ed. Denys Pringle; British Historiography on the Crusades and Military Orders: from Barker and Smail to Contemporary Historians, in: Runciman-Conference; The Suppression of the Templars in Cyprus, 1307–1312, in: St John Historical Society Proceedings; Crusader Sources from the Near East, in: Byzantium and the Crusades: the Non-Greek Sources 1025–1204; A new text of the Annales de Terre Sainte, in a festschrift; introduction for: Europe 2000 Crusades exhibition catalogue; Society and Ethnicity: the Franks, in: A History of Cyprus under Latin Rule, ed. Angel Nicolaou-Konnari and Christopher Schabel; entries for EncycCru; 1191: Conquest, Continuity and Change, in: Essays on the History of Cyprus.

EDGINGTON, Susan B., Albert of Aachen, edition and English translation (Oxford: OMT, 2005).

EKDAHL, Sven, Crusades and Colonization in the Baltic, in: The Palgrave Guide to the Crusades, ed. Helen Nicholson (Basingstoke: Palgrave Macmillan, 2005); The Battle of Tannenberg-Grunwald-Żalgiris (1410) as Reflected in Monuments of the 20th Century, in: MO3; entries on Tannenberg, battle (1410), warfare in Baltic crusades, castles in Baltic region, for: EncycCru.

FAVREAU-LILIE, Marie-Luise, Die italienischen Handelsniederlassungen in den Kreuzfahrerstaaten (12./13. Jh.), in: Die Kreuzfahrer und der Orient, Katalog und Essayband zur Ausstellung Mannheim (Reiss-Engelhorn-Museum) 15.10.2005–29.01.2006 / Oldenburg (Landesmuseum für Natur und Mensch) März–Juni 2006 / Halle (Landesmuseum für Vorgeschichte) September–Dezember 2006 (Mainz, 2005); Die Wahrnehmung des Vierten Kreuzzugs außerhalb Venedigs: Perspektiven der Geschichtsschreibung im 13. Jahrhundert, in: The Fourth Crusade Revisited, Papers of an International Conference on the Fourth Crusade (1204), Andros, 27–30 May 2004, ed. Evangelistos Chrysos, Otto Kresten, Walter Brandmüller (Paderborn: Schöningh, 2005); articles on Geroldo di Losanna (Valenza), patriarcha di Gerusalemme, Gerusalemme, patriarcato di, in: Enciclopedia Federiciana, ed. Arnoldo Arnaldi et al., vol. 1 (Roma, 2005); entries on Caffaro, Embriachi, Tyre, for: EncycCru.

FLORI, Jean, Islam et fin des temps: la place de l'islam dans l'interprétation prophétique de l'Histoire au Moyen Âge (Paris: Éditions du Seuil, 2005).

FOLDA, Jaroslav, The Figural Arts in Crusader Syria and Palestine, 1187–1291: Some New Realities, in: Dumbarton Oaks Papers 58 (2005); East Meets West: The Art and Architecture of the Crusader States, in: A Companion to the Medieval Art, ed. Conrad Rudolph (Oxford: Blackwell, 2005).

GARDNER, Christopher, entries on France, The Peace and Truce of God, Toulouse, for: EncycCru; Heretics or Lawyers? Propaganda and Toulousan Identity Through the Albigensian Crusade, in: The New Middle Ages, ed. Stephanie Hayes (London: Palgrave/St Martin's Press, 2005); Négocier le pouvoir: Toulouse et son gouvernement sous les Capétiens (vers 1200–vers 1340), in: Annales du Midi (2005/06).

GERTWAGEN, Ruthy, Harbours and Port Facilities along the Sea Lanes to the Holy Land, in: Logistics of Warfare in the Age of the Crusades, ed. John Pryor (Aldershot: Ashgate); Venice, in: Encyclopedia of World Trade since 1450, ed. John J. McCusker.

GUTH, Klaus, Zwischen Heimat und Welt: Positionen der Volkskunde / Europäischen Ethnologie als Kulturwissenschaft (Berlin, 2005).

HARRIS, Jonathan, Introduction, in: Chronology of the Byzantine Empire, ed. Timothy Venning (Basingstoke: Palgrave Macmillan); ed., Palgrave Advances: Byzantine History (Basingstoke: Palgrave Macmillan); entries on Greek sources, Manuel II, John V, Bessarion, Paul II, Innocent VIII, for: EncycCru; with Heleni Porphyriou, The Greek Diaspora in Europe after the Fall of Constantinople, in: The Place of Exchange: Cities and Cultural Transfer in Europe, 1400–1700, ed. Donatella Calabi and Stephan Turk Christensen (Cambridge UP).

HOCH, Martin, entry Hattin, battle (1187), for: EncycCru.

HOUBEN, Hubert, Wie und wann kam der Deutsche Orden nach Griechenland?, in: Néa Rhòme 1 (2004) = Festschrift Vera von Falkenhausen.

HOUSLEY, Norman J., Crusading indulgences, 1417–1517, in: Indulgences in Late-Medieval Europe, ed. Robert Swanson (Leiden: Brill, 2005); Contesting the Crusades (Oxford: Blackwell, 2005); Perceptions of Crusading in the Mid-Fourteenth Century: the Evidence of Three Texts, in: Viator (2005).

HUNYADI, Zsolt, with József Laszlovszky, The Crusades and the Military Orders: Expanding the Frontiers of Medieval Latin Christianity (Budapest: CEU Department of Medieval Studies, 2005) [revised 2nd edition + bibliography on CD-ROM]; Hospitallers in the Medieval Kingdom of Hungary, c.1150–1387 (Budapest – Szeged: METEM Books – CEU Medievalia, 2005).

JASPERT, Nikolas, Zwei unbekannte Hilfsersuchen des Patriarchen Eraclius vor dem Fall Jerusalems (1187), in: Deutsches Archiv für Erforschung des Mittelalters; Carlomagno y Santiago en la memoria histórica catalana, in: El camí de Sant Jaume i Catalunya: historia, art i cultura, ed. Maria Teresa Ferrer i Mallol and Pere Vergés (Barcelona, 2005); Forgotten Brethren – Historiography on the Non-Military Orders and Congregations of the Crusader States, in: Medio siglo de estudios sobre cruzadas y órdenes militares, ed. Luis García Guijarro-Ramos; Kleinere Ritterorden Palästinas – und der Kanonikerorden vom Heiligen Grab, in: Las órdenes militares en la Europa medieval (Barcelona, 2005); Von Karl dem Grossen bis Kaiser Wilhelm: Die Erinnerung an vermeintliche und tatsächliche Kreuzzüge in Mittelalter und Moderne, in: Konfrontation der Kulturen? Saladin und die Kreuzfahrer, ed. Bernd Schneidmüller and Stefan Weinfurter (2005); Jerusalem und sein Königshaus, in: ibid.; Jerusalem und die Kreuzfahrerherrschaften im Leben und Denken des Maimonides, in: Die Trias des Maimonides: Jüdische, arabische und antike Wissenskultur, ed. Georges Tamer; several entries for EncycCru.

JENSEN, Janus Møller, Denmark and the Crusades, 1400–1650, for a festschrift.

JOTISCHKY, Andrew, The Franciscans, the Holy Land and the End of Crusading, in: Medieval Encounters – Special Edition Essays in Honour of Kenneth M. Setton, ed. Larry Simon (2006).

JUBB, Margaret, The Crusaders' Perceptions of their Opponents, in: Advances in the Crusades, ed. Helen Nicholson (Basingstoke: Palgrave Macmillan, 2005).

KEDAR, Benjamin Z., Dimensioni comparative del pellegrinaggio medievale, in: Roma e Gerusalemme nel Medioevo: Paesaggi umani ed ambientali del pellegrinaggio meridionale, Salerno 26–29 Ottobre 2000, ed. Massimo Oldoni; Some Reflections on Maps, Crusading and Logistics, in: The Logistics of Crusading, Sydney 2002, ed. John Pryor; I due *Montes Gaudii* di Gerusalemme, in: La Puglia tra Gerusalemme e Santiago di Compostella, Bari 2002, ed. Maria Stella Calò Mariani; The Voyages of Giuàn-Obadyah in Syria and Iraq and the Enigma of his Conversion, in: Giovanni-Obadyah da Oppido, proselito, viaggiatore e musicista dell'età normanna, Oppido Lucano 2004, ed. Antonio De Rosa; The Fourth Crusade's Second Front, in: The Fourth Crusade and its Consequences, Athens 2004, ed.

Angeliki Laiou; Ramla: The Evidence of World War I Aerial Photographs, in: History and Archaeology of Ramla, ed. Denys Pringle; with Daniella Talmon-Heller, Did Muslim Survivors of the 1099 Massacre of Jerusalem Settle in Damascus? The True Origins of the a-Salihiyya Suburb, in: Al-Masāq.

LIMOR, Ora, ed. with Guy G. Stroumsa, Christians and Christianity in the Holy Land (Turnhout: Brepols); 'Holy Journey': Pilgrimage and Christian Sacred Landscape, in: ibid.; ed. with Meir Litvak, Religious Radicalism (Jerusalem: Merkaz Shazar) [Hebrew]; ed. with Elchanan Reiner, Pilgrimage: Jews, Christians, Moslems (Tel Aviv) [Hebrew and English]; Pelagia's Tomb on the Mount of Olives: Sin, Repentance, Salvation; Mary and the Jews: Three Witness Stories (Alpaym) [Hebrew].

MADDEN, Thomas F., The New Concise History of the Crusades (Lanham: Rowman and Littlefield, 2005); Food and the Fourth Crusade: A New Approach to the 'Diversion Question', in: Logistics of Warfare in the Age of the Crusades, ed. John H. Pryor (Aldershot: Ashgate).

MESCHINI, Marco, Innocenzo III e il "negotium pacis et fidei" in Linguadoca (1198–1215) [PhD thesis]; Validità, novità e carattere della decretale *Vergentis in senium* (Reg. II, 1) di Innocenzo III (25 marzo 1199), in: Bulletin of the Medieval Canon Law; Innozenz III. und der Kreuzzug als "Mittel" im Kampf gegen die Häresie, in: Deutsches Archiv für Erforschung des Mittelalters; Pourquoi Béziers: La chute de Béziers (22 juillet 1209), in: Mieux vaut mort que vif vaincu: Sièges et batailles méridionales (1209–1250), Toulouse; Note sull'assegnazione della viscontea Trencavel a Simone di Montfort nel 1209, in: Mélanges de l'École Française de Rome, Moyen Âge.

MITCHELL, Piers D., A Population Study of Health in the Crusader Period Inhabitants of Tel Jezreel (Le Petit Gérin), Israel, in: Levant; with Y. Nagar and Ronnie Ellenblum, Weapon Injuries in the 12th Century Crusader Garrison of Vadum Iacob Castle, Galilee, in: International Journal of Osteoarchaeology; with J. Huntley and E. Stern, Bioarchaeological Analysis of the 13th Century Latrines of the Crusader Hospital of St John at Acre, Israel, in: MO3; entries on Disease, War injuries, for: EncycCru; The Infirmaries of the Order of the Temple in the Medieval Kingdom of Jerusalem, in: The Medieval Hospital and Medical Practice: Bridging the Evidence, ed. B. Bowers (Aldershot: Ashgate); Challenges in the Study of Health and Disease in the Crusades, in: Diachronic Patterns in the Biology and Health Status of Human Populations of the Eastern Mediterranean, ed. M. Faerman; The Torture of Military Captives during the Crusades to the Medieval Middle East, in: Noble Ideals and Bloody Realities: Warfare in the Middle Ages, 378–1492, ed. N. Christie and M. Yazigi (Leiden: Brill).

MÖHRING, Hannes, Saladin: Der Sultan und seine Zeit (München, 2005).

MORRIS, Colin, The Sepulchre of Christ and the Medieval West (Oxford: UP, 2005).

NICOLLE, David, Byzantine, Western European, Islamic and Central Asian Influence in the Field of Arms and Armour from the 7th to the 14th Century AD (Cambridge: UP) [article]; The Fall of Acre 1291, Osprey Campaign series; Carolingian Cavalryman, Osprey Warrior series; Crusader Fortifications in the Holy Land, 1192–1302, Osprey Fortress series; Overcoming Walls: The Technology of Breaching and Scaling Walls in Medieval Europe, in: De Re Militari website; The Military Finds, in: Final Report on the Excavations in part of the Citadel of Damascus carried out by the French Institute for Oriental Studies in Damascus.

NIELEN, Marie-Adélaïde, Nouvelles preuves de l'historie des vicomtes de Tripoli: tentative de reconstitution de la généalogie de la famille Visconte, in: Actes du colloque Le comté de

Tripoli: état multi-culturel et multi-confessionnel, Université du Saint-Esprit de Kaslik, 2–3 décembre 2002; entries on Lignanges d'Outremer, Assises de Jérusalem, for: EncycCru.

O'MALLEY, Gregory, The Knights Hospitaller of the English Langue, 1460–1565 (Oxford: UP, 2005) [PhD thesis]; Collective Image and Indiviual Insufficiency among the Hospitallers of the English *Langue* in the Fifteenth and Sixteenth Centuries, in: OM 2003.

OTTEN-FROUX, Catherine, Les Occidentaux dans les villes de province de l'empire byzantin: le cas de Chypre, in: Actes du 21e congrès international des études byzantines, Paris 2001; Famagouste génoise, in: Lacrimae Cypriae, ed. B. Imhaus.

PAHLITZSCH, Johannes, The People of the Book, in: Ayyubid Jerusalem, ed. Robert Hillenbrand and Sylvia Auld; Mediators between East and West: Christians under Mamluk Rule, in: Mamluk Studies Review 9 (2005).

PAVIOT, Jacques, La croisade bourguignonne aux XIVe et XVe siècles: un idéal chevaleresque?, in: Francia (2005); Projets de croisade, fin XIIIe s.–déb. XIVe s. (Paris, 2005/06) [Documents relatifs à l'histoire des croisades: Fidence de Padoue, Liber recuperationis Terre Sancte; Via ad Terram Sanctam; Memoria; La Devise des chemins de Babiloine; (Hôpital) Qualiter Terra Sancta possit per Christianos recuperari; (Temple) Consilium; Henri II, roi de Chypre, Tractatus de subsidio et felici recuperatione Terre Sancte; Roger de Stanegrave, Li Charboclois d'armes du conquest precious de la Terre sainte de promission].

PIANA, Mathias, The Castle of Toron (Qal'at Tibnîn) in South Lebanon: Preliminary Result of the 2000/2003 Campaigns, in: Bulletin d'Archéologie et d'Architecture Libanaises (2005); Konfrontation der Kulturen? Saladin und die Kreuzfahrer, Kolloquium am 4./5. November 2005 in den Reiss-Engelhorn-Museen Mannheim, in: Kunstchronik (2005); ed., Castles and Bazaars: Medieval Forms of Life in the Eastern Mediterranean (Regensburg: Schnell & Steiner, 2005).

PRINGLE, Denys R., The Chapel of the Holy Sepulchre in the Castle of Tripoli (Mont-Pèlerin), in: Egypt and Syria in the Fatimid, Ayyubid and Mamluk Eras, vol. 5, ed. U. Vermeulen and J. Van Steenbergen (Leuven: Peeters, 2006); entries on Aila, Arsuf, Ascalon, Belfort, Belvoir, Blanchegarde, Caesarea, Chastelneuf, Château Pèlerin, Cresson, battle (1187), Gaza, Habis Jaldak, Kerak, Magna Mahumeria, Mirabel, Montfort, Montreal, Ramla, Toron de los Caballeros, for: EncycCru; see Bulletin 24 (2004), 30.

PURKIS, William, Elite and Popular Perceptions of *imitatio Christi* in Twelfth-Century Crusade Spirituality, in: Elite and Popular Religion, ed. K. Cooper and J. Gregory, Studies in Church History 42 (2006).

SARNOWSKY, Jürgen, Die Schuldbücher und Rechnungen der Großschäffer des Deutschen Ordens in Preußen, vol. 1: Das erste Schuldbuch der Königsberger Großschäfferei von 1400–1402 [book]; ed. with Roman Czaja, Selbstbild und Selbstverständnis der geistlichen Ritterorden, OM 2003; Hospitaller Brethren on 15th-Century Rhodes, in: International Mobility in the Military Orders, ed. Jochen Burgtorf and Helen Nicholson (Cardiff: University of Wales Press) [article]; Kirche und Krieg im Mittelalter, for a festschrift [article].

SCHABEL, Christopher, The Status of the Greek Clergy in Early Frankish Cyprus, in: Volume in Memory of Constantine Leventis, ed. J. Chrysostomides et al. (Camberley/Surrey: Porphyrogenita, 2005); with Nicholas Coureas and Gilles Grivaud, The Capital of the Sweet Land of Cyprus: Frankish and Venetian Nicosia, in: A History of Nicosia, ed. Demetrios Michaelides (Nicosia, 2005); with Gilles Grivaud, Nicosie, in: Camille Enlart, L'art gothique et la renaissance en Chypre, ed. Alain Erlande-Brandenberg (Athens: BEFAR); The Myth of

Queen Alice and the Subjugation of the Greek Church of Cyprus, in: Identités croisées en un milieu méditerranéen: le cas de Chypre, ed. Gilles Grivaud (2005); Attitudes toward the Greeks and the History of the Filioque Dispute in 14th Century Oxford, in: The Fourth Crusade Revisited, Papers of an International Conference on the Fourth Crusade (1204), Andros, 27–30 May 2004, ed. Evangelistos Chrysos, Otto Kresten, Walter Brandmüller (Paderborn: Schöningh, 2005); co-ed. with Angel Konnari, Cyprus: Society and Culture, 1191–1374 (Leiden: Brill, 2005).

SEEBERG SIDSELRUD, Kaare, An Armorial of the Catholic Hierarchy in the Nordic Countries Post-Reformation.

TESSERA, Miriam Rita, Alessandro III e l'enigma dell'Instructio fidei al sultano di Iconio, in: Atti del convegno Fedi a Confronto: ebrei, cristiani e musulmani fra X e XIII secolo, ed. S. Gensini.

TOUATI, François-Olivier, La Terre sainte: un laboratoire hospitalier au Moyen Âge, in: Sozialgeschichte mittelalterlicher Hospitäler, ed. N. Bulst, Tagung auf der Reichenau, Konstanzer Arbeitskreis für Mittelalterliche Geschichte; La géographie hospitalière médiévale: des modèles aux réalites, Orient-Occident, IVe–XVe siècles, in: Hôpitaux et maladreries au Moyen Âge, espace et environnement, Amiens, Université de Picardie, Laboratoire d'archéologie, 22–24 novembre 2002; ed., Vocabulaire historique du Moyen Âge (Orient-Occident), 5th, revised and enlarged edition (Paris: La Boutique de l'Historie), 336pp.

5. Work in progress

EL-AZHARI, Taef, The Career of Balak the Artukid.

BALARD, Michel, The Latins in the Near East [book]; Spices in the Middle Ages [book].

BEREND, Nora, Christianization and State-Formation in Northern and Central Europe $c.900$–$c.1200$.

BIRD, Jessalyn, The History of the West (Historia Occidentalis) of Jacques de Vitry, a translation; Women and the Crusades (London Books); Christian Society and the Crusades, 1198–1274, a sourcebook in collaboration with Edward Peters and James Powell (Univ. of Pennsylvania Press); Paris Masters and the Preaching of the Early Phases of the Albigensian Crusades [not the crusade of Louis VIII]; Organization and Recruiting for the Crusade of Frederick II; The Impact of Prophecy on the Outcome of the Fifth Crusade and the Crusade of Frederick II [three articles].

BOMBI, Barbara, Innocent III and the 'praedicatio' to the Heathen in Northern Europe: Mission and Crusade (1198–1216), revised and extended PhD thesis; see Bulletin 24 (2004), 32.

BORCHARDT, Karl, ed., with Anthony Luttrell and Ekhard Schöffler, Hospitaller Documents concerning the History of Cyprus, First Half of the 15th Century (Cyprus Research Centre); ed., with Nikolas Jaspert and Helen Nicholson, a festschrift for Anthony Luttrell.

CARR, Annemarie Weyl, ed. with Andreas Nicolaides, Asinou: The Church and the Frescoes of the Panagia Phorbiotissa.

CONGDON, Eleanor A., Wool Shipped from Aragon/Catalonia to Venice, $c.1400$; Antonio Contarini, Merchant and/or Procurator; An Early Ship-Board Cannon: Niccolo Rosso's Gun, $c.1403$ [articles].

COUREAS, Nicholas S., The Latin Church in Cyprus 1313–1378 (Ashgate, 1997); The Chronicle of George Boustronios: A New English Translation (Cyprus Research Centre and

Greece and Cyprus Research Centre, Univ. of Albany); The Life of Peter Thomas by Philippe de Mézières: A Translation into English (Cyprus Research Centre).

CRAWFORD, Paul, The Involvement of the University of Paris in the Trial of the Templars [article]; The Templars and the Hospitallers [book].

DEMURGER, Alain, Prosopographie des Templiers d'après les données des interrogatoires du procès, so far about 600 Templars present in Paris and interrogated by the papal commission whose report was edited by Michelet.

EDBURY, Peter, The Third Crusade [book]; A Critical Edition of Philip of Novara's Legal Treatise [book]; The Manuscript Tradition of the French Translation of William of Tyre [article]; with E. Walker, A Translation into English of the Chronique d'Amadi [book].

EDGINGTON, Susan B., with Carol Sweetenham, Chanson d'Antioche, English translation and commentary (Aldershot: Ashgate, 2007); Guido da Vigevano's *Regimen sanitatis*, comparative edition and commentary; edition and translation of OF regs of Jerusalem Hospital Vat. 4852; Crusader Medicine (London Books).

FOLDA, Jaroslav, Crusader Art in the Holy Land, 1187–1291 (Cambridge – New York: Cambridge UP, 2005).

FOREY, Alan, Desertions and Transfers from Military Orders (12th to Early 14th Centuries); The Papacy and the Spanish Reconquest; Marriage and Sexual Relations between Western Christians and Outsiders in the Crusading Period.

GERTWAGEN, Ruthy, Struggles for Survival or for Power? The Venetian Maritime Empire up to 1500 [book]; Corfu and its Port in the Venetian Polcy in the Eastern Mediterranean in the Late Medieval and Early Modern Period (14th and 15th Centuries), in: Journal of International Maritime History; The Walls of Acre, in: Festungsjournal: Deutsche Gesellschaft für Festungsforschung; The Contribution of Venice's Colonies to its Naval Warfare in the Eastern Mediterranean in the 15th Century, in: Rivista Mediterranea: Ricerche storiche (Palermo) [articles].

HIESTAND, Rudolf, Oriens Pontificius Latinus.

HOCH, Martin, Saladin, in: Kriegsherren der Weltgeschichte: Von Xerxes bis Nixon, ed. Stig Förster et al. (München: Beck).

HOUSLEY, Norman J., Experiencing the Crusades (Yale UP) [book].

HUNYADI, Zsolt, contributions for MIL.ORD: Dictionnaire critique des Ordres militaires européens au Moyen Âge.

JASPERT, Nikolas, The Order of Montjoie [article].

JENSEN, Janus Møller, A List of Brethren from the Final Decades of the 12th Century in Scandinavia [book].

JOTISCHKY, Andrew, with Bernard Hamilton, Monasticism in the Crusader States (Cambridge: UP).

KRÜGER, Jürgen, Architectural History of the Hospitals of the Order of St John and the Teutonic Order; The Setting Out of the Holy Places in the Holy Land; Architectural Copies of the Holy Places in Europe.

LIGATO, Giuseppe, Sibilla, regina crociata [book].

MADDEN, Thomas F., Religion and Religiosity in Medieval Venice.

MAIER, Christoph T., with Nicole Bériou, The Sermons of the Albigensian Crusade of 1226 (Oxford Medieval Texts); Crusades against Christians (Hambledon and London).

MITCHELL, Piers D., Analysis of a cesspool from crusader period Acre for evidence of intestinal diseases in those who originally used it; Archaeological study of health and disease in the crusader period population of Caesarea.

NICOLAOU-KONNARI, Angel, The Encounter of Greeks and Franks in Cyprus in the Late Twelfth and Thirteenth Centuries: Phenomena of Acculturation and Ethnic Awareness (Birmingham UP – Ashgate, 2006).

NICOLLE, David, Arsuf 1191, Osprey Men-at-Arms; Crusader Castles in Cyprus, the Aegean and Black Sea regions, Osprey Fortress; co-author, Russian Armies late 15th to early 17th Centuries, Osprey Men-at-Arms; co-author, Scandinavian Baltic Crusades, Osprey Men-at-Arms; Warfare in the Crusader World (Hambledon); Costume and medieval military equipment research for the Royal Jordanian Institute for Furusiya Research; in collaboration with the British Museum and the Syrian Department of Antiquities research in recently recognised medieval leather helmets and related materials from the Citadel of Damascus, currently in store in the National Museum in Damascus.

OTTEN-FROUX, Catherine, Publication of sources concerning Cyprus; History of Famagusta.

PAVIOT, Jacques, The idea of crusade in France, end 13th to beginning 16th centuries.

PHILLIPS, Jonathan P., The Second Crusade: Extending the Frontiers of Christianity (Yale UP, 2006).

PRINGLE, Denys R., ed., History and Archaeology of the City of Ramla (c.715–1917) [book]; Pilgrimage to Jerusalem and the Holy Land, 1187–1291, Crusader Texts in Translation (Aldershot: Ashgate); with G. Ewart, 'There is a castle in the west ...': Dundonald Castle Excavations 1986–93; The Pottery of the Crusader States, in: Medieval Archaeology; The Protestant Cemetery in Tunis: Catalogue of the Gravestones of the 17th to 19th Centuries; with Lucy-Anne Hunt, The Artistic Programme of the Medieval Wall-Paintings surrounding the Tomb of the Virgin Mary in Jerusalem; Castles, Churches and Landscape in the Frankish East, Variorum Collected Studies series (Aldershot: Ashgate); see Bulletin 24 (2004), 34.

RICHARD, Jean, Au-delà de la Perse et de l'Arménie: la découverte de l'Asie centrale par l'Orient latin; Aux origines de l'alliance franco-mongole (1145–1262).

SARNOWSKY, Jürgen, Die Schuldbücher und Rechnungen der Großschäffer des Deutschen Ordens in Preußen, vols. 2 and 3 for the officials in Königsberg, second part, and in Marienburg; a critical edition of the statutes of the Hospitallers from 1493, Guillaume Caoursin, based on a manuscript from the National Library of Malta and further sources, presenting the text of the statutes itself and at least some of the earlier statutes which were the basis of this revision, financed by the Deutsche Forschungsgemeinschaft.

SCHABEL, Christopher, St Theodore Abbey, Nicosia: A Cistercian Monastery of Women; Martyrs and Heretics, Intolerance of Intolerance: The Azymo Dispute and the Execution of 13 Greek Monks in Cyprus in 1231; with Jean Richard, Bullarium Cyprium: Papal Letters Involving Cyprus 1196–1378, Texts and Studies in the History of Cyprus (Nicosia: Cyprus Research Centre, 2007/2008); with William Duba, Bullarium Hellenicum I: Pope Honorius III's Letters Involving Frankish Greece (Leiden: Brill).

SEEBERG SIDSELRUD, Kaare, An Armorial of the Catholic Hierarchy in the Nordic Countries Pre-Reformation.

TESSERA, Miriam Rita, see Bulletin 24 (2004), 34–35.

TOKO, Hirofumi, Byzantium, in: A Companion to the History of the Mediterranean World.

TOUATI, François-Olivier, Hypergamie endogamique? Sexualité et conjugalité dans les États latins d'Orient.

URBAN, William, The Samogitian Crusade, revised and enlarged 2nd edition.

6. Theses in progress

BRIDGER, Heidi, The Conquest and Settlement of Frankish Greece, 1204–61, supervised by Jonathan Phillips, Royal Holloway, University of London.

CARLSSON, Christer, The Religious Orders of Knighthood in Medieval Scandinavia 1291–1536.

CHRYSSIS, Nikolaos, Public and Private Opinion in Byzantine-Western Relations, 13th–15th Centuries, with special reference to crusading in the Greek lands, supervised by Jonathan Harris, Royal Holloway, University of London.

JENSEN, Janus Møller, Denmark and the Crusades, 1400–1650, Univ. of Southern Denmark at Odense.

JINKS, Alison, Philip Augustus and the Crusades, supervised by Jonathan Phillips, Royal Holloway, University of London.

LIAKOPOULOS, Giorgios, The Late Byzantine and Ottoman Peloponnese, supervised by Jonathan Harris, Univ. of London.

MAIOR, Balazs, The Medieval Settlement Pattern of the Syrian Littoral, 11th to 13th Centuries, PhD, Cardiff Univ., supervised by Denys Pringle.

MORTON, Nicholas, The Teutonic Knights in the Holy Land, supervised by Jonathan Phillips, Royal Holloway, University of London.

PETRE, James, Crusader Castles of Cyprus: The Fortifications of Cyprus under the Lusignans, 1191–1489, MPhil, Cardiff Univ., supervised by Denys Pringle.

PURKIS, William, Crusade and Pilgrimage Spirituality, c.1095–c.1187, PhD in History, Emmanuel College, Cambridge, supervised by Jonathan Riley-Smith.

ROBINSON, Dana, John of Brienne and the Brienne Dynasty, supervised by Jonathan Phillips, Royal Holloway, University of London.

THOMPSON, Jennifer, Death and Burial in the Latin East: A Study of the Crusader Cemetery at 'Atlit, Israel, PhD, Cardiff Univ., supervised by Denys Pringle.

WAGNER, Thomas, Krankheiten und Krankenversorgung zur Zeit der Kreuzzüge: Epidemien, Verwundetenpflege, historische Krankheitsbilder, Univ. Würzburg.

7. Fieldwork planned or undertaken recently

Dan Bahat: starting in the summer of 2005 a six year project of digging at Tell-Yavneh, the crusader Ibelin.

Christer Carlsson: excavation of Årsta, a Teutonic Order commandery on the eastern coast of Sweden, during the summer of 2005.

Jaroslav Folda: research during the summer of 2004 in New York, Washington/DC, London and Istanbul on medieval silk with regard to the ornamental decoration of luxury textiles.

Piers D. Mitchell: trip to Israel in October 2004 firstly to obtain archaeological samples for a project on diet in the crusader period, and secondly to research a number of medieval pilgrimage destinations.

David Nicolle: photographic surveys of the battlefields of Arsuf 1191 and Acre 1291, of Islamic fortifications in Syria.

Mathias Piana: third campaign of excavation and survey of the castle of Toron/Lebanon, and survey of crusader fortifications in Southern Lebanon.

8. News of interest to members

a) Conferences and seminars

2005 May: Regards croisés sur la guerre sainte dans le monde latin du XIe au XIIIe siècle, conference and seminar at the Casa de Velázquez, Madrid, organized by Philippe Josserand in collaboration with Daniel Baloup.

2005 June 27–29 Al Akhawayn University in Ifrane, Morocco, The Mediterranean in World History and Africa in World History, further information at www.thewha.org, or by Alfred.Andrea@uvm.edu

2005 July 1 Sydney, Symposium at the Centre for Medieval Studies, organized by John H. Pryor on 'From the West to the Holy Land in the Age of the Crusades'.

2005 July 4 Sydney, 20th International Congress of Historical Sciences, session organized by Michel Balard and Benjamin Z. Kedar on 'Peoples and Cultures of the Levant in the Age of the Crusades'.

2005 July 15–19, IV Medieval Chronicles Conference, Univ. of Reading, offers for papers on any aspect of chronicles welcome or requests to be added to mailing list lfsnoble@ reading.ac.uk

2005 September 8–11 Clerkenwell, London, The Military Orders on Land and by Sea, The Fourth International Conference of the London Centre for the Study of the Crusades, the Military Religious Orders and the Latin East, organized by a committee under the chairmanship of Jonathan Riley-Smith; conference administrator Miss H.E. Gribble, 13 Highcombe Close, London SE9 4QH, he@gribblehe.fsnet.co.uk

2005 September 23–25, Toruń, Ordines militares – Colloquia Torunensia Historica XIII, Die Ritterorden als Träger von Herrschaft: Territorien, Grundbesitz und Kirchen, organized by Roman Czaja and Jürgen Sarnowsky, Instytut historii i archiwistyki universytetu Mikołaja Kopernika w Toruniu, rc@his.uni.torun.pl

2006 January 27–29, Marksburg/Germany, International Symposium Castles and Towns of the Crusader Period in the Eastern Mediterranean, organised by Europäisches Burgeninstitut der Deutschen Brugenvereinigung in cooperation with the Gesellschaft für Internationale Burgenkunde / International Castle Research Society, Aachen

b) Other news

Taef el-Azhari is an advisor to the documentary film 'Crusades – The Crescent and the Cross' produced in Damascus, Aleppo and Maarat al-Numaan during November 2004 and broadcast in November 2005 by The History Channel. The programme consultant was Jonathan Phillips and he filmed in Istanbul, Acre, Hattin and Jerusalem. Other contributors were Professor John France, Dr Tom Asbridge, Dr Paul Crawford and Tariq Ali.

Zsolt Hunyadi invites to visit, comment on and/or contribute to http://www.sscle.org

The Palgrave Series 'Studies in the Crusades' is a new monograph series publishing the best new research on the Crusades, defined in their broadest sense to include wars in the Iberian Peninsula and the Baltic, and campaigns against heretics and Christians. This series will encourage innovative scholarly work in research areas such as prosopography, gender, cross-cultural exchange, the societies founded or ruled by the crusaders, slavery within those societies, and the role and function of crusading in European society. It is not intended to include volumes of essays, editions of primary texts (except as part of a critical analysis) nor revised Ph.D. theses. Initial proposals may be addressed to Dr Helen Nicholson (Cardiff Univ.), email: nicholsonhj@cardiff.ac.uk

The Syrian Department of Antiquities plans to open a small museum in the Citadel of Damascus after this reopens to the public; the museum will contain medieval and late medieval military artefacts, textiles and other objects discovered by French archaeologists within the Citadel over recent years (notice by David Nicolle).

Exposition 'Sceaux et usages de sceaux: images de la Champagne médiévale', avec en particulier des documents relatifs aux Champenois aux Croisades (familles de Joinville, Brienne, Champlitte, Villehardouin, etc.), Châlons (Marne): Paris, Centre historique des Archives nationales, automne 2005 (notice par Marie-Adélaïde Nielen).

The Gesellschaft für Internationale Burgenkunde / International Castle Research Society in Aachen/Germany prepares for an exhibition Castles and Bazaars – Medieval Forms of Life in the Levant, where a great-scale model of the Krak des Chevaliers, based on recent research, will be shown. It starts at the Archaeological Museum in Frankfurt am Main/Germany, 4 November 2005 to 15 February 2006, and afterwards will be shown at the Museum of the National Geographic Society, Washington/DC, 4 April to 4 September 2006 (notice by Mathias Piana).

9. Members' queries

In 1993, Sotheby's auctioned off the Abousson collection. The sale included a large number of Venetian merchant letters, including some very fine letters by or to Marco Bembo, c.1482. These were all bought by one particular buyer, probably acting as an agent for someone else. If anyone knows the current owner, Eleanor A. Congdon would very much like to include those letters in her research. If anyone knows of any other letters (besides those in Venice, Cambridge and Minnesota) she would be grateful for a citation.

10. Officers of the Society

President: Professor Michel Balard. Honorary Vice-Presidents: Professor Benjamin Z. Kedar, Professor Jean Richard, and Professor Jonathan Riley-Smith. Secretary: Professor Sophia Menache. Assistant Secretary: Professor Luis García-Guijarro Ramos. Editor of the Bulletin: Professor Karl Borchardt. Treasurer: Professor James D. Ryan. Website: Dr Zsolt Hunyadi.

Committee of the Society: Professor Antonio Carile (Bologna), Professor Robert Huygens (Leiden), Professor Hans Eberhard Mayer (Kiel).

11. Income and expenditure account for the Society

The accounts starting from 18 September 2002 will be established by the new treasurer.

12. List of members and their addresses

Shawn D. ABBOTT, 924 Greenbriar Road, Muncie IN 47304-3260, U.S.A.; sdbabbott@hotmail.com

Prof. Baudouin van den ABEELE, Rue C. Wolles 3, B-1030 Bruxelles, BELGIUM; vandenabeele@mage.ucl.ac.be

Dr Anna Sapir ABULAFIA, Lucy Cavendish College, Cambridge CB3 0BU, ENGLAND, U.K.

Prof. David S. H. ABULAFIA, Gonville and Caius College, Cambridge CB2 1TA, ENGLAND, U.K.

Gabriella AIRALDI, Dipartimento di Scienze dell'antichità e del medioevo (DISAM), Università di Genova, Via Lomellini 8, I-16124 Genoa, ITALY; tel.: 0039-010-2465897 and 2099602, fax: 0039-010-2465810

Brian ALLISON LEWIS, c/o Sabic, PO Box 5101, Riyadh 11422, SAUDI ARABIA.

Prof. Reuven AMITAI-PREISS, Dept. of Islamic and Middle Eastern Studies, Hebrew Univ., Jerusalem 91905, ISRAEL; amitai@h2.hum.huji.ac.il

Dr Monique AMOUROUX, 2, Avenue de Montchalette, Cassy, F-33138 Lanton, FRANCE

Prof. Alfred J. ANDREA, 161 Austin Drive #3, Burlington VT 05401, U.S.A.; aandrea@uvm.edu

Prof. Benjamin ARBEL, School of History, Tel-Aviv Univ., Tel-Aviv 69978, ISRAEL; arbel@ccsg.tau.ac.il

Dr Marco AROSIO, Università del Sacro Cuore, Milano, ITALY; marco_arosio@tin.it

Dr Thomas S. ASBRIDGE, Dept. of History, Queen Mary and Westfield College, Univ. of London, Mile End Road, London E1 4NS, ENGLAND, U.K.; t_asbridge@qmul.ac.uk

Dr Hussein M. ATTIYA, 20 Ahmed Sidik Street, Sidi Gaber El-Shiek, Alexandria, EGYPT

Prof. Taef K. EL-AZHARI, 6/14 Zahraa El-Maadi, Second Sector, Cairo 11435, EGYPT; taef@tedata.net.eg

Dr Mohammed AZIZ, PO Box 135513, Beirut, LEBANON.

Prof. Bernard S. BACHRACH, Univ. of Minnesota, Dept. of History, 633 Social Sciences Building, Minneapolis MN 55455, U.S.A.

Dr Dan BAHAT, PO Box 738, Mevasseret Zion 90805, ISRAEL; danbahat@yahoo.com

Prof. Michel BALARD, 4, rue des Remparts, F-94370 Sucy-en-Brie, FRANCE, Michel.Balard@univ-paris1.fr

Prof. Laura BALLETTO, Via Orsini 40/B, I-16146 Genoa, ITALY; Laura.Balletto@lettere.unige.it

Paul Walden BAMFORD, 2204 West Lake of the Isles Parkway, Minneapolis MN 55405-2426, U.S.A.

Prof. Malcolm BARBER, Dept. of History, Univ. of Reading, PO Box 218, Whiteknights, Reading RG6 6AA, ENGLAND, U.K.; m.c.barber@reading.ac.uk

Prof. John W. BARKER, Dept. of History, Univ. of Wisconsin, 3211 Humanities Building, Madison WI 53706, U.S.A.; jwbarker@wisc.edu

Sebastian BARTOS, 6762 4th Avenue, Brooklyn NY 11220, U.S.A.; sebartos@hotmail.com

The Rev. Fr. Robert L. BECERRA, Senior Associate Pastor, St Luke Catholic Church, 2892 South Congress Avenue, Palm Springs FL 33461-2170, U.S.A.; SinaiPantocrator@aol.com

Dr Bruce BEEBE, 1490 Mars Lakewood OH 44107, U.S.A.; lgbeebe@aol.com

Prof. George BEECH, Dept. of History, Western Michigan Univ., Kalamazoo MI 49008, U.S.A.; beech@wmich.edu

Elena BELLOMO, via dei Rospigliosi 1, I-20151 Milano, ITALY; elena.bellomo@libero.it

Jacob BEN-CNAAN, 52 Katz Street, Petakh-Tikva 49374, ISRAEL; ponar@zahav.net.il

Matthew BENNETT, 58 Mitchell Avenue, Hartley Wintney, Hampshire RG27 8HG, ENGLAND, U.K.; mattbennett@waitrose.com

Dr Nora BEREND, St Catharine's College, Cambridge CB2 1RL, ENGLAND, U.K.; nb213@cam.ac.uk

Jessalynn BIRD, 1514 Cortland Drive, Naperville IL 60565, U.S.A; jessalynn.bird@iname.com

Prof. Nancy BISAHA, Dept. of History, Vassar College, Maildrop 81, 124 Raymond Avenue, Poughkeepsie NY 12604, U.S.A.; nabisaha@vassar.edu

Prof. John R. E. BLIESE, Communication Studies Dept., Texas Tech Univ., Lubbock TX 79409, U.S.A.

Dr Adrian J. BOAS, Institute of Archaeology, Hebrew Univ. of Jerusalem, Jerusalem 91905, ISRAEL; adianjboas@yahoo.com

Prof. Mark S. BOCIJA, Columbus State Community College, 550 E. Spring Street, Columbus OH 43216-1609, U.S.A.; mbocija@cscc.edu

Louis BOISSET, Université Saint-Joseph de Beyrouth, BP 166 778, Achrafieh, Beirut, LEBANON.

Brenda M. BOLTON, 8 Watling Street, St Albans AL1 2PT, ENGLAND, U.K.; brenda@bolton.vianw.co.uk

Barbara BOMBI, via Leonardo da Vinci 26, I-27029 Vigevano (PV), ITALY; bbombi@libero.it

Pierre BONNEAUD, Carretera de Sant Vicenç 47, E-08394 Sant Vicenç de Montalt (Barcelona), ESPAÑA; pierrebonneaud@yahoo.es

Prof. Karl BORCHARDT, Wiesenstraße 18, D-91541 Rothenburg ob der Tauber, GERMANY; stadtarchiv@rothenburg.de

Prof. Charles R. BOWLUS, History Dept., Univ. of Arkansas, 8081 Mabelvale, Little Rock AR 72209-1099, U.S.A.; carolus22000@yahoo.com

Prof. Charles M. BRAND, 508 West Montgomery Avenue, Haverford PA 19041-1409, U.S.A.; cmbrand4@earthlink.net

Dr Michael BRETT, School of Oriental and African Studies, Univ. of London, Malet Street, London WC1E 7HP, ENGLAND, U.K.

Robert BRODIE, 61 St Saviours Wharf, 8 Shad Thames, London SE1 2YP, ENGLAND, U.K.; robert@dbrodie.demon.co.uk

Dr Judith BRONSTEIN, Ilanot 29/2, Haifa 34324, ISRAEL; Judith_Bronstein@hotmail.com

Prof. Elizabeth A. R. BROWN, 160 West 86th Street PH4, New York NY 10024, U.S.A.; rsbrown160@aol.com

Prof. James A. BRUNDAGE, 1102 Sunset Drive, Lawrence KS 66044-4548, U.S.A.; jabrun@ku.edu

Dr Marcus G. BULL, Dept. of Historical Studies, Univ. of Bristol, 13-15 Woodland Road, Clifton, Bristol BS8 1TB, ENGLAND, U.K.; m.g.bull@bris.ac.uk

SSG Almyr L. BUMP, 7070 Austrian Pine Way #1, Portage MI 49204, U.S.A.

Dr Jochen BURGTORF, California State Univ., Dept. of History, Fullerton CA 92834-6846, U.S.A.; jburgtorf@fullerton.edu

Olivier BURLOTTE, Appartment 79, Smolensky Boulvard 6-8, Moscow 119 034, RUSSIA, oburlotte@yahoo.com

Prof. Charles BURNETT, Warburg Institute, Woburn Square, London WC1H 0AB, ENGLAND, U.K.; ch-burne@sas.ac.uk

The Rev. Prof. Robert I. BURNS, History Dept., UCLA, Los Angeles CA 90095, U.S.A.; fax: (310) 338-3002.

Dr Peter BURRIDGE, Harmer Mill, Millington, York YO4 2TX, ENGLAND, U.K.

Ane Lise BYSTED, Dept. of History, Univ. of Southern Denmark, Campusvej 55, DK-5230 Odense M, DENMARK; bysted@hist.sdu.dk

Dr J. P. CANNING, History Dept. Univ. College of North Wales, Bangor, Gwynedd, WALES, U.K.

Prof. Franco CARDINI, PO Box 2358, I-50123 Firenze Ferrovia, ITALY.

Christer CARLSSON, Medieval Archaeologist, Institut for Historie, Kultur og Samfundsbeskrivelse, Syddansk Universitet, Campusvej 55, DK-5230 Odense, DENMARK; cc_arch75@hotmail.com

Alan Brady CARR, 2522 20th Street, Lubbock TX 79410, U.S.A.

Dr Annemarie Weyl CARR, Division of Art History, Southern Methodist Univ., PO Box 750356, Dallas TX 75275-0356, U.S.A.; acarr@mail.smu.edu

Marc CARRIER, 500 Alexandre-Dumas, Granby Quebec J2J 1B2, CANADA.

Jennifer CASTEN, 875 Western Avenue, Apt. 3, Brattleboro VT 05301, U.S.A.; nulla@macol.net

Prof. Brian CATLOS, Univ. of California Santa Cruz, Stevenson Academic Center, 1156 High Street, Santa Cruz CA 95064, U.S.A.; bcatlos@ucsc.edu

Prof. Fred A. CAZEL Jr., 309 Gurleyville Road, Storrs Mansfield CT 06268-1439, U.S.A.

Dr Simonetta CERRINI[-ALLOISIO], Via Antonio Gramsci 109/32, I-15076 Ovada (Alessandria), ITALY; alloisiocerrini@inwind.it

Anton CHARLTON, 16 Muswell Hill, Muswell Hill, London NJ0 3TA, ENGLAND, U.K.

Dr Martin CHASIN, 1125 Church Hill Road, Fairfield CT 06432-1371, U.S.A.; mchasin@worldnet.att.net

Dr Katherine CHRISTENSEN, CPO 1756 Berea College, Berea KY 40404, U.S.A.; katherine_christensen@berea.edu

Dr Niall G. F. CHRISTIE, Dept. of Classical, Near Eastern and Religious Studies, The Univ. of British Columbia, BUCH C260-1866 Main Hall, Vancouver B.C. V6T 1Z1, CANADA; niall.christie@yahoo.com

Ioanna CHRISTOFORAKI, Aristotelous 26, Chalandri, Athens 15234, GREECE; joanna.christoforaki@archeology.oxford.ac.uk

Dr Juliana CHRYSOSTOMIDES, Dept. of History, Egham Hill, Egham, Surrey, ENGLAND, U.K.; j.chysostomides@rhul.ac.uk

Padre Giulio CIPOLLONE, B.S.S.T., Padri Trinitari, Piazza S. Maria alle Fornaci 30, I-00165 Roma, ITALY; cipolloneunigre6009@fastwebnet.it

Dr G. H. M. CLAASSENS, Departement Literatuurwetenschap, Katholieke Universiteit Leuven, Blijde Inkomststraat 21, Postbus 33, B-3000 Leuven, BELGIUM.

Pierre-Vincent CLAVERIE, 9, rue du Bois-Rondel, F-35700 Rennes, FRANCE; pvclaverie@minitel.net

Dr Penny J. COLE, Trinity College, 6 Hoskin Avenue, Toronto, Ontario M5S 1HB, CANADA; pjcole@trinity.utoronto.ca

Prof. Eleanor A. CONGDON, Youngstown State Univ., One University Plaza, Youngstown OH 44555, U.S.A.; eacongdon@ysu.edu

Prof. Giles CONSTABLE, 506 Quaker Road, Princeton NJ 08540, U.S.A.

Prof. Olivia Remie CONSTABLE, Dept. of History, Univ. of Notre Dame, Notre Dame IN 46556-0368, U.S.A.; constable1@nd.edu

Prof. Robert F. COOK, French Language and General Linguistics Dept., Univ. of Virginia, 302 Cabell Hall, Charlottesville VA 22903, U.S.A.

Prof. Rebecca W. CORRIE, Phillips Professor of Art, Bates College, Lewiston ME 04240, U.S.A.; rcorrie@bates.edu

Prof. Ricardo Luiz Silveira da COSTA, Rua Joao Nunes Coelho 264 apto. 203, Ed. Tom Jobim – Bairro Mata da Praia – Vitória – Espírito Santo (ES), CEP 29.065-490, BRAZIL; riccosta@npd.ufes.br or ricardo@ricardocosta.com

Dr Nicholas S. COUREAS, PO Box 26619, Lykarittos, CY-1640 Nicosia, CYPRUS.

The Rev. H. E. J. COWDREY, 19 Church Lane, Old Marston, Oxford OX3 0NZ, ENGLAND, U.K.; fax (0)1865 279090.

Dr Paul CRAWFORD, History Dept., Alma College, 614 West Superior Street, Alma MI 48801, U.S.A.; crawford@alma.edu

Prof. Larry S. CRIST, 6609 Rolling Fork Drive, Nashville TN 37205, U.S.A.

B. Thomas CURTIS, 36 Brockswood Lane, Welwyn Garden City, Herts. AL8 7BG, ENGLAND, U.K.; btcurtis@btinternet.com

Dana [DENNIS-]CUSHING, PO Box 9088, Waukegan IL 60079, U.S.A.

Charles DALLI, Dept. of History, Faculty of Arts, Univ. of Malta, Msida MSD06, MALTA; cdalli@arts.um.edu.mt

Philip Louis DANIEL, Archivist, Equestrian Order of the Holy Sepuchre of Jerusalem, 37 Somerset Road, Meadvale, Redhill, Surrey RH1 6LT, ENGLAND, U.K.; fax: 01737-240722.

Dr Béatrice DANSETTE, 175, Boulevard Malesherbes, F-75017 Paris, FRANCE.

Nicole DAWE, 21 New Road, Okehampton, Devon EX20 1JE, ENGLAND, U.K.; ndawe@hotmail.com

Julian DEAHL, c/o E. J. Brill, PO Box 9000, NL-2300 PA Leiden, THE NETHERLANDS; deahl@brill.nl

Dr Bernhard DEMEL O.T., Leiter des Deutschordenszentralarchivs, Singerstraße 7, A-1010 Wien, AUSTRIA; tel. 513 70 14.

Prof. Işin DEMIRKENT, Head of Middle Ages History Dept., İstanbul Üniversitesi Edebiyat Fakültesi Tarih Bölümü, Beyazkt – İstanbul, TURKEY; address for all correspondence: Darkca, Tuzla Cad. 67 Kocaeli, TURKEY; fax: 212.6290312.

John A. DEMPSEY, 218 Edgehill Road, Milton MA 02186-5310, U.S.A.; milton1@bu.edu

Prof. Alain DEMURGER, 5, rue de l'Abricotier, F-95000 Cergy, FRANCE; ademurger@wanadoo.fr

Prof. George T. DENNIS, Loyola Marymount Univ., PO Box 45041, Los Angeles CA 90045-0041, U.S.A.; nauarchos@aol.com

Americo DE SANTIS, 88 East Main Street, Box Number 141, Mendham NJ 07945, U.S.A.; ricodesantis@hotmail.com

Dr M. Gary DICKSON, History, School of History and Classics, Univ. of Edinburgh, Wm. Robertson Building, 50 George Square, Edinburgh EH8 9JY, SCOTLAND, U.K.; GaryDickson77404@aol.com

Prof. Richard DIVALL, 301 Arcadia, 228 The Avenue, Parkville, Victoria 3052, AUSTRALIA; naestro@spin.net.au

Dr Erica Cruikshank DODD, 4208 Wakefield Place, Victoria, B.C. V8N 6E5, CANADA.

César DOMÍNGUEZ, Universidad de Santiago de Compostela, Facultad de Filología, Avda. Castealo s/n, E-15704 Santiago (La Coruna), ESPAÑA.

Dr Cristina DONDI, 128 Berkeley Court, Glentworth Street, London NW1 5NE, ENGLAND, U.K.; cfd@bodley.ox.ac.uk

Ara DOSTOURIAN, Box 420, Harmony RI 02829, U.S.A.

Mary DOUROU-ELIOPOULOU, Kephallenias 24, Althea 36km.Sounion Ave., 19400 Attiki, GREECE; meliop@cc.uoa.gr

Dr Jean DUNBABIN, St Anne's College, Oxford OX2 6HS, ENGLAND, U.K.

Mark DUPUY, 119 South Sixth Avenue, Apartment A, Clarion PA 16214, U.S.A.; mdupuy@clarion.edu

John DURANT, 32 Maple Street, PO Box 373, West Newbury MA 01985, U.S.A.

Dr Valerie EADS, 308 West 97th Street, New York NY 10025, U.S.A.

Prof. Richard EALES, School of History, Univ. of Kent, Canterbury CT2 7NX, ENGLAND, U.K.; rgel@ukc.ac.uk

Ana ECHEVARRÍA ARSUAGA, Facultad de Geografía e Historia, Departimento de Historia Medieval, C/ Senda del Rey, E-28040 Madrid, ESPAÑA; anaevjosem@wanadoo.es

Prof. Peter W. EDBURY, School of History and Archaeology, Cardiff Univ., PO Box 909, Cardiff CF10 3XU, WALES, U.K.; edbury@cardiff.ac.uk

Dr Susan B. EDGINGTON, 3 West Street, Huntingdon, Cambs PE29 1WT, ENGLAND, U.K.; s.b.edgington@btinternet.com

Axel EHLERS, Berdingstraße 4a, D-30451 Hannover, GERMANY; aehlers1@gwdg.de

Prof. Sven EKDAHL, Sponholzstraße 38, D-12159 Berlin, GERMANY; Sven.Ekdahl@t-online.de

Prof. Ronnie ELLENBLUM, 13 Reuven Street, Jerusalem 93510, ISRAEL; msronni@pluto.mscc.huji.ac.il

Prof. Kasper ELM, Koserstraße 20, D-14195 Berlin, GERMANY.

Prof. Steven A. EPSTEIN, Dept. of History, 204 Hellems, Campus Box 234, Univ. of Colorado, Boulder CO 80309-0234, U.S.A.; steven.epstein@colorado.edu

Dr Helen C. EVANS, The Medieval Dept., The Metropolitan Museum of Art, 1000 Fifth Avenue, New York NY 10028, U.S.A.; helenevans@metmuseum.org

Michael EVANS, Flat 6, Marston Ferry Court, Oxford OX2 7XH, ENGLAND, U.K.; m_r_evans@hotmail.com

Prof. Theodore EVERGATES, 146 West Main Street, Westminster MD 21157, U.S.A.

John C. FARQUHARSON, 19 Long Croft Lane, Cheadle Hulme, Cheadle Cheshire SK8 6SE, ENGLAND, U.K.; johnfarquharson@easicom.com

Prof. Marie-Luise FAVREAU-LILIE, Kaiser-Friedrich-Straße 106, D-10585 Berlin, GERMANY; mlfavre@mail.zedat.fu-berlin.de

Jack FERGUSSON, Dept. of Chemistry, Univ. of Canterbury, Christchurch, NEW ZEALAND; j.fergusson@chem.canterbury.ac.nz

P. J. FLAHERTY, 9 Oak Street, Braintree MA 02184, U.S.A.

Prof. Jean FLORI, Docteur d'État des Lettres et Sciences Humaines, Directeur de Recherche au Centre d'Études Supérieures de Civilisation Médiévale de Poitiers, 69 rue Saint Cornély, F-56340 Carnac, FRANCE; flori.jean@wanadoo.fr

Prof. Jaroslav FOLDA, Dept. of Art, Univ. of North Carolina, Chapel Hill NC 27599-3405, U.S.A.; jfolda@email.unc.edu

Michelle FOLTZ, M.D., PMB 33, PO Box 1226, Columbus MT 59019, U.S.A.

Dr Alan FOREY, The Bell House, Church Lane, Kirtlington, Oxon. OX5 3HJ, ENGLAND, U.K.

Edith FORMAN, 38 Burnham Hill, Westport CT 06880, U.S.A.

Barbara FRALE, via A. Gramsci 17, I-01028 Orte (VT), ITALY; barbara-frale@libero.it

Dr John FRANCE, History Dept., Univ. of Wales, Swansea SA2 7PP, WALES, U.K.; j.france@swansea.ac.uk

Dr Peter FRANKOPAN, Worcester College, Oxford OX1 2HB, ENGLAND, U.K.; peter.frankopan@worcester.ox.ac.uk

Prof. Yvonne FRIEDMAN, Dept. of History, Bar-Ilan Univ., Ramat-Gan 55900, ISRAEL; yfried@mail.biu.ac.il

Stuart FROST, 44 Ratumore Road Charlton, London SE7 7QW, ENGLAND, U.K.; stuartfrost@fsmail.net

R. FROUMIN, Neve Eitan, D. N. Beit Shean 10840, ISRAEL; froumin@yahoo.com

Michael and Neathery FULLER, 13530 Clayton Road, St Louis MO 63141, U.S.A.

Prof. Luis GARCÍA-GUIJARRO RAMOS, Professor titular de Historia Medieval, Facultad de Huesca, Plaza de la Universidad 3, E-22002 Huesca, ESPAÑA; luguijar@posta.unizar.es

Dr Christopher K. GARDNER, Postdoctoral Fellow in History, George Mason Univ., MS: 3G1, Fairfax VA 22030, U.S.A.; cgardner@jhu.edu

Giles E. M. GASPER, Wolfson College, Linton Road, Oxford OX2 6UD, ENGLAND, U.K.

F. Gregory GAUSE Jr., 207 Bayard Avenue, Rehoboth Beach DE 19971, U.S.A.; prgause@aol.com

Sabine GELDSETZER, M.A., Westheide 6, D-44892 Bochum, GERMANY; sabine.geldsetzer@ruhr-uni-bochum.de

Prof. Maria GEORGOPOULOU, Dept. of the History of Art, Yale Univ., PO Box 208272, New Haven CT 06520-8272, U.S.A.; maria.georgopoulou@yale.edu

Deborah GERISH, Dept. of Social Sciences Box 32, Emporia State Univ., 1200 Commercial, Emporia KS 66801, U.S.A.; dgerish@netscape.net

Dr Ruthy GERTWAGEN, 30 Ranas Street, PO Box 117, Qiryat Motzkin 26317, ISRAEL; ruger@macam.ac.il

Prof. John B. GILLINGHAM, 49 Old Shoreham Road, Brighton, Sussex BN1 5DQ, ENGLAND, U.K.; john@jgillingham.wanadoo.co.uk

Prof. Anne GILMOUR-BRYSON, 1935 Westview Drive, North Vancouver, B.C. V7M 3B1, CANADA; annegb@telus.net

J. L. GILS, Gouden Leeuw 820, NL-1103 KS Amsterdam, THE NETHERLANDS.

Prof. Dorothy F. GLASS, 11 Riverside Drive, Apartment 6-OW, New York NY 10023, U.S.A.; dglass1@att.net

Prof. Aryeh GRABOIS, History Dept., Univ. of Haifa, Mount Carmel, Haifa 31905, ISRAEL; arag@research.haifa.ac.il

Michael GRAYER, 192 York Road, Shrewsburg Shropshire SY1 3QH, England, U.K.

Gilles GRIVAUD, 8 rue de Général de Miribel, F-69007 Lyon, FRANCE.

The Rev. Joseph J. GROSS, Trinitarian History Studies, PO Box 42056, Baltimore MD 21284, U.S.A.; jjg62osst@aol.com

Prof. Klaus GUTH, Greiffenbergstraße 35, D-96052 Bamberg, GERMANY.

Dr Mark E. HALL, 6826 Walso Avenue, El Cerrito CA 94530, U.S.A.; markhall@gol.com

Adina HAMILTON, 469 Albert Street, Brunswick West Victoria 3055, AUSTRALIA or History Dept., Univ. of Melbourne, Parkville Victoria 3052, AUSTRALIA.

Prof. Bernard HAMILTON, 7 Lenton Avenue, The Park, Nottingham NG7 IDX, ENGLAND, U.K.

Peter HARITATOS Jr., 1500 North George Street, Rome NY 13440, U.S.A.

Jonathan HARRIS, Dept. of History, Royal Holloway, Univ. of London, Egham, Surrey TW20 0EX, ENGLAND, U.K.; jonathan.harris@rhul.ac.uk

Kathryn D. HARRIS, 6 Gallows Hill, Saffron Walden, Essex CB11 4DA, ENGLAND, U.K.

Dr Alan HARVEY, Dept. of Historical and Critical Studies, Univ. of Northumbria, Newcastle-upon-Tyne NE1 8ST, ENGLAND, U.K.; alan.harvey@unn.ac.uk

David HAY, 164 McCaul Street Apt. 1, Toronto, Ontario M5T 1WA, CANADA.

Dr Bodo HECHELHAMMER, Erzbergerstraße 8, D-64823 Groß-Umstadt/Heubach, GERMANY; bodo.hechelhammer@t-online.de or Institut für Geschichte, Residenzschloß, D-64283 Darmstadt, GERMANY; bh@polihist.pg.tu-darmstadt.de

Prof. Thérèse de HEMPTINNE, Universiteit Gent, Faculteit van de Letteren, Vakgroep Middeleeuwse Geschiedenis, Blandijnberg 2, B-9000 Gent, BELGIUM.

Michael HESLOP, 2, Boulevard J.-Dalcroze, CH-1204 Geneva, SWITZERLAND; michaelheslop@atlworld.com

Dr Paul HETHERINGTON, 15 Luttrell Avenue, London SW15 6PD, ENGLAND, U.K.; phetherington@ukonline.co.uk

Dr Avital HEYMAN, 12 Herzel Street, Ness-Ziona 74084, ISRAEL; avital-h@internet-zahav.net

Prof. Rudolf HIESTAND, Brehmstraße 76, D-40239 Düsseldorf, GERMANY.

Charles A. HILKEN, PO Box 4825, St Mary's College, Moraga CA 94575, U.S.A.; chilken@stmarys-ca.edu

Dr George HINTLIAN, Armenian Patriarchate, PO Box, Jerusalem 14001, ISRAEL.

Dr Martin HOCH, Konrad-Adenauer-Stiftung, Rathausallee 12, D-53757 Sankt Augustin, GERMANY; Lobebaer@web.de

Dr Catherine HOLMES, University College, Oxford OX1 4BH, ENGLAND, U.K.; catherine.holmes@univ.ox.ac.uk

Prof. Peter M. HOLT, Dryden Spinney, Bletchington Road, Kirtlington, Kidlington, Oxon OX5 3HF, ENGLAND, U.K.

Prof. Hubert HOUBEN, Via Marugi 38, I-73100 Lecce, ITALY; houben@sesia.unile.it

Prof. Norman J. HOUSLEY, School of Historical Studies, The Univ. of Leicester, Leicester LE1 7RH, ENGLAND, U.K.; hou@leicester.ac.uk

Prof. Lucy-Anne HUNT, Dept. of History of Art and Design, Righton Building, Cavendish Street, Manchester M15 6BK, ENGLAND, U.K.; l.a.hunt@mmu.ac.uk

Zsolt HUNYADI, 27 Szekeres u., H-6725 Szeged, HUNGARY; hunyadiz@hist.u-szeged.hu

Prof. Robert B. C. HUYGENS, Witte Singel 28, NL-2311 BH Leiden, THE NETHERLANDS.

Sheldon IBBOTSON, PO Box 258, Rimbey, Alberta T0C 2J0, CANADA; bronwen@ telusplanet.net

Robert IRWIN, 39 Harleyford Road, London SE11 5AX, ENGLAND, U.K.; robert@ robertirwin.demon.co.uk

Prof. Peter JACKSON, History Dept., Univ. of Keele, Keele, Staffs. ST5 5BG, ENGLAND, U.K.; hia08@keele.ac.uk

Martin JACOBOWITZ, The Towers of Windsor Park, 3005 Chapel Avenue – 11P, Cherry Hill NJ 08002, U.S.A.

Prof. David JACOBY, Dept. of History, The Hebrew Univ., Jerusalem 91905, ISRAEL; jacobgab@mscc.huji.ac.il

Dr Kay Peter JANKRIFT, Institut für Geschichte der Medizin der Robert Bosch Stiftung, Straußweg 17, D-70184 Stuttgart, GERMANY.

Dr Nikolas JASPERT, Institut für Geschichte, Universität Erlangen-Nürnberg, Kochstraße 4, D-91056 Erlangen, GERMANY; nsjasper@phil.uni-erlangen.de

Prof. Carsten Selch JENSEN, Dept. of Church History, Univ. of Copenhagen, Købmagergade 46, POB 2164, DK-1150 Copenhagen K, DENMARK; csj@teol.ku.dk

Janus Møller JENSEN, Institute of History and Civilization, Univ. of Southern Denmark, DK-5230 Odense M, DENMARK; jamj@hist.sdu.dk

Prof. Kurt Villads JENSEN, Dept. of History, Odense Univ., Campusvej 55, DK-5230 Odense M, DENMARK; kurt.villads.jensen@humanities.dk

Prof. William Chester JORDAN, Dept. of History, Princeton Univ., Princeton NJ 08544, U.S.A.; wchester@princeton.edu

Philippe JOSSERAND, 1 rue Rubens, F-44000 Nantes, FRANCE; philippe.josserand@ humana.univ-nantes.fr

Dr Andrew JOTISCHKY, Dept. of History, Univ. of Lancaster, Bailrigg, Lancaster LA1 4YG, ENGLAND, U.K.; a.jotischky@lancaster.ac.uk

Dr Margaret A. JUBB, Dept. of French, Taylor Building, Univ. of Aberdeen, Old Aberdeen, AB24 3UB, SCOTLAND, U.K.; m.jubb@abdn.ac.uk

Dr Fotini KARASSAVA-TSILINGIRI, Chrysostomou Smyrnis 14, N. Smyrni, Athens 17121, GREECE.

Prof. Benjamin Z. KEDAR, Dept. of History, The Hebrew Univ., Jerusalem 91905, ISRAEL; fax (home): 972-8-9700802, bzkedar@h2.hum.huji.ac.il

Prof. Nurith KENAAN-KEDAR, Dept. of Art History, Tel-Aviv Univ., Tel-Aviv 69978, ISRAEL.

Dr Hugh KENNEDY, Medieval History Dept., Univ. of St Andrews, St Andrews, Fife KY16 9AL, SCOTLAND, U.K.

Dr Andreas KIESEWETTER, Via La Sila 16/8, I-00135 Roma, ITALY; leonidas@ilink.it

Sharon KINOSHITA, Associate Professor of Literature, Univ. of California Santa Cruz, Santa Cruz CA 95064, U.S.A.

Dr Klaus-Peter KIRSTEIN, Lerchenstraße 60, D-45134 Essen, GERMANY; kirstein-musemeyer@t-online.de

Dr Michael A. KOEHLER, Hertogenlaan 14, B-1970 Wezembeek-Oppem, BELGIUM.

Prof. Athina KOLIA-DERMITZAKI, Plateia Kalliga 3, Athens 11253, GREECE; akolia@ arch.uoa.gr

Wolf KONRAD, 6240 Phillips Road, Mundaring 6073, West Australia, AUSTRALIA; wolf17.telstra.easymail.com.au

Prof. Barbara M. KREUTZ, 1411 Orchard Way, Rosemont PA 19010, U.S.A.

Prof. Jürgen KRÜGER, Edelsheimstraße 2, D-76131 Karlsruhe, GERMANY; juergen.krueger@ geist-soz.uni-karlsruhe.de

Hans-Ulrich KÜHN, Silcherstraße 9/1, D-71254 Ditzingen-Schöckingen, GERMANY; hans-ulrich.kuehn@web.de

Sarah LAMBERT, 35 Cromer Road, London SW17 9JN, ENGLAND, U.K.; slambert@ gold.ac.uk

The Rev. William LANE, Charterhouse, Godalming Surrey GU7 2DF, ENGLAND, U.K.; wjl@peperharow.freeserve.co.uk

Dr Robert A. LAURES, 1434 West Maplewood Court, Milwaukee WI 53221-4348, U.S.A.; dr001@voyager.net

Stephen LAY, c/o Dept. of History, Monash Univ., Melbourne, AUSTRALIA.

Eric LEGG, PSC 98 Box 36, Apo AE 09830, U.S.A.; ericlegg@hotmail.com

Robert D. LEONARD Jr., 1065 Spruce Street, Winnetka IL 60093, U.S.A.; rlwinnetka@ aol.com

Dr Antony LEOPOLD, 62 Grafton Road, Acton, London W3 6PD, ENGLAND, U.K.

Richard A. LESON, 2720 St Paul Street #2FF, Baltimore MD 21218, U.S.A.; ral2@ jhunix.hef.jhu.edu

Dr Yaacov LEV, PO Box 167, Holon 58101, ISRAEL; yglev@actcom.net.il

Dr Christopher G. LIBERTINI, 27 Lombard Lane, Sudbury MA 01776, U.S.A.; clibertini@ aol.com

Dr Giuseppe LIGATO, Viale San Gimignano 18, I-20146 Milano, ITALY; giuseppeligato@ virgilio.it

Prof. Ralph-Johannes LILIE, Kaiser-Friedrich-Straße 106, D-10585 Berlin, GERMANY; mlfavre@zedat.fu.berlin.de

Prof. Ora LIMOR, The Open Univ., 16 Klausner Steet, Tel Aviv 61392, ISRAEL; orali@ openu.ac.il

Prof. John LIND, Dept. of History, Univ. of Odense, Campusvej 55, DK-5230 Odense M, DENMARK; john_lind@hist.ou.dk

Dr Simon D. LLOYD, Dept. of History, Univ. of Newcastle-upon-Tyne, Newcastle Upon Tyne NE1 7RU, ENGLAND, U.K.; s.d.lloyd@ncl.ac.uk

Prof. Peter W. LOCK, 9 Straylands Grove, Stockton Lane, York YO31 1EB, ENGLAND, U.K.; p.lock@venysj.ac.uk

Scott LONEY, 4153 Wendell Road, West Bloomfield MI 48323, U.S.A.; scottloney@ ameritech.net

Prof. Graham A. LOUD, School of History, Univ. of Leeds, Leeds LS2 9JT, ENGLAND, U.K.; g.a.loud@leeds.ac.uk

Prof. Michael LOWER, Dept. of History, Univ. of Minnesota, 614 Social Sciences Building, 267 19th Avenue South, Minneapolis MN 55455, U.S.A.; mlower@umn.edu

Zoyd R. LUCE, 2441 Creekside Court, Hayward CA 94542, U.S.A.; zluce1@earthlink.net

Dr Svetlana LUCHITSKAYA, Institute of General History, Leninski pr. 89-346, Moscow 119313, RUSSIA; svetlana@mega.ru

Andrew John LUFF, Flat 3, The Hermitage, St Dunstans Road, Lower Feltham, Middlesex TW13 4HR, ENGLAND, U.K.; andrew@luffa.freeserve.co.uk

Dr Anthony LUTTRELL, 20 Richmond Place, Bath BA1 5PZ, ENGLAND, U.K.

Christopher MACEVITT, Dumbarton Oaks, 1703 32nd Street NW, Washington DC 20007, U.S.A.

Merav MACK, Lucy Cavendish College, Cambridge CB3 0BU, ENGLAND, U.K.

Dr Alan D. MACQUARRIE, 173 Queen Victoria Drive, Glasgow G14 7BP, SCOTLAND, U.K.

Prof. Thomas F. MADDEN, Dept. of History, Saint Louis Univ., 3800 Lindell Boulevard, PO Box 56907, St Louis MO 63108, U.S.A.; maddentf@slu.edu

Ben MAHONEY, 19 Bond Street, Mount Waverly, Victoria 3149, AUSTRALIA; BMahoney@abl.com.au

Dr Christoph T. MAIER, Sommergasse 20, CH-4056 Basel, SWITZERLAND; ctmaier@hist.unizh.ch

Chryssa MALTEZOU, Istituto Ellenico di Studi Bizantini e Postbizantini di Venezia, Castello 3412, I-30122 Venezia, ITALY; hellenic.inst.@gold.ghnet.it

Prof. Lucy Der MANUELIAN, 10 Garfield Road, Belmont MA 02178-3309, U.S.A.; lucy.manuelian@tufts.edu

Prof. Michael MARKOWSKI, Dept. of History, Westminster College, 1840 South 1300 East, Salt Lake City UT 84105, U.S.A.

Dr Christopher J. MARSHALL, 8 Courtyard Way, Cottenham, Cambridge CB4 8SF, ENGLAND, U.K.

Dr Carlos de Ayala MARTINEZ, Historia Medieval, Ciudad Universitaria de Cantoblanco, Ctra. De Colmenar, E-28049 Madrid, ESPAÑA.

Prof. Laurence W. MARVIN, History Dept., Evans School of Humanities and Social Sciences, Berry College, Mount Berry GA 30149-5010, U.S.A.

Dr John F. A. MASON, Christ Church College, Oxford OX1 1DP, ENGLAND, U.K.

Kathleen MAXWELL, 4016 26th Street, San Francisco CA 94131, U.S.A.; kmaxwell@scu.edu

Prof. Hans Eberhard MAYER, Historisches Seminar der Universität Kiel, D-24098 Kiel, GERMANY.

Robert MAYNARD, Cuba Villa, 146 Wick Road, Bristol BS4 4HQ, ENGLAND, U.K.; robian@btinternet.com

Andreas MAZARAKIS, Rizou 3, Athens 10434, GREECE; amazarakis@tee.gr

Prof. Rasa MAZEIKA, 48A Arcadian Circle, Toronto, Ontario M8W 4W2, CANADA.

Arthur H. S. MEGAW, 27 Perrins' Walk, London NW3 6TH, ENGLAND, U.K.

Prof. Sophia MENACHE, Dept. of History, Univ. of Haifa, Haifa 31905, ISRAEL; menache@research.haifa.ac.il

Marco MESCHINI, Via Fé 15, I-21100 Varese, ITALY; marco.meschini@libero.it

Margaret MESERVE, Assistant Professor of History, Univ. of Notre Dame, 219 O'Shaughnessy Hall, Notre Dame IN 46556, U.S.A.; margaret.h.meserve.1@nd.edu

Prof. D. Michael METCALF, Ashmolean Museum, Oxford OX1 2PH, ENGLAND, U.K.

Françoise MICHEAU, 8bis, rue du Buisson Saint-Louis, F-75011 Paris, FRANCE; fmicheau@univ-paris.fr

Prof. Klaus MILITZER, Winckelmannstraße 32, D-50825 Köln, GERMANY; klaus.militzer@uni-koeln.de

Peter John MILLS, 3 Huxley Road, Leyton, London E10 5QT, ENGLAND, U.K.; petermills@lireone.net

Prof. Laura MINERVINI, Dipartimento di Filologia Moderna, Università di Napoli Federico II, Via Porta Di Massa 1, I-80133 Napoli, ITALY; lrminer@unina.it

Dr Piers D. MITCHELL, 84 Huntingdon Road, East Finchley, London N2 9DU, ENGLAND, U.K.; p.mitchell@clara.co.uk

PD Dr Hannes MÖHRING, Wilhelm-Bode-Straße 11, D-38104 Braunschweig, GERMANY; hannes_moehring@web.de

Dr Johannes A. MOL, Grote Dijlakker 29, NL-8701 KW Bolsward, THE NETHERLANDS; zeemol@oprit.rug.nl

Dr Kristian MOLIN, 38 Vessey Terrace, Newcastle-under-Lyme, Staffordshire ST5 1LS, ENGLAND, U.K.; kristian.molin@nulc.ac.uk

Lisa K. MONROE, 7417 Park Terrace Drive, Alexandria VA 22307, U.S.A.; nlmonroe@earthlink.net

Dauvergne C. MORGAN, 235 Tooronga Road, Glen Iris, Melbourne, Victoria 3142, AUSTRALIA.

Dr David O. MORGAN, 302 Orchard Drive, Madison WI 53705, U.S.A.; domorgan@facstaff.wisc.edu

Jonathan C. MORGAN, 19 Elia Street, Islington, London N1 8DE, ENGLAND, U.K.; jonathan.morgan@whb.co.uk

J. Diana MORGAN, 64 Victoria Avenue, Swanage, Dorset BH19 1AR, ENGLAND, U.K.

Hiroki MORITAKE, Kami-Ono 371, Hiyoshi-mura, Kitauwa-gun, Ehime-ken 798-1503, JAPAN; jerus@hiroshima-u.ac.jp

The Rev. Prof. Colin MORRIS, 12 Bassett Crescent East, Southampton SO16 7PB, ENGLAND, U.K.; cm5@soton.ac.uk

Cécile MORRISSON, 36, chemin Desvallières, F-92410 Ville d'Avray, FRANCE.

Roger D. MULHOLLEN, Center for Study of Ancient Religious History, 13217 W. Serenade Circle, Sun City West AZ 85375-1707, U.S.A.; audrog@aol.com

Prof. M. E. MULLETT, Institute of Byzantine Studies, Queen's Univ. of Belfast, Belfast BT7 1NN, NORTHERN IRELAND, U.K.; n.mullett@aub.ac.uk

Dr Alan V. MURRAY, International Medieval Institute, Parkinson 103, The Univ. of Leeds, Leeds LS2 9JT, ENGLAND, U.K.; a.v.murray@leeds.ac.uk

Stephen R. A. MURRAY, Apartment 2419, 77 Huntley Street, Toronto, Ontario M4Y 2P3, CANADA; sramurray@hotmail.com

Claude MUTAFIAN, 216 rue Saint-Jacques, F-75005 Paris, FRANCE; claude.mutafian@wanadoo.fr

Alan NEILL, 13 Chesham Crescent, Belfast BT6 8GW, NORTHERN IRELAND, U.K.; neilla@rescueteam.com

Prof. Robert S. NELSON, Dept. of Art, Univ. of Chicago, 5540 South Greenwood Avenue, Chicago IL 60637, U.S.A.

Michael de NÈVE, Laubacher Straße 9, D-14197 Berlin, GERMANY or Freie Universität

Berlin, FB Geschichts- und Kulturwissenschaften, Koserstraße 20, D-14195 Berlin, GERMANY; michaeldeneve@web.de

Dr Helen J. NICHOLSON, School of History and Archaeology, Cardiff Univ., PO Box 909, Cardiff CF10 3XU, WALES, U.K.; nicholsonhj@cardiff.ac.uk

Angel NICOLAOU-KONNARI, 10 Philiou Zannetou Street, 3021 Limassol, CYPRUS; an.konnaris@cytanet.com.cy

Dr David NICOLLE, 67 Maplewell Road, Woodhouse Eaves, Leics. LE12 8RG, ENGLAND, U.K.; david.nicolle@tesco.net

Mark John NICOVICH, 4497 Pershing Avenue #201, St Louis MO 63108, U.S.A.

Marie-Adelaïde NIELEN, 254, avenue Daumesnil, F-75012 Paris, FRANCE; marie-adelaide.nielen@culture.gouv.fr

Torben K. NIELSEN, History Dept., Aalborg Univ., Fibigerstraede 5, DK-9220 Aalborg, DENMARK; histkn@i4.avc.dk

Yoav NITZAN, 4 Ha-Adereth Street, Jerusalem 92343, ISRAEL; famnitzan@altavista.com

Prof. Peter S. NOBLE, Dept. of French Studies, SML, Univ. of Reading, Whiteknights, Reading RG6 6AA, ENGLAND, U.K.; p.s.noble@reading.ac.uk

Dr Gregory O'MALLEY, 87 Lovel Road, Cambridge, ENGLAND, U.K.; OMalley_Greg_J@cat.com

Prof. Mahmoud Said OMRAN, History Dept., Faculty of Arts, Univ. of Alexandria, Alexandria, EGYPT; msomran@dataxprs.com.eg

Col. Erhard (Erik) OPSAHL, 5303 Dennis Drive, McFarland WI 53558, U.S.A.; epopsahlw@aol.com

Dr Catherine OTTEN, 9, rue de Londres, F-67000 Strasbourg, FRANCE; otten@umb.u-strasbg.fr.

Prof. Robert OUSTERHOUT, School of Architecture, Univ. of Illinois, 611 Taft Drive, Champaign IL 61820-6921, U.S.A.; rgouster@unic.edu

Dr Johannes PAHLITZSCH, Parallelstraße 12, D-12209 Berlin, GERMANY; pahlitz@zedat.fu-berlin.de

Tivadar PALÁGYI, Tapolcsanyi u. 8, H-1022 Budapest, HUNGARY; tivadarp@hotmail.com

Dr Aphrodite PAPAYIANNI, 40 Inverness Terrace, London W2 3JB, ENGLAND, U.K.; aphroditepapayianni@hotmail.com

Dr Peter D. PARTNER, 17 Clausentum Road, Winchester, Hampshire, S023 9QE, ENGLAND, U.K.; pdp4@aol.com

Prof. Jacques PAVIOT, 21, rue de Vouillé, F-75015 Paris, FRANCE; jacques.paviot@wanadoo.fr or paviot@univ-paris12.fr

Peter Shlomo PELEG, 2 Mordhai Street, Kiryat Tivon 36023, ISRAEL; fax: 972 4 9931 122; ppeleg@netvision.net.il

Nicholas J. PERRY, PO Box 389, La Mesa NM 88044, U.S.A.; nicholasperry@earthlink.net

Theodore D. PETRO, 517 McAlpin Avenue, Cincinnati OH 45220, U.S.A.; petrod@email.uc.edu

Dr Jonathan P. PHILLIPS, Dept. of History, Royal Holloway Univ. of London, Egham, Surrey TW20 0EX, ENGLAND, U.K.; j.p.phillips@rhul.ac.uk

Simon D. PHILLIPS, 1 Turtle Close, Stubbington, Hampshire PO14 3JG, ENGLAND, U.K.; phillips_s_d@lycos.co.uk

Dr Mathias PIANA, Benzstraße 9, D-86420 Diedorf, GERMANY; mathias.piana@phil.uni-augsburg.de

Brenda POCHNA, 17 Berryhill, Eltham Park, London SE9 1QP, ENGLAND, U.K.

Dr John PORTEOUS, 52 Elgin Crescent, London W11, ENGLAND, U.K.

Prof. James M. POWELL, 5100 Highbridge Street, Apartment 18D, Fayetteville NY 13066, U.S.A.; mpowell@dreamscape.com

Jon POWELL, 711 SE 11th #43, Portland OR 97214, U.S.A.; jonp@pdx.edu

Dr Karen PRATT, French Dept., King's College London, Strand, London WC2R 2LS, ENGLAND, U.K.

Jennifer Ann PRICE, Dept. of History, Univ. of Washington, PO Box 353560, Seattle WA 98195-3560, U.S.A.; japrice@u.washington.edu

Prof. R. Denys PRINGLE, School of History and Archaeology, Cardiff Univ., PO Box 909, Cardiff CF10 3XU, WALES, U.K.; pringlerd@cardiff.ac.uk

Dragan PROKIC, M.A., Rubensallee 47, D-55127 Mainz, GERMANY; dp.symbulos@t-online.de

Prof. John H. PRYOR, History Dept., Univ. of Sydney, Sydney, N.S.W. 2006, AUSTRALIA; john.pryor@arts.usyd.edu.au

William J. PURKIS, 46 Fennec Close, Cherry Hinton, Cambridge CB1 9GG, ENGLAND, U.K.; william_purkis@hotmail.com

Ian D. QUELCH, 27 Barn Meadow Lane, Great Bookham, Surrey KT23 3EZ, ENGLAND, U.K.; Ian.Quelch@ntlworld.com

Yevgeniy / Eugene RASSKAZOV, Worth Avenue Station, PO Box 3497, Palm Beach FL 33480-3497, U.S.A.; medievaleurope@apexmail.com

Prof. Geoffrey W. RICE, History Dept., Univ. of Canterbury, Private Bag 4800, Christchurch, NEW ZEALAND; g.rice@hist.canterbury.ac.nz

Prof. Jean RICHARD, 12, rue Pelletier de Chambure, F-21000 Dijon, FRANCE.

Maurice RILEY Esq., PO Box 15819, Adliya, BAHRAIN, Arabian Gulf; mriley@batelco.com.bh

Prof. Jonathan S. C. RILEY-SMITH, The Downs, Croxton, St Neots, Cambridgeshire PE19 4SX, ENGLAND, U.K.; jsr22@cam.ac.uk or jonathan.rileysmith@btinternet.com

Rebecca RIST, 50 Roseford Road, Cambridge CB4 2HD, ENGLAND, U.K.; raw2@corn.ac.uk

The Rev. Leonard Stanley RIVETT, 47 Ryecroft Avenue, Woodthorpe, York YO24 2SD, ENGLAND, U.K.

Prof. Louise Buenger ROBBERT, 709 South Skinker Boulevard Apartment 701, St Louis MO 63105, U.S.A.; lrobbert@mindspring.com

Jason ROCHÉ, Seaview, Kings Highway, Largoward, Fife KY9 1HX, SCOTLAND, U.K.; sharon@showard1.fsnet.co.uk

José Manuel RODRÍGUEZ-GARCÍA, C/ San Ernesto 4.5° C, E-28002 Madrid, ESPAÑA; anaevjosem@wanadoo.es

Prof. Israel ROLL, Dept. of Classics, Tel-Aviv Univ., Ramat Aviv, Tel-Aviv 69978, ISRAEL; rolli@post.tau.ac.il

Dean Richard B. ROSE, 119 Grandview Place, San Antonio TX 78209, U.S.A.

Prof. Myriam ROSEN-AYALON, Institute of Asian and African Studies, The Hebrew Univ., Jerusalem 91905, ISRAEL.

Dvora ROSHAL, PO Box 3558, Beer-Sheva 84135, ISRAEL; devorahr@afikim.co.il

Linda ROSS, Dept. of History, Royal Holloway Univ. of London, Egham, Surrey TW20 0EX, ENGLAND, U.K.; linde@lross22.freeserve.co.uk

Prof. John ROSSER, Dept. of History, Boston College, Chestnut Hill MA 02467, U.S.A.; rosserj@bc.edu

Prof. Miri RUBIN, Dept. of History, Queen Mary, Univ. of London, Mile Ende Road, London E1 4NS, ENGLAND, U.K.; m.e.rubin@qmw.ac.uk

James RUEL, Ground Floor Flat, 63 Redland Road, Redland, Bristol B56 6AQ, England, U.K.; james-ruel@hotmail.com

Prof. Frederick H. RUSSELL, Dept. of History, Conklin Hall, Rutgers Univ., Newark NJ 07102, U.S.A.; frussell@andromeda.rutgers.edu

Prof. James D. RYAN, 100 West 94th Street, Apartment #26M, New York NY 10025, U.S.A.; james.d.ryan@verizon.net

Dr Andrew J. SARGENT, 33 Coborn Street, Bow, London E3 2AB, ENGLAND, U.K.; andrewsargent@newham.gov.uk

Prof. Jürgen SARNOWSKY, Historisches Seminar, Universität Hamburg, Von-Melle-Park 6, D-20146 Hamburg, GERMANY; juergen.sarnowsky@uni-hamburg.de

Christopher SAUNDERS OBE, Watery Hey, Spring Vale Road, Hayfield, High Peak SK22 2LD, ENGLAND, U.K.

Prof. Alexios G. C. SAVVIDES, Aegean Univ., Dept. of Mediterranean Studies, Rhodes, GREECE; or: 7 Tralleon Street, Nea Smyrne, Athens 17121, GREECE; savvides@rhodes.aegean.gr

Christopher SCHABEL, Dept. of History and Archaeology, Univ. of Cyprus, PO Box 20537, CY-1678 Nicosia, CYPRUS; schabel@ucy.ac.cy

Jochen SCHENK, Emmanuel College, Cambridge CB2 3AP, ENGLAND, U.K.; jgs29@cam.ac.uk

Prof. Paul Gerhard SCHMIDT, Seminar für lateinische Philologie des Mittelalters, Albert-Ludwigs-Universität Freiburg, Werderring 8, D-79085 Freiburg i. Br., GERMANY.

Dr Beate SCHUSTER, 19, rue Vauban, F-67000 Strasbourg, FRANCE; beaschu@compuserve.com

Prof. Rainer C. SCHWINGES, Historisches Institut der Universität Bern, Unitobler-Länggass-Straße 49, CH-3000 Bern 9, SWITZERLAND.

Kaare SEEBERG SIDSELRUD, Solbergliveien 87 B, NO-0683 Oslo, NORWAY; kaares@mail.hf.uio.no

Iris SHAGRIR, Dept. of History, The Open Univ., 16 Klausner Street, POB 39328, Tel Aviv 61392, ISRAEL; irissh@openu.ac.il

Prof. Maya SHATZMILLER, Dept. of History, The Univ. of Western Ontario, London, Ontario N6A 5C2, CANADA.

Karl W. SHEA, Unit 6, 93 Avocca Street, Randwick 2031, New South Wales, AUSTRALIA; sangrail@bigpond.com

Dr Jonathan SHEPARD, 14 Hartley Court, Woodstock Road, Oxford OX2 7PF, ENGLAND, U.K.; nshepard@easynet.co.uk

Dr Elizabeth J. SIBERRY, 28 The Mall, Surbiton, Surrey KT6 4E9, ENGLAND, U.K.

Alicia SIMPSON, 8 Karaiskaki Street, Athens GR-18345, GREECE.

Dr Gordon Andreas SINGER, PO Box 235, Greenbelt MD 20768-0235, U.S.A.; andysinger@att.net

Dr Corliss K. SLACK, Dept. of History #1103, Whitworth College, Spokane WA 99251, U.S.A.; cslack@whitworth.edu

Rima E. SMINE, 25541 Altamont Road, Los Altos Hills CA 94022, U.S.A.

Sheila R. SMITH, 111 Coleshill Road Chapelend, Nuneaton Warwickshire CV10 0PG, ENGLAND, U.K.

Simon SONNAK, PO Box 1206, Windsor 3181, Victoria, AUSTRALIA; heliade@bigpond.com.au

Arnold SPAER, PO Box 7530, Jerusalem 91079, ISRAEL; hui@spaersitton.co.il

Brent SPENCER, 3 9701 89 Street, Fort Saskatchewan, Alberta T8L IJ3, CANADA; ktcrusader@yahoo.com

Dr Alan M. STAHL, 11 Fairview Place, Ossining NY 10562, U.S.A.

Prof. Harvey STAHL, Dept. of the History of Art, Univ. of California, Berkeley CA 94720, U.S.A.; hstahl@socrates.berkeley.edu

Dr Alexandra STEFANIDOU, 35 Amerikis Street, Rhodos 85100, GREECE; aleste@otenet.gr

Eliezer and J. Edna STERN, Israel Antiquities Authority, PO Box 1094, Acre 24110, ISRAEL; fax: 04-9911682 or 9918074.

Alan D. STEVENS, Campbell College, Dept. of History, Belmont Road, Belfast BT4 2ND, NORTHERN IRELAND, U.K.; alan.d.stevens@ntlworld.com

Paula STILES, Dept. of Medieval History, 71 South Street, Univ. of St Andrews, St Andrews, Scotland KY16 9AJ, SCOTLAND, U.K.; thesnowleopard@hotmail.com

Myra STRUCKMEYER, 29 Flemington Road, Chapel Hill NC 27517, U.S.A.; struckme@email.unc.edu

Shaul TAMIRI, Hachail-Halmoni #8, Rishon le Zion 75255, ISRAEL.

Olivier TERLINDEN, Avenue des Ramiers 8, B-1950 Kraaïnem, BELGIUM; olivierterlinden@yahoo.com

Miriam Rita TESSERA, via Moncalvo 16, I-20146 Milano, ITALY; monachus_it@yahoo.it

Kenneth J. THOMSON, Edessa, 8 Salterfell Road, Scale Hall, Lancaster LA1 2PX, ENGLAND, U.K.; kenneth@thomsonk91.fsnet.co.uk

Prof. Peter THORAU, Historisches Institut, Universität des Saarlandes, Postfach 15 11 50, D-66041 Saarbrücken, GERMANY.

Prof. Hirofumi TOKO, 605-3 Kogasaka, Machida, Tokyo 194-0014, JAPAN; ttokou@toyonet.toyo.ac.jp

Prof. John Victor TOLAN, Département d'Histoire, Université de Nantes, B.P. 81227, F-44312 Nantes, FRANCE, or: 2, rue de la Chevalerie, F-44300 Nantes, FRANCE; john.tolan@humana.univ-nantes.fr

Prof. François-Olivier TOUATI, Le Navril, F-49250 La Ménitré, FRANCE; francoistouati@aol.com

Catherine B. TURNER, Flat 3, 1055 Christchurch Road, Boscombe East, Bournemouth BH7 6BE, ENGLAND, U.K.

Dr Judith M. UPTON-WARD, Flat 6, Haywood Court, Reading RG1 3QF, ENGLAND, U.K.; juptonward@btopenworld.com

Prof. William L. URBAN, Dept. of History, Monmouth College, 700 East Broadway, Monmouth IL 61462, U.S.A.; urban@monm.edu

Theresa M. VANN, Hill Monastic Manuscript Library, St John's Univ., Collegeville MN 56321, U.S.A.; www.hmml.org

Dr Marie-Louise von WARTBURG MAIER, Paphosprojekt der Universität Zürich, Rämistraße 71, CH-8006 Zürich, SWITZERLAND; paphos@hist.unizh.ch

Benjamin WEBER, 1, Residence du Parc, F-31520 Ramonville, FRANCE; benyi_tigrou@hotmail.com

Dr Daniel WEISS, History of Art Dept., Johns Hopkins Univ., 3400 North Charles Street, Baltimore MD 21218, U.S.A.; dweiss@jho.edu

Brett E. WHALEN, 119 Quillen Court, Stanford CA 94305, U.S.A.

Dr Mark WHITTOW, St Peter's College, Oxford OX1 2DL, ENGLAND, U.K.

Timothy WILKES, A. H. Baldwin & Sons Ltd., 11 Adelphi Terrace, London WC2N 6BJ, ENGLAND, U.K.; timwilkes@baldwin.sh

The Rev. Dr John D. WILKINSON, 7 Tenniel Close, London W2 3LE, ENGLAND, U.K.

Dr Ann WILLIAMS, 40 Greenwich South Street, London SE10 8UN, ENGLAND, U.K.; ann.williams@talk21.com

Prof. Steven James WILLIAMS, Dept. of History, New Mexico Highlands Univ., PO Box 9000, Las Vegas NM 87701, U.S.A.; stevenjameswilliams@yahoo.com

Gayle A. WILSON, PO Box 712, Diamond Springs CA 95619, U.S.A.; gayle@inforum.net

Peter van WINDEKENS, Kleine Ganzendries 38, B-3212 Pellenberg, BELGIUM.

Prof. Johanna Maria van WINTER, Brigittenstraat 20, NL-3512 KM Utrecht, THE NETHERLANDS; j.m.vanwinter@let.uu.nl

Prof. Kenneth B. WOLF, Dept. of History, Pomona College, Pearsons Hall, 551 North College Avenue, Claremont CA 91711-6337, U.S.A.

Dr Noah WOLFSON, 13 Avuqa Street, Tel-Aviv 69086, ISRAEL; noah@meteo-tech.co.il

Peter WOODHEAD, Tarry Cottage, Church Lane, Daglingworth near Cirencester, Gloucestershire GL7 7AG, ENGLAND, U.K.

Dr John WREGLESWORTH, Fountain Cottage, 98 West Town Road, Backwell, North Somerset BS48 3BE, ENGLAND, U.K.; john@wreg.freeserve.co.uk

Prof. Shunji YATSUZUKA, 10-22 Matsumoto 2 chome, Otsu-shi, Shiga 520, JAPAN

William G. ZAJAC, 9 Station Terrace, Pen-y-rheal, Caerphilly CF83 2RH, WALES, U.K.

Prof. Ossama Zaki ZEID, 189 Abd al-Salam Aref Tharwat, Alexandria, EGYPT; ossama_zeid@hotmail.com

Prof. Monique ZERNER, Villa Stella, Chemin des Pins, F-06000 Nice, FRANCE; zernerm@unice.fr

Institutions subscribing to the SSCLE

Atatürk Kültür, Dil ve Tarih Yüsek Kumuru, Türk Tarih Kumuru, Baskanligi, TURKEY.

Brepols Publishers, Steenweg op Tielen 68, B-2300 Turnhout, BELGIUM.

Bibliothécaire Guy Cobolet, Le Bibliothécaire, École Française d'Athènes, 6, Didotou 10680 Athènes, GREECE.

Centre de Recherches d'histoire et civilisation de Byzance et du Proche-Orient Chétien, Université de Paris 1, 17, rue de la Sorbonne, 75231 Paris Cedex, FRANCE.

Centre for Byzantine, Ottoman and Modern Greek Studies, Univ. of Birmingham, Edgbaston, Birmingham B15 2TT, ENGLAND, U.K.

Couvent des Dominicains, École Biblique et Archéologique Français, 6 Nablus Road, Jerusalem 91190, ISRAEL.

Deutsches Historisches Institut in Rom, Via Aurelia Antica 391, I-00165 Rome, ITALY.

Deutschordenszentralarchiv (DOZA), Singerstraße 7, A-1010 Wien, AUSTRIA.

Dumbarton Oaks Research Library, 1703 32nd Street North West, Washington D.C. 20007, U.S.A.

Germanisches Nationalmuseum, Bibliothek, Kornmarkt 1, D-90402 Nürnberg, GERMANY.

History Department, Campbell College, Belfast BT4 2 ND, NORTHERN IRELAND, U.K.

The Jewish National and University Library, PO Box 34165, Jerusalem 91341, ISRAEL.

The Library, The Priory of Scotland of the Most Venerable Order of St John, 21 St John Street, Edinburgh EH8 8DG, SCOTLAND, U.K.

The Stephen Chan Library, Institute of Fine Arts, New York Univ., 1 East 78th Street, New York NY 10021, U.S.A.

Metropolitan Museum of Art, Thomas J. Watson Library, Serials Dept., 5th Avenue at 82nd Street, New York NY 10028, U.S.A.

Museum and Library of the Order of St John, St John's Gate, Clerkenwell, London EC1M 4DA, ENGLAND, U.K.

Order of the Temple of Jerusalem, The Autonomous Priory of England, Affiliate Order of the Industrial Temple, 151 Glebe Road, Norwich, Norfolk NR2 3JH, ENGLAND, U.K.

Serials Department, 11717 Young Research Library, Univ. of California, Box 951575, Los Angeles CA 90095-1575, U.S.A.

Sourasky Library, Tel-Aviv Univ., Periodical Dept., PO Box 39038, Tel-Aviv, ISRAEL.

Teutonic Order Bailiwick of Utrecht, Dr John J. Quarles van Ufford, Secretary of the Bailliwick, Springweg 25, NL-3511 VJ Utrecht, THE NETHERLANDS.

The Warburg Institute, Univ. of London, Woburn Square, London WC1H 0AB, ENGLAND, U.K. [John PERKINS, Deputy Librarian, jperkins@a1.sas.ac.uk]

Eberhard-Karls-Universität Tübingen, Orientalisches Seminar, Münzgasse 30, D-72072 Tübingen, GERMANY.

University of California Los Angeles Serials Dept. / YRL, 11717 Young Research Library, Box 951575, Los Angeles CA 90095-1575, U.S.A.

University of London Library, Periodicals Section, Senate House, Malet Street, London WC1E 7HU, ENGLAND, U.K.

University of North Carolina, Davis Library CB 3938, Periodicals and Serials Dept., Chapel Hill NC 27514-8890, U.S.A.

Universitätsbibliothek Tübingen, Wilhelmstraße 32, Postfach 26 20, D-72016 Tübingen, GERMANY.

University of Reading, Graduate Centre for Medieval Studies, Whiteknights, PO Box 218, Reading, Berks. RG6 6AA, ENGLAND, U.K.

University of Washington, Libraries, Serials Division, PO Box 352900, Seattle WA 98195, U.S.A.

University of Western Ontario Library, Acquisitions Dept., Room M1, D. B. Weldon Library, London, Ontario N6A 3K7, CANADA.

W. F. Albright Institute of Archaeological Research, 26 Salah ed-Din Street, PO Box 19096, Jerusalem 91190, ISRAEL.

Guidelines for the Submission of Papers

The editors ask contributors to adhere to the following guidelines. Failure to do so will result in the article being returned to the author for amendment, or may result in its having to be excluded from the volume.

1. Submissions. Submissions should be made on 3.5 inch, high-density IBM compatible disks and in two typescripts, double-spaced with wide margins. Please send these to one of the editors. Remember to include your name and address on your paper.

2. Length. Normally, the maximum length of articles should not exceed 6,000 words, not including notes. The editors reserve the right to edit papers that exceed these limits.

3. Notes. Normally, notes should be REFERENCE ONLY and placed at the end of the paper. Number continuously.

4. Style sheet. Please use the most recent *Speculum* style sheet (currently *Speculum* 75 (2000), 547–52). This sets out the format to be used for notes. Failure to follow the *Speculum* format will result in accepted articles being returned to the author for amendment. In the main body of the paper you may adhere to either British or American spelling, but it must be consistent throughout the article.

5. Language. Papers will be published in English, French, German, Italian and Spanish.

6. Abbreviations. Please use the abbreviation list on p. ix–x of this journal.

7. Diagrams and Maps should be referred to as figures and photographs as plates. Please keep illustrations to the essential minimum, since it will be possible to include only a limited number. All illustrations must be supplied by the contributor in camera-ready copy, and free from all copyright restrictions.

8. Italics. Words to be printed as italics should be italicised if possible. Failing this they should be underlined.

9. Capitals. Please take every care to ensure consistency in your use of capitals and lower case letters. Use initial capitals to distinguish the general from the specific (for example, 'the count of Flanders' but 'Count Philip of Flanders').

Editors

Professor Benjamin Z. Kedar
Department of History
The Hebrew University
Jerusalem 91905, Israel

Professor Jonathan S. C. Riley-Smith
Emmanuel College
Cambridge CB2 3AP
U.K.

SOCIETY FOR THE STUDY OF THE CRUSADES AND THE LATIN EAST MEMBERSHIP INFORMATION

The primary function of the Society for the Study of the Crusades and the Latin East is to enable members to learn about current work being done in the field of crusading history, and to contact members who share research interests through the information in the Society's Bulletin. There are currently 420 members of the SSCLE from 30 countries. The Society also organizes a major international conference every four years, as well as sections on crusading history at other conferences where appropriate.

The committee of the SSCLE consists of:
Prof. Michel Balard, *President*
Prof. Jean Richard, Prof. Jonathan Riley-Smith and Prof. Benjamin Z. Kedar, *Honorary Vice-presidents*
Prof. Sophia Menache and Luis Garcìa-Guijarro Ramos, *Secretary and Assistant Secretary*
Prof. James D. Ryan, *Treasurer*
Prof. Karl Borchardt, *Bulletin Editor*
Dr Zsolt Hunyadi, *Website*.

Current subscription fees are as follows:
- Membership and Bulletin of the Society: Single £11, $15 or €17;
- Student £6, $9 or €10;
- Joint membership £15, $23 or €25;
- Membership and the journal *Crusades*, including the Bulletin: £20, $30 or €33.